Lustful Appetites

LUSTFUL APPETITES

An Intimate History of
Good Food and Wicked Sex

Rachel Hope Cleves

polity

The right of Rachel Hope Cleves to be identified as Author of this Work has been asserted in accordance with the UK Copyright, Designs and Patents Act 1988.

First published in 2025 by Polity Press

Polity Press
65 Bridge Street
Cambridge CB2 1UR, UK

Polity Press
111 River Street
Hoboken, NJ 07030, USA

ISBN-13: 978-1-5095-5363-1

A catalogue record for this book is available from the British Library.

Library of Congress Control Number: 2024938463

Typeset in 11.5 on 14pt Adobe Garamond
by Cheshire Typesetting Ltd, Cuddington, Cheshire
Printed and bound in Great Britain by CPI Group (UK) Ltd, Croydon

The publisher has used its best endeavours to ensure that the URLs for external websites referred to in this book are correct and active at the time of going to press. However, the publisher has no responsibility for the websites and can make no guarantee that a site will remain live or that the content is or will remain appropriate.

Every effort has been made to trace all copyright holders, but if any have been overlooked the publisher will be pleased to include any necessary credits in any subsequent reprint or edition.

For further information on Polity, visit our website:
politybooks.com

For all my fellow hungry greedy people. *Bien vivre et mourir gras!*

Contents

Acknowledgments

I don't even know where to begin. This book has been so long in the cooking that I can't possibly recall all the hands that took a turn stirring the pot.

The project began during a sabbatical year in Paris, during 2013–2014, when I thought I was working on a book about Americans who learned to cook in France only to keep coming across sex in the sources. During that year, on some of my archive visits, I had the company of Natasha Lehrer, a great reader, writer, cook, and friend, who is reason enough for me to keep engineering research projects that bring to me Paris until I can't swallow one more single bite of foie gras (never!).

Despite the newness of my project, in 2015 the team at Notches blog, including Gill Frank and Justin Bengry, invited me to guest-edit a series of blog posts on the theme of food and sex. The wonderful submissions that came in, from Benjamin Carp, Gustavo Corral, Robert Gamble, Christopher Hommerding, Scott Larson, and Laika Nevalainen, persuaded me that this new direction in my research had legs.

I took further encouragement from travel grants that I received from the Schlesinger Library, which allowed me to read through the papers of Julia Child, Elizabeth David, and M. F. K. Fisher, and from the Harry Ransom Center at the University of Texas, Austin, which allowed me to read the papers of Sylvia Beach and Sybille Bedford. The research for this book would not have been possible without the support of the Social Sciences and Humanities Research Council (SSHRC), which funded a multi-year project I called "Parmesan and Pleasure." I didn't realize just how many years it would take to turn that project into a book. I blame Norman Douglas, who distracted me and demanded that his own book take precedence.

With the support of SSHRC, I was able to employ a series of wonderful research assistants who combed through sources including magazines, newspapers, and diaries, with enthusiasm and dedication. Thank you to

Katey Flechl, Alexie Glover, Lauren Irvine, Jamey Jesperson, Michelle Snidal, and Sal Wiltshire. The book gained immeasurably in depth and richness from your contributions. Thanks also to my adored friend and occasional research assistant Amy Glemann.

Thank you to all the editors and anonymous peer reviewers – yes, even you, reader B – who helped me hone my arguments in article and chapter form: Tracey Deutsch, Anne Ewbank, Craig Friend, Heidi Gengenbach, Lorri Glover, Amanda Herbert, Frank Jacob, Alex Lichtenstein, Wilhelm Meusburger, Shauna Sweeney, and Vanessa Warne. Thank you, thank you to Emily Contois, who generously provided feedback on my work on *Real Men Don't Eat Quiche* while she was publishing her own article on the topic. A true act of scholarly commensality. The book also benefited enormously from the feedback I received at talks, delivered everywhere from community centers, to classrooms, to libraries, to international conferences.

Thank you to all the archivists who make the work of historians possible – this includes the keepers of family archives, like David Marchasani who shared scans of his aunt Thelma Wood's dog-eared cookbooks. Thanks also to Jonathan Ned Katz for talking with me about his aunt, Cecily Brownstone.

Thank you to the commentators on the blog I kept during my year in Paris, and to the community of hungry people who engaged my tweets during the good years when I was constantly posting my discoveries in the archives. You persuaded me that one day there would be an audience for this book.

Special shout-out to the following tweeps: Celia Sack, owner of Omnivore Books on Food, who allowed me to use her amazing San Francisco bookstore as an archive of rare cookbooks; Guillaume Coatalen, who helped with my French when I was working on my *Vocabula Amatoria* scholarship; and Bri Watson and Robert Davis, who pointed me to fun sources. Thanks to all the people on all the platforms who came up with creative titles for the book. I have saved you, gentle reader, from so many bad puns.

Thanks to the many food writers and scholars I've had the good fortune to communicate with – even briefly! – while working on the book: Annabel Abbs, Ken Albala, John Birdsall, Aaron Bobrow-Strain, Emily Contois, Adam Federman, Julieta Flores Jurado, Jonathan Kauffman,

Alex Ketchum, Rachel Laudan, Joy Hui Lin, Sylvia Lovegren, Amanda Moniz, Zachary Nowak, Lisa Jordan Powell, Kyla Wazana Tompkins, Helen Zoe Veit, Stephen Vider, and Ashley Rose Young. It's easy to feel isolated when working from a tree house on Vancouver Island, but you made me feel like part of a larger community.

A few truly generous souls read the full book in draft form and gave me detailed feedback. Thank you to Jamey Jesperson, Adam Shprintzen, and Masha Zager. Thank you to Pascal Porcheron for inviting me to publish with Polity, and thank you to Julia Davies for taking over the reins, with assistance from Helena Heaton and Maddie Tyler. To all the friends who helped me in the important process of choosing the best book cover: I think we nailed it.

How can I possibly thank all the people who cooked me wonderful sensuous meals and fed my appetites? Top of that list is Tim Cleves. Thank you from the bottom of my heart for all the love along the journey. My parents deserve better than the quick dismissal they get in the introduction. It wasn't their fault they worked full time! They still managed to fill my belly with many delicious meals. As a child, I particularly loved my mom's Chinese spare ribs and my stepmother's manicotti. I would like to pretend to have loved my father's peanut butter, bacon, and banana sandwiches but I just can't. What a delight it is to now be the mother of two adult children who love to cook. They should move back to Victoria so they can cook for me and fatten me up (you especially, Maya).

I've eaten so many wonderful meals with friends over the past decade. I am thankful to each and every person in every kitchen, domestic and commercial, who has fed me. It is my greatest aspiration that this book will generate many more dinner invitations in the future. Please feed me! I eat everything and I'm happy to wash up afterwards.

Introduction: Good Food, Wicked Sex

In the beginning, according to a familiar story, a single, delectable, irresistibly ripe piece of fruit plucked fresh from the branch awakened humanity's sexual appetite. Scholars may debate whether the fruit was an apple or a fig or an apricot or a pomegranate, but who doubts that biting into a fruit's taut, sun-warmed, sweet flesh could make Adam's and Eve's juices flow? As Milton describes the scene in *Paradise Lost*, when Adam and Eve ate from the fruit, "carnal desire enflaming, hee on *Eve*/Began to cast lascivious Eyes, she him/As wantonly repaid." Adam and Eve progress from eating the fruit of temptation to burning in lust in a few short lines.[1]

If you need persuasion that eating fruit might enflame the passions, just watch Alan Bates devour a fig in the 1969 film adaptation of D. H. Lawrence's *Women in Love*. At a summer picnic table in the verdant English countryside, the handsome, dark-haired, dark-eyed Bates grabs a purple fig from the fruit bowl, pushes his thumbs into its ripe center until it splits open, and presses his mouth directly to the red flesh inside. Bates tells the others that the Italians say the fig stands for "the female part, the fig-fruit; the fissure, the yoni, the wonderful moist conductivity toward the centre." He then lifts his juicy fingers to his lips and describes the smell to the table. Several of his dining companions are swooning by the scene's end.[2] Or, for a more recent example, consider Timothée Chalamet's lustful interlude with a peach, followed by Armie Hammer's hungry bite from the same peach, in the 2017 film *Call Me by Your Name*.[3]

The link between food and sex is a story told and retold in many times and places. In ancient Chinese poetry, hunger serves as a symbol for sexual appetite. The *Shijing*, a collection of folk songs and verse dating to the fourth or fifth century BCE, includes a poem that describes a girl starving for a boy who does not consummate their attraction: "There is a pelican on the bridge./It does not wet its beak./That boy there/does not

1

consummate his coition./Oh, dense! Oh, lush!/The morning rainbow on South Mountain./Oh, pretty! Oh, lovely!/This young girl is starving."[4] The fourth-century BCE Chinese philosopher Gaozi said "appetite for food and sex is nature." But the anthropologist Judith Farquhar, who studies modern China, challenges Gaozi, arguing that appetites for food and sex "are far from natural – in the sense of being ineluctable, everywhere the same, or determined outside of human history." Food and sex may have an "inherent comradeship," but their comradeship takes different forms across historical contexts.[5]

Like their Chinese counterparts, fourth-century BCE Athenians associated fish and lust in their poetry and treatises, but they applied their own distinct spin. For the Greeks, fish was not an appropriate sacrificial offering; it represented an indulgence that could only be justified by love for pleasure. Fish were considered irresistible, like sex itself, and gifts of fish were an instrument of seduction. Despite the rich Athenian discourse about food and sex, the topics have received little attention from classicists. The widely shared belief that food and sex are connected by nature has led scholars to neglect the topic as one requiring no explanation.[6]

The oversight can also be attributed to moral anxieties that date back to the classical era. Proper control of the alimentary and sexual appetites was a central concern of classical philosophy.[7] Ancient philosophers and medical authorities warned that luxurious foods stimulated dangerous lustful appetites. That concern shaped early Christian philosophy, and continues to feed a widespread unease today, contributing to ongoing neglect of the topic.[8]

This book traces the history of our modern belief system linking good food to wicked sex, from the invention of the restaurant in late eighteenth-century France through the emergence of the foodie in late twentieth-century Great Britain and the United States. The book ends where this research journey began for me. I was born in New York City in the mid-1970s and raised by parents who worked full-time jobs and had neither the time nor the inclination for performing great feats in the kitchen. Good food held little importance at the tables of my childhood. The first "gourmets" I met were my stepmother's first cousin, David, and his lover, Jerry, who loved to bake and would bring rich desserts to holiday meals. My stepmother's parents were old-school Jewish Marxists who came of age during the Great Depression. They reused tea bags and stocked a dusty case of off-brand soda in their garage, which no one would drink, which meant they never had to restock. At holidays, my step-grandfather would put out a *teiglach*, an inedible pile of hard little pastry nuggets stuck together with tooth-breaking honey syrup. One bite was all it took to abandon any thought of ever eating *teiglach* again, which inspired the theory that my step-grandfather brought the same inedible *teiglach* to every holiday, offering up the food equivalent of his undrinkable soda. Jerry's decadent desserts opened my eyes to a queer world where food's pleasure mattered more than its convenience or economy.

My childhood impression that all gay men were gourmets was reinforced by my favorite television show, *Three's Company*, about a cooking-school student named Jack Tripper who fools his landlord into letting him live with his two female roommates by pretending to be gay. In an earlier treatment for the series, the main character is a chef in a French restaurant.[9] In both versions, the character's gourmet cooking establishes his homosexual alibi, even as the show's humor depends on treating this association as an outdated stereotype. One of the most popular bestsellers of my childhood, *Real Men Don't Eat Quiche* (1982) by Bruce Feirstein, negotiated the same tension, its humor hinging on the association between gourmet French food and homosexuality, even as it implicitly made fun of that stereotype. In short, I came of age in a world where good food was still very gay, but there was a strong sense that times were changing.

I became a beneficiary of that change in the late 1980s when my mother started living with a man who loved to cook French food. Then I met my future husband, who set about trying to seduce me with his cooking (it worked). He made me a brook trout with lemons the first time I went to his apartment; the Athenians would have approved. Today, my students, born in the twenty-first century for the most part, don't associate gay men and gourmet food. They may not associate indulgent food with any of the varieties of illicit sexuality that I explore in this history – including prostitution, libertinism, lesbianism, and promiscuity.[10] But the social pressure my female students feel not to eat too much or too richly on first dates suggests that the belief system lingers on.[11] The popularity of the hashtag #foodporn on TikTok (more than 41 billion views!) reveals how this historic association survives in the English language. By unpeeling the onion and revealing the historical logic behind the often-unspoken rules that continue to influence our attitudes toward food and sex today, I hope this book will starve our moral discourses of some of their power and free readers to feed their appetites with less worry.

From Puritans to foodies

In the decade that I've spent researching the history of food and sex, I've frequently fielded skeptical questions from people who want to know how I can possibly squeeze such a vast topic into a single book. I can't, of course. I've limited myself to making a sweeping argument that covers two centuries and two continents. Briefly, *Lustful Appetites* argues that the emergence of the restaurant in late eighteenth-century France, and its popularity as a site for prostitution and adultery, prompted middle-class moralists in Britain and the United States during the nineteenth century to fixate on the dangerous link between French food – then the standard for good food – and immoral sex. Anglo-American Victorianism rejected the pleasures of the table as sexually suspect, especially for women. That attitude created the conditions for late nineteenth- and twentieth-century sexual outlaws, like bohemians, lesbians, and gay men, to claim a taste for good food as an identity marker. If loving good food made a person sexually suspect, then men and women who resisted sexual orthodoxy could claim their identity by indulging at the table. The first half of the book focuses on restaurants and sex work in the late eighteenth and nineteenth centuries; the second half of the book focuses on epicureanism and sexual rule-breakers in the late nineteenth and twentieth centuries.

Not until the sexual revolution of the 1960s and 1970s did this Anglo-American system of beliefs, or "alimentary-sexual regime," begin to fall apart.[12] In the late twentieth century, straight men and women claimed the new identity of the foodie, decoupling a taste for good food from sexual immorality. Even today, Anglo-Americans have a reputation for being "puritanical" about food and sex. By opening in the late eighteenth century, however, *Lustful Appetites* challenges the idea that the actual Puritans were to blame for this rejection of pleasure.

Victorian precepts against alimentary indulgence drew on a deep well of beliefs, dating back to ancient Greek and early Christian medicine and philosophy.[13] The fourth-century desert fathers tried to temper their lusts by fasting, even by giving up salt. Evagrius of Pontus (345–399 CE) warned that "gluttony is the mother of lust, the nourishment of evil thoughts."[14] Saint Basil (330–379 CE) believed that "through the sense of touch in tasting – which is always seducing toward gluttony by swallowing, the body, fattened up and titillated by the soft humors bubbling uncontrollably inside, is carried in a frenzy toward the touch of sexual intercourse." Similar beliefs circulated within medieval Catholicism, which defined gluttony as one of the seven deadly sins. Thomas à Kempis, the fifteenth-century author of *The Imitation of Christ*, the most widely read devotional book of the late medieval era, warned that "[w]hen the belly is full to bursting with food and drink, debauchery knocks at the door."[15]

Anglo-American culture began to develop a distinctive aversion to luxurious food during the early modern period. The Protestant Reformation rejected the Catholic practice of alternating feasting with fasting in favor of a new steady daily regime of plain food.[16] The slave trade, which justified enslavement, in part, by characterizing Black people as orally and sexually indulgent, contributed to a new ideal of slender, white female embodiment.[17] Later, the growing availability of food for the working classes during the Industrial Revolution led elites to distinguish themselves not by eating more than the poor, but by eating with greater refinement and delicacy.[18]

It's true that when the Puritans came to power in mid-seventeenth-century England, they attacked gluttony and feasting, which were associated with whoredom and adultery in English culture.[19] In 1645, the Puritan-dominated Long Parliament forbade the celebration of Christmas, a ban that lasted for fifteen years until the Restoration of the monarchy. The ban extended to mince pies, a traditional holiday food. Defenders of the feast day complained loudly. A 1646 pamphlet ridiculed the Puritans, complaining that in previous years Father Christmas could be found in every house, surrounded by "roaste Beefe and Mutton, Pies and Plum-porrige, and all manners of delicates," but the Parliament had locked him in prison where he became "much wasted, so that he hath looked very thin and ill."[20] Even after the Restoration, the Puritans' enemies continued to make fun of the mince pie ban. Samuel Butler's mock-heroic poem *Hudibras* scorned the Puritans as men who "quarrel with *minc'd Pies*, and disparage/Their best and dearest friend *Plum-Porridge*;/Fat *Pig* and *Goose* it self oppose./And blaspheme *Custard* through the *Nose*."[21] Butler's poem helped fix the reputation of the Puritans as haters of good food.

The Puritans who settled New England not only attacked gluttony, they linked it directly to illicit sexual behaviors. In a 1674 execution sermon delivered at the hanging of a seventeen-year-old boy caught committing bestiality with a mare, Puritan minister Samuel Danforth warned the community to "Beware of Fulnes of Bread, i.e., *Gluttony* and *Drunkenness*, This was another of the sins of *Sodom*, and it is the very fodder and the fuel of the sin of *uncleanness*." Danforth expanded on this theme in typical Puritan fashion by citing a large number of biblical passages linking excessive eating to sexual uncleanness: chapter 5, verse 7, from Jeremiah, about how the backsliding people of Jerusalem had fed to the full and then committed adultery; Book 2 of Peter, chapter 2, verses 13 and 14, about unclean people who feasted with their eyes full of adultery; Luke, chapter 21, verse 34, in which Jesus warned his followers not to let their hearts be overcharged by eating or drinking to excess. Danforth summed up these passages' moral lesson in his own distinctive phrase: "'Tis a lamentable thing to see Christians Belly-gods."[22]

Even after the Puritan era came to a close, their eighteenth-century descendants, New England Congregationalists and Presbyterians, continued to attack gluttony. One of the most frequently cited scriptural passages in New England between 1690 and 1740 was the warning against "eating and drinking unworthily" from Book 1 Corinthians, 11:29.[23] During the early eighteenth century, "there was a growing sense that an excess of food and nourishment was a vice." Revivalist ministers warned their flocks that "surfeiting," or consuming food to excess, would make them susceptible to lusts and passions.[24]

Unsurprisingly, many modern epicures, like André Simon the founder of the Wine & Food Society, complained that "the Puritans were responsible for the destruction of what sound gastronomic traditions existed" in England and the United States.[25] The Puritan hypothesis has had its defenders among food historians, but there are strong counterpoints against this seemingly logical argument.[26] In the first place, modern scholarship has complicated the Puritans' image as a people haunted "by the fear that someone, somewhere, may be happy," in H. L. Mencken's famous axiom. In fact, New England Puritans enthusiastically defended sexual pleasure within marriage, and they ate diverse diets that exploited the rich oceans and lands where they settled.[27] Neither sex nor food under the Puritans was as bland as they are depicted in the popular imagination.

In the second place, non-Puritans attacked the alimentary appetites in terms just as strenuous as their Puritan counterparts. In his *Manuall of Daily Prayers* (1655), Jeremy Taylor, an opponent to Puritanism, included a prayer to "Let my appetites be changed into spiritual desires, that I may hunger after the food of Angels . . . Lord let me eat and drink so, that my food may not become a temptation."[28] The Catholic priest Thomas Wright wrote in his book *The Passions of the Mind in General* (1601) that gluttony was "the forechamber of lust" and "great repasts swim under the froath of lust."[29] Similar sentiments can be found in non-religious seventeenth-century English texts. The playwright Thomas Middleton wrote, "if gluttony be the meat, lechery is the porridge; they're both boiled together."[30] In short, anti-gastronomic discourse was widespread in seventeenth-century Anglo culture, not confined to the Puritans.

A third weakness of the Puritan hypothesis is that there were similar currents of religious thought condemning gluttony in France, but they didn't lead to a lasting antagonism against eating for pleasure in French culture. In the sixteenth century, both French Protestants and French Catholics joined in the condemnation of gluttonous appetites, but eating well became a positive virtue in France by the seventeenth century, regardless of those critiques.[31]

The fourth and final problem with the Puritan hypothesis is that arguments that "food, like sex, is something necessary, but definitely not to be enjoyed by the virtuous," were far more common in nineteenth- and twentieth-century English texts than in their seventeenth- and eighteenth-century predecessors.[32] Between the early 1800s and the 1960s, the dominant middle-class Protestant culture in Britain and the United States ratcheted its hostility against the enjoyment of good food to unprecedented extremes. Although men also experienced its effects, this anathema fell particularly harshly on women.

Nothing was quite so distasteful, in the eyes of polite Victorian society, as the sight of a woman enthusiastically enjoying the taste of her food. In 1859, the American cookbook author Eliza Leslie advised ladies never to pour butter sauce over their fish, never to ask for food in a conspicuous voice, never to bite into a bread roll but to tear it into little bits, never to gnaw a bone, never to eat an orange except with a teaspoon, never to bite corn from the cob, never to drink two glasses of champagne, and never ever to utter the word *stomach* at table.[33] Even these guidelines were insufficient for the truly persnickety.[34] "A woman should never be seen eating or drinking," Lord Byron insisted, "unless it be lobster salad and champagne, the only truly feminine and becoming viands."[35] That even a notorious immoralist like Lord Byron shared his culture's revulsion for women's appetites points to the power this alimentary-sexual regime held.

In short, the roots of Anglo-American antipathy to the appetites stretched millennia deep, but the tree didn't reach full fruit until the early 1800s. Apple, pomegranate, apricot, or fig, the tree of temptation simultaneously haunted and enticed Anglo-American culture during the next two centuries. Only recently have we stepped out from beneath its shadowed branches. Even now, the fruit's sweet and poisonous taste lingers in our mouths.

ONE

The Pleasures of the Table

On a blustery chill day in the winter of 1947, a broken-hearted English woman sat down at her writing desk in a lonely hotel room in Ross-on-Wye under the watchful eye of John Wesley, the founder of Methodism, whose image was stamped on a frail white jug she had purchased at a local antique shop. Disconsolate about the hotel's rations-limited menu of flour-and-water soup, and rissoles made of bread and gristle, she dreamed of the flavorful Mediterranean food she had eaten in Egypt, where she spent the war years. In "a furious revolt" against the "terrible, cheerless, heartless food" served at the hotel, she wrote "words like apricot, olives and butter, rice and lemons, oil and almonds." The words acted like a ray of sun breaking through the grey skies that had flooded the West Country since her arrival, warming her skin and assuaging her grief. Looking back years later, Elizabeth David realized, "those were dirty words that I was putting down."[1] John Wesley would have agreed.

In the mid-eighteenth century, John Wesley published a popular diet book that prescribed exactly the sort of flavorless cuisine David mournfully encountered on her return to England. His 1751 *Primitive Physick* mixed the health teachings of the doctor and early vegetarian advocate George Cheyne with a Protestant religious message. Wesley warned his followers against the moral injury not only of meat eating, but of eating "pickled or smoked or salted food," or in fact any "high-season'd" dishes.[2] Physical *and* moral health, according to Wesley, depended on sticking to a plain diet. *Primitive Physick*'s impact reached far beyond the confines of Methodism, becoming a powerful gospel within Anglo-Protestantism writ large.

The Anglican minister and popular essayist Vicesimus Knox, for example, echoed Wesley in his writings, warning readers against the "pleasures of the table." Any person who ate beyond the point of moderation, like a "voracious and impure animal," according to Knox, should be grouped with "the loose, the profligate, the libidinous, [and] the drunkard."[3]

Benjamin Franklin, who published Wesley's sermons in the colonies, translated this Anglo-Protestant consensus into a pithy aphorism for American readers of his *Poor Richard's Almanack*: "a full Belly is the mother of all evil." During his youth, Franklin had fallen under the influence of another early vegetarian, the mystic Thomas Tryon, who believed that human passions had to be tamed through avoidance of meat. A lover of fine food and women (fine or otherwise), Franklin often strayed from his own best intentions, but his alter ego Poor Richard enthusiastically spread the gospel of "a sober diet" which "mitigates the Passions and Affections" and "allays the Heat of Lust."[4] *Poor Richard's Almanack* was one of the most popular books of the colonial era, selling up to ten thousand copies a year. Franklin's bestseller turned Tryon's esoteric advice into common sense for white, Protestant, middling-class Americans.

After the Revolution, America's leading physician, Benjamin Rush, recommended a sober diet for combating venereal desire and promoting wellbeing.[5] An Enlightenment thinker, Rush did not condemn pleasure as impure. He argued that embodied pleasures were designed by "a wise and good Being" to promote human health. But, he warned, pleasure in excess was a "frequent cause of disease." According to Rush, "riotous eaters of flesh" suffered liver obstructions, dropsy, low fevers, and unslakable thirst. When it came to diet, he recommended simplicity: one substantial meal a day, featuring a single plain dish.[6] Rush enshrined dietary temperance as a republican virtue, a contrast to the aristocratic gluttony of the old world.[7] A citizen's capacity for participating in self-governance was indicated by his regulation of his body. "A simplicity in diet, whether it be considered with reference to the happiness of individuals or the prosperity of a nation, is of more consequence than we are apt to imagine," the Massachusetts poet Joel Barlow wrote in the preface to his 1793 mock heroic, "Hasty Pudding," which celebrated New England's common cornmeal mush.[8] It was a dish often ridiculed by Europeans, who denigrated maize as animal feed, which in turn inspired American nationalists to elevate hasty pudding as a symbol of patriotic resistance. For citizens in the new United States, plain food became not simply a moral imperative but a nationalist commitment.[9]

Nothing represented excessive eating to Anglo-Americans more than French food. Over the course of the long eighteenth century, in the context of repeated wars fought between Britain and France for global domination, British identity coalesced around its distinctions from French culture. This process of cultural self-differentiation took hold in Britain's North American colonies as well as in the British Isles. British identity at home and abroad focused on Protestantism, as distinct from French Catholicism; around the parliamentary system, as distinct from French absolutism; and around plain food, as distinct from French gastronomy.[10]

Anglo complaints about French "licentiousness of eating" first appeared in the early eighteenth century. Eliza Smith's 1727 cookbook *The Compleat Housewife*, originally published in London and the first cookbook to be printed in the American colonies, proudly compiled "wholesome" recipes for "English palates" and rejected "French messes," or French food. She made a few exceptions when it came to baking, including recipes for French bread and French cake.[11] Hannah Glasse's *The Art of Cookery Made Plain and Easy* (1747), also popular in the colonies, voiced a similar bias against the fashion for French cooking and held up the "good English cook!" for admiration.[12] If most readers of Smith and Glasse were women, men encountered the same sentiments in popular periodicals like the *London Magazine* and the *Spectator*, both of which circulated in North America.[13] In sum, more than a century of war between France and Britain stigmatized French food as licentious and elevated a taste for plain cooking into a key facet of Anglo-American identity.[14]

For a brief window during the Revolution, patriotic pushback against British cultural dominance led Americans to re-evaluate the prejudice against French food. When American diplomats were posted to France following the 1778 military alliance, several discovered a taste for French cuisine. Thomas Jefferson's epicureanism is well known and entirely in keeping with his general spendthrift love for luxuries of all sorts. But his more dour colleague John Adams also enjoyed French food during his diplomatic posting to Paris, writing back to Abigail Adams in 1779 that "the cookery and the manner of living here, which you know Americans were taught by their former absurd masters to dislike, is more agreeable to me than you can imagine."[15] This window of rapprochement shut, however, after the French Revolution's violent turn during the Reign of Terror. A new wave of Francophobia in the United States renewed longstanding suspicions of the licentiousness of French cuisine and strengthened the republican argument for the virtue of plain food.[16]

Cabinets particuliers

The guillotine scared many Americans and Britons off French politics, but another French invention turned their opinions against French cuisine: the restaurant. The problem was not that the food served in restaurants was bad. The problem was that the sex served alongside it was very, very wicked. The development of an eroticized French gastronomic culture in the late eighteenth century was the grain of sand, or irritant, around which the pearl of a new Anglo-American alimentary-sexual regime took shape in the nineteenth century.

To a purist, the kitchen might seem like the most important room in a restaurant, but to the impurists who frequented restaurants in their early days, the *cabinet particulier* held that distinction. The *cabinet particulier* was a small private room, typically furnished with a table, chairs, and a couch, where a man could dine in the company of a woman who was not his wife. *Cabinets particuliers* could be luxurious, like the infamous upstairs rooms at Lapérouse, on Paris's Left Bank, where women tested the diamonds they received from lovers by scratching the stones' facets against the mirrored walls.[17] Or they could be basic cribs, just four walls and a couch. Sumptuous or stark, *cabinets particuliers* were as common in nineteenth-century French restaurants as wine cellars. For many male diners – and during the nineteenth century most diners-out were male – the restaurant was a place to have sex, as much as a place to eat.

Sex figured prominently in conceptions of the restaurant from the beginning. The word *restaurant* originated in the mid-eighteenth century as a French term for a meat bouillon sold in Paris eateries to refined gentlemen who supposedly required delicate foods to restore their sensitive constitutions.[18] The *restaurant* was an elixir intended to reinvigorate the drooping male. This treatment was supported by classical Galenic physiology, which linked hot and humid foods, like meat broth, to spermatic production and increased virility.[19] Women also consumed *restaurants*, but with less frequency than men, whose needs and appetites drove the expanding trade.[20] In a satirical etching from 1782 titled "Le Restaurant," a man is shown amorously clutching a woman on a settee, while a maid

A gentleman amorously clutches a woman on a divan in a luxurious room meant to represent a *cabinet particulier*, while a maid servant serves a bowl of *restaurant*. "Le Restaurant," 1782. Jeanne Deny or Martial Deny after Niclas Lafrensen II (Nicolas Lavreince). Widener Collection.
Courtesy National Gallery of Art, Washington

servant hovers nearby holding a bowl of broth on a serving platter. The man's sword is propped against a chair, pointing upwards. The setting is a *cabinet particulier*, although it could easily be mistaken for a bedroom.[21]

The word "restaurant" soon shifted from describing a type of broth to the type of place that served the broth. Restaurants were distinct from other public eating places at the time, like the communal *tables d'hôte* in hotels, because they permitted a diner to enter at any time, sit at a private table, and order from a menu that priced each dish individually.[22] *Tables d'hôte*, on the other hand, had set mealtimes, prices fixed per meal, and public tables. In the late eighteenth century, restaurateurs expanded their menus beyond broths to offer other delicate foods. The first grand restaurants in the city opened in the 1780s in the Palais-Royal, a popular cruising ground for sex workers. Male pleasure-seekers could satisfy both their alimentary and sexual appetites in a single visit. The connection between restaurants and sex workers became even more entangled after the Revolution when new restaurants emerged along the grand boulevards of Paris's Right Bank. Many of these luxurious establishments, decorated with immense mirrors and smokeless oil lamps, also included *cabinets particuliers* where men could bring prostitutes and mistresses. By the beginning of the nineteenth century, Parisian bourgeois men would not bring their wives to restaurants with private rooms.[23]

The rise of restaurants in France coincided with the emergence of a new genre of "gastronomic" literature that celebrated pleasurable eating as a social good.[24] This literature departed from traditional Christian doctrines that regarded eating for pleasure as morally problematic. According to those teachings, eating for the purpose of sustaining the body was ethically good; eating for the purpose of self-pleasuring was ethically wrong because it was a conduit for lust. Stigmatization of the unbridled appetite for indulgent cuisine persisted in France during the early decades of the Enlightenment but later loosened.[25] In the late eighteenth century, the secular turn of the French Revolution toppled the last religious proscriptions on eating for pleasure.

The writer Joseph de Berchoux captured this shifting sensibility in an 1801 poem titled "La Gastronomie", coining a new term for the art and science of eating for pleasure, freed from the imputations of sinfulness that clung to the old term *gourmanderie* (gluttony).[26] "Gastronomy" celebrated the interconnections between food and sex. An early edition of Berchoux's popular poem included a frontispiece depicting a man having his cup filled at a café by a pretty waitress whom he is clinching lasciviously.[27] The verses that followed continued in the same erotic vein, for example describing an old man gazing at his favorite dish with "an amorous leer."[28]

The word "gastronomy" soon spread among French food writers. The most famous food writer of the early nineteenth century, Jean Anthelme Brillat-Savarin, subtitled his *Physiologie du Gout*, "*méditations de gastronomie transcendante*."[29] Like the restaurant, gastronomy had as much to do with sex as food from the outset. Writers could not resist incorporating erotic themes in their food writing, and few things absorbed their attention as much as the pleasures of the *cabinet particulier*.

According to the nineteenth-century writers Francisque Michel and Édouard Fournier, authors of *Histoire des Hôtelliers, Cabarets, Hôtels Garnis, Restaurants et Cafés* (1851), the first Paris establishment to offer customers a *cabinet particulier* was a seventeenth-century cabaret named L'Écharpe, in the Place Royale (the Place des Vosges today). Michel and Fournier drew their information from a 1635 book by Charles Sorel that recommended L'Écharpe as a place where men could pay the proprietor to rent "the prettiest room in the house" and drink sweet wines with their mistresses without being troubled or cheated by anyone.[30] This genealogy was repeated in a history of cafés and cabarets by Alfred Delvau, a nineteenth-century Paris journalist famous for his accounts of daily life in the French capital, and in another history of cabarets by Albert de La Fizelière, a friend of Baudelaire. Delvau called the *cabinet particulier* a diabolical invention, the pitfall of virtues and fortunes – but considering his fascination with the Paris underworld, it's hard to take him too seriously as a moralist.[31]

In the 1800s, *cabinets particuliers* became commonplace in Paris.[32] The journalist Georges Touchard-Lafosse wrote in 1821 that for several years past, all the restaurants in Paris had painted the words "*cabinets particuliers*" prominently on their signs.[33] This included many of the city's earliest restaurants, including La Galiote, which dated back to the Revolution. The number of restaurants that had private rooms expanded over the course of the century and reached a peak of popularity during the Second Empire, 1852–70. By 1861, Pierre Larousse, the famous dictionary writer and encyclopedist, insisted that *cabinets particuliers* were "*the* principal attraction of renowned restaurants" in Paris, including the Café Anglais, the Maison Dorée, and the Café Riche, which were frequented by aristocrats and the very wealthy.[34]

Private rooms were famous for their waiters' discretion. In a one-act French vaudeville titled *Les Cabinets Particuliers* (1832), a waiter tells the restaurateur that he thinks a young man and a woman dining in one of the rooms must be lovers, but the restaurateur forbids him from making any such interpretations, telling him a waiter must be deaf and mute. Later, when confronted by a suspicious husband searching for his wife, the restaurateur refuses to say where she is, insisting that it's his professional obligation to be discreet.[35] The waiters were to keep their eyes averted from anything they shouldn't see in the private rooms, and after serving dessert, they wouldn't enter the room again without first loudly announcing their arrival. To protect the diners' privacy, the rooms could even be locked from the inside, preventing any possible interruption of the guests' enjoyment. The lock also allowed men to trap their female guests. Unsurprisingly, the private rooms were notorious for sexual coercion.

Georges Touchard-Lafosse reported eavesdropping on a seduction taking place in the private room next to his own on a visit to La Galiote. The man began by saying "You defend yourself in vain, you must cede, the moment has arrived," to which the woman replied "Don't demand it; I swore I wouldn't." After a little more back and forth, including the woman's confession that she had betrayed similar oaths twelve times since she was fifteen years old, the woman acknowledged her weakness and gave way.[36] In Touchard-Lafosse's dialogue, the coercion is part of the flirtation, but other sources acknowledged the violence that such encounters could entail. In an otherwise humorous book titled *Mémoires d'un Cabinet Particulier* (1863), a private room recalled its varied guests, including a serial rapist. The unpleasant man arrived each time with a different modestly dressed working-class girl who hardly dared to lift her eyes. After the food was served, the man would slip the waiter a five-franc piece and tell him not to come in, no matter what he heard. Several months later, the girl would return, this time dressed in silks and makeup, and always on the arm of a different man. To the author, the rapes were a catalyst for the women's greater misfortune, their descent into prostitution.[37] A similar scene is described in Gustave Flaubert's

L'Éducation Sentimentale (1869), when Rosanette, a courtesan, tells the story of how her mother sold her virginity to a married man who took her to a *cabinet particulier* and raped her on the divan after the waiter had plied her with wine.[38]

The waiters who served the *cabinets particuliers* may have been discreet when it came to the occupants' sexual encounters, but that's not to say they were disinterested. In addition to hosting liaisons, the *cabinets particuliers* were used for literary salons, business meetings, and political gatherings, all of which could generate conversation of interest to the state. According to Larousse, during the waning days of the July Monarchy (1830–1848), conspirators gathered in private rooms in restaurants to plan their coups while the waiters, in the pay of the police, eavesdropped avidly. Never, Larousse wrote, had the expression "the walls have ears" been truer.[39] The government also paid informants to listen in on the amorous encounters transacted within the private rooms. Keeping track of the sexual peccadillos of powerful men could prove just as useful as listening in on their political loose talk.[40] During the Second Empire, the Paris police surveilled both the moral and political goings-on in the cabinets.[41]

In a book about policing, Gustave-Placide Macé, commander of the Sûreté, or investigative bureau of the Paris police, from 1879 to 1884, wrote that "wine, gambling, girls, disease, and adultery" were the foundations of the *cabinet particulier*. The rooms varied in luxury and cost. At the lower end of the economic scale, wine-sellers furnished rooms with bare cots and served marked-up bad wines to men enjoying the company of dishevelled and dirty prostitutes. At the high end, the grand restaurateurs of the boulevards provided luxurious rooms and sold overpriced weak champagne to wealthy men in the company of finely made-up courtesans. Differences in accommodations, however, could not disguise the fundamental commonalities across the economic spectrum. In all the rooms, according to Macé, bestiality and brutishness reigned supreme. Even in the finest restaurants, the courtesans carved obscene pictures into the mirrors with the diamonds they were gifted and left piles of dirty dishes stacked on the pianos.[42]

La cuisine d'amour

The menus offered in the *cabinets particuliers* tended toward lighter fare. The authors of *Paris-Restaurants*, one of fifty short illustrated volumes on Parisian life from 1854, ridiculed the food served in private rooms, such as small morsels pickled in vinegar, fried peaches, cucumbers in oil, and pineapple sauce. The rooms were not intended for serious eating but for canoodling. What did it matter if the truffles were losing their scent or the wines were bad, as long as there were two burning hearts and a bottle of champagne on ice? "Le divan est le plat de résistance du cabinet particulier," they explained. The couch was the dish of choice.[43] A later article on the "decline of French cooking" echoed this complaint. The young men who patronized the city's prostitutes were "not gourmets, and when they order dinners in those private rooms which every Parisian restaurant must have, they often regard the divan as the *plat de résistance*." As a result of their bad influence, the city's restaurants had been taken over by unartistic cooking and economical sauces.[44]

This assessment was overly harsh. While it was "understood that the *cabinet particulier* was not precisely invented for the work of chewing," many restaurants nevertheless provided a wide menu, often with a focus on aphrodisiac foods.[45] Larousse listed champagne, oysters, crawfish bisque, and truffled young partridge as standard offerings.[46] Many of these foods had long been associated with the sexual appetite. The oyster's reputation as an aphrodisiac dated back to ancient Rome, owing to the mollusk's resemblance to female genital anatomy. Pliny the Younger wrote in the first century CE of treating a friend to a dinner featuring oysters and erotic dancers from Cadiz.[47] The Roman satirist Juvenal jokingly compared eating oysters to cunnilingus.[48] The association between oysters and sex persisted throughout the centuries. Early modern medical literature credited oysters with the power of sexual invigoration. Felix Platter's *A Golden Practice of Physick* recommended oysters as a curative for "want of Copulation."[49] And Casanova famously devoured dozens of oysters at a time in the company of girls and women whom he was seeking to seduce.[50] At the time Larousse was writing, the French word for oysters, *huître*, was a familiar euphemism for the vulva.[51]

The sexual symbolism of the oyster also drew from the classical myth that Aphrodite, or Venus, the goddess of love, was born from the ocean, arising from the foam in a seashell. In most classical depictions, the shell is a scallop, but the erotic association spilled over onto the oyster. Venus rising from the sea was a popular theme in Renaissance art, most famously in Sandro Botticelli's *The Birth of Venus* (1485), where the nude goddess is depicted standing daintily on a scallop shell, and in Titian's *Venus Anadyomene* (1520), where the scallop shell floats near her rounded hips. Nineteenth-century French artists frequently adapted this Renaissance theme. In 1838, James Pradier sculpted a Venus in bronze, reclining gracefully in a shell that looks more like an oyster than a scallop. William-Adolphe Bouguereau's *The Birth of Venus* (1879), consciously echoes Botticelli's composition, with the fully nude goddess counter-poised in a scallop shell, surrounded by fawning attendants, one blowing on a conch.

The famous scene held understandable appeal for restaurateurs and dinner-party hosts. Eugène Briffault, one of the most prominent food writers in nineteenth-century France, described a famous supper held for *viveurs,* or sensualists. In the middle of the table stretched a platter covered by a pink veil. When all the male guests were seated, the servants lifted the veil and revealed a young woman lying on a conch shell sur-rounded by marine plants. She was draped in coral and appeared to be sleeping, but when the carvers came to carry her away she jumped to her feet and "assumed the pose of a nymph as if she were going to perform the dance of the naiads," then bounded over the heads of the guests and disappeared. Such suppers for *viveurs,* according to Briffault, became popular during the 1820s and were frequently hosted in the *cabinets particuliers* of famous restaurants, like the Café Anglais. But Briffault complained that these suppers inclined too greatly toward flirtation and seduction, detracting from what he considered to be the proper focus of a good dinner: the food.[52]

Like oysters, crawfish (or crayfish) also had an aphrodisiac reputation connected to their watery origins. The word "aphrodisiac," of course, derives from Aphrodite, and all foods of the sea, her birth element, were thought to promote sexual potency.[53] In the nineteenth century, crawfish became the archetypal seduction food served in the *cabinet particulier*. According to the American food historian Waverley Root, "a young lady invited to dine out, if she was ushered into one of those private restaurant dining rooms so popular at the period, remarkable for the tact and discretion of their staffs, to find a bucket of champagne and a bowl of crawfish on the table, knew what she had to expect." The French historian Robert Courtine concurs that "crayfish, in those days, were inseparable from lover's feasts."[54]

A short illustrated comedic monologue from 1879 titled *Les Écrevisses* (The Crawfish), written by Jacques Normand, a friend of Alexandre Dumas *fils*, celebrated the crustacean's connection to the *cabinet particulier*. The poem tells the story of a provincial young man's dream of eating an amorous meal of crawfish in a Paris *cabinet particulier*. He travels to Paris to collect his inheritance and, on what is meant to be his final night in town, he takes a young woman to a meal of crawfish in a private room. The meal is such a success that he repeats it for the next week, and soon six months have passed and still he lingers in Paris. The poem includes a picture of two lovers sharing a kiss in a *cabinet particulier*, their faces obscured by an enormous crawfish standing on its fanned tail. Beneath the image, the poem explains that while the hair colors of the women with whom the young man shares his *tête-à-têtes* might change – sometimes blonde, sometimes brunette – the menu always stays the same: "*C'étaient toujours des écrevisses, en cabinet particulier!*" It's always crawfish in the *cabinet particulier*.[55] Predictably, the French word for crawfish, *écrevisse*, like oyster, doubled as slang for women's genitalia.[56]

The dish of young truffled partridge included by Larousse on the menu of the *cabinet particulier* also had erotic associations dating back to classical roots.[57] Many birds, including partridges, pigeons, ducks, and turkeys, were believed to be hot and humid and, therefore, aphrodisiac. There were exceptions to this rule. Peacocks, quail, and thrush were hot birds but did not augment sexuality.[58] In French literature, partridges in particular figured frequently as a sexual symbol. Medieval bestiaries described partridges as highly sexual birds, because the females laid many eggs and the males purportedly engaged in sex with other males.[59] The association between partridges and erotic activity persisted in gastronomic writings in the nineteenth century. Jean Anthelme Brillat-Savarin, rhapsodized about the erotic sight of a pretty woman nibbling on a partridge wing in *The Physiology of Taste*:

> Nothing is more agreeable to look at than a pretty gourmande in full battle-
> dress: her napkin is tucked in most sensibly; one of her hands lies on the

A dissolute young man wastes his fortune over amorous crawfish dinners in a
cabinet particulier with young sex workers in this illustration by S. Arcos from
Jacques Normand, *Les Écrevisses* (Tresse: Paris, 1789).

table; the other carries elegantly carved little morsels to her mouth, or perhaps
a partridge wing on which she nibbles; her eyes shine, her lips are soft and
moist, her conversation is pleasant, and all her gestures are full of grace.[60]

Brillat-Savarin does not locate this sight in a particular place, but it
is easy to imagine the encounter in a *cabinet particulier*, where far from
the prying eyes of the public a woman might feel comfortable to rest her
hand on the table and eat meat from the bone (but only nibble; it would
have been unseemly to put the entire bone in her mouth).

Brillat-Savarin also wrote about "the erotic properties of truffles" in
The Physiology of Taste. He attributed the great love of truffles among
French women to "the general conviction that the truffle contributes
to sexual pleasures." Not content with relying on its reputation, Brillat-
Savarin decided that further research was required to determine whether
"the truffle's amorous effects were real." When he asked his women
friends, they gave ironical or evasive answers. Only one woman was

willing to answer straightforwardly, telling him that one time after a meal of truffled fowl she almost succumbed to the seductions of a friend of her husband. When she woke in the morning, she felt ashamed by her infamous behavior. "I blame the whole thing on the truffles," she confessed. From that point on, she had never eaten them without mistrust.[61] This anecdote was too risqué for some early English translations. Fayette Robinson who published an American translation in 1854 excised Brillat-Savarin's conversation with his woman friend, explaining "the Translator here has thought it best to omit a very BROAD dialogue, which Brillat-Savarin introduced into his book."[62] Along with the *cabinet particulier*, the gastronomic writings that explicitly celebrated its erotic pleasures fixed the association between French restaurants, French cuisine, and illicit sexuality in the Anglo-American imagination.

Turning tricks

The many tricks that sex workers and restaurateurs used to part patrons from their money did nothing to redeem the reputation of French restaurants in the nineteenth century. Many restaurants operated on a kickback system to reward women guests for ordering expensive items, chief among them champagne, the drink of choice to wash down the delicate morsels served up in the *cabinet particulier*. Champagne's popularity owed less to its reputation as an aphrodisiac than to its association with luxury. Champagne at a meal signaled indulgence, both alimentary and erotic. The nineteenth-century journalist Paul Mahalin claimed that one of the most respectable restaurateurs in Paris put his mark on champagne corks, allowing women to return the morning after an evening spent in a *cabinet particulier* and exchange each cork for cash.[63]

Gustave Macé, the Paris police chief, described an elaborate system in which prostitutes received commissions on drink and food from restaurants. In one scam, a restaurant might have two sets of prices: less expensive for the regulars, including the prostitutes, and more expensive for the occasional visitors, like the clients the women brought in. A prostitute might pay the restaurateur for her own meal at the discounted rate, then bring the bill for the full meal at the higher price to her client, who would pay for her meal a second time. Later, the prostitute would recoup the second cost of her meal from the restaurateur.[64] In another scam, restaurateurs would pay women commissions for ordering dishes that weren't selling well and that needed to be offloaded from the kitchen before they spoiled.[65] Even high-end restaurants engaged in these tactics. An English guide to Paris nightlife published in 1877 claimed that the *cocottes*, or high-class prostitutes who were frequent guests in the *cabinets particuliers* at the Maison Dorée and the Café Anglais, earned commissions on the total bills for the evening. Female guests typically ordered the most expensive dishes, like truffles, game, lobster salad, and champagne, to drive the cost up. Sometimes they would beseech their hosts to buy them one of the elegant fans or other pricey items that decorated the mantelpieces. The next day, the women would return to the restaurant, exchange the fan for cash, and receive a payout on the meal.[66]

The category of French sex workers who specialized in making money by eating with men in the private rooms of restaurants came to be known as *soupeuses*. Roughly translated, this word means female diners. Nineteenth-century slang dictionaries defined the *soupeuse* as a type of prostitute, a profession for which the French language had hundreds of words. According to Albert Barrère's *Argot and Slang* (1889), the *soupeuse* was a prostitute fond of eating in *cabinets particuliers*.[67] Within the grand hierarchy of nineteenth-century Paris sex workers, *soupeuses* fell in the middle, beneath the celebrated *grandes horizontales* or most expensive courtesans, like Marie Duplessis or Cora Pearl, but above the denigrated *pierreuses*, or streetwalkers, who proliferated in the city. The journalist Ali Coffignon positioned *soupeuses* within the category of *femmes galantes*, or courtesans. *Soupeuses* had flash and style. They dressed in colorful and gaudy clothes, which were often beyond the means of ordinary streetwalkers. Becoming a *soupeuse* took the assistance of an *ogresse*, a woman who made her money renting or selling expensive clothes to sex workers.[68] A couple of images of *soupeuses* from the turn of the twentieth century show them dressed in pink, with big hats and feathers and eye-catching ruffles.

Soupeuses were ubiquitous at "night restaurants," which stayed open after the theaters closed between ten at night and three or four in the morning. These night restaurants illuminated the Boulevard des Italiens and other grand avenues of the city long after all the other shops had extinguished their lights. They existed to entertain men on the town, not simply to feed them, and that entertainment required women. "Pour le souper il faut la *soupeuse*. Un souper sans femme serait un simple dîner

Two images of *soupeuses*, French sex workers who specialized in dining in *cabinets particuliers* with their customers. The *soupeuses* wear large flashy hats and gaudy pink clothes that advertise their availability. Edgar Chahine's 1901 *Un Couple de Soupeuses*, (left), and Georges Bottini 1903 *La Soupeuse* (right).
Wikimedia Commons (left) and Rosenwald Collection, Courtesy National Gallery of Art, Washington (right)

nocturne," explained an author of the time, or in rough translation: *a supper requires a soupeuse; a supper without women would be simply a nighttime dinner.*[69] Naturally, most night restaurants offered *cabinets particuliers* for the convenience of their customers.

Owners of night restaurants worked in conjunction with the *soupeuses*. Some owners of night restaurants were married to madams who operated *maisons de tolérance*, or licensed brothels.[70] Night restaurateurs would go to concert halls and theaters and pass out vouchers to pretty women, or slip them a few francs for a meal. The voucher covered an inexpensive meal like *choucroute* (sauerkraut and sausage), a half-bottle of wine, and a dessert. The expense to the restaurateur paid dividends since the men who frequented night restaurants chose them on the basis of the *soupeuses* they attracted. Restaurateurs also reimbursed *soupeuses* for the price of drinks consumed on site while waiting to attract a customer to take her to a private room. The elevated prices in the *cabinets particuliers* compensated for the loss on the price of drinks.[71]

There were probably as many different compensation schemes as restaurants. The *soupeuse* might earn a price on each man she brought to a restaurant, or receive commissions on champagne, or pocket the difference between the price of her meal and the elevated price on the *cabinet* menu. A *soupeuse* might have several different meals with several different men over the course of the evening, bringing her final client home with her.[72] Some *soupeuses* earned money primarily through their work within the restaurant, but there were also sex workers who used meals in a restaurant as a means to gauge the depth of their clients' wallets before committing to an evening together.

While many texts and images depicted the *soupeuse* as a glamorous figure, social critics cast a more withering eye. In his slang dictionary *Vocabula Amatoria* (1896), John Stephen Farmer acidly defined the *soupeuse* as a "variety of prostitute well-known in certain restaurants provided with private rooms. They dress well, are amusing, but are not necessarily young."[73] Macé likewise described some of the *soupeuses* as older women who could no longer earn a decent income from sex work, and depended on generous men to buy them meals in order to eat. The real *soupeuse*, he wrote, was "*bouffie, molle, viande de seconde catégorie,*" or puffy, soft, second-rate meat. They floated, he wrote, from table to table, having a chop here, a radish there, stealing away a glass of wine and fobbing off the bills on male diners.[74] Particularly rapacious *soupeuses* were known as *flibocheuses*. The word was a portmanteau of *flibustière*, the French word for a filibuster or pirate, and *rigolbocheuse*, or a licentious woman.[75] A satirist described the *flibocheuse* as half-woman, half-sponge.[76]

One school of French social science theorized that women became prostitutes because of their inordinate appetites for food. Alphonse Esquiros, a socialist writer and friend of Victor Hugo, published an 1840 study of prostitutes that drew on the pseudoscience of phrenology, or study of cranial characteristics, to analyze sex workers. The cerebral organ that predominated in prostitutes, according to Esquiros, was the organ of alimentivity, which controlled the appetites. Esquiros explained that working-class women with enlarged organs of alimentivity who couldn't endure the routine starvation typical of their social status became prostitutes in order to satisfy their hungers. In other words, nineteenth-century French society denied poor women an honest means to fill their stomachs, so they resorted to sex work instead. An immoderate need for food led women to become sex workers, and once the work began filling their stomachs, their hunger kept them in the profession. The great majority of brothels, according to Esquiros, kept well-stocked tables. The proof that it was hunger for food, not sex, that drove working-class women to become prostitutes could be observed from their bodies. Prostitutes were inclined to embonpoint, with large and protruding breasts, fleshy shoulders, ample pelvises, abundant firm flesh, and devouring mouths.[77]

Grandes horizontales *at the Grand Seize*

The idea that women became prostitutes because of their alimentary appetites played out in popular narratives about celebrated nineteenth-century courtesans as well. Stories of the famous *grandes horizontales* of the mid-nineteenth century entertained audiences in Britain and the United States as well as in France and helped fix the association between French food and illicit sex in the Anglo-American imagination. For example, Marie Duplessis, one of the most famous demimondaines of the mid-nineteenth century and the inspiration for the writer Alexandre Dumas *fils*'s heroine Marguerite in *La Dame aux Camélias* (1848), arrived in Paris as an impoverished teenager and was standing on a corner staring at a street vendor selling fried potatoes, "like a peasant craving gold coins," when she was discovered by the famed dandy and theater director Nestor Roqueplan. Roqueplan bought her the potatoes, which she devoured. After this auspicious introduction to the fast life, Duplessis became the mistress of a restaurateur named Nollet, who owned an establishment in the Palais-Royal. She climbed the ranks from there and became a famous guest of the *cabinets particuliers* of the Café Anglais and the Maison Dorée. She had a sweet tooth, and a passion for cookies and iced meringues.[78]

Similar stories about the grand appetites of the *grandes horizontales* appear throughout the literature of the Second Empire. The English-born demimondaine Cora Pearl, who became famous in Paris for her marvelous equestrianism as she rode out mornings in the Bois de Boulogne, rivaled Marie Duplessis in her love for fine food. Pearl could frequently be found in the private rooms of restaurants. Auguste Escoffier, the most celebrated French chef of the nineteenth century, cooked for her at Le Petit Moulin Rouge, the first restaurant he worked at in Paris. He invented a dish that he called Noisettes d'Agneau Cora, which was lamb served within artichoke hearts, a pun on the term *coeur d'artichaut* used for men who fell in love with every woman they met. On another occasion, Escoffier created a menu for Pearl and a young lover that included a dish of *pigeon en cocotte*, another French pun: a pigeon was a word for a sucker, and a *cocotte* meant a courtesan. Escoffier described Pearl as "particularly talented in the art of plucking these little birds."[79] Sometimes the little birds took offense. In 1872, the grandson of the proprietor of France's first restaurant chain, the Bouillons Duval, accidentally shot himself at Pearl's apartment (he meant to shoot her), leading to her temporary exile from Paris. This incident did little to temper her extravagance. According to a famous story, Cora Pearl once had herself served up naked, garnished with a few sprigs of parsley, on an enormous silver platter in the Grand Seize room at the Café Anglais.[80]

The chef at the Café Anglais, Adolphe Dugléré, also named a dish after one of the *grandes horizontales* who frequented the Grand Seize. *Pommes Anna*, a dish made from layered sliced potatoes cooked in butter to make a cake, was named for Anna Deslions.[81] During Dugléré's sojourn in the kitchen, the Grand Seize became the most legendary of Paris's *cabinets particuliers*. According to Charles-Albert comte de Maugny, who subtitled his memoir about Paris in the Second Empire the "memories of a sybarite," the city's leading demimondaines ended every day in the Grand Seize.[82] In addition to Pearl and Deslions, the room was patronized by Esther Guimond, Blanche d'Antigny, and their royal and aristocratic lovers, the Prince of Wales, the Prince of Orange, the Duke of Rivoli, and Prince Auguste d'Arenberg.

The restaurants Brébant-Vachette and Bonnefoy also attracted many celebrated courtesans of the Second Empire. According to Maugny, the *cocottes* were "really at home there. The frills of their silk dresses brighten the echoes of the private rooms, and their light songs escape cheerfully through the half-open windows."[83] The mirrors in the private rooms at Brébant-Vachette were scratched with the names of countless *soupeuses*.[84] Many of the *soupeuses* who frequented Vachette were young and "appetizing," according to Alfred Delvau, but there were plenty who showed the marks of their years. And yet, Delvau remarked acidly, these experienced women were quite successful at luring men into *cabinets*.[85] Delvau's 1867 guidebook to the pleasures of Paris made note of which cafés and restaurants were most visited by *cocottes* and their male companions. These ranged from upscale establishments like Maison Dorée, which had as many *cocottes* as Egypt had grasshoppers, to dubious, even dangerous, places, like Le Café du Rat Mort (the Dead Rat Café).

The association between sex workers and restaurants was so powerful that by 1860, according to the nineteenth-century French historian Jules Michelet, a single woman could "hardly go out in the evening; she would be taken for a prostitute . . . She would never dare enter a restaurant."[86] Michelet overstated the case, reifying bourgeois norms that were more prescriptive than descriptive. But the linkage between sex workers and food was very strong, and hardly limited to restaurants and cafés. The most successful demimondaines were also famous for the extravagant meals they served at parties. A guidebook to Paris at night described the menus at such "cocottes' balls" as a parade of delicacies, including dishes like truffled partridge, baked quail, the delicate sausage known as a *boudin à la Richelieu*, and sole with shrimp, all washed down with champagne and great wines like Château Lafite.[87]

The literary brothers Edmond and Jules de Goncourt attended a dinner at the house of the courtesan Giulia Beneni (known as La Baruccione) and described the menu she served of turtle soup, truffles, pheasant, asparagus, and crawfish, all of which were considered aphrodisiacs. The menu was designed to excite, they commented in their journal, with the dishes heavily spiced and peppered, as was typical of the food served in bordellos.[88] Some called this style of cooking *cuisine de cocotte*, a pun since the word *cocotte* meant both courtesan and a type of cooking vessel. One friend of the Prince of Wales defined *cuisine de cocotte* as truffles, shellfish, champagne, and other expensive luxuries.[89] The high-society gossip columnist Frederick Cunliffe-Owen, who wrote under the pen name "Marquise de Fontenoy," described *cuisine de cocotte* as "highly seasoned" and of a "florid character."[90] True gourmands, these literary men all agreed, shuddered at this style of cooking as being in poor taste.

The *cabinet particulier* proved as irresistible to French writers, like the Goncourts, as it did to French gourmands. Often enough, when they could afford it, the writers were gourmands. Honoré de Balzac collaborated with Horace Raisson to publish a restaurant guide.[91] Alexandre Dumas *père* authored a twelve-hundred-page cookbook.[92] A friend of Dumas, who witnessed the great writer with his sleeves rolled up in the kitchen, wrote, "I verily believe that Dumas took a greater pride in concocting a stew than in constructing a novel or a play."[93] Dumas took his gastronomy to extremes, but he was one among many French writers of the mid-nineteenth century who lived their lives in restaurants and took gastronomy seriously. Restaurants naturally found their way into the works of these writers, and the Grand Seize room of the Café Anglais laid particular claim to their imagination. It appeared again and again in French literature, ranging from operas, to plays, to novels. "The dramatists and novelists have used and abused the famous private room known as *le grand seize*," observed an American critic in 1893. The observation proved true of his countrymen as well.[94]

The first French authors to write about the Grand Seize were the chroniclers of Paris's high life during the Second Empire. *La Vie Parisienne*, a weekly magazine founded in 1863 that enchanted readers with its bountiful illustrations and articles about theater, fashion, and gossip, mentioned the room in a risqué 1864 piece about a comic "actress" named Lolo. She was the type who knew all of Paris, and all of Paris knew her. Her affections were fleeting and the day after a love affair she would burst out laughing and run to the Grand Seize to party with her friends.[95] The room makes a similar appearance in Jacques Offenbach's 1866 operetta *La Vie Parisienne*, the libretto for which was written by Henri Meilhac and Ludovic Halévy. Offenbach, Meilhac, and Halévy are synonymous with the musical theater of the Second Empire. Their erotic fictions about the lives of the city's demimondaines contributed enormously to the women's golden legend. In *La Vie Parisienne*, the heroine Métella sings a tribute to brilliant champagne-drunk nights spent at the Grand Seize.[96]

The room also appeared repeatedly in French crime fiction published in the late nineteenth century. Scholars date the origins of the French detective novel to Émile Gaboriau's *Monsieur Lecoq* novels of the 1860s.[97] His success swiftly inspired imitators, including Adolphe Belot, Pierre Alexis Ponson du Terrail, Fortuné du Boisgobey, and Charles Mérouvel. The Grand Seize appeared in novels by each of these authors. In Adolphe Belot's *Le Drame de la Rue de la Paix* (1867), an aspiring detective prepares to confront the suspect in a murder at a dinner party he has arranged in the Grand Seize, a room that the author describes as well known to the fashionable world.[98] Ponson du Terrail, whose popular Rocambole

The only surviving photograph of the Grand Seize, by Jean Barry, 1913, captures
the infamous *cabinet particulier* long after its heyday as the most glamorous
private dining room frequented by the *grandes horizontales* of the Second Empire.
Paris Musées / Musée Carnavalet – Histoire de Paris

novels made him one of the bestselling novelists of the day, set a part of
the third volume in his series *Les Voleurs du Grand Monde* at the Grand
Seize. Since most of his readers were unlikely to ever be able to afford
a meal in the notoriously expensive *cabinet*, Ponson du Terrail opened
with the question: "Qu'est-ce que le Grand-Seize?" – What is the Grand
Seize? – and explained that it was a room in the Café Anglais that was
well known to all *viveurs* (high livers) in Paris, where every night the sons
of the best families chewed their way through their inherited fortunes.[99]
Charles Mérouvel's *Les Secrets de Paris: Angèle Méraud* (1883) told the
story of an "excessively pretty" daughter of a fish merchant who was led
into a life of debauchery, including "orgies romaines du Grand Seize"
where she feasted on fine wines and truffles.[100] Fortuné du Boisgobey's
La Bande Rouge (1886), relating the adventures of a young girl during the

1870 siege of Paris, described the Grand Seize as so famous it was well known from the Caucasus to Kentucky.[101]

French literary novelists of the late nineteenth century, many of whom looked down on the work of popular novelists like Belot and Ponson du Terrail, also could not resist the Grand Seize as a setting in their fiction. Honoré de Balzac, Gustave Flaubert, and Émile Zola each mentioned the Café Anglais in their novels. Flaubert's *L'Éducation Sentimentale* includes a love scene set at an unspecified private room in the restaurant. The fickle hero Frédéric Moreau visits the Anglais with his demimondaine lover Rosanette, who seduces him by putting a flower petal between her lips and holding it out for him to nibble, while he's seated on a red divan beneath a mirror (the furnishings in the Grand Seize). He pulls her onto his lap and she orders a meal of steak, crayfish, truffles, pineapple salad, and vanilla ice. Zola's famous courtesan novel, *Nana* (1880), inspired by the life of Anna Deslions among others, included the private rooms at the Café Anglais, as did his earlier novel *La Curée* (1871). Alphonse Daudet mentioned the Grand Seize by name in *Les Rois en Exil* (1879), a novel that he dedicated to the gastronome Edmond de Goncourt.[102] Goncourt met with Flaubert, Zola, Daudet, and the Russian writer Ivan Turgenev every month for a meal they called the "Dinner of the Five," that was not held at the Café Anglais but at the Café Riche, which was also known for its *cabinets particuliers*.[103]

The Grand Seize caught the imagination of foreign writers as well. After all, its guests included British aristocrats, Russian boyars, and American millionaires as well as the gilded youth of France. The room made its appearance in English-language newspapers, fiction, and travel guides. The British magazine *Once a Week* included a letter from Paris in 1869 that reported on meals in the capital city's eateries, ranging from "a supper in the Grand Seize to a dinner at eleven sous in the rue Ste. Anne."[104] The British sensation novelist Mary Elizabeth Braddon described the "famous supper room," with its "flaming windows shining upon the Boulevard," for her titillated readers.[105] The scandalous American socialite Julian Osgood Field, who wrote fiction under the pen name X. L., included the Grand Seize in two of his sophisticated short stories, as well as in his gossipy memoirs.[106] Francis Bourne-Newton's *Gastronomic Guide to Paris* (1903) and Nathaniel Newnham-Davis's *Gourmet Guide to Europe* (1908) both included the room. Newnham-Davis insisted that "the history of the Anglais has never been written because, as the proprietor will tell you, it never *could* be written without telling tales anent great men which should not be out into print," especially stories "of dinners given in the Grand Seize."[107] Even long after the building which housed the Café Anglais was torn down in 1913, its famed *cabinet* survived in literature, appearing in historical novels by the British romance writer Barbara Cartland and the American author Frank Wilkinson.[108]

The literature of the Grand Seize illustrates the role that writing played in the ascendance of French food culture in the nineteenth century. As the sociologist Priscilla Parkhurst Ferguson has argued, "the avid readers of nineteenth-century culinary texts were as essential to French culinary culture as the voracious eaters of nineteenth-century gastronomic practice."[109] French restaurants, with their *cabinets particuliers*, and French gastronomic writing, with its positive attitude toward pleasure, combined to create the idea of French cuisine and imbued it with erotic resonance both in France and beyond its borders. British and American audiences proved especially receptive audiences to this gastro-erotic mythos. They eagerly consumed translations of French novels from the sensational to the literary. Zola, Flaubert, Belot, and Mérouvel were all republished in English. English and American writers also contributed to this discourse with their own accounts of the pleasures to be enjoyed in the *cabinets particuliers* of Paris.

The appetite for reading about the restaurants of Paris translated almost immediately into a desire on the part of Britons and Americans to experience the multifaceted pleasures of French gastronomy for themselves. During the nineteenth century, a steadily growing flood of Britons and Americans visited the city's restaurants and wrote to their friends and family back home about their experiences. Their reactions revealed a complicated mixture of longing and loathing for the restaurant's twinned pleasures, contributing to the growing fixation in Victorian culture that good food encouraged illicit appetites and that eating for pleasure was especially inappropriate for respectable women.

TWO

Innocents Abroad

No sooner had the ink dried on the preliminary draft of the Treaty of Amiens in fall 1801, ending almost a decade of war between Britain and France, than the English journalist Francis William Blagdon packed his bags for Paris. Cut off from visiting since the early years of the French Revolution, British tourists were eager to experience the pleasures that France had to offer, and restaurants ranked high on that list. In his account of his travels, *Paris as It Was and as It Is* (1803), Blagdon described the attractions of the restaurant for his countrymen who had yet to experience the pleasure. To pass by a restaurant and smell the delicious odors pouring out of its kitchens without having money enough to pay for a meal was "worse than the punishment of Tantalus, who, dying with thirst, could not drink, though up to his chin in water." Restaurants were that amazing. "Really, my dear friend, I would advise every rich epicure to fix his residence in this city," he continued. Having whetted his readers' appetites, Blagdon went on to list the amazing variety of dishes offered at his favorite restaurant, Beauvilliers:

> Soups, thirteen sorts. – *Hors-d'oeuvres*, twenty-two species. – Beef, dressed in eleven different ways. – Pastry, containing fish, flesh and fowl, in eleven shapes. Poultry and game, under thirty-two various forms. – Veal, amplified into twenty-two distinct articles. – Mutton, confined to seventeen only. – Fish, twenty-three varieties. – Roast meat, game, and poultry, of fifteen kinds. – Entremets, or side-dishes, to the number of forty-one articles. – Desert, thirty-nine. – Wines, including those of the liqueur kind, of fifty-two denominations besides ale and porter. – Liqueurs, twelve species, together with coffee and ices.

Convinced that his readers would not believe this extraordinary list, Blagdon included a full reproduction of Beauvilliers' menu, which took up nine pages of his book.

An honest reporter, Blagdon also acknowledged that restaurants served more than food. They attracted deep-pocketed men of all professions, including stock traders, speculators, and gamblers, who had appetites that were not easily satiated, and "where rich rogues abound, luxurious courtesans are at no great distance." Blagdon explained to his Anglo-American audience that courtesans were common at restaurants, especially at those which had *cabinets particuliers*, where diners could "enjoy all possible privacy." The waiters took caution never to enter these "snug little rooms" until they heard themselves called. The rooms were asylums to love. To these rooms, many husbands owed "the happiness of paternity," and many a "gay wife" owed the happiness of time spent with her lover.[1] In short, the very first reporting on restaurants in English presented these new temples to good food as dens of wicked sex.

Blagdon's call to the epicures of the world to follow him to Paris received an enthusiastic reception. Unfortunately, peace between Britain and France proved short-lived. War broke out again in 1803 and lasted until 1814 (before resuming briefly in 1815). As soon as Napoleon abdicated, thousands of British tourists flocked to France.[2] They were joined by thousands of American tourists, who had also been held off by the decade-plus Napoleonic Wars.[3] "It was natural," according to one British tourist who made the trip in 1814, "that they would rush towards it at the first moment of admission," driven by romantic impressions of the country.[4]

This new wave of travelers reported back to their compatriots confirming Blagdon's accounts of the wonders of the French restaurant. Henry Matthews, who visited Paris in 1819, explained in a published account of his travels that

> it may be possible, in London, to get the substance of a dinner at a chop-house for as small a sum as two shillings; but in a wretched form, and without any of the accessories of luxury, or even comfort. In Paris, however, you may dine at the Salon Français in the Palais Royal in a superb *salon*, as well fitted up, and better lighted, than the Piazza coffeehouse in Covent-garden, and be served with soup, three dishes *au choix*, bread *à discretion*, a pint of burgundy, and dessert, all for the sum of twenty-pence.[5]

An English guidebook to France published in 1816 struck a similar tone, explaining "the English epicure can form no conception of the rich and almost innumerable dishes which there invite his taste."[6] The French restaurant offered a new domain of alimentary pleasure to Anglo-American travelers.

As eager as these visitors were to sample the rich and sophisticated cuisine coming out of French restaurant kitchens, they were equally attracted by the thrilling opportunity to witness, and perhaps partake in, the dynamic sexual commerce that accompanied the meals. The history of tourism has not sufficiently reckoned with the role of sex as one of the major motivators of travel in the eighteenth, nineteenth, and twentieth centuries.[7] The initial wave of Anglo-American tourists to Paris after the Napoleonic Wars consisted largely of single men, many of whom were on the hunt for new erotic experiences. From the beginning, their descriptions of their visits to restaurants mixed the gastronomic and the erotic. Later, as more wives and daughters and even single women made the journey, female tourists struggled between their desire to experience the pleasures of the restaurant for themselves and the need to preserve their reputations from the restaurant's association with sex work and adultery.

Dames de comptoir

Many Anglo-American tourists' accounts of their visits to Paris's restaurants and cafés began with descriptions of these eating places' erotic pleasures. As soon as a visitor walked in the door, one of the first sights that met his eyes was a sort of throne on which sat an attractive woman who prepared the bills and collected payments from the waiters.[8] The use of pretty women to act as hostesses and cashiers overseeing a restaurant's operations dated back to the very beginning. The Enlightenment philosophe and encyclopedist Denis Diderot described falling in love with a "belle restauratrice," or pretty restaurant hostess, when he dined in a new Paris restaurant in 1767.[9] He was not alone. Anglo-American tourists' obsession with these women soon became notorious.

The women who sat in the front of restaurants and cafés were often referred to as *limonadières* or *dames de comptoir*, lemonade sellers or cashiers. The first term dated back to the early eighteenth century and referred to women who worked in cafés that sold lemonade along with coffee and liqueurs.[10] In the 1803 edition of *Almanach des Gourmands*, the famous French food writer Grimod de La Reynière included praise not only for the refreshments served at the café Corazza, but for the beauty of its cashier, Madame Lenoir, whom he called one of the prettiest *limonadières* in Paris.[11] The term *dame de comptoir* began to appear in the nineteenth century. In the sixth edition of his *Almanach*, La Reynière described a woman who worked at a specialty grocery in Paris as a *dame de comptoir*, and explained that her gracious, intelligent presence made the store dear to gourmands.[12] A French guidebook from 1828 succinctly described the *dame de comptoir* as "un petit morceau du sexe," or a little piece of sex, whose presence excited male diners' appetites.[13]

The beauty of the *limonadières* and *dames de comptoir* attracted tourists as well as locals. The Scottish editor John Scott, who visited Paris in 1814 at the first possible opportunity and quickly published a volume about his trip, described the famous settings of the Revolution for readers but acknowledged that "historical interest" alone did not compel his or others' travels. British tourists were drawn to Paris for its ability "to satisfy the sensualist" and "delight the gay" in "dispensing a profusion of captivating pleasures." Highest among Paris's sensual attractions were the "restaurateurs" in the Palais-Royal, all of which had at their entry a "Madame, who sits in state, to diffuse the consciousness of a female presence." In Paris, the softer sex was in attendance wherever men came together. Like many men, Scott was especially drawn to the "priestess" who presided over the Café des Mille Colonnes "with even more than the usual pomp of such persons. She is a fine woman, and admits the stare of her visitors as a part of the entertainment which they have a right to expect."[14]

Madame Romain, the cashier who worked at the Mille Colonnes, was the most famous *dame de comptoir* of the early nineteenth century. Known colloquially as la Belle Limonadière, she had even, reputedly, attracted the attention of Napoleon's brother. According to Stephen Weston, who visited Paris in 1814, "the great attraction . . . of the Mille Colonnes, that rivals in numbers the pillars of Persepolis and of Cordova, is the Lady, or Belle Limonadiere, set up in her splendid bar, by a Russian Prince, with a profusion of diamonds in her hair, and a gold bell in her hand, with which she summons her aide-de-café, and gives change."[15] A hand-colored etching by British humorist Thomas Rowlandson shows Madame Romain seated on a high throne while men at nearby tables gaze up rapturously at her impervious face. Paintings of male and female nudes hang on the walls at the same level as Romain's throne.[16] Rowlandson's is only one of several early nineteenth-century etchings depicting *la belle limonadière*. An unsigned 1816 etching of the Café des Mille Colonnes shows Madame Romain's breasts spilling out from her low-cut dress, stupefying the men who cluster around her throne.[17] It's possible that her erotic fame may have contributed to the French slang *café des deux colonnes* being used as a euphemism for female genitalia, and the expression to take one's coffee at the *café des deux colonnes* being used for performing oral sex on a woman.[18]

After Madame Romain retired from the Mille Colonnes, she was succeeded by other beautiful *dames de comptoir*. When American journalist Nathaniel Hazeltine Carter visited Paris in 1825, on a tour to recover his health, he had a chance to see one of Madame Romain's successors.[19] Like the male tourists who came before him, Carter focused significant attention in his 1827 travelogue on the restaurants and cafés of the Palais-Royal, calling them "one of the peculiar features of Paris." Astonished at the hundreds of dishes listed on the restaurant menus, Carter equally enjoyed seeing the pretty women who handled payments:

> In some conspicuous part of the room, a throne is erected to the height of several feet from the floor, ornamented in the most tasty manner, and furnished with silken or velvet cushions. Here the presiding goddess sits in state, dressed with all the showy elegance of the French women. On entering and leaving the room, each person takes off his hat and bows to her with as much reverence as he would manifest in approaching or taking leave of a princess. She returns the salute, and sometimes deigns a smile or whispers a soft word to those whom she recognizes. But generally she sits in silent and motionless dignity, overlooking the tables beneath her, and frowning at any impoliteness. It is a great point to procure the prettiest women for these places, who never fail to attract company. Some of them have held their thrones much longer than eastern monarchs, and received more marks of homage than any of the Bourbons. The Mille Colonne, so called because its mirrors reflect a thousand gilded columns, has long been celebrated for the beauty of its incumbent. Every pretty girl is an heir-apparent to this species of dominion.[20]

Another *dame de comptoir* who received a great deal of attention from British and American tourists was Madame Véry, the proprietress of

Véry's restaurant in the Palais-Royal. In 1802, when Francis Blagdon visited, he described Madame Véry as "a *beau corps de femme*, or, in plain English, a very desirable woman." According to Blagdon, her husband owed his business to the erotic charms of his wife, who presented herself to the Minister of the Interior in order to secure the passage of their application for tenancy of their establishment.[21] Ten years later, Madame Véry's buxom figure continued to attract the eye of customers and artists. Thomas Rowlandson's sketch of *Madame Véry Restaurateur* was often printed on the same sheet as his *Belle Liminaudière.* [22]

Madame Véry's popularity with English tourists also caught the eye of French cartoonists. Louis Marie Yves Queverdo's *Milord Bouffi payant sa Carte à Madame Veri* (1815) depicts a fat Englishman paying his bill at Véry's. He has his hand in his pocket, ostensibly to retrieve his wallet, in a gesture suggesting male masturbation. Madame Véry looks on impassively, like la Belle Limonadière, her large breasts prominent beneath her fashionable green dress.[23] A third hand-colored etching from the same period, by Aaron Martinet, shows a fat Englishman asleep on a chair in front of Véry's restaurant, his right hand tucked into his pocket, directly above his crotch, a smile splitting his pink, swollen face.[24] These three sketches of Madame Véry, as well as the similar sketches of Madame Romain, illustrate how the sexual appeal of women workers drew male customers to early French restaurants. Pretty *dames de comptoir* rivaled the *cabinet particulier* as a defining feature of the early restaurant's erotic allure.[25]

Madame Romain and Madame Véry elevated Paris's *dames de comptoir* into erotic celebrities. After the women retired, their successors attracted devotion from a new wave of tourists. John Sanderson, an American teacher who visited Paris in 1835, noted that in every restaurant and café of the Palais-Royal, "there is a woman of choice beauty, mounted on a kind of throne. She is present always, and may be considered as one of the fixtures of the shop."[26] An 1842 London writer similarly enthused about "the lady, who sits enthroned, the presiding divinity of the restaurant." He described how the huge mirrors in restaurants picked up dazzling reflections from the *dames de comptoir's* earrings as they waved their heads.[27] *Dames de comptoir* and *limonadières* attracted attention even when they were away from their stations. An American tourist in 1833 admired the "fairer goddess[es] of the *café*" as they strolled through

Thomas Rowlandson's 1814 hand-colored etching "Madame Very, Restaurateur,
Palais Royal, Paris, and La Belle Liminaudiere au Caffee de Mille Collone, Palais
Royale Paris," highlights Anglo-American tourists' fixation on the restaurant's
erotic attractions from their first encounters with new French invention.
Rowlandson's etchings call far more attention to the *dames de comptoir*'s breasts
than to the food or drink served at either famous institution.
The Elisha Whittelsey Collection, The Elisha Whittelsey Fund, 1959

Louis Marie Yves Queverdo's "Milord Bouffi payant sa carte à madame Véri," satirizes the Anglo-American obsession with Paris restaurants' pretty *dames de comptoir*, depicting a fat Englishman reaching suggestively into his pocket while staring at the prominently displayed breasts of Madame Véry.
Wikimedia Commons

the Tivoli Gardens, an amusement park located on the city's Right Bank.[28]

The attraction that the *dames de comptoir* and *limonadières* provided was primarily visual. Their prettiness graced the restaurants and cafés and titillated the male customers who supped under their gaze. Another erotic visual experience could be gleaned from just visiting the Palais-Royal where many restaurants were located, and looking at the "dense mass of abandoned women" who circulated the area, in the words of one tourist.[29] The American writer Washington Irving first visited Paris in 1805 (Americans continued to travel in small numbers to France during the Napoleonic Wars, in which the United States remained officially a neutral party until the war of 1812), and he went immediately to the Palais-Royal. He observed with great interest the "frail nymphs" who paraded the grounds. During his stay in Paris, he returned repeatedly to the Palais, both to eat at the restaurants, including Beauvilliers and Les Deux Frères, and to observe the prostitutes who frequented the gardens.[30] Of course, visits to Parisian restaurants offered more than sights to please the eye.

Feeding the appetites

Restaurants were designed to feed all men's senses: the visual, with their employment of pretty women and their use of mirrors and gas lighting; the auditory, with their hard surfaces refracting the busy chatter of fellow diners; the olfactory, with the smells emanating from their kitchens; the gustatory, with the rich cooking of their popular dishes; and the tactile, with their private rooms set aside for amatory encounters. It did not take Anglo-American tourists long to discover the pleasures of the *cabinets particuliers*, where they could enjoy hands-on experiences of the restaurant's erotic attractions. Their interest in these rooms swiftly drew the same ridicule as their obsession with the pretty cashiers. A French cartoon from 1818, titled "Le facheux contretems ou l'anglais surpris par sa femme" (the unfortunate setback, or the Englishman surprised by his wife), shows a scrawny and unattractive Englishwoman grabbing her husband by the ear as he follows an attractive French woman wearing a flashy hat (clearly a *soupeuse*) into a doorway from which hangs a sign reading "Restaurateur Cabinets Particuliers."[31] By the doorway, two eels hang from a hook, alluding to the French use of *anguille* (eel), as a euphemism for penis, and leaving no doubt as to the man's amorous intentions.[32]

First-person accounts by British and American tourists during the nineteenth century tended to be more discreet than the French caricatures ridiculing them. Hezekiah Hartley Wright, an American who published his reminiscences of traveling through the Continent in 1835–6, described his visits to every restaurant of note in Paris, including Véry's, Périgord, Trois Frères Provençaux, Grignon's, Rocher de Cancale, and Grand

An unattractive Englishwoman grabs her startled husband by the ear as he follows a flashily dressed *soupeuse* through the doorway of a restaurateur advertising *cabinets particuliers*. Two eels hanging by the front door leave no doubt as to the man's amorous intentions. "Le facheux contretems ou l'anglais surpris par sa femme" (1818).
Sir John Soane's Museum, London

Vatel. His favorite was the Rocher de Cancale, where he confessed that he liked to dine in the *cabinets particuliers* because diners in the private rooms were permitted to "make as much noise" as they wanted, and "no one says *nay* or enters with rueful countenance." Although Wright, who was traveling alone, acknowledged the existence of Paris's women of easy virtue, including *grisettes*, the grey-cloaked working-class women who often lived with students and unmarried young men, he didn't elaborate to readers on who joined him making noise in his *cabinets*.[33]

Many Anglo-Americans in France during the first half of the nineteenth century made the journey on the recommendation of their doctors, who prescribed travel as a treatment for various ailments, including consumption (tuberculosis). Wright, who died in 1840, most likely came for this purpose. Not satisfied simply to recommend travel to their patients, many medical students and doctors themselves traveled to Paris in the early nineteenth century to improve their skills by studying at the city's hospitals with the leading doctors of the day. Around seven hundred American medical students studied in Paris between 1830 and 1860.[34]

L. J. Frazee traveled to Paris in 1844 with a couple of doctor companions to spend three months of study in Paris. On their very first evening in the city, the trio paid a visit to a restaurant in the Palais-Royal. Frazee marveled over the menu, the waiters, and the mirrors. Soon he took up lodgings in the Latin Quarter, the student neighborhood near the Sorbonne. Disdaining the *table d'hôte* offered by his landlady, Frazee ate in local restaurants each night, which he admitted were full of *grisettes* eating with their student lovers. Frazee didn't mention whether he enjoyed the company of a *grisette* during his nightly meals, but he did warn readers that he "would not advise that any young man be sent to Paris to improve his morals." That was as close to a confession as a respectable medical student was likely to make in a published memoir.[35]

Virginia medical student Philip Claiborne Gooch was far more forthcoming in his unpublished Paris diary from the late 1840s. Gooch had a *grisette* lover named Clementine, and they socialized together in restaurants with his friend Theodore, who had a *grisette* lover named Emeline. In one diary entry, Gooch described a dinner enjoyed by the four of them: "I uncork the bottle of champagne. Theodore begins to eat. We drink. I take Emeline, who has the shivers, in my arms and put her on her knees. We kiss. We start to cry. They kiss. We kiss also." By the evening's end, the friends had finished three bottles of champagne before retiring to bed and "what follows." The next morning, they ate an enormous breakfast and Gooch returned to the hospital to observe dissections.[36]

Similar scenes of debaucherous meals enjoyed by students and their favorite *grisettes* in the Latin Quarter became a staple in romantic fiction during the second half of the nineteenth century, after the publication of Henri Murger's *Scènes de la Vie de Bohème* in 1845. The text was quickly translated into English and inspired scores of imitators.[37] The *grisette* turned into such a common trope that Mark Twain skewered their reputation in his satirical travel book, *The Innocents Abroad* (1869). During a visit to Paris, Twain kept asking his guide to point out the city's *grisettes*, who were (if you let the books of travel tell it,) always so beautiful – so neat and trim, so gracefull – so naive and trusting – so gentle, so winning – so faithful to their shop duties, so irresistible to buyers in their prattling importunity – so devoted to their poverty-stricken students of the Latin Quarter – so light hearted and happy on their Sunday picnics in the suburbs – and oh, so charmingly, so delightfully immoral!

But when the guide finally showed him the true *grisettes* of Paris, Twain was disappointed to discover that the women were homely. He "knew by their looks that they ate garlic and onions." *Grisettes* were a "romantic fraud" in Twain's opinion; "it would be base flattery to call them immoral." Ending with a little flattery of his own, Twain opined that American women were far more handsome than French women.[38]

Twain's mockery aside, many Americans found a great deal to enjoy in the opportunities for good food and illicit sex that Paris provided. The expression "Good Americans, when they die, go to Paris," is often attributed to Oliver Wendell Holmes, Sr., who studied medicine in Paris in the 1830s, but the witticism belonged to his dear friend whom he met on the ship over, Thomas Gold Appleton.[39] The son of a wealthy merchant, Appleton didn't need to work for a living, and had plenty of time to visit to Paris over the years. On his very first visit, Appleton dined at Les Trois Frères Provençaux, the Rocher de Cancale, the Café de Paris, and the city's other fine restaurants, which he returned to often in the years that followed. According to Hale, Appleton believed in "the gospel of good-eating, maintaining that the pleasures of the palate were given us to enjoy, as much as those of sight and sound." This defense set Appleton apart from Victorian society, which was turning sharply against alimentary indulgence.

Appleton's friend Julia Ward Howe (author of "The Battle Hymn of the Republic") said that he "cultivated a Byronic distaste for the Puritanic ways of New England," indicating just how immoral his epicureanism appeared at the time.[40] Appleton disliked his home country's bland food and its restrictive attitude toward sex. He "set a bright spice-loving table at home" and said the only way he would get married would be if he were held down and under the effects of chloroform.[41] Appleton did have a strong appreciation for pretty actresses. His repeat visits to Paris gave him many opportunities to enjoy both the city's cuisine and its theater, as well as to observe the ups and downs of both entertainments. On a visit in 1856, he complained that the city was unusually lacking in talent "on the stage, in opera, [and] in the cabinet," referring to the "actresses" who moonlighted as courtesans and frequented restaurant private rooms.[42]

The Irish writer Thomas Moore, who moved to Paris with his wife Bessy and their children in 1820, was not just Byronic – he was friends with Byron. Moore's first book of verse, published in 1800 when he was twenty, was a loose English translation of ancient Greek "anacreontic" verse dedicated to the twinned pleasures of wine and love. On its fame, he moved to London, and the next year he published a volume of erotic poetry (under a pen name) that won him the admiration of Lord Byron.[43] In his daily diary, Moore records frequent visits to the city's restaurateurs including Beauvilliers, Véry's, and the Rocher de Cancale, among other grand establishments. On a couple of occasions, Moore noted that he took particularly pleasurable meals in *cabinets particuliers*, including with his wife. Whether he dined with women not his wife in the restaurants' private rooms he left unsaid, but he did frequently note the pretty women he encountered in the restaurants, including the *dames de comptoir*.[44]

Women's appetites

Thomas Moore's wife Bessy was wary of eating out at restaurants when they arrived in Paris in 1820. Moore noted her "reluctance to enter the room" when he first took her to dinner at Véry's. Previously an actress, Bessy's reputation was already vulnerable to rumor, but perhaps her experience in that disreputable profession made it easier for her to take the adventurous leap into dining in restaurants.[45]

The French restaurant's association with sex workers and adultery made it dangerous to the reputations of Victorian women travelers, presenting a real challenge to these adventurous souls. At home in Britain and the United States, public eating places like chophouses and coffeehouses tended to be frequented entirely by men.[46] Respectable women belonged in the private domestic sphere. An 1816 guidebook for British tourists warned that in Paris "the mixture of ladies with the gentlemen at many of the coffeehouses will surprise the English traveller" accustomed to "the retired and unassuming delicacy" of English women.[47] Even more shocking to the English traveler was the sight of French women dining without male chaperones in the public rooms of restaurants, "a custom which would be reckoned grossly unbecoming in London, but is by no means uncommon in Paris," as an English minister huffed.[48]

Anglo-American tourists frequently commented on the surprising presence of French women in such public spaces. John Scott, who traveled to Paris in 1814, admired the city's great restaurants, but he confessed that "the appearance of ladies sitting among crowds of men in these public rooms startles the English visitor, as a custom that trenches on the seclusion that he is inclined to think necessary to the preservation of the most valuable female qualities." Seeing French women eating in restaurants led Scott to question, "Can a woman lose her virtue by dining in this promiscuous assemblage?" or "[C]an we better shew our regard for women, than by making them our inseparable companions?" In other words, Scott suggested that Englishmen could show respect for their wives by taking them to restaurants and thus forswearing the opportunity to take advantage of the restaurant's erotic opportunities.[49]

The English traveler W. Stewart, who visited Paris at the same time as Scott, arrived at a similar conclusion. As soon as he and his traveling companions arrived in the city, they left the women at a hotel and ventured out to the boulevards. They soon discovered both the streets and the "coffee house full (*inside and out*) with well dressed women and as well dressed beaux." After taking note of this difference in norms, Stewart and his companions returned to collect their wives and went out all together. Their party of seven sampled a number of restaurants, including moderately priced places close to their hotel, and also the most expensive restaurants in the city, Véry's and the Trois Frères Provençaux. Stewart delighted in these restaurants' extensive menus and excellent champagnes. For most of their visit, however, they arranged to have a local restaurateur deliver meals to their private apartments.[50]

American travelers also felt startled at the presence of French women in the city's eating places. When the American schoolteacher John Sanderson traveled to Europe for his health in 1835, he marveled that Parisian restaurants were frequented by the "best bred ladies." In Britain and the United States, he noted, there was "a public separation of the sexes" and a strong prejudice against the sight of "eating women." Sanderson, however, was a liberal-minded fellow, and he considered the women who ate in Paris restaurants to be attractions, alongside the sparkling mirrors, marble tabletops, and snowy white linen.[51] Medical student L. J. Frazee also took note that in Paris "restaurants like the *cafés* are frequented by ladies as well as gentlemen." He didn't entirely approve of the practice. Frazee judged the French to be immoral, given "to act almost entirely from the promptings of animal passion."[52] A Southern gentleman, born and raised in Kentucky, Frazee was accustomed to a far more restrictive gender order in which white women of property kept close to home. That might explain why, according to a French author, Southern men were particularly enthusiastic visitors to the city's night restaurants.[53]

Several accounts published by nineteenth-century women travelers describe their trepidation about eating in Paris restaurants in their own words. Emma Hart Willard, the famous American educator and women's rights advocate, scandalized her male traveling companions by threatening to eat at a Paris restaurant during a European tour in 1830–1. She looked in through the large clear windows of the restaurants in the Palais-Royal, gazing on the men who ate at the tables inside. "The Parisians say, that respectable ladies, especially strangers, go there occasionally," she wrote in a letter to her students back in Troy, New York, but Willard's male traveling companions would not believe it. "I have not yet made such a violent out-break: and doubt whether I shall have the courage" she admitted. The disapproval of her male countrymen was too daunting.[54]

For women who worked up the courage to walk through the doors, sitting down at a restaurant table could be a nerve-wracking experience. Caroline Kirkland, an American writer who traveled to Europe in the late 1840s, described the physical anxiety her countrywomen experienced when dining out:

> Dining at a restaurant is one of the novelties of the lady-traveller in Paris. Taking a sandwich or a plate of oysters at Thompson and Weller's is a considerable feat, and some of our ladies at home roll up their eyes at the boldness which can venture thus far. But to sit down in a public room, to a regular dinner of an hour's length or more, is quite another affair, and it really requires some practice before one can refrain from casting sly glances around during the process, to see whether anybody is looking.

The fine silver, elegant China, and delicate cuisine at the grand Parisian restaurants went a long way toward assuaging elite women's moral reservations about dining out, but luxurious table settings couldn't erase their anxiety altogether. It took a certain type of woman to enjoy this boundary-pushing behavior. Kirkland, who lived in New York City and hosted a literary salon, was adventurous enough to take pleasure in the experience: "One feels at first as if it was a transgression; but after a while this subsides into a feeling of agreeable *abandon*." Yet, lest anyone get the wrong idea, Kirkland reassured her readers that she hadn't done anything *truly* naughty by eating out.[55]

Caroline Wilde Cushing, a young married woman from the conservative New England town of Newburyport, Massachusetts, offered similar reassurances to her father in an 1829 letter from Paris. The French capital, she explained, had a large number of restaurateurs, and "their establishments deserve to be seen as a matter of curiosity, by those who would not otherwise frequent them." As a respectable woman, she wouldn't ordinarily visit such risqué establishments, but for the purpose of being a good tourist, she was willing to briefly relax her standards of propriety. With those apologies, Cushing launched into a fulsome account of Parisian restaurants' large gracious rooms, beautiful *dames de comptoir*, and extensive à la carte menus. The restaurants of the Palais-Royal and the Boulevards were the most luxurious, she noted, and served cuisine "prepared in the highest perfection of the gastronomic art." Women were seldom to be seen dining at restaurants without male companions. Their need to be chaperoned illustrated the erotic atmosphere of even respectable restaurants. But, Cushing reassured her father, one really did encounter so many people in the restaurants, it wasn't too terrible of her to have indulged.[56]

Only in their private writings could women express pleasure in their Paris restaurant adventures without carefully scaffolding their descriptions in layers of apologies. Jane Bigelow, the wife of the American consul to Paris, John Bigelow, wrote about eating in the city's restaurants in her diary. In an 1858 entry, she recorded having a meal with a man at the largest café in Paris, noting she had an "excellent dinner and great amusement."[57] Bigelow was an unusual woman, who was almost uniquely indifferent to public opinion, a fact frequently commented on by people who met her and were shocked by her manners. She didn't act like a diplomat's wife. She was close friends with Charlotte Cushman, the Sapphic actress, and she filled scrapbooks with articles about the cross-dressing female novelist George Sand. Bigelow wasn't the sort of woman to feign modesty.

Writing publicly about the pleasure of dining in restaurants took a very special type of woman. Julie de Marguerittes, a London-born, Italian-Jewish divorcée, opera singer, journalist, and music critic, who was married to George Foster, an American author who wrote about New York City's seedy nightlife, took the bold step of writing a guidebook for Anglo-American travelers to Paris that included commentary on the city's *cabinets particuliers*.[58] In *The Ins and Outs of Paris* (1855), Marguerittes informed readers that the great restaurants of the Palais-Royal like Véry's and Véfour's had long since become tourist traps. However, one could still catch a sight of a Parisian gentleman dining in the famous old restaurants when he was in the company of a woman with whom he wished to eat in private. As Marguerittes explained, the gentleman and his lady friend would approach the private entrance of such restaurants, "where, at a well-known signal, the garçon will show them into a *cabinet particulier*, the prettiest little boudoir imaginable." Marguerittes also described for her readers the handkerchief trick played by enterprising young prostitutes. Dropping their handkerchief for a man to see, they would strike up conversation with the gallant who retrieved the item, and soon the *soupeuse* would ask him whether he had yet eaten, prompting an invitation from the gallant to dine together in a *cabinet particulier* at Véry's, Véfour's, or the Trois Frères. To write so openly of the sex trade, as Marguerittes did in her guidebook, removed her from the ranks of respectability. But by virtue of being Jewish, divorced, an opera singer, and a journalist, she was already excluded from that category.[59]

Nightlife guides

Marguerittes was one of a kind, but her guidebook was one in a popular mid-nineteenth-century genre that served the ever-growing number of Anglo-American tourists in Paris.[60] Respectable guidebooks were rarely upfront about the sexual attractions of restaurants, avoiding the topic of *cabinets particuliers* or the *soupeuses* who solicited men for meals. Galignani's and Baedeker's, two of the most popular nineteenth-century guides to Paris, kept entirely mum on the subject. *The Stranger's Guide to Paris*, published in 1837, briefly mentioned the existence of rooms where "families or small parties may dine in private," but most commercial guidebooks avoided the topic.[61]

An appetite for information about the most risqué of Paris's attractions drove the emergence during the second half of the nineteenth century of a new genre of underground American and English nightlife guides. *Paris and Brussels after Dark* (1865), *Paris by Gaslight* (1867), *Nocturnal Paris* (1877), and *The Nocturnal Pleasures of Paris* (1889) provided explicit information to male tourists about the erotic offerings of the city's restaurants. The first of these books, which was subtitled *The Cocottes, or, Gay Women of Paris and Brussels*, included profiles of famous flashy young women and descriptions of the dance halls, cafés, and restaurants where one might encounter and entertain them. The book included a list of six "night restaurants" with *cabinets particuliers* that remained open until dawn: Brébant's, Bonnefoy's, Café Anglais, Maison Dorée, Peter's, and Hill's Tavern. All of the restaurants were located on the Right Bank, near the opera.[62] Hill's specialized in serving English and American customers by offering up familiar Anglo foods like ham, sandwiches, and pale ale. The restaurant named all of its dozen-plus private rooms after famous poets, leading Alfred Delvau to joke in a guidebook about the ugly things Shakespeare and Lord Byron must have heard, even if the sights were beautiful.[63]

Many of the guidebooks warned credulous readers against the scams that the young women used in these night restaurants to empty their hosts' pockets. For example, while a gentleman was dining with a young woman, a flower seller might come by and the young woman would beg for flowers, only later to resell them to the vendor. Or a cab driver might come by and present her with a tradesman's bill which she would then implore the young man to pay (and later recoup from her accomplice). If he were particularly unlucky, the young man might be dragged along by his date after dinner to a friend's party where, shortly after his arrival, cards would be produced and game playing would continue until his pockets were emptied.

Paris by Gaslight offered instructions for tourists in how to enjoy restaurant private rooms without getting fleeced. The author, "Peeping Tom," encouraged readers to "sally forth to participate in some of the nocturnal amusements of the gay capital," but he warned them to be careful. The prices in *cabinets particuliers* were double those of the restaurants' main salons. In an entertaining anecdote lifted from a French guidebook, he explained the notorious "sob trick." A young woman would enter a train carriage crying discreetly behind her veil. If a curious gentleman asked about her troubles, the young woman would reluctantly reveal that she was running away from home and an unnatural stepfather. She would then allow herself to be persuaded to take a meal with the male passenger at a restaurant in Paris, in a *cabinet particulier*, to preserve her modesty. Only later, after the gentleman had gone to great expense, would he discover that the young woman was no fair maiden but a practiced prostitute.[64] *Nocturnal Paris*, published a decade later, explained to readers that, after dessert was served in the *cabinets particuliers* of grand restaurants, waiters would leave the couples undisturbed. "What an incentive to vice!" exclaimed the guidebook, in what might be read as an advertisement, rather than a warning, considering the list of night restaurants that followed.[65]

By the end of the century, when *The Nocturnal Pleasures of Paris* was published, the advice literature had become even more frank. The guidebook's author, Captain Wray Sylvester, affected a tone of wry disenchantment. Too many English visitors were disappointed by Paris because they traveled from one tourist trap to another without ever stumbling onto the real pleasures the city had to offer. Sylvester promised to give readers the secret to enjoying themselves without getting cheated. Considering the fact that three of his guidebook's five chapters were devoted to dining, cafés, and suppers, it's clear where he thought the city's true pleasures lay.

Sylvester didn't simply list restaurants with *cabinets particuliers*, he differentiated between the type of erotic entertainments offered at Paris restaurants across the spectrum. The women in ground-floor night restaurants were not very high class. While Hill's restaurant offered *cabinets particuliers* furnished with tables, chairs, piano, and "a very suggestive divan or sofa," the female company had a decidedly low tone. Instead, Sylvester recommended Duchesne's, a *café à femme* with female waitstaff who were "so pretty" that they couldn't be blamed for exchanging sexual favors for tips. Duchesne's had well-furnished private rooms upstairs which sold food and drink at reasonable prices, although Sylvester warned readers that "these short loves are objectionable for hygienic reasons," and it might be better to avoid them. Sylvester also praised the Café Américain but warned of the high prices in the private rooms. Café Sylvain, on the other hand, had "seen its day." Most readers were probably grateful for Sylvester's granular advice on which restaurants had the best *cabinets particuliers*, and his encouragement to enjoy what the city had to offer and "get rid of all your foolish Puritanical prejudice (English or American)."[66]

It wasn't their Puritanical heritage, however, that held Anglo-American tourists back. The moral anxieties which troubled Americans and Britons were distinctly Victorian in nature. As they traveled to Paris in ever greater numbers during the nineteenth century and became more and more familiar with French restaurants and their erotic pleasures, their attitudes toward the pleasures of the table became more and more restrictive at home. Like an image in a funhouse mirror, the rise of the restaurant and French gastronomy in the nineteenth century was reflected by an intensifying Anglo-American moral antagonism to the pleasures of the table and to women's appetites in particular.

THREE

Perverted Appetites

As Anglo-Americans abroad shared accounts of the new Parisian gastronomy with readers back home, many middle-class moralists in the United States and Great Britain recoiled. Instead of piquing their curiosity, the travelers' tales of long menus, private rooms, and pretty cashiers prompted their repugnance. In Norwich, Connecticut, a concerned correspondent, who declared himself to be not "much of a gastronian," wrote to his local paper in 1828 sounding the alarm against the new French fashion. He opened with a poem:

> Happy the man, who is not looking
> To know each different kind of cooking:
> For otherwise his dinner were spoiled
> If his meat were boiled instead of broiled.[1]

The author's defiant rejection of the pleasures of the table encapsulated what soon became a dominant theme in Victorian bourgeois culture. To take too much notice of food was unmanly, even effete. For women, taking too much notice of food had even worse implications. In the nineteenth century, Anglo-Americans treated the female appetite as a "barometer of sexuality."[2] A woman who publicly indulged her alimentary appetite encouraged suspicions about how she privately indulged her erotic appetite.

Ever since Adam and Eve's fall from grace, the Connecticut letter writer explained, humanity had been subject to "unnatural" appetites. In the Garden of Eden, Adam and Eve had eaten for pleasure alone, but after their expulsion from Paradise, eating was tainted by death. In the postlapsarian world, eating had become dissipated. The wealthy continually sought new ways to heighten their unnatural pleasures. Cleopatra spiced her soups with costly jewels. Roman emperors ate ridiculous animals seasoned with great delicacy. Now the French were initiating a new era of gastronomic indulgence characterized by the restaurant and rhapsodic writing about flavorful dishes. If the United States followed in France's fashionable footsteps, moral ruin would be sure to follow. "Heaven grant that our country may preserve her simplicity of manners!" the Connecticut letter writer prayed. For the sake of their moral health and civic survival, Americans should stick to simple diets. Returning to the message in his opening verses, the writer concluded that "thrice happy are those, who, enjoying a healthy appetite, keenly relish whatever is placed before them, not pausing to inquire how it was cooked, and hardly knowing what it is."[3] To many travelers who visited the United States in the mid-nineteenth century, it would appear that the writer had been granted his wish.

While French gastronomy embraced the erotics of the table, British and American alimentary ethics moved in the opposite direction, condemning good food for its excitatory qualities. Anglo-American moral prohibitions against eating for pleasure shaped food tastes on both sides of the Atlantic, prompting the insistence on plain cooking that came to dominate the Victorian kitchen in Britain and in the United States. By the late nineteenth century, Anglo-American food was infamous for its blandness. But the cultural dominance of this anti-hedonic ideal also gave rise to hearty dissent. By tying together good food and illicit sexuality, Victorian moral discourse ultimately opened the possibility for the rise of countercultures that enacted their rebellions against the norm by enthusiastically embracing epicureanism.

Moral diets

Anglo-American antipathy to flavorful food began rising to a fever pitch in the 1830s. In 1838, the New England lawyer Isaac Appleton Jewett, who had traveled widely around the United States and Europe and thoroughly enjoyed his meals in Paris restaurants, described his fellow Americans as "anxious to the extremest point" about their "moral diets." The expression "moral diets" had previously been used to describe the regular consumption of religious texts, like daily Bible readings, but in the 1830s Jewett and others began using the phrase to describe Anglo-American attitudes toward what they ate. Those attitudes were unforgiving. Judging the pleasures of the table as unworthy and suspicious, "Americans pay little attention to cooking," Jewett complained. They gobbled down their meals with dyspeptic consequences.[4] During the first half of the nineteenth century, the United States and Great Britain became known as countries with poor cooking and gross eaters. Visitors to the United States in particular frequently commented on how Americans shoveled down their food, inhaling vast quantities in record time so they could return to business as quickly as possible.[5]

Religious leaders put a more positive spin on Americans' growing obsession with their moral diets. An 1839 essay by a Presbyterian minister encouraged young readers to attend to their "moral diet. Eat the bread of life."[6] By eating correctly, American youth could preserve themselves from the growing dangers of a rapidly urbanizing nation and all the city's attendant seductions. No foodstuff was more heavily laden with moral implications in the antebellum era than bread, and no man was more responsible for that association than Sylvester Graham.

In 1831, Graham, an evangelical minister and temperance reformer, published his first book of dietary essays, *Lectures on the Science of Life*, which advocated a meatless diet as a means to control the passions. Drawing on the theories of the early national doctor Benjamin Rush, Graham argued that sexual excitement led to debility. Good health depended on the suppression of sexual energy or, more concretely, the suppression of masturbation and excessive sex. Even sex within marriage was dangerous if it took place more than once a month. Strange as it may seem, Graham's teachings found a receptive audience, especially after the terrifying outbreak of a cholera epidemic in 1832, which Graham blamed on "dietetic intemperance and lewdness."[7] His most enthusiastic followers opened "Graham boardinghouses" in the mid-1830s, which served vegetarian cuisine to young single men working in the cities. His supporters also published a health journal named for him.

Vegetarianism was a tough sell in the antebellum United States, but Graham's recipe for coarse unleavened brown bread spread widely, even among people unwilling to give up meat. Graham's claim that his loaf was the keystone to a moral diet earned him the moniker "the prophet of bran bread." His 1837 *Treatise on Bread, and Bread-Making* opened with the assertion that bread was "the most important article of diet which enters into the food of man." Refined bread had been invented "to gratify *wanton* and *luxurious* persons." Bread made from unrefined grain required more chewing, prevented excessive eating or gluttony, and would save man from his lusts. Such bread couldn't be bought. Only wives and mothers had the moral sensibility to bake bread for their families; they alone could "appreciate the importance of good bread to their physical and moral welfare." Wives and mothers might complain they lacked the time, or ability, to bake good bread, but the greater impediment was that "the perverseness of our sensualism" led them to disregard sound dietary advice.[8]

Graham's list of dietary don'ts also extended to condiments, spices, sweets, grease, coffee, tea, and alcohol. The Grahamite diet avoided all stimulation in the form of strong flavors, prescribing a bland palate. This preference for minimally flavored foods was reproduced in many American and British cookbooks of the era written by middle-class women. In one food historian's harsh judgment, "It does not seem unfair to describe the food of the nineteenth-century English domestic cookery books as rather monotonous, and above all lacking in any sense of the *enjoyment* of food."[9] Other scholars have found more evidence of pleasure in cookbooks authored by Victorian women like Eliza Acton and Lady Clark of Tillypronie. Perhaps so, but the recipes in these domestic compendiums focused on moral and physical health, which were understood to exist in tension with pleasure. The cookbooks also shared an emphasis on thrift, which could not be separated from moral concerns about the appetite. Practicing economy was more than a matter of saving money, it was a method of moral self-fashioning through sober self-control over temptations to pleasure.

As Lydia Maria Child, author of the 1829 *Frugal Housewife*, one of the most popular early American cookbooks, explained, "I have attempted to teach how money can be *saved*, not how it can be *enjoyed*." Child's instructions for making use of every scrap of food from fish skin (throw it in coffee to clarify the hot drink), to leftover vegetable and meat scraps from boiled dinners (chop them fine and turn them into mincemeat), demonstrated her prioritization of economy over taste. She told readers to reconsider their dislike for the "much despised" liver since it was "the cheapest of all animal food." Chicken livers, gizzards, and necks could be cut up very fine and made into gravy. Child criticized "epicures" who cared only about fine distinctions of flavor. She gave her best advice for making frugal cooking taste good, but taste had only secondary importance when it came to feeding a household.[10]

Child's close friend Abigail Alcott, the mother of *Little Women* author Louisa May Alcott, embraced Grahamite theories with even greater ferocity. Abigail Alcott and her husband, the transcendentalist philosopher Bronson Alcott, were both vegans, eating only grains, vegetables, and fruit. The family often ate only bread and water, twice a day, a diet shaped by penury as well as morality. Like Graham, the Alcotts saw this diet as key to chaste behavior. Celibacy held so much appeal to Bronson Alcott that it threatened to end his marriage, leading to a short separation between him and Abigail. Bronson also used food to teach moral lessons to their children. When Louisa was two years old and her sister Anna was four, Bronson attempted to recreate the lesson of the Garden of Eden by giving each girl an apple and forbidding them to eat it. Louisa failed the test, little surprise for a hungry toddler being raised in a household where food was in short supply. At other times, Bronson punished the girls' misbehavior by starving himself as a moral lesson.[11] (He used a similar tactic at his experimental school, forcing students to beat *him* when they misbehaved.)

Across the Atlantic, the literary Brontë sisters received similar dietary training in the religious school they attended in the early 1820s. Drawing on Lockean childrearing advice promoting a starchy, low-salt diet as a means to control children's "primitive, untamed appetites," as well as currents in contemporary Anglo-Protestant thought, the school subjected the Brontës and their peers to a starvation diet accompanied by regular lectures "on the sin of caring for carnal things and of pampering greedy appetites." These moral lessons were applied most vigorously against female children, who suffered the most extreme constrictions on the expression of their appetites.[12]

The growing anathema to flavorful food in Victorian culture spread through multiple channels: in schools, cookbooks, health guides, periodicals, sermons, and speeches. In 1837, Bronson Alcott's cousin William A. Alcott founded the American Physiological Association to spread Bronson's moral dietary theories throughout the United States. William Alcott considered himself a "medical missionary." He aimed to educate the public and lift humankind "toward the Eden whence we came" through the power of the written word. He advertised his 1838

The Young House-Keeper, or, Thoughts on Food and Cookery as a "moral work," unlike typical cookbooks that were just "bundles of recipes for fashionable cookery." According to William Alcott, a proper diet was key to moral rectitude. "Appetites become perverted by exciting food and drink," he warned. How could a person live a moral life when "every thought, and feeling, and motion which is kindled in the kitchen or the parlor, savors of some sensual gratification"? Bad food was to blame for filling the brothels of the antebellum city. Like Lydia Maria Child, whose writings he admired, Alcott prescribed a diet of "mild and bland" foods. These offered better nutrition than flesh, fish, and high-seasoned food. According to Alcott, adding pepper, mustard, horseradish, or vinegar to potatoes was an abuse of great "magnitude and flagrance." Potatoes should only be seasoned with a little salt. The object of food was to nourish man, "not merely to give him pleasure in eating." It goes without saying that Alcott thought the only legitimate drink for washing down his recommended diet of grains and vegetables was water.[13]

Health reformers grew even more explicit in their warnings against the linkage between bad food and illicit sexuality later in the century, as norms around sexual speech loosened. Popular narratives of Victorian censorship overlook how the social concern with illicit sexuality actually expanded speech and writing about sex as a problem. As Michel Foucault famously argued, the Victorians put sex into discourse.[14] The American health reformer Diocletian Lewis, who succeeded Sylvester Graham as the most popular lecturer on the health reform circuit during the second half of the nineteenth century, started his 1874 book *Chastity* by expressing a longing for "a full, frank discussion and comprehension of the subject of sex."[15] Like his predecessors, Dio Lewis believed that sexual excess, which he defined as sex within marriage more than twice a month or any sexual expression (including masturbation) outside of marriage, caused a wide range of physical debilities from backache to neuralgia, deafness, and blindness.

To control sexual excess, a good diet was key. "The excitability and intensity of sexual passion is largely dependent on what we eat and drink," Lewis wrote. And the first concern was far more important than the latter: "Gluttony counts one hundred victims where drunkenness counts one."[16] Much of Lewis's nutritional advice was familiar. "Nutritious food, plainly cooked, is the general rule," he explained. He recommended brown bread, cracked wheat mush, and other bland grains. He wasn't a vegetarian, but he advocated limiting meat to once a day. Those who were "afflicted with abnormal sexual longings" should skip meat altogether. Lewis also recommended avoiding known aphrodisiacs like eggs, oysters, crabs, and all kinds of shellfish, as well as a laundry list of vegetables including tomatoes, asparagus, celery, beets, turnips, and the "odious onion." Strong flavors were dangerous. "Everything which inflames one appetite is likely to arouse the other also. Pepper, mustard, ketchup and Worcestershire sauce – shun them all. And even salt, in any but the smallest quantity, is objectionable; it is such a goad toward carnalism that the ancient fable depicted Venus as born of the salt sea-wave." Finally, he recommended using simple recipes, nothing that could be described as a "triumph of culinary arts." Baking, boiling and roasting were preferable to frying. And absolutely no coffee.[17]

Not every medical authority agreed with the health reformers. Dio Lewis morosely related the tale of a young man who went to the doctor, concerned about the problem of ejaculating at night, and the doctor told him to get a mistress. When the young man objected to the immorality of this solution, the doctor responded: "If a man chose to live on bran-bread and moonshine, it was all very well, but, for his part, he preferred a good steak and a bottle of champagne."[18] Lewis's advice was extreme. It's unlikely that many people followed it to the letter, either in the bedroom or the kitchen. But even those who failed to meet the ideal could uphold its value. Ministers and doctors, including medical school professors like James Aitken Meigs of Jefferson Medical College in Philadelphia, praised his books. Lewis also influenced the nutritional theology of Ellen White, the Seventh-Day Adventist leader, and her most famous follower, health reformer John Harvey Kellogg.[19]

Perverted appetites

As a member of the millennialist Millerite movement, Ellen White rose to prominence as a prophet in the 1840s, when she began receiving visions on health and instructing her followers not to eat meat or greasy foods, nor to drink tea, coffee, or alcohol. After she founded the Seventh-Day Adventist Church in 1861, her visions about diet picked up pace, and she published a series of texts developing her theories about the interconnection between food and sex.[20] Like the Puritan minister Samuel Danforth two centuries earlier, White condemned Christians who made "a god of their bellies." In her 1864 essay "Health," White used the story of Adam and Eve as evidence that bad eating was the root cause of sexual sin.

In the Garden of Eden, Adam and Eve had eaten only plant food but, after the fall, humanity "ate animal food, and gratified their lusts until their cup of iniquity was full." White connected immoral eating to the crime of Sodom, in particular. "The destruction of Sodom and Gomorrah was on account of their great wickedness," White explained, "They gave loose rein to their intemperate appetites, then to their corrupt passions." Indulging their lust for flesh had led men to commit the abominable sin of sodomy. Hunger for animal flesh, according to White, was evidence of a "perverted appetite." Some people's appetites were so perverted that mere flesh would not suffice; "they crave highly-seasoned meats, with rich gravies." The remedy was to eat plain, simple food, twice or at most three times a day, allowing the stomach to rest in between.[21]

White returned to the theme of "perverted appetites" in later writings.[22] She may have got this term from William Alcott, who in several books of advice for young women insisted that "only your perverted appetite is ever and anon calling for rich dishes."[23] Alcott warned young women that indulging their perverted appetite for rich and flavorful food would lead to masturbation, painful menstrual cycles, and scrofula (tubercular swellings on the neck). The phrase also circulated in health reform periodicals, like the *Graham Journal* and the *American Vegetarian and Health Journal*.[24] The American Vegetarian Society, publisher of the latter journal, declared that its "grand objects" were to launch "an attack . . . on perverted Appetite."[25] Later the phrase appeared in the writings of Dio Lewis.[26] Of course, as a prophet, White insisted that her dietary advice came solely from her visions, and that she only became aware of the teachings of health reformers like Graham, Alcott, and Lewis after experiencing her own spiritual revelations.[27] Regardless of where it originated, the concept of "perverted appetites" traveled from White's writings to those of her most famous acolyte, John Harvey Kellogg.

From his perch as the superintendent of the Battle Creek Sanitarium (the Mayo Clinic of its day), Kellogg extended significant influence over the moral physiological beliefs of the late nineteenth century.[28] Kellogg grew up in the Seventh-Day Adventist Church, and was sent by the Church to study medicine in the 1870s. He returned home in 1875 and took over as superintendent of the Western Health Reform Institute, founded by the Church, which he swiftly renamed the Battle Creek Sanitarium. Kellogg used his position to advance his philosophy of "biologic living," which "was at the bottom a religious and moral system."[29] Biologic living mixed the Christian physiology of Sylvester Graham and William Alcott with the new insights of germ theory. For example, Kellogg was a militant vegetarian and justified this position by arguing that animal food was a site for the prolific replication of bacteria, which, he argued, had been created in the wake of Adam's fall. Like Graham and Alcott, Kellogg linked bad eating to wicked sex. The body had only a finite amount of energy, and expending that energy in masturbation (the worst sin) or excessive sex within marriage (also bad) would cause a permanent decline in health. Kellogg followed these arguments to the most extreme conclusions, recommending that boys who masturbated excessively be circumcised without anesthesia, and that girls who did the same have their clitorises burned with carbolic acid.[30]

Embracing a philosophy of medical mission, the Battle Creek Sanitarium published a journal, *Good Health*, to spread the doctrine of biologic living. Kellogg also published medical books and served as the national superintendent of the Women's Christian Temperance Union's department of social purity. His ideas did not stay confined to Battle Creek. Articles in *Good Health* often took up Ellen White's battle cry against the "perverted appetite."[31] Eating anything rich or flavorful fell into this category, as did simply the act of eating with gusto:

> We can leave off meats, and yet err and injure our health by eating too largely of butter, cream, sugars, rich sauce, pies, cakes, and nuts of various kinds. We can eat our food spiced with hurtful condiments, as peppers, mustard, etc., and we can use salt and other articles more freely than we should. We can eat pickles and other indigestible articles in the vegetable kingdom, greatly to our injury, whether we are sickly or well, but especially if we suffer from ill health. We can eat the best diet with intemperance; in too large quantities, at improper times, and too frequently. We can eat too fast, without stopping to masticate our food, and we can eat too large an assortment at one time.[32]

According to the doctrine of biologic living, a person's moral and physical health were both endangered by eating foods that excited sensation. Eating for pleasure was an act of transgression, a sin against God, for which a person would be punished with bad health. True happiness consisted in right feelings, in suppressing the perverted appetites that led to bad eating, bad sex, and disease.

Kellogg succeeded in spreading Ellen White's message far and wide. Under Kellogg's influence, warnings against the immoral consequences of eating rich and flavorful foods became commonplace in late nineteenth-century parenting magazines and medical journals.[33] Kellogg's philosophy found enthusiastic adherents in Britain, like the angry reader who wrote into *The Woman Worker* magazine scolding them for publishing a pickles recipe that pandered to "perverted appetites," and insisting that "the use of vinegar, spices, and condiments is not only unnecessary but positively harmful, and should be banished from the house."[34] Or the essayist for the Salvation Army magazine who railed against perverted appetites, selfish dispositions, and sensual propensities, spreading the gospel of self-denial in matters of food and drink.[35] Or the letter writer to a Newcastle-area newspaper who recommended vegetarianism for the working classes and athletes, and admonished readers against gluttonous feasting at Christmas driven by their perverted appetites.[36]

As Christian alimentary asceticism spread in the late nineteenth century, it became thoroughly entangled with modern medical discourse. Methodist minister C. F. Clymer's 1880s sermon on "Food and Morals" exemplifies the often-bizarre mix of religious and physiological language in Victorian moral dietary advice. Opening with a verse from Deuteronomy that condemned gluttons and drunkards, Clymer promised that after listening to his sermon, followers would "see the connection more clearly between vice and victuals" and "how food may damage our bodies and demoralize our souls." He then shifted from typical warnings against eating meat, which spurred people to animalistic behaviors, to an explanation of the scientific properties of gluten and an advertisement for gluten suppositories. He also recommended a diet of cucumbers and watermelons for people with desk jobs. At the end of his sermon, Clymer returned to this original message. "Eating and drinking are always associated with the bar and brothel," he thundered.[37]

The ladies were supposed only to nibble

Belief in the connection between bad food and wicked sexuality reached far beyond Adventists and food faddists in the Victorian era, shaping how ordinary people ate and how they thought about eating. Since the onus to maintain sexual respectability fell particularly hard on Victorian women, whose virtue was defined by their purity, women experienced the harshest restrictions on their diet. As early as the 1790s, a British writer instructed that "As eating a great deal is deemed indelicate in a lady; (for her character should be rather divine than sensual,) it will be ill manners to help her to a large slice of meat at once, or fill her plate too full."[38] To preserve their good names, middle-class and upper-class women exercised tight control over how they ate in public. When they didn't, people gossiped about them.

The Scottish minister Archibald Alison was surprised when he traveled through France after the Napoleonic Wars to see how French women enjoyed food in public gatherings, like parties. At a ball supper, "it is often impossible in England to prevail upon the ladies to taste a morsel," whereas in France the women "regale themselves with dressed dishes, swallow with incredible avidity," and "sit down to potations of hot punch, strong enough to admit of being set on fire." Alison did not approve of the way that French women conducted themselves. "Nothing can certainly be more destructive of all ideas of feminine delicacy, than to see a beautiful woman with one of these midnight bowls burning before her." The reflected light on her complexion made her look like a "voracious inhabitant of another world" or, in other words, a demon.[39]

Men like Alison did not just cast judgment on strangers. They scrutinized the eating habits of their wives and daughters. John Bigelow, a New York lawyer and politician, grew concerned when his young wife Jane became pregnant in 1851 and she refused to moderate her eating. "I cannot induce her to abstain from meat. She has a keen appetite," he noted in his diary. "And yet it does not seem to be a morbid one," he reassured himself.[40] Unfortunately, Jane's behavior never stopped troubling John.

Unusually resistant to social pressure, and famous for her unconventionality, Jane Bigelow kept her "hungry appetite," as she wrote in her diary, throughout her life.[41] She filled her scrapbooks with recipes and menus, served as an officer of the Pot Luck Club, and eventually founded the first cooking school in New York City in 1876 as a philanthropic endeavor. She blithely disregarded the advice of etiquette writers like Eliza Leslie: instead of stopping at one glass, she always gleefully noted when a dinner party involved an "abundance of champagne."[42] Jane's refusal to repress her appetites garnered criticism from men she encountered, especially after her husband became a diplomat, serving first as the American Consul in Paris, and later as the American Ambassador to France. Rev. H. R. Haweis, a British minister who met her several times, wrote scathingly of Bigelow's behavior during a meal at his house, but also remarked on her singular charisma. She was a "most fascinating but somewhat embarrassing lady."[43] And yet Jane Bigelow's lack of convention where her own appetites were concerned did not inspire her to overlook other women's failures of dining etiquette. She noted caustically in her diary that Julia Dent Grant, wife of the Civil War general, "eats too much when she goes visiting."[44]

Fully aware of the judgment cast upon them, many women described guilt and shame about their appetites in their diaries and letters. Sylvia Drake, a devout Congregationalist who for years kept a religious diary in which she bemoaned her sinful ways, frequently found cause for self-criticism in her enjoyment at table. She described a meal in August 1838, at the height of her kitchen garden's production, when she ate roast turkey, squash, beans, sweet corn, cucumbers, potatoes, good bread, butter, cheese, swamp whortle berries, custard pie and good ice water. She noted that she ate everything with a fine relish "and enjoyed it better than I should, with an unnatural appetite which cannot be satisfied."[45] The fact that Drake, who was frequently sick, struggled to keep her weight within spitting distance of one hundred pounds didn't make her feel any less guilty about her "unnatural" appetite. Her self-recrimination on this count likely connected to the greatest source of guilty feeling in her life, her romantic relationship with her life partner Charity Bryant.[46]

Similarly, Frank (Frances) Ann Shimer, a young teacher from New York, wrote to her sister in the 1850s bemoaning the "unhealthy craving appetite" that made it hard for her to resist extra helpings at the dinner table of the boarding house in Illinois where she lived.[47] Like Sylvia Drake, Shimer may have connected this "unhealthy craving" for food with her romantic feelings for another woman, Cindarella Gregory. In fact, it was

Shimer's passion for Gregory that had prompted her to accept the offer from a group of investors in western Illinois to move to their frontier town and run a co-educational seminary for the new settlement's youth, requiring her residence in the boarding house. The move allowed Shimer and Gregory to share a bed (frontier necessity) for the next two decades.[48]

Guilty feelings about indulging their appetites appear in the diaries of British women as well. Harriet Sanderson Stewart accompanied her father, the Reverend Francis Stewart, on a trip around the world in the early 1900s when she was in her thirties. In her diary, she recorded a dinner that the two of them ate at a Washington, DC restaurant, which specialized in seafood. The restaurant, she raved, prepared oysters sixty different ways. They started with oysters, then had turtle soup, terrapin Maryland style, broiled lobster with butter, and a green salad with capers and cheese, all washed down with "old musty ale." Feeling uneasy about the indulgence, and the bill, Harriet was reassured by her father's consolation that "we do not often indulge our carnal appetites." Plus, they deserved such a fine meal considering the state of "semistarvation" they had been experiencing at their poorly selected hotel.[49]

The denial of female appetites turned up as a constant theme in Victorian fiction. Authors signaled their heroines' moral continence by emphasizing their thinness and pallor, the same qualities that made consumptive girls into idealized beauties during the nineteenth century.[50] In novels, women were frequently depicted seated at the dinner table, but rarely were they permitted to eat.[51] Abba Goold Woolson, author of the 1873 feminist text *Woman in American Society*, noted that "the familiar heroines of our books, particularly if described by masculine pens, are . . . never to commit the unpardonable sin of eating in the presence of a man."[52] Living, breathing women might have found it harder to resist eating than their textual counterparts, but if moral theories of the appetite didn't lead to a widespread wasting away of nineteenth-century white womanhood, it did make their expressions of hunger into a problem.

It's clear from Victorian fiction that the pressures on women to repress their appetites extended far beyond the ranks of religious enthusiasts and health reformers. The bohemian actress and writer Ada Clare captured this moral dietary system in her 1866 novel *Only a Woman's Heart*. The novel's heroine Laura, who Clare based on herself, appears at the beginning of the novel as a wild "hoydenish" girl, given to fist-fighting and devouring vast amounts of food. The novel's love interest, a young man named Victor Doria, observes her at dinner:

> She had an omnipotent appetite. Every minute she seemed to help herself from some new dish, and the next minute it was gone. After she had apparently consumed all the substantial viands, she calmly commenced a career on the sweets, and then pies and cakes vanished like stars before the breaking dawn. He stood there – this most refined and fastidious young man – in rapt astonishment, wondering that so young and slender a creature could appropriate such a quantity of the world's productions.

After Victor rejects Laura's love, she tries to refine herself into a model of civilized femininity, hoping to win his affections. She learns "that the extent of her appetite was vulgar" and begins eating large private lunches so that at dinners in company she can eat only a little. The novelist, however, reveals her bohemian rejection of these conventions later in the novel when Laura, having failed in her efforts to win Victor's love, defends her youthful appetites from a schoolmate's insults. At least, she says, "I never fed behind the curtain. I was a Goth and Vandal at the dinner table, but no smuggling in of pies and pancakes for me, and hiding them in bed, to be consumed surreptitiously at midnight." Clare treats the impossible demands placed on women's appetites as a source of tragedy, and the melodramatic book ends with the sensitive Victor's death from sunstroke, and the passionate Laura's death from a broken heart. Quite literally: she has an aneurysm of the heart.[53]

The famous Gilded Age New York author Edith Wharton's novella *False Dawn* describes the constraints placed on women's appetites in similar terms. Set in New York during the 1840s, the story includes a dinner party hosted by a wealthy society man on a summer day. The meal includes "heaped-up cookies, crullers, strawberry short-cake, piping hot corn-bread and deep golden butter in moist blocks," as well as Virginia ham, scrambled eggs on toast, broiled blue-fish, tomatoes, heavy silver jugs of butter-colored cream, floating islands, slips and lemon jellies, and towering piles of maple syrup. Wharton captures the abundance of the rich man's hospitality and his male guests' enjoyment of what was set before them: "They ate – oh, how they all ate!" But Wharton's *they* extends only to the masculine guests. "The ladies were supposed only to nibble," she reminds readers, who in 1924, when the story was published, might not have grasped the severity of the restrictions on women eating in the antebellum era.[54]

Wharton's fiction also suggests how those restrictions applied to restaurant culture when it finally spread beyond the boundaries of France, making inroads in the United States and Great Britain during the second half of the nineteenth century. In *The House of Mirth* (1905), the decline of Wharton's heroine Lily Bart is signified through her appearances at restaurants. Bart is born into the waning days of old money society; beautiful but impoverished, her exquisite sensibilities set her apart from the nouveaux riches, and ultimately doom her to extinction. Early in the novel she turns down an invitation to dine at the luxurious New York restaurant Sherry's with a male admirer, Lawrence Selden, in favor of taking tea with him in the privacy of his rooms. Later, at the critical moment of her downfall, Selden encounters Bart in the corrupt European city of Monte Carlo in the "strident setting of the restaurant." Back in New York City after her downfall, Bart finally starves to death (although the *coup de grâce* arrives via a lethal overdose of chloral hydrate). Wharton's complicated text illuminates the high costs to women of the social anxieties around their appetites.[55]

Born in 1862, Wharton came of age in a world where respectable women dined in private homes and ate sparingly in public. Anglo-American encounters with restaurants and gastronomy in Paris during the early nineteenth century had prompted an anti-epicurean reaction among Victorians. When the first French-style restaurants opened in cities like New York, London, and San Francisco, offering private rooms modeled on the *cabinets particuliers* of Paris, they reinscribed the link between French cuisine and sexual wickedness, intensifying anxieties about the morality of the alimentary appetites. The stigma against restaurants placed them largely out of bounds for respectable women until a new generation of independent women, like Wharton herself, insisted on their right to feed their appetites rather than die from starvation.

FOUR

Private Rooms and Rooms Private

"Americans have no restaurants," Isaac Appleton Jewett grumbled in an 1838 travelogue. The young lawyer had been raised in Vermont and practiced law in Cincinnati and New Orleans, making a pretty wide circuit of the antebellum United States. He'd also traveled to Paris, where, like so many Americans before him, he'd admired the *dames de comptoir* and sampled the finest restaurants the city had to offer. He knew whereof he spoke when he drew his sad conclusion about the deficits of his homeland. Jewett conceded only one exception to his general rule: Delmonico's in New York City. There alone could an American find an eating house that operated on the Parisian model.[1]

Perhaps Jewett exaggerated, but not by much. It took a surprisingly long time for restaurants to spread to the United States. A French émigré opened a health-oriented eating house in Boston in 1794 which he called "Julien's Restorator," but no restaurants resembling those in Paris opened in the United States until the 1820s.[2] Only when urbanization and industrialization separated the workplace from home in the antebellum era, drawing large migrations of single young men to the nation's growing cities, did a local restaurant culture begin to emerge. By then, the restaurant was so fixed in the American imagination as a French invention that chefs in the United States often gave their restaurants French names, wrote their menus in bad French, and copied the Parisian precedent of offering private rooms to amorous diners.

Delmonico's followed the French example in each of these regards. Its founders, brothers Giovanni and Pietro Del'Monico, were immigrants from Berne who opened their first confectionery and catering house in downtown Manhattan in the 1820s. By the 1830s, they had opened a proper restaurant on South William Street, with a French menu, *cabinets particuliers* on the third floor, and a customer base that, according to one journalist, was "of a questionable character." Diners in the restaurant's private rooms could order the aphrodisiac foods common on

Parisian menus, including partridges, truffles, and champagne, as well as celebrated American ingredients, like terrapins and canvasback ducks.[3] Delmonico's attracted an almost entirely male clientele since any women or children who dined there during its early decades were "apt to witness practices which are not likely to benefit their morals," as a magazine writer put it politely in 1853.[4]

The closest that Britain came to restaurants before the mid-nineteenth century were its chophouses, mentioned frequently in James Boswell's *London Journal*, which served simple food quickly and cheaply but were not "genteel."[5] London's chophouses bore no comparison to the airy, mir-rored, and marbled restaurants with extensive menus that were common in Paris. Wealthy British men took meals at private gentlemen's clubs, which were not open to the public and did not permit women. French chefs who received their training in Paris's grand restaurants emigrated to Britain to cook for the gentlemen's clubs, like Alexis Soyer who ran the kitchen at the Reform Club from 1837 to 1850 and wielded a profound influence over nineteenth-century British gastronomy. As late as 1879, the entry on "restaurants" in *Dickens's Dictionary of London* explained that "a very few years ago the expectant diner, who required, in the public rooms of London, something better than a cut off the joint, or a chop or steak, would have had but a limited number of tables at his command." As few tables as were available at *his* command, there were even fewer to be had in London at *her* command. Before the 1870s, "with one or two exceptions, respectable restaurants, to which a lady could be taken, may be said hardly to have existed at all," the dictionary's editor Charles Dickens, Jr. reported.[6] He may have exaggerated, but he captured the anxieties that restaurants provoked when they finally arrived in London, carrying with them the sexual associations drawn from their French origins.[7]

Private rooms

When the restaurant was transplanted from France to the United States, its erotic reputation traveled along with it. The sexual disreputability of the restaurant created a need for restaurateurs in the United States to offer private rooms to customers, while at the same time the very existence of those private rooms transplanted the disreputability of the restaurant to its new environs. Aware that the restaurant's erotic reputation was a major factor in its appeal, canny restaurateurs walked a fine line between attending to male diners' appetites and assuring their protection from the reputational risks of those appetites.

In 1837, Joseph Boulanger, a Belgian chef, opened one of the nation's first French restaurants, in Washington, DC. Boulanger had trained at the renowned Maison Chevet in Paris's Palais-Royal and then worked as head chef in the Jackson White House. He was celebrated for his soups, cakes, ice creams, and candies.[8] When he opened his restaurant, Boulanger advertised its elegantly furnished "private rooms," and emphasized his willingness to serve gentlemen who were living in the city without their families.[9] During the 1830s, most congressmen and senators lived alone in boarding houses in the rough-hewn capital city, leaving their wives and children at home, and taking part in a bachelor culture that included intercourse with the city's sex workers, who may have been guests in the private rooms at Boulanger's (as they were at the restaurants of the Palais-Royal).[10]

While the capital city's culture of male sociability created a demand for restaurants, it was in the nation's rapidly growing financial capital, New York City, that a true restaurant culture first took hold in the United States. By 1840, there were a dozen or more private supper rooms in New York City restaurants.[11] Private rooms could be found in restaurants from the seedy streets of the Bowery to the tony reaches of Fifth Avenue. There were sumptuous private rooms decorated in velvet carpets and lace curtains, attached to fashionable restaurants, and there were downscale private rooms, with stained white tablecloths and a simple cot, attached to working-class oyster cellars. The rowdy eating houses that clustered in the Wall Street area had private boxes where customers took "girls of the town." According to an 1866 vice guide, "private box saloons" could be found along the major avenues at most of the street corners above Sixteenth Street. The city also had all-night restaurants, with upstairs rooms rented out to "lady boarders of questionable morals" who sang "flash" (sexy) songs and decorated their windows with red and white curtains in the shape of fans.[12] The Lafayette Restaurant, on Water Street, advertised that its private rooms were open until midnight.[13] The *New York Clipper*, which reported on the city's erotic entertainments, cheerfully boasted that "in the *menage* of public dinners New York is not behind even Paris."[14]

Whether they served up luxuries like roast beef, roast goose, partridges, pigeons, and lobsters, or simple food like pork and beans, mutton chops, fish balls, pickled salmon, and sour eels, prices in private rooms doubled those in public rooms. However, as in France, the menus were not the main attraction of private rooms. "They are, in reality, nothing more than places for assignations," explained the author of an 1869 book about New York City's sex trade. Private rooms were "much resorted to by men who aim to seduce young girls."[15] Another New York City vice guide, from 1866, laid the blame on sex workers rather than their clients. Restaurants with private rooms, the guide explained, were favored by "bewitching creatures, of sweet seventeen" who dragged complacent old gentlemen there to part them from their money.[16] The ubiquity of illicit sex in New York City's restaurant private rooms was widely enough known that a new restaurant which opened on Broadway in 1850 stressed that its "twenty elegantly fitted supper apartments for ladies and gentlemen" were the "most superb and chaste thing of the kind in the country."[17]

The South Carolina writer William M. Bobo noted that there was a wide difference between restaurant "private rooms" and "rooms private," explaining that "the waiters understand what is meant, when a party orders "a room private,"" copying the word order from the French *cabinet particulier*.[18] The private room, rendered in ordinary English, might have respectable purposes, but the translated-from-French "room private" denoted a place for sex.

Just to call a restaurant French or Parisian, in the mid-nineteenth-century United States, suggested the possibility that sex commerce took place at the establishment. Alonzo Welsh's "Parisian Restaurant" in 1850s Baltimore was frequented by the city's prostitutes, who were welcomed by the owner since they attracted male customers.[19] Chicago's "Parisian Restaurant" advertised a "private room for ladies."[20] Portland, Oregon's Parisian restaurant, a "strictly first-class French restaurant," offered "elegant private boxes" for the accommodation of ladies.[21]

While private rooms ostensibly existed to protect women diners' reputations, it was the rooms themselves, with their potential use for sexual encounters, which made restaurants disreputable for women. Nineteenth-century restaurant advertisements gestured ambiguously at their rooms' multiple potential uses. Boston's Maison Dorée, which took its name from the Paris restaurant famous for its *cabinets particuliers*, advertised the availability of "private supper rooms" and a "rear entrance" in the pages of the *Harvard Lampoon*, whose young readers were far more likely to dine with lovers than wives.[22] E. Denechaud's restaurant in Vicksburg, a Mississippi River city notorious for prostitution, advertised its "private rooms for the accommodation of private parties," the doubly stressed *private* sending a clear message to readers.[23] The "Restaurant Francais" in Honolulu's Globe Hotel advertised "nice private rooms," as well as "Wines, Spirits, [and] Liquors," alcoholic offerings that likely kept away respectable women who favored dry establishments.[24] The Bourse restaurant in Philadelphia, named after a building in Paris, offered a spacious public "ladies' dining room," and also four private dining rooms for small parties. In short, the restaurant offered separate spaces for men to bring their wives and their mistresses.[25] The "Restaurant du Commerce" in Sacramento stated that its private supper rooms were provided "for the accommodation of Families and others."[26] Who was meant by *others* might be gleaned from the frequent reports in contemporary Sacramento newspapers on the Gold Rush city's booming sex trade.[27]

The Gold Rush city most notorious for its thriving sex trade and restaurant culture was San Francisco. The city's rapid growth and slapdash construction in the 1850s provided few luxurious accommodations for hosting parties, which made the private rooms at the Poodle Dog, the city's first French restaurant, critical to the town's early social life.[28] As the city grew and developed, offering more reputable venues for gatherings, however, the men of the city never gave up the Poodle Dog. An 1869 item in the *San Francisco Chronicle* poked fun at the married men who ate sumptuous dinners with "fast women" in the famous restaurant's private rooms.[29]

The Poodle Dog set a precedent, according to an early chronicler of the city's dining scene. It was "one of the earliest of the type known as 'French Restaurants,'" so-called because "convivial parties of men and women found its private rooms convenient for rendezvous." One of the Poodle Dog's waiters opened a spin-off called "the Pup," which was famous for its frogs' legs *à la poulette*. Respectable women wouldn't eat at the Poodle Dog or the Pup, and limited themselves to sneaking in the side doors of less notorious restaurants for secretive meals in private rooms.[30]

By the turn of the century, the Poodle Dog and the Pup had been joined by many other French restaurants in San Francisco that had

A menu illustration for San Francisco's Poodle Dog restaurant features a black
poodle carrying a tray with a bottle of champagne and two filled coupe glasses
in an elevator to one of the restaurant's notorious upstairs private rooms. The
illustration was reproduced as the cover of a promotional book produced by the
restaurant; Louis Roesch, ed., *The Tale of a Poodle* (Louis Roesch Co.,
San Francisco, 1915).
Courtesy Carpe Diem Fine Books

private rooms for their male customers, including St Germaine, Pierre's,
and Blanco's. To differentiate itself, the Poodle Dog installed an elevator
that allowed women to be delivered directly to a private room. An anonymous poem from the early 1920s celebrated the legendary restaurant:
"In the Poodle Dog a crowd/Out in 'Frisco;/Disturbs your nerves with
noises loud/Out in 'Frisco/And you will go just one floor up,/And in
privacy you'll sup/Close beside your buttercup,/Out in 'Frisco."[31] The
Poodle Dog even spotlighted its famous upstairs rooms in its marketing,
with an advertisement depicting a poodle carrying a tray with a bottle of
champagne and two crystal coupes, riding an elevator to deliver drinks

to waiting lovers.[32] Not to be outdone, Blanco's installed an elevator that was so large a cab could be driven into it to deliver a woman upstairs to the room where the impatient customer waited.[33]

Well into the twentieth century, according to one of San Francisco's most infamous madams, the term "French restaurant" was defined as an eating place where men could have sex: "the particular characteristic of the French restaurants was neither the sauces nor the accents of the maître-d', but rather the rooms and the bedrooms upstairs."[34] Nor was San Francisco alone in this regard. At the turn of the twentieth century, the term "French restaurant" was commonly used as a euphemism for a brothel. This linkage made eating out anywhere beyond the pale as far as many women were concerned. As one historian has put it, "The family Sunday dinner and a meal eaten in a men's chophouse might bear some superficial resemblance to one another as food, but socially and morally they were as the marriage bed is to the brothel."[35] Restaurants could not be extricated from the sex-work culture that haunted their origins.

Sex on the menu

The fact that many nineteenth-century brothels served fine food and even hosted supper balls further fixed the association between gastronomy and wicked sex. In the winter of 1842, New York City's flash newspapers reported on a competition among local brothels to host the most elegant suppers. "There is at present a feeling of ambition or jealous rivalry existing between the high courtesan hostesses of the city," an article in *The Whip* explained. A brothel on Anthony Street hosted a "Queen Sweets Assembly," featuring an elegant cake topped by two white doves sipping from each other's lips and accompanied by two pyramids of coconut and candied oranges. Willoughby's brothel hosted a supper ball where all the male guests wore military uniforms. And Williams's brothel hosted a ball and supper that were "sumptuous in the extreme – exceeding anything of the kind we ever witnessed." The luxury of these meals far outclassed the fare on offer in the city's oyster cellars and box saloons.[36] Fancy food continued to be served in the city's high-end brothels throughout the century. A surviving menu from an 1890s New York hotel that catered to extra-marital sex reveals a luxurious kitchen on a par with the best restaurants of the Gilded Age.[37]

Another American city where sex work and restaurants remained tightly intertwined throughout the nineteenth century was New Orleans. The city's eighteenth-century French history and nineteenth-century French immigrants had made a strong impact on its Creole cuisine, inspiring its celebrated *étouffées* and *beignets*. Meanwhile, the city's role as a center of the domestic slave trade before 1865, and its post-emancipation significance as a port city for the Caribbean trade, attracted large numbers of single men who provided a market for a thriving commercial sex industry. Prostitution "flourished uncontrolled throughout the antebellum period" and became concentrated in Storyville, an area north of the French Quarter, after the passage of the first Lorette Ordinance of 1857.[38] By the late nineteenth century, New Orleans "had a reputation as the wickedest city in America," which drew huge numbers of visitors, from around the United States and Europe who were eager to sample its twinned pleasures of good food and wicked sex.[39]

Advertisements for the city's French restaurants that offered "private rooms" for visitors filled the back pages of the local newspapers.[40] Charles Boster's Casino Beer Saloon and Restaurant at the corner of Carondelet and Union Streets advertised its French cook, Madame Abels, and its "private rooms" for "parties wishing to be undisturbed."[41] Nearby Denechaud's Restaurant, at Carondelet near Canal Street, advertised "private rooms up stairs for private dinners."[42] The Cotton Exposition saloon, operated by E. F. Denechaud's son, E. A. Denechaud, advertised its private rooms upstairs as suitable for "card parties," a clear sign he was not catering to respectability.[43] The Maison Dorée, another American restaurant to take its name from the Paris institution, advertised its availability to "Ladies and Gentlemen, on leaving the Opera or the Theater," highlighting its "Private Rooms, choice Waiters, [and] the best Parisian cookery."[44] Americans who could not afford a trip to Paris could experience the French city's infamous gastro-sexual pleasures on local shores. And, as in Paris, meals served in the city's private rooms came at extraordinary prices. The proprietors of Pizzini's Restaurant, at the corner of Dryades and Canal, sued a New Orleans newspaper for suggesting that the high prices in their private rooms were a form of extortion, a pay-off for keeping quiet about the illicit goings-on that took place behind closed doors.[45]

New Orleans restaurateurs did not deny the erotic reputations of their establishments, just the allegation that they extorted their customers.

One of the city's most famous restaurants, Begué's, published a cookbook filled with erotic poems that customers had written about eating there. The restaurant, which bordered the city's French Market, was established in the 1860s by a butcher's wife, Madame Begué (née Elizabeth Kettenring), who had emigrated from Bavaria to New Orleans in the 1850s. She opened her first restaurant in 1867, preparing second breakfasts for butchers to enjoy after they closed their shops for the day. Following the death of her first husband, she remarried a Gascon butcher named Hypolite Begué, and together they opened Begué's restaurant at the corner of Decatur and Madison streets.[46] Often credited with inventing brunch, Begué's specialized in serving hearty omelets and wine. Meals lasted for three hours. In the words of an early twentieth-century journalist, Begué's served "Epicurean breakfasts in the Quartier Latin for the *bon-vivants* of the nation."[47] The restaurant was a famous first stop for tourists who arrived in the city on overnight trains.

The restaurant was also famous for its leather-bound registers where tipsy guests were encouraged to scribble extemporaneous verses after their meals. The verses in Begué's registers overflowed with hedonistic celebrations of New Orleans' alimentary and sexual pleasures. "Here's to Begué's when you're hungry/Champagne when you're dry/A pretty girl when you need one/And Heaven when you die," one satisfied diner wrote, capturing a widely shared sentiment. Some customers abandoned attempts at verse under the influence of too many glasses of wine. "Here is to your good health/Drink wine get drunk/And never get married," a presumably inebriated diner added. Horace Fletcher, the manager of the New Orleans Opera House, wrote "I love this town, and all its ways/I love its girls so sweet/But best of all I love Begué's/When it comes time to eat." At the French Market restaurant, residents and visitors alike could indulge to excess. Even women contributed naughty verses to the registers. Leona Roos wrote, "Chickens like corn/Birds like seed/Boys like me/And I like 'feed.'" The bohemian actress Dorothy Usner, who later became a restaurateur in Greenwich Village, struck a scandalous note in the register, writing: "My only regret when I dined at Begue's/Was this – I forgot/To first discard my stays."[48] Far from embarrassed by these paeans, the restaurant reprinted them in a cookbook distributed on the night train to the city.[49]

Stag restaurants

Many French Quarter institutions excluded women diners. Maylié's, on Poydras Street, hosted a "strictly Stag Table d'Hote dinner" from its opening, in 1876, until Prohibition forced the restaurant to remove the wine cellar and build "another dining room where at last ladies could be served."[50] The Gem Saloon, the French Quarter restaurant where six wealthy young men calling themselves the Mystick Krewe of Comus met in January 1857 to plan the first modern Mardi Gras, also limited itself to male customers, offering a "Ladies Annex" upstairs.[51]

So-called stag restaurants, where women weren't just discouraged from the public rooms but excluded entirely, could be found across the United States. The New Era Restaurant in Ohio advertised itself as "strictly a Stag Restaurant," as did James Bell's restaurant in Oakland, Maryland.[52] Herbert's and Schroeder's restaurants in San Francisco were open to men only; Herbert's stayed open all night.[53] Hotels often maintained stag restaurants to keep prostitutes from the premises. The Breevort Hotel in Chicago had a men's restaurant modeled on a Moorish palace.[54] New York's Waldorf-Astoria had two men's restaurants, one of them the North Café, which was decorated with carved pillars and beams.[55] Many men's restaurants went by the name "grills" to differentiate them from restaurants that were open to both sexes.

While hotels may have offered men-only public rooms to discourage sex workers from crowding the premises, late nineteenth-century stag dinners at private clubs and in restaurant private rooms could also feature erotic entertainment. Newspapers frequently reported on stag dinners, leaving unreported the possible presence of any women who were paid to be there. Any traces that made it to the newspaper were carefully couched in euphemism. A satirical "diary of a congressman" published in the *Biloxi Daily Herald* included an entry: "Went last night to a swell stag dinner" given by a lobbyist, "Some regular tobasco-sauce vaudeville turns between the courses."[56] In other words, the diners had been entertained with saucy performances by quote–unquote dancers. The ubiquity of such entertainment is hinted at by a set of pre-printed menu cards from the 1890s, designed to be used at stag dinners, decorated with "a sugges-tive champagne cork with an acrobatic young woman poised upon it."[57] Stag dinners featuring women performers were protected by a veil of secrecy, rarely pierced except in the case of scandal, as that of a stag dinner at Sherry's restaurant in Manhattan that became notorious following a police raid.

The dinner, thrown by one of P. T. Barnum's grandsons for his brother, who was soon to be married, included thirteen courses served to twenty of the city's wealthiest men. It also featured a series of female dancers who were paid to lose their clothes over the course of their performances, culminating in an appearance by a performer known as "Little Egypt" who had become famous for her belly-dancing show at the Chicago World's Columbian Exposition. When one of the other dancers felt insulted by the low fee she was offered in comparison to Little Egypt, her stepfather/manager tipped off the police, who raided the restaurant. Accidentally bursting into the women's dressing room rather than the private supper room, the police ended up wrong-footed and forced to leave without making arrests. Later, Little Egypt danced the "couche couchee" (belly dancing), adorned only in "gaslight and melody" for all the guests.[58] The police raid led to an ongoing scandal and an unusual amount of reporting about exactly what took place at the stag dinner. At other dinners, less well reported, the performances went even further than Little Egypt's – extending to public sex and animals copulating.[59] In short, men-only restaurants and stag dinners excluded or included sex workers according to the appetites of their male customers. Since men's social reputations were largely impervious to sexual gossip, as long as they confined their sexual encounters to girls and women, the single-sex environment at stag restaurants and dinners was less about men's protection and more about their desires.

The culinary desert of England

Restaurants spread to Britain even later than they did to the United States. The first French restaurant in London, Verrey's, opened in 1825, but it remained almost one of a kind for the next half-century.[60] An 1849 London guidebook listed Verrey's as the city's only French restaurant.[61] The English actor and fervent Francophile Charles Selby complained in his 1860 book *The Dinner Question* that

> [u]ntil within the last few years a comfortable, well-served and withal genteel *table-d'hôte* at a moderate cost was not to be found in all London. Shilling

ordinaries at one, or at the latest two o'clock, where the fare consisted of our proverbial "gory joints" and badly cooked cheap fish, served on a second day's tablecloth, with steel forks, and leaden spoons, in a dingy room with a sanded or sawdust-strewed floor, garnished with spittoons, and reeking with the fumes of stale tobacco, were the only attempts at *social* dinners in public, and their frequenters were nearly all coarse feeders of a vulgar stamp, careless of everything but the *quantity* of meat and pudding they could swallow for their shilling.[62]

The situation for diners in London improved in the 1860s, but, as late as 1872, an article about cooking in Britain described Verrey's as an "oasis in the culinary desert of England."[63] Over the next decade, restaurant culture in the city expanded until, in 1885, the situation had changed so drastically that a guidebook boasted that there was probably no capital in Europe that had "so many spacious and splendid restaurants as London." Even so, the food served in London often didn't rise to the level of the decor, tending toward English standards of plain boiled or fried fish and joints of meat, plus one or two soups.[64]

Many of the earliest British restaurants to operate on the French model, serving fine food from an extensive menu priced per dish to guests seated at their own tables in a public room, also followed the Parisian example of providing private rooms upstairs. Among the most famous were the Café Royal, the Savoy, Romano's, and Kettner's. The upstairs private rooms at the Café Royal became the subject of public scandal at the end of the century when they were exposed as a meeting spot for Oscar Wilde and his male lovers.[65] As late as the 1930s, the Savoy was known as a *"mauvais lieu,"* a "wicked place where wicked men take wicked women" to eat oysters and drink champagne.[66] Kettner's, in Soho, opened by the former chef to Napoleon III, had private rooms decorated with green and gold wallpaper, ornaments on the mantelpiece that could be purchased for female guests, and oil paintings of Italian scenery. Going upstairs at Kettner's put a woman's reputation at risk.[67] Romano's private rooms were Japanese themed. Scott's restaurant had a private room in its turret. The private rooms in the Etoile in Charlotte Street were famous for their fold-down beds.[68]

Like their American counterparts, the private rooms in London's French restaurants served a dual purpose. By keeping diners free from prying eyes, the rooms could preserve women's reputations, or they could provide space for illicit encounters, exacerbating respectable women's need to hide in private rooms. This tension comes to light in Nathaniel Newnham-Davis's 1899 *Dinners & Diners*, a memoir-style guidebook to eating out in London. In several chapters, Newnham-Davis describes escorting a married woman out to meals. In an early scene, he reassures her husband, who likes to stay home in the evening, that he will take his wife to private rooms to guard her respectability. But as Newnham-Davis waxes poetic about all the private rooms in London restaurants, the wife suggests there's something scandalous about the extent of his knowledge. In other words, she hints that he has been conducting affairs with immoral women in the private rooms where he proposes to take her to protect her reputation. Her husband, unbothered by this ambiguity, approves of the outings. Yet when Newnham-Davis takes the wife to Kettner's Restaurant in Soho, they access the private room through the kitchen so she won't have to parade through the public room first. She remarks that this mode of access is "quite wrong" and asks Newnham-Davis, "[O]ughtn't we to have slipped up the stairs like a couple of guilty things?" In short, the wife takes pleasure in imagining herself visiting a private room for illicit purposes, while the stated purpose for her eating in the room is the opposite. Even eating in private rooms for prudish reasons could bring a sexual thrill. Respectable women could enjoy the erotics of the private room while protecting their moral reputations.[69]

Newnham-Davis's married companion sailed close to the wind just by eating in a restaurant. Many nineteenth-century British women abstained altogether. The theater critic Clement Scott said women's presence at restaurants was "considered fast, if not disreputable."[70] The British magazine the *Lady* claimed that before the 1870s "women had never dined in public except with their husbands on very rare occasions and, even then, in only one or two select establishments."[71] Auguste Escoffier recounted that "in Victorian London of the 1880s and 1890s actresses, singers, and demimondaines were the kinds of women seen in public places. Wives or English ladies were reluctant to dine in public restaurants for fear of being mistaken as mistresses." The situation in London differed remarkably from the Paris of Escoffier's youth, when he cooked at Le Petit Moulin Rouge, one of the city's finest restaurants, which was frequented by both high-society ladies and notorious demimondaines.[72]

Women in London did eat out during the nineteenth century, but their public dining generated anxiety.[73] As late as 1899, the *Lady* called it an open question whether respectable women should eat in restaurants.[74] Women were typically on safe ground if they ate in public rooms with their fathers or husbands. There was a short list of London restaurants where respectable women felt comfortable, including Epitaux's on Pall Mall and Verrey's on Regent Street. An 1885 guidebook described Verrey's as one of "half a dozen London restaurants or confectioner's shops" in which respectable women could eat.[75] But, even at Verrey's, women restricted their visits to lunches. In the evenings, the restaurant served a typically male clientele from a menu of French dishes like *bisque d'écrevisse*, many of which had erotic associations.

Well into the twentieth century, many London restaurants continued to exclude women even during lunch. In mystery writer Dorothy L. Sayer's 1933 *Murder Must Advertise*, gentleman detective Lord Peter Wimsey takes a female acquaintance to lunch at Simpson's-in-the-Strand because it is one of the few London restaurants with an "upper room where ladies are graciously permitted to be entertained."[76] At least it was an elegant room, with marble pillars and great bouquets of flowers.[77]

While London's respectable women avoided eating out at night, the city's demi-monde flocked to the city's French restaurants that stayed open late. An 1888 account of London's late-night dining scene noted the "décolleté damsels" and "ageing roués" who frequented these establishments. The author also recorded the presence of girls who ordered their meals, then waited patiently for an interested man to come along and foot the bill, echoing the tactics of French *soupeuses*.[78]

Feminine appetites

As Anglo-American cities expanded in the mid-nineteenth century, enticing women into the streets as workers and consumers, the need grew for respectable public dining options where they could refresh themselves when out of the house. In the United States and Great Britain, specialized restaurants catering to women emerged to serve that demand and allow women to participate in the consumer pleasure of dining out without compromising their reputations. The rise of the women's restaurant represented an Anglo-American innovation in restaurant culture, unprecedented in France.

The first women's restaurants to emerge were ice cream saloons or confectioneries, which served sweet and delicate foods and, most importantly, didn't serve alcohol. Victorian mothers routinely advised their daughters when dining in public to opt for light, dainty foods like sweets rather than meat and heavily spiced dishes.[79] Many confectioneries were modest establishments where a woman who was out shopping could stop for tea and a sandwich, or, if she were feeling brave, a sherry cobbler (perhaps because this drink was sweetened, it escaped the ice creameries' general ban on alcohol).[80] Their sugary alcohol-free menus, however, did not de-eroticize ice cream saloons as thoroughly as moralists might have hoped. The presence of women eating together in public invited sexual commentary, regardless of what they ate.

The most famous ice cream saloon in mid-nineteenth-century New York City, Taylor's Epicurean Palace, was a 7,500-square-foot room, with 18-foot ceilings, marble counters, bronze and gilt statuary, gilt-framed mirrors, and crimson and gold chairs and sofas.[81] By the early 1850s, a visitor to New York City observed that Taylor's had become "not only a place where you can get what you want in the way of the delicacies of the season, but a trysting ground for all sorts of lovers."[82] Taylor's didn't have private rooms, but it did have tucked-away tables. An anecdote published in a flash paper described a "young lady and gentleman cosily seated together in one of the cubby holes of that famous establishment."[83] Eventually, ice cream itself came to be seen as an instrument of seduction. In an 1875 ditty, "The Cream-Venders' Crime," a young man told the plaintive story of how his girlfriend ran away with "a feller that peddled ice-cream." Anything that roused the female alimentary appetite held the potential to rouse her amatory appetites as well.[84] Foods marked as "innocent" like ice cream could become wicked if women enjoyed them too much.

Ice cream's French and Italian associations heightened Americans' growing anxieties about this food they initially regarded as appropriate for female consumption. In Paris, the famous Café Tortoni on the Boulevard des Italiens, which served sherbets and ices, went from family restaurant to dangerously risqué, once *cocottes* and courtesans started flocking there at night.[85] Brief notices in the American scandal papers suggest that a similar dynamic occurred in the United States.

Not long after their first appearance, American ice cream saloons and confectioneries began to be used as fronts for selling sex and gambling. In Baltimore, some "confectioneries" were little more than brothels, a letter to a New York paper claimed. "You may walk into many of our confectioneries and you will be saluted with, will you take a private room, sir?" If you answered in the positive, you would be whisked into "a splendidly furnished chamber with every thing to cause an excitement, when, in the heat of passion, you may do that deed."[86] In New York, Alick Hoag was known for "keeping under the name of an ice cream garden, an improper resort for males and females."[87] In Philadelphia, the girlfriend of a gambler supposedly kept "a sort of ice cream saloon, for a sham" to entrap innocents.[88] Brothels or not, women's confectioneries continued to hold erotic fascination through the end of the century. When a women's lunch-counter opened in New York in 1891 to provide a reputable place for ladies to eat, a male reporter gleefully described the sight of the customers struggling to modestly get on and off the hard stools, and took note of the women's "feminine appetites" for pie and ice cream.[89] The idea of women eating ice cream unchaperoned still carried enough of an erotic charge to sell copy.

In Britain, the sexual suspicions about confectioneries persisted well into the twentieth century. In *Hatter's Castle*, a 1932 novel by A. J. Cronin set in Dumbarton, Scotland, a young man pulls his lover into an Italian ice cream café and, as she passes through the doors, she feels "she had finally passed the limits of respectability, that the depth of her dissipation had now been reached." Expecting a sordid den crowded with bacchanalian revelers, the young woman is surprised to find instead a clean bright room served by a fatherly proprietor. While the scene pokes fun at the young woman's naivety, she was not alone in fretting about the danger of ice cream parlors. The rise of Italian-operated ice cream parlors in Scotland produced such a moral panic that the British Women's Temperance Association led a campaign against them in the early 1900s.[90]

The end of private rooms

Ice cream saloons and confectioneries did not resolve the problem of the restaurant's sexual associations. To enjoy the new consumer culture of dining out that spread in nineteenth-century Anglo-American cities, respectable women didn't need restaurants set aside for them alone, they needed all restaurants to exclude disreputable women. They needed to abolish the private room as a space for sex.

Feminist moral campaigns against private rooms in the United States began as early as the post-Civil War era. In New York City, members of the Sorosis Club, the first organization for women professionals and writers, began engaging the private rooms at Delmonico's to host their meetings. At one of their first Delmonico's lunches, in 1869, they took up the question of the "social evil," or prostitution, and debated whether laws to criminalize "seduction" would be more or less effective at curtailing male sexual abuse of girls than changing social norms to "mete out to men the same measure of justice and retribution as fell upon women." A notice of the meeting that appeared in the *New York Times* joked about "the male monsters served up after lunch" by the ladies.[91] The following year, at a Sorosis lunch, one member gave a report attesting "that men and women [could] dine together, without either being injured by the experiment." Moreover, the Sorosis member insisted that women could engage in the sorts of commensality long reserved for male epicureans, like giving toasts and singing songs, without being "unwomanly."[92] The women's daring pushed the outermost boundaries of the norms of respectability, as signified by its coverage in the newspaper.

Jane Cunningham Croly, a journalist and one of Sorosis's founders, spread this feminist argument to her middle-class readers, encouraging them to assert their right "to engage a private room and lunch, for a certain number of guests, at a stylish restaurant." In a cookbook Croly published in 1878, she included a chapter of "Sorosis" recipes, many inspired by Delmonico's kitchens, such as *lobster à la cordelaisé, aubergine farcis,* and *soup à la condé.*[93] The pressure from elite women customers like Croly led Delmonico's to bar prostitutes from its private rooms. One young man who brought a disreputable female guest to a private room in contravention of the new house rules was presented at the end of his meal

84

with a bill that was so high he refused to pay, thus effecting the intended punishment – exiling him forever.[94]

Anglo-American women who traveled abroad shared in this revolution, crowding French restaurants, despite their private rooms. In 1878, Annie S. Wolf, a young Philadelphia woman who toured Europe with her husband, described Paris restaurants as filled with French, English, and American women. The English women she caricatured as "robust" and poorly dressed. The French women were fashionable and had "a combination of grace and wit, that in other females would seem disreputable daring *insouciance*." The American women sat at the table with perfect elegance and propriety, despite the fact that "flash gentleman" were constantly arriving at the door of the fanciest restaurants asking for *cabinets particuliers* where they could be seated with their female companions. Wolf sniffed that "There is no attempt to screen these vices. They are spread before the public in all their attractions." In other words, Paris restaurants had not lost their erotic function in the late 1870s, but respectable English women and American women had become more capable of sharing space with such sexual expression without losing their own respectability.[95]

At the end of the century, as increasing numbers of American girls traveled to Paris to study, they followed the example of the male students who had preceded them by flocking to the city's restaurants. This daring behavior inspired rebuke from American moralists who accused them of letting down their countrywomen's reputation for being "pure of womanhood." But such mean-spirited attacks inspired equally fulsome defenses from commentators who were more sympathetic to changing times. "In Paris when girls or women go into a private room at a public cafe it is a pretty sure sign that they are not as good as they ought to be," admitted an American journalist, but he defended two American girls who had been subjected to public rebuke for eating in a private room with a couple of American men. As newcomers to the city, "they never dreamt that it was compromising their good names to go into a 'cabinet particulier' with two Americans, both of whom they knew had respectable standing in the community." The men turned out to be scoundrels but that could not be laid at the feet of the girls, who shouted for help out the window and were rescued before they could be injured.[96]

By the early 1900s, young female American students in the Latin Quarter could even be witnessed eating together in the local bistros without the presence of a male chaperone.[97] Dining out at restaurants became a way to flex their independence, along with smoking cigarettes and going abroad in the first place. And yet, even well into the twentieth century, the most upright among American women in Paris thought twice before eating in a public room without a male protector. According to Elizabeth Dryden, a newspaper correspondent who lived on the Right Bank for more than two decades, it took "the leveling hand of war" to dispense with the old conventions. Only in the heady days of August 1914, as the city's American colony fled from the coming conflagration, did the sight of "an American woman's dining alone" become a non-event.[98]

In Britain, New Women at the turn of the century protested the outdated dynamics of the restaurant private room and the sexual double standard that excluded them from public entertainment and subjected them to sexual coercion when they did go out.[99] In a 1900 short story by the risqué British novelist Violet Hunt, an adventurous young woman, who is the daughter of an aristocrat and a bohemian (and thus free to do anything she chooses), is asked to dinner by a writer she has been trying to impress with her daring. Although she has "never dined alone with a man at a restaurant in my life before," she agrees to the meal. A female friend who witnesses the dinner expresses shock, telling the heroine "I am old-fashioned enough to think that a woman's dining alone at a public restaurant, even with her *fiancé* is a rather exceptional proceeding." The friend is not alone in her shock. The heroine's daring scares the male writer so deeply that he abandons the flirtation and immediately gets engaged to an innocent, traditional young woman instead. Hunt's story skewered the hypocrisies of the double standard.[100]

Turn-of-the-century New Women fought back. This generational shift is captured in H. G. Wells's 1909 novel *Ann Veronica*. An older man invites the young heroine to dinner at Rococo's, a fictive London restaurant perhaps modeled after Romano's. "We'll go to a place where we can have a private room," he promises her. A French waiter with "discretion beyond all limits in his manner" ushers them into an upstairs apartment with a "silk crimson-covered sofa" and hothouse flowers. The naive heroine is surprised by the obtrusive sofa. "One can talk without undertones, so to speak," the older man reassures her. "It's – private." After the meal, which includes wine, the waiter presents the bill and then closes the door with "ostentatious discretion." The man stands up and locks the door. The naive heroine feels afraid but doesn't act, thinking "after all, what could happen?" Of course, the older man immediately pounces on the heroine.

Then the story takes an unexpected turn. Ann Veronica is no nineteenth-century exemplar of "frail" womanhood. She is a New Woman and she knows "ju-jutsu." She punches her would-be seducer hard in the jaw, forcing him to let her go. The older man is shocked by the blow and cannot understand why she has violently rejected him. Why, he asks the heroine, if she didn't want to be his lover, did she "come to a *cabinet particulier* with me?" When he renews his effort to have sex with her, she breaks a glass on the table and the waiter returns, giving her an opportunity to escape (after more angry remarks from the older man about the relations between the sexes).[101]

Ann Veronica captured a profound shift in middle-class norms.[102] The older man considers it obvious that his invitation to dinner in a private room comes with the expectation of sex, paid for by the meal and wine. In the eyes of her male companion, by eating French food and drinking French wine Ann Veronica has signaled her availability. By the nineteenth-century moral codes under which he'd been raised, indulgence in good food marked a woman as sexually indulgent. But to the young heroine, this moral equation between food and sex is not obvious. She doesn't see sharing a meal with the older man as an invitation for him to make sexual advances. Partly, that's an expression of her sexual naivety, as a well brought-up daughter in a middle-class family. But it's also an expression of a broader cultural shift that was taking place in Britain and the United States, which was not only reimagining sex and gender, but also challenging the moral regulation of food and sex that had governed throughout the previous century.

Of course, women did not penetrate the restaurant only as diners. In the mid-nineteenth century, they began to appear on the floors of restaurants in the United States, France, and Great Britain as workers. Women's entry into the waiting profession, however, did not increase the respectability of women in restaurants. If anything, the rise of the waitress intensified the disreputability of the restaurant during the second half of the nineteenth century, reinforcing the association between good food and wicked sex.

FIVE

Pretty Waiter Girls

In the beginning, all waiters were men. When customers sat down at Café Anglais, Delmonico's, or Verrey's, they called *garçon* for the menu. Men served the food, in public rooms and private rooms. Even if an alluring *dame de comptoir*, seated on her throne, calculated the final bill, it was a male waiter who brought it to the satiated diners. Waiters played a role in the sale of sex as well as the sale of food. They respected the closed door of the private room and kept the secrets of their male customers. They served the bottles of overpriced champagne and pulled the corks that female guests pocketed to redeem the next day. But for the most part, they weren't on the menu.

Then came the waitress. In the second half of the nineteenth century, as moderately priced restaurants mushroomed up in towns and cities, small and large, throughout the United States, Great Britain, and France, restaurateurs turned to women for cheap labor. While waiters at the original grand restaurants delivered food with a performance of hauteur and obsequiousness that gave diners a sense of privilege, waitresses offered an illusion of invitation and availability that sparked appetites and left customers hungry for more. The waitress seemed to be on the menu, even if she wasn't listed there.

Nineteenth-century waitressing can be classified as a "parasexual" profession, a form of sexuality that was "deployed but contained, carefully channelled rather than fully discharged."[1] At a time when social intercourse was often strictly segregated by gender, the waitresses' smiles and friendly conversations offered men a sexual frisson. At racier venues, male customers could touch waitresses on their waists, or backs, or in other sensitive spots forbidden to the touch in encounters with respectable women. Men often asked waitresses to meet them outside of the workplace for sexual encounters, perhaps in exchange for gifts or cash. But if some waitresses moonlighted as prostitutes, waitressing was not itself sex work. The job did not involve the exchange of sex for cash.

Waitresses earned money from expertly giving the impression of sexual availability.

The sexual reputation of waitressing created a market for purity. Victorian middle-class bourgeois society demanded eating places that were unstained by sexual enterprise. Entrepreneurs launched chain restaurants where food was served by women dressed in unadorned black uniforms and clean, white aprons designed to communicate their unblemished respectability. A graffiti artist can't resist a clean wall, and nineteenth-century diners couldn't resist projecting new erotic fantasies onto those clean, white aprons. The innocent waitress became a subject of erotic fascination, an irresistible invitation to despoilment that attracted customers as surely as the women's more provocatively attired counterparts in racier establishments.

At the raciest establishments, the waitresses weren't all female, at least in a biological sense. Some of the most desirable waitresses spent their early years as boys. Their combination of maleness and femininity came as a surprise to unwitting customers, but that surprise held its own potent allure. The male barmaid or waitress became a figure of fantasy just like her female counterpart. And perhaps she opened the door to a remodeled role for the waiter. If sexologists are to be believed, in the late nineteenth century waiting tables was one of the professions most favored by gay men, who, like their female counterparts, often served customers with an inviting smile that hinted at the possibility of something more.

Waiter girl saloons

The idea of employing women, not only behind the bar but to run food and drink to tables of men, appears to have originated in the United States. "Pretty waiter girls," as they were first known, added an innovative sexual attraction to draw male customers to restaurants. San Francisco restaurateurs used waiter girls as early as 1849. The Gold Rush flooded the California port city with single men who slept in tents, shanties, and shops. They took their meals in eating houses of every description: American *dining-rooms*, English *lunch-houses*, French *cabarets*, Spanish *fondas*, German *Wirtschaften*, Italian *osterie*, Chinese *chow-chows*, and so on. The most expensive and fashionable restaurants, which served luxurious delicate fare like game and oyster, first innovated hiring women to wait on customers.

At the time, the skewed sex ratios in San Francisco made it "quite a luxury to be spoken to and waited upon by a pretty girl." Sometimes all the waiter girls offered customers was feminine conversation, but the men's desire for more intimate converse brought them back for repeat visits. "Money was foolishly squandered upon them in presents of jewelry and dress, and the regard of the giver in most instances was the gratification of an occasional deceitful word or smile, and the deep mortification of discovering at last that he had been outwitted, jilted, and fooled," an early recorder of San Francisco history wrote in 1855.[2] According to one historian, during the first two years of the Gold Rush, "San Francisco waiter girls earned an ounce of gold for merely sitting and drinking with a customer or standing by a man while he gambled."[3] Waiter girls grew rich from mining forty-niners.

If pretty waiter girls originated in San Francisco, they became an institution in New York, America's first restaurant city.[4] Junius Henri Browne's 1869 exposé of the city's entertainment scene credited New York as the birthplace of the waiter girl concert saloon.[5] Concert saloons served drinks and light fare to accompany variety entertainment, including music and comedy acts. What distinguished concert saloons from respectable theaters was "their incorporation of feminine sexuality as part of the entertainment."[6] Frank Rivers's Melodeon Concert Saloon, near the corner of Broadway and Spring, which opened in summer 1859, may have been the first to use female singers to run food and drink between acts. The Gaieties, which opened on Broadway soon after, institutionalized the use of theatrically dressed pretty waiter girls.[7] As the *Clipper* explained, waiter girls were "engaged to carry refreshments to those who may prefer to take a 'nip' in their seats, rather than be jostled by a crowd of all sorts of people generally to be found in a bar-room."[8] The innovation drew so many customers to the Melodeon and the Gaieties that new pretty waiter girl saloons immediately "sprang up, immoral mushrooms, all over town." Within a year, there were hundreds of the saloons in New York, according to Browne.[9]

Advertisements for concert saloons in the *New York Daily Herald* repeated the words "pretty waiter girls" in all caps, line after line after line.[10] A January 5, 1861 ad for the Gaieties Concert Room on Broadway

The superior quality of the refreshments served.

The length of the performance.

The privacy those who elect can enjoy, though surrounded by hundreds of people.

And the youth, beauty and accomplishments of the

PRETTY WAITER GIRLS
PRETTY WAITER GIRLS,
PRENTY WAITER GIRLS,
PRETTY WAITER GIRLS,
PRETTY WAITER GIRLS,
PRETTY WAITER GIRLS,
PRETTY WAITER GIRLS,
PRETTY WAITER GIRLS,
PRETTY WAITER GIRLS,
PRETTY WAITER GIRLS,
PRETTY WAITER GIRLS,
PRETTY WAITER GIRLS,
PRETTY WAITER GIRLS,
PRETTY WAITER GIRLS,
PRETTY WAITER GIRLS,
PRETTY WAITER GIRLS,
PRETTY WAITER GIRLS,
PRETTY WAITER GIRLS,
PRETTY WAITER GIRLS,
PRETTY WAITER GIRLS,
PRETTY WAITER GIRLS,
PRETTY WAITER GIRLS,
PRETTY WAITER GIRLS,
PRETTY WAITER GIRLS,
PRETTY WAITER GIRLS,
PRETTY WAITER GIRLS,
PRETTY WAITER GIRLS,
PRETTY WAITER GIRLS,
PRETTY WAITER GIRLS,

Who attend to all the wants of the gentlemen, while every branch of the business receives its full share of attention and the best and most talented performers are engaged regardless of the price. Especial attention is paid to the engagement of the
YOUNG LADIES

The Gaieties, a Broadway concert saloon, drew repeated attention to its pretty waiter girls in advertisements from the early 1860s.
New York Daily Herald, Jan 28, 1861.

listed the "PRETTY WAITER GIRLS!" who worked its room ten times in a row.[11] The advertisement must have been successful because ten days later the Gaieties advertised its PRETTY WAITER GIRLS twenty times in a row.[12] In March, the Gaieties ran an advertisement in the *Herald* listing the "PRETTIEST WAITER GIRLS" no fewer than one hundred times.[13] The advertisements themselves became a point of controversy. The *New York Times* accused the *Herald* of acting as a "pimp-puffer to these vile dens" by advertising the "seductive charms" of the pretty waiter girls.[14] But profit won out over morals, and other newspapers followed suit with copycat ads.[15] Even the *New York Times* gave in and began printing advertisements with the magic words.[16]

Charges that newspapers were acting as "pimp-puffers" by accepting advertisements for pretty waiter girls highlight how fuzzy the line was between parasexual work and sex work. Some nineteenth-century sources used "waiter girls" as a synonym for prostitutes. The *Clipper* published an 1868 police survey of the city that counted 525 houses of prostitution, 90 houses of assignation, 33 waiter girl saloons, 2,070 public prostitutes, and 345 waiter girls.[17] Waiter girls appeared in the report as a type of prostitute, who differed from public prostitutes by virtue of their connection to a particular saloon or restaurant, rather than by the nature of the work they did. Five years later, a New York nightlife guide stated that pretty waiter girls "belong to the lowest and very worst class of prostitutes."[18] This opinion finds support in the work of some historians of sex work, who have treated the "waiter girl" as an "occupational group within the profession" of prostitution, rather than as a separate profession altogether.[19] Such sweeping equivalencies, however, are overstated.

Waiter girls varied. So too did waiter girl saloons, which ran the gamut from elegant palatial establishments to small filthy cellars. The high-end saloons clustered around Broadway, while according to one critic, "those of the Bowery, and Chatham street, are mere brothels."[20] Signs outside saloons advertised "the prettiest waiter girls in the city."[21] Past the front doors, many of their entryways were decorated with paintings of dancing women in tights, stylized along such exotic themes as Ottoman "houris" or the goddess Venus.[22] The nicer establishments had marble-topped tables and parquet floors. The racier establishments had paintings of nudes or "engravings of the French schools" (pornographic images) decorating the walls.[23]

In the 1870s, concert saloons escaped their downtown confines and began to open in some of the city's toniest neighborhoods. The Louvre, at the corner of Fifth Avenue and Twenty-Third Street, was the finest concert saloon in the city. Its walls were frescoed with baskets of luscious purple grapes, golden apples, and sunny flowers. In the center of the room, a fountain sent up sprays of water that sparkled in the artificial lights. The waiter girls dressed neatly and modestly, some of them even elegantly. But the Louvre's waiter girls, like those employed by less elegant saloons, were happy to drink with customers, sipping rum "with very fresh and pretty lips, through the delicatest of hollow straws and from the rosiest of goblets." The Louvre's waiter girls worked on commission, earning a percentage on alcohol sales, encouraging customers to buy expensive bottles of Veuve Clicquot champagne.[24] High-end waiter girl saloons like the Louvre also served delicate cuisine, similar to that served in Parisian *cabinets particuliers*, such as fricaseed frogs' legs, oysters, and boned turkey.[25] In fact, the largest concert saloons had private rooms, often labeled as "wine rooms," furnished with couches just like the *cabinets*.[26]

At the most expensive concert saloons, the waiter girls dressed at the apex of fashion, in silks and crinolines.[27] More rumbustious saloons competed for customers by dressing their waiter girls in theatrical costumes: short skirts, red boots with tassels or bells, highland plaids, Irish green, Spanish peasant dresses, and even "Turkish trouserloons."[28] Waiter girls wore dresses made of lightweight materials that accentuated their bodies.[29] Low necklines revealed bare shoulders and décolletage.[30] Short skirts showed far more than ankles. One exposé described waiter girls as wearing "microscopic dresses" that left them "half-naked."[31] Waiter girls wore makeup and gaudy jewelry. Junius Browne called waiter girls "painted and bedizened wantons."[32] The journalist Mark Mills Pomeroy thought that waiter girls were good-looking "except that the wanton is lurking deep in her eyes."[33] Harsher critics denied that waiter girls, as a class, were pretty. According to George Ellington, the waitresses at the Louvre were "very coarse, fat and prodigiously ugly."[34] Gustav Lening described them as "bloated" by drink.[35]

Pretty or not, waiter girls' costumes, revealing dresses, and use of makeup marked them as sexually disreputable, freeing male customers to speak to them crudely and touch them in intimate places. Waiter girls used physical touch to cajole customers into drinking more, earning commissions off the sales. Mark Pomeroy described how the waiter girl "gently lays her hand on your arm to whisper something, or to ask a question. Her soft hand plays with yours on the sly. She pulls imaginary splinters or chips of tooth-picks from your whiskers, and 'purrs' like a

INTERIOR OF A CONCERT-SALOON.

Pretty waiter girls service male customers in a New York City saloon. The girls wear short skirts that reveal their lower calves, and plunging necklines that reveal their breasts. Some hang over customers encouraging them to drink more. Others can be seen seated at men's tables. "Illustration 34: Interior of a Concert Saloon," in George Ellington, *The Women of New York; Or, the Under-World of the Great City* (New York, 1869).
New York Public Library

love-asking kitten."[36] A reporter who visited McGlory's Armory Hall in the 1870s described how the waiter girls "plump themselves on our laps and begin to beg that we put quarters in their stockings for luck. There are some shapely limbs generously and immodestly shown in connection with this invitation."[37] In an illustration from George Ellington's *The Women of New York*, the waiter girls lean over customers' shoulders, placing their breasts close to the men.

Customers did not always take kindly to being milked by waiter girls. In 1862, a sailor who had emptied his pockets at the 444 Saloon while courting a waiter girl named Kate White went back to the bar and shot another waiter girl who had been helping White handle him. The *National Police Gazette* reported that White was the wife of a "confidence operator." The reporter couldn't keep himself from getting a dig in at waitresses as a profession, describing the "pretty waiter girl" witnesses in the subsequent court trial for felonious assault and battery as "the homeliest looking crowd." According to the reporter, conflicts between disgruntled male customers and waitresses often ended in violence against customers, who refused to press charges because of their shame at being conned.[38]

Waiter girls soon leapt from the barroom floor to the stage and print as they became characters in concert-saloon songs, sensationalist reporting, and melodramatic poems and fiction. A tragic poem in three cantos about a pretty waiter girl named Susie Knight, first published in 1862 in the *Clipper*, related the "true and romantic story" of the young woman's betrayal by a "son of New York" who placed her in a "palace of sin" before she eventually shifted to waiting tables. When the poem appeared as a chapbook the following year, it outsold all other poetic productions on the market.[39] Waiter girls also crafted their own tales, of innocence and seduction and cruel abandonment, to win the sympathy, affections, and cash of customers.[40] Reporters described how the waiter girls would tell their stories to reel men in, casting themselves as frail and fallen women in need of rescue.[41] The waiter girls' parasexual work was "very much the product of a male agenda and male management, yet its women subjects were accomplished managers too," as a historian of Victorian barmaids has argued.[42]

The explosion of pretty waiter girl saloons in New York City in the early 1860s alarmed moralists, who claimed it was impossible for waiter girls to "remain virtuous." The system presented "every possible temptation to sin and degradation."[43] The new system also threatened the interests of ordinary theater owners, who saw their revenues decline. Under the combined pressures of religious and business interests, the New York State legislature passed a "Concert Bill" in 1862 banning the waiter girl system (despite rumors that saloon owners sent a troupe of waiter girls to Albany to lobby against the bill).[44] Shortly after its passage, a waiter girl named Josephine Bailey was arrested for serving lager at an upscale concert saloon called Canterbury Hall, putting the law to the test.[45] The charges against Bailey were later dismissed.[46] Ultimately, the Concert Bill hampered the pretty waiter girl business, but did not succeed in eliminating it. Many smaller establishments shut down immediately after the law's passage, but powerful saloon owners in the city evaded the law by claiming their performances weren't concerts, by pretending they didn't sell alcohol, by disguising the waiter girls as customers, or by bribing police and inspectors.[47]

Meanwhile, pretty waiter girl saloons spread throughout North America. Newspapers in the 1860s and 1870s reported on pretty waiter girl music halls opening in Washington, DC; New Orleans, Louisiana; Fort Wayne, Indiana; Chicago, Illinois; Nashville, Tennessee; Elko, Nevada; Norfolk, Virginia; and countless other small and large cities across the United States.[48] Beale Street, in Memphis, Tennessee, was well known in 1866 for the pretty waiter girls who worked in its free-and-easies.[49] The spread of waiter girl establishments to new cities was often followed by new ordinances to prohibit them, adopting New York's example, with equivalent success.[50] Hotels and resorts across the United States also started to hire female waitresses in the 1860s.[51] The White Mountain Hotel in New Hampshire dressed its "pretty waiter girls" in ruffled busts and expanding crinolines, earning appreciative glances from "many an amorous Yankee" over his dinner of beef or mutton.[52] Even charitable organizations made use of pretty waiter girls at their fundraising dinners.[53]

Personating a woman

Not all the pretty waiter girls who worked at concert saloons were raised as girls. In 1865, news broke that a well-known pretty waiter girl in New York City had been revealed to be "a young man." According to the *Clipper*, Jennie Lamont, who worked at Charley Grovesteen's Champion Music Hall, was arrested for "impersonating a female *woman* without any title thereto, either anatomically or otherwise." Lamont claimed that her legal name was Jim Day, and that she was eighteen years old and originally from Canada. She had worked at Champion Music Hall for three months without remark, until one evening when she agreed to go out to supper with some young male customers. During dinner, "a 'tussle' occurred in which the discovery was made that Jennie Lamont was not Jennie Lamont, but a young man in disguise." The *Clipper* presented Lamont's story as a warning to readers. Dehumanizing Lamont by referring to her as "it," the newspaper called the story "a warning to all dead struck after 'pretty waiter girls.'"[54] More sympathetic readers might have read the story as a warning to waiter girls about the dangers of sexual assault if they went out with customers, and a special warning to trans women like Lamont to be careful about whose invitations they accepted.

Jennie Lamont was not singular. Only a few months later, the *New York Times* reported the exposure of another waitress for "personating a woman." The "young girl of pleasing looks and address," who called herself "Miss Addie," had worked as a "pretty waiter girl" at a Broadway Varieties until the passage of the Concert Bill, after which she moved to Cleveland and became a waitress at a concert saloon there. Miss Addie became an instant sensation among the men of Cleveland, who "beseiged [sic] her in droves," presenting her with handkerchiefs, bonnets, garters, and other fancy gifts. Men lined up to take her out for carriage rides, ice cream and strawberries, and other entertainments, until at last "the astounding discovery was made that 'Miss Addie' was a man!" According to the newspaper report, Miss Addie said she had been dressing as a woman for fourteen years, and that she "looks as much like a woman when in male attire as when dressed in bonnet and gown." Miss Addie's discovery does not appear to have harmed her career in Cleveland. It may even have increased her appeal on stage. Following the news, she appeared each evening at the Cleveland Varieties in the first act.[55]

Intriguingly, theater programs from early 1860s music halls separately advertised performances by two actresses, Miss Jennie Lamont and Miss Addie Lamont, who both appeared on stage as Mazeppa, a risqué role that required an actress to ride across stage, tied to a horse, dressed in nude tights and no skirt.[56] The diarist Alfred Doten wrote about seeing Addie Lamont in this role in Virginia City, Nevada, in 1868. He observed that she was a "small woman − good legs & hips, but no arms, bosom or even a graceful erect attitude."[57] The description of Addie Lamont's lack of "bosom" raises the possibility that this performer was the same trans woman who appeared on stage in New York and Cleveland. There are also notices from the 1880s of another trick-rider named Addie Lamont who performed a "hurricane slide" trick from the top of an elephant, and was perhaps the same person.[58] Or maybe the Addie Lamont who performed as Mazeppa was the same Addie Lamont who opened the first brothel in Denver, Colorado, after supposedly being abandoned by her minister husband while on the wagon road west.[59]

As for Jennie Lamont, a group of performers in San Francisco staged a rebellion in 1864, refusing to appear with her, and calling her a "woman of bad repute."[60] Perhaps this points to a sexual secret or a secret sex. Whatever the objections to Jennie Lamont, they didn't hamper her career. In 1865, she returned to perform in her "native city," New York.[61] A notice in Chicago in 1866 described her as "the queen of comedy and song."[62] In the 1870s, she performed an aerial act with her husband "Albert Lamont" as part of various minstrel troupes.[63] The name "Jennie Lamont" continued to appear on playbills well into the twentieth century, perhaps capturing several different performers' careers. Whether Jennie Lamont the waiter girl, Miss Jennie Lamont the actress, Miss Addie the waiter girl, Miss Addie Lamont the actress, and Miss Addie Lamont the madam were one, two, three, four, five, or more different people is impossible to determine from the sources.

Female impersonator acts, as they were known at the time, were popular on the concert saloon stage, so it makes sense that trans women might enjoy popularity as waiter girls at concert saloons as well.[64] Francis Leon earned esteem as a "clever impersonator of female characters," first in minstrel shows and later in opera burlesque. A profile described Leon as a graceful "*prima donna*" and as a "*danceuse*," mixing these feminine descriptors with male pronouns, seemingly without concern.[65] Charles Heywood was also billed as a "burlesque prima donna and female impersonator." Minstrel shows often featured female impersonators in blackface. Charles Villiers and Fred Abbott both appeared under the title "female impersonator and wench dancer."[66] Justin Robinson specialized as an "impersonator of African feminine affections." Myron Lewis, Fernando Fleury, and W. H. Rice performed in touring minstrel troupes that appeared in cities across the nation.[67]

While minstrel acts lampooned Black femininity to make racist white audiences laugh, prima donnas like Leon and Heywood performed femininity in a more seductive light. In Britain, the character of the barmaid also became popular for male performers. Victor Rosenberg performed in the "character of the Male barmaid," as did Sydney Stevens.[68] An advertisement for Harold Shromburg's act at the Wire Mason's Arms in Blackburn announced "world renowned male barmaid, golden-haired beauty, costly dresses." Acts like Shromburg's carried a sexual frisson for audiences.[69]

Men's erotic appetite for trans women could translate to profits for the waiter girl saloons that employed them. That appetite is evident in the observation by the nineteenth-century sexologist Havelock Ellis that in Germany "the highest proportion of inverts is found among male actors and music hall artists who take women's parts."[70] Ellis used the term "invert" to capture what he saw as the gender reversal inherent to men who sought sex with other men. It is very likely that the percentage of "female impersonators" oriented toward sex with men was as high in Britain and the United States as it was in Germany. Nineteenth-century US press coverage of impersonator acts, male and female, often alluded to performers' same-sex affairs.[71]

More evidence of trans feminine waiter girls turns up erratically in the sources. An 1864 *Clipper* feature on the "Reveille" music hall in Manhattan casually mentioned twenty "shemales" who worked there as waitresses. The article offered no explanation of the term. In its numerous feature stories on other waiter girl saloons, the *Clipper* never used the term "shemale." The article about the Reveille may have employed "shemale" just as derogatory slang to denigrate the women workers who took on the male role of waiting tables, or it's equally possible that the article records how the Reveille drew in men by hiring "impersonators" as servers.[72] Bars in San Francisco's "Barbary Coast" vice district were known to hire female impersonators to sell alcohol and sex. Police in San Francisco arrested a "pretty waiter girl" in 1874 who they said was really a man named John Roberts.[73]

Billy McGlory's Armory Hall, a notorious New York concert saloon on Hester Street near the Bowery that operated on and off throughout the 1870s and 1880s, hired male waiter girls who dressed in short skirts and high red boots and makeup, "and who in falsetto voices exchanged disgusting badinage among themselves and with the patrons."[74] Armory Hall also attracted customers by cross-dressing some of its female waiter girls in masculine Zouave costumes, a uniform worn by the French artillery in North Africa. The Zouave waiter girls waited tables with the "mingled slouchiness and jauntiness" typical of Bowery b'hoys, the neighborhood's working-class youth. Periodically throughout the evening, the Zouave girls assembled as a troupe to perform lightning drills for customers. Armory Hall also held female boxing and wrestling matches for the entertainment of guests.[75]

After McGlory's concert saloon shut down for good, a new concert saloon specializing in hiring trans women opened near the Bowery. Columbia Hall, popularly known as "Paresis Hall" (a reference to a paralytic disorder caused by syphilis), hired trans women as performers. According to Jennie June's [Ralph Werther] *Autobiography of an Androgyne*, the saloon became a meeting place for an organization of trans women who called themselves the "circle hermaphroditos."[76]

An intriguing reference from an 1890s textbook on medical jurisprudence suggests that pretty waiter girls were also associated with another queer sexual expression. The physician and professor of nervous diseases Irving C. Rosse reported accounts of "biuterine marriages" between waiter girls in beer gardens.[77] Rosse didn't offer any specific examples of these biuterine marriages, a phrase he apparently coined. Havelock Ellis also noted lesbianism's "frequency among waitresses" in Germany, and wrote that he had received "the history of a homosexual waitress from Sydney, New South Wales" as well. At the time he published his groundbreaking *Studies in the Psychology of Sex*, Ellis did not yet have information about the frequency of lesbianism among waitresses in Britain, where women had just begun to make inroads as professional servers.[78]

Brasseries à femmes

It didn't take long for the waiter girl system to spread beyond American concert saloons back to the continent where restaurants first appeared. For once, France followed the United States in a new innovation combining the sale of food and sex. According to the nineteenth-century French journalist and moralist Ali Coffignon, French women first emerged from behind the counter and began serving drinks to men's tables in 1860 at the little cafés in Paris known as *caboulots*. These women servers received meals and were paid 150–200 francs a month. The *caboulots* were harmless, according to Coffignon, but after the 1867 World Exposition in Paris a new variety of restaurant appeared, the *brasserie à femmes* (or *brasserie de femmes*), which posed a new and unrivaled danger to public morality and health. The women who worked at brasseries serving food and drink (often *choucroute*, or sausages and sauerkraut, and beer) were more akin to prostitutes than to the relatively innocent *dames de comptoir* found in Paris cafés and restaurants before 1860. In fact, Coffignon blamed the *brasseries à femmes* for leading to the shuttering of licensed brothels, or *maisons de tolérance*, throughout the city.[79]

Coffignon's censorious commentary should be taken with a grain of salt. Historians of the *brasseries à femmes* have argued that the women servers who gave these restaurants their appellation were, like the pretty waiter girls of the United States, parasexual workers rather than sex workers. The job did not involve the exchange of sex for money; rather, the waitresses' tips depended on their openness to sexual flirtation and intimate touch.[80] That flirtation could be quite outrageous by nineteenth-century standards. An 1889 Paris nightlife guide described a night at the Domino Rose, a *brasserie à femmes* in the rue Cujas, across from the Sorbonne, when "a student poured his *bock* into the slipper of the girl who was waiting at his table and drank it off," an act that went far "beyond the more than ordinary shamelessness and bold-facedness of the girls in attendance."[81]

The waitresses provided male diners with sexual entertainment, but not necessarily with sex. This entertainment was so popular that the number of *brasseries à femmes* rapidly multiplied. Women fled their work as chambermaids, seamstresses, and cashiers to become waitresses. The brasseries reached their peak of popularity in the 1890s, when they could be found clustered in the Latin Quarter where students lived, and in the Tenth Arrondissement near the Gare du Nord and Gare de l'Est train stations.[82]

The geographic clustering of the brasseries in locations with high numbers of unmarried men and transient men suggests that a fair number of the brasserie waitresses did supplement their incomes with sex work. According to Coffignon, the waitresses could be divided into two categories: prostitutes and the merely debauched. Prostitutes were drawn to the brasseries because they were safer places to work than the streets. Critics also offered harsher explanations for why prostitutes worked at the brasseries.

A 1903 guidebook claimed that the typical waitress was "a faded, worn-out girl of uncertain age, who in her earlier days has led a gay life, but has ceased to be attractive to the men about town and who is glad to take up with this miserable work for a bare subsistence." The guide alleged that these washed-up prostitutes schemed to get customers so drunk they passed out, and then robbed the unconscious men. Departing from previous sections, which listed places *to* go, the guidebook's section on "cafes of women" included a list of "places against which the English visitor is warned," including the Domino Rose, the Chat Noir, the Brasserie Ferdinand, the Brasserie des Sirènes, and the Brasserie Coquette. Of course, if the reader found the description of the brasseries more exciting than alarming, the proscribed list could double as a guide.[83]

Another allegation against brasserie waitresses was that they engaged in sexual relations with each other. Ali Coffignon levied this charge in a chapter on "le saphisme" in his book *Paris Vivant: La Corruption à Paris* (1888). Sapphism was an ancient practice, Coffignon acknowledged, but it had recently made remarkable progress (not in a good way). The city did not yet have fixed rendezvous for sapphists as it did for men who sought sex with men. But Coffignon claimed that female couples could be found working as waitresses at the brasseries. They were identifiable by their matching dresses, ribbons, and jewelry. They called themselves "little sisters." The presence of sapphists among brasserie waitresses made sense to Coffignon since, he claimed, sapphists were numerous within the prostitute class, and the majority of brasserie waitresses were, or had been, prostitutes.[84]

Waitresses

Not all French restaurants that employed women as servers were disreputable or dangerous. Women also worked as waitresses at France's first casual restaurant chain, the Bouillons Duval. Pierre Louis Duval began to open these spacious inexpensive soup houses in the 1850s. There were over two hundred Bouillons in Paris by the turn of the century, primarily staffed by women. The waitresses dressed modestly in black with white aprons and bonnets.

Nevertheless, some had questionable reputations. Many made a career of waitressing, but others "soon found their way into different professions; and a number, naturally, went on the stage."[85] Even the waitresses who stuck to restaurant work acted in ways that defied bourgeois respectability. By tradition, on New Year's Day the Bouillon waitresses presented their cheeks to male diners to be kissed. As an observer described the scene, "There is a continual smacking of kisses, varying in sound from the popping of champagne corks to a cow pulling her foot out of the mud." This kissing privilege was so titillating that "men have been known to eat five meals at the Duvals on New Year's Day for the mere sake of these embraces."[86] Soon enough, like other waitresses, the women who worked at the Bouillons became subjects of erotic fascination. Pierre-Auguste

Renoir's 1875 portrait *A Waitress at Duval's Restaurant* captures their allure, picturing a pretty young woman in a close-fitting black dress and clean white apron, one hand jauntily perched on her hip, smiling knowingly at the viewer.[87]

British restaurants and bars began hiring female waiters sometime in the mid-nineteenth century. Family-run taverns and public houses had employed daughters and wives to serve drinks and *tables d'hôte* for centuries. In the 1830s, new elegant "gin palaces" began to employ women barmaids, who served drinks from behind counters. But when the restaurant appeared in Britain, it followed the French model of using waiters. Along with the à la carte menu, the public room, and the private tables, the waiter was part of the package that defined the restaurant.

The English writer Thomas De Quincey observed a growing number of women "waitresses" in English eating houses in the mid-1850s. Twenty-five years earlier, De Quincey wrote, the word "waitress" would have been "simply ludicrous," but since then the new word had become "as indispensable to precision of language" as the word heiress.[88] The spread of waitresses in Britain remained limited until the spread of restaurants in the 1870s. An 1879 publication referred to the mass employment of female servers as "essentially a modern institution," a new phenomenon of the last quarter of the nineteenth century.[89]

The shift in terminology from "waiter girl" to "waitress" did not signal a shift away from the work's parasexual associations. The new word – which soon spread to the United States – continued frequently to be paired with the adjective "pretty." Many entertaining anecdotes about "pretty waitresses" circulated in the pages of magazines and newspapers.[90] As soon as waitresses became widespread, they aroused men's erotic imaginations.

Popular British tea shop chains, like Lyons' and the Aerated Bread Company (or A.B.C.), which offered light food, were quick to hire women to serve customers. Waitresses at these tea shops wore modest uniforms and were not encouraged to be bold-faced in their flirtations, like the servers at the *brasseries à femmes*, but they were expected to chat a little with male diners. Managers hired women servers for their physical appeal. An industry magazine reported in 1895 that "pretty girls are eagerly taken as waitresses in certain restaurants and cafés, no matter how ignorant of their duties they may be."[91] Unsurprisingly, waitresses soon became subjects of public fascination in Britain, inspiring comic operas, music hall songs, and fiction.

In *The Bachelors*, a comic opera printed in Manchester in 1880, a member of a bachelor club persuades the steward to hire waitresses instead of waiters. When the women appear on stage, they sing, "We're single girls all out of places,/Of employment we're in quest:/Seeking work where pleasing faces/Most are in request." The steward does his best to "choose a beauty/Lustrous eyes, and lips as fruity/As the ripest cherry plum." One of the candidates squeezes the steward's "thumb" to win her case. The sexual innuendo would have been plain to audiences.[92] The serialized novel *Peggy of Lyons: A Romance of the Famous Tea-Shops* (1910) took a less raunchy, more romantic, approach. The novel related the story of the daughter of a Scottish peer who traveled to London and took a job at a Lyons' tea shop chain while pursuing her love for a suitor rejected by her father.[93]

By the end of the nineteenth century, waitressing had spread throughout Europe. In an 1894 article, the young American travel writer Sterling Heilig entertained readers with the varieties of waitresses around the world. Germany was "the real home of the pretty waiter girl." At beer halls and concert saloons, "blonde girls of the Fatherland, pink-cheeked, blue-eyed and laughing" dressed in "pink skirts and short-sleeved bodices," took drinks from customers' steins, and sat chatting at their tables. In Hungary, the waiter girls danced with customers. Turkish waiter girls served customers at the island resort of Orsova, south of Budapest. In Belgium, the Flemish maidens were "the mildest, modestest and most domestic types of waiter girls the world had yet seen." At the Antwerp Exposition, British barmaids were serving drinks in a new costume: a sailor suit of blue and white, with a Union Jack on the apron. In Spanish cities there were as yet no waitresses, but in the villages of Andalusia girls "go to service in the Fonda and wait on the village boys and traveling mule drivers." Heilig even reviewed the charms of waitresses beyond European borders, reporting that in Japan, tea shop waitresses wore "crackling silk."[94]

Heilig's fixation on the costumes of waitresses was widely shared. Their uniforms designated waitresses as working women, and therefore as public women, a category understood as synonymous with prostitutes. The act of wearing a uniform marked a woman as a subject of erotic potential, regardless of the modesty or immodesty of the design. The waitresses at America's first restaurant chain, the Harvey House, which operated at train stations across the west, dressed modestly in uniforms similar to those worn by the waitresses at the Bouillons Duval and the A.B.C. Their black dresses and clean white aprons signaled both the cleanliness of the establishments and the respectability of the girls. But the Harvey Houses waitresses' reputation as "upright Christians of high standards" didn't make them undesirable to customers. Instead, they became the restaurants' "most popular dish."[95] Just as ice cream saloons that were designed to preserve women's sexual reputations became sites of erotic fascination, restaurants that advertised the purity of their waitresses aroused the erotic interest of male customers.

By the turn of the twentieth century, waitressing had expanded far beyond its early roots in the sexually risqué context of the concert saloon. While grand restaurants remained almost exclusively the preserve of male waiters, female waitresses could be found everywhere else. But taking waitresses out of their sexualized context did not take the sex out of waitressing.

The pioneering sociologist Frances Donovan wrote an ethnography of waitressing based on nine months she spent working as a server in 1917–18 at a wide range of Chicago restaurants, including Jewish delis, tea rooms, hash houses, and country club grills. In a chapter titled "The Sex Game," Donovan wrote that across the spectrum "restaurants want women who are young and good looking; the advertisements announce it and most managers insist on it." Donovan, who was a widow in her late thirties at the time of her research, was advised by fellow waitresses to take off her wedding ring if she wanted good tips. She found out that it was routine for customers to leave a card with their number along with their tips. Waitresses could be choosy about who they went on dates with since they earned "the necessaries of life for themselves."[96] Most of Donovan's coworkers used dates for their ability to provide tickets to entertainment and gifts like clothing and accessories, but some also took cash for sex.

Donovan was surprised by the sexuality of the waitresses she worked with, whose behavior did not conform to her middle-class expectations. The women frequently engaged in "dirty jokes and unclean conversation" among themselves, passed around obscene poetry, and "pointed out to each other men who indulged secretly in perverse sexual practices."[97] Unfortunately, Donovan refrained from recording their jokes or conversation, which she considered offensive. She blamed the conditions of city life for perverting the waitresses' healthy sexuality into an "unnatural expression." In their hearts, she argued, most waitresses aspired to domesticity, but the economic inefficiency of the men in their lives led waitresses to take on "a life of semi-prostitution."[98] Donovan thought that the women paid a harsh price for this behavior, suffering from high rates of venereal disease and endangering their lives with risky abortions. But a few little snippets of dialogue she recorded in her ethnography suggest that the women were less bothered by their situations. One of the waitresses joked with Donovan about her venereal disease, saying "I don't make no claims to being decent." Generally, "they appeared to be happy, too, not cast down and ashamed of their degradation."[99]

The ongoing parasexual expectations for waitresses at the beginning of the twentieth century created the conditions for the restriction of women as workers at expensive restaurants. In North America and Europe, expensive restaurants requiring formal service remained the preserve of waiters. Labor unions that organized waiters frequently excluded waitresses, associating them with prostitution. Unions even sought to prohibit women from working in restaurants in France, Britain, and Belgium.[100] Excluding women from waiting tables, however, did not desexualize the profession. By the early twentieth century, waiting tables had become notable as a profession that attracted queer men, along with hairdressing and interior decorating. In sexological case studies, homosexual men often reported work histories as waiters, many in hotel restaurants which created opportunities to meet for sex in customers' rooms.[101] At some restaurants in early twentieth-century London and New York, the entire waitstaff consisted of gay men.[102]

Eventually, proprietors' desires to pay low wages overcame moral resistance to hiring women, and waitresses became the majority of servers at lower-priced restaurants like cafeterias, drugstores, coffee shops, and truck stops. Once waitresses became ubiquitous, the profession gradually lost its stigma. In the United States, in 1900, only a third of waiters were women. By 1970, 92 percent of people who served food were female. But even if over the course of the twentieth century waitresses ceased to be seen as akin to prostitutes, the profession retained elements from its origins. Restaurant managers continue to express preference for hiring "women who are young and good-looking," mild flirtation remains an effective strategy for earning tips, and customers continue to ask their servers, female and male, out on dates.[103]

SIX

Dinners in Bohemia

Charles Astor Bristed didn't care what other people thought about him; he had "an entire indifference to the opinion of mere masses of men."[1] As a young man in his twenties, he broke from social conventions by publishing the first original serious American work of gastronomy, an 1848 essay titled "Table Aesthetics." He confessed that he was well aware "many very worthy persons . . . will consider my purpose in this essay frivolous at best, if not absolutely mischievous." The article came at the heyday of American anti-epicureanism. But rather than defend himself, he ridiculed his critics: "'The art of eating and drinking!' cries one. 'Animal propensities! sensual! making a beast of one's self!'" Bristed called these attacks on the appetite "rubbish."[2] Instead of apologizing, Bristed defended eating and drinking as vital subjects of inquiry because they were intimately associated with the experience of joy. Some called Bristed a "dandy."[3] He preferred the label "bohemian."[4]

The origins of the term "bohemian" are cloudy. Its earliest recorded usage was in a little-known 1790 novel, *Les Bohémiens*, an erotic adventure story with strong anti-clerical themes written by a disgraced marquis who was "a scoundrel, a reprobate, a rogue, [and] a thoroughly bad hat."[5] The hero of *Les Bohémiens* embodied the antipathy to social conventions that became central to the culture of bohemianism. The novel had few readers, but the word "bohemian" spread in the nineteenth century. By the 1830s, it had become common in Paris literary circles as an adjective for young convention-defying artists and writers.[6]

The word reached wide circulation with the publication of the French journalist Henri Murger's wildly popular sketches, *Scènes de la Vie de Bohème*, in 1845. Drawing from his own life, Murger told the story of four hungry and broke young friends – a composer, a philosopher, a painter, and a poet – who lived in the Latin Quarter of Paris. Each had a *grisette* mistress, except for the inconstant Colline, for whom "every day was the day of Saint Appetite." Lacking money to heat their garret apartments, the friends met daily at the Café Momus, where they drank endless cups of coffee so they could shelter in the restaurant's warmth. When they had cash, they ate at La Mère Cadet, famed for its stewed rabbit, sauerkraut, and "a thin white wine with a smack of brimstone." Murger's work popularized the romantic myth of the bohemian life, dedicated to the pleasures of art, women, and food, without regard to the judgments of Church, state, or family.[7]

Charles Astor Bristed, who visited Paris in the mid-1840s, adored Murger's *Scènes* and translated them into English, publishing selections in the *Knickerbocker* magazine in 1853–4 under the title "The Gypsies of Art."[8] One translated scene, recounting the four friends' spirited conversation over a breakfast of artichokes and pepper sauce, appeared alongside an unsigned review of Brillat-Savarin's *Physiologie du Gout*, also likely by Bristed.[9] The review quoted at length from Brillat-Savarin's defense of eating for pleasure: "gastronomy sustains us from the cradle to the grave; increases the gratification of love and the confidence of friendship; disarms hatred, and offers us, in the short passage of our lives, the only pleasure which, not being followed by fatigue, makes us weary of all others."[10] With his translations, reviews, and original works, Bristed led the charge to spread the gospel of bohemian gastronomy to the United States.

Skeptics scoffed at the idea that crass materialistic Americans could ever personify the bohemian ideal, but Bristed defended his compatriots. Bohemianism, he wrote, was just another word for "unconventionalism," or a "strong disbelief in Mrs. Grundy." There was nothing particularly French about the philosophy. Bohemians were men (only men, according to Bristed), who had literary or artistic tastes and an incurable proclivity to debt. By these standards, he wrote, "I do claim to be a Bohemian." After all, he was a writer, and he had "never been out of debt but twice since the age of sixteen."[11] Considering that his grandfather was John Jacob Astor, the richest man in America, Bristed must have racked up some pretty sizable restaurant bills to get himself into such trouble.[12]

Shortly before his death, in 1874, Charles Astor Bristed published a "casual cogitation" about the future of food in the United States. "Will the coming American eat and drink?" he asked. Sylvester Graham was dead and gone, but the ascetic tendency was "far from extinct." Many Americans continued to regard taking pleasure in good food as a form of "depravity." This widespread antipathy to eating for pleasure had resulted in America's "singularly and deplorably low state of the culinary art." Bristed argued against asceticism by comparing puritanical diets to sleep deprivation and argued that only a robust diet produced genius. "Vegetables and water have never given us more than one true poet – Shelley," he argued. Byron had pretended to live off biscuits and soda water, but he'd privately eaten and drunk more heartily, and "if we proceed to prose fiction, great novelists, as a class, may be called lusty livers." Thackeray and Dickens, according to Bristed, were made brilliant by their sensuous appetites, which tempered their tendencies toward bitter iconoclasm and cynicism.[13]

It was no accident that Bristed used the example of writers to illustrate the salutary effects of good food. Many aspiring journalists, novelists, and poets of the age embraced bohemianism. The journalist Junius Henri Browne remarked in 1869 that "all persons of literary or artistic proclivities" had come to be seen as bohemians, although Browne thought the term should be reserved more narrowly.[14] Skeptics debated whether wealthy libertines had the right to call themselves bohemians, or whether sexual freedom fit within bohemianism. Everyone, however, agreed that a taste for good food was central to the bohemian sensibility.

The Parisification of New York

Although Murger had claimed that "Bohemia only exists and is only possible in Paris," by the early 1850s, writers and artists in London and New York City were claiming the identity for themselves. The novelist William Makepeace Thackeray is often credited with having "introduced both the word and the concept of bohemia to England from Paris."[15] After losing his inheritance on gambling and failed publishing ventures, Thackeray studied art in Paris before becoming a successful writer. He gained fame with his novel *Vanity Fair* (1847–8), whose "seminal Bohemian protagonist," Becky Sharp, shocked readers.[16]

Thackeray's *Bildungsroman, The History of Pendennis*, published serially in 1848–50, further spread the gospel of bohemianism by romanticizing his youthful years spent striving to make his way in London's literary scene, eating and drinking with friends, and going deeply into debt. After a morning of work, Pendennis and his young writer friends "sally out upon the town with great spirits and appetite, and bent upon enjoying a merry night."[17] The sexual frankness of Thackeray's novels and his personal renown for gluttony cast his own reputation under suspicion. The Anglo-Irish author Fitz-James O'Brien called Thackeray a "British Bohemian, a man really capable of excesses and of coarseness, a man really familiar with the sins and the degradations, the acute sufferings and the morbid ill-health of the modern world."[18]

These charges could have been levied against O'Brien himself, who moved to the United States in 1852 and became a key figure in the nation's first self-proclaimed bohemian crowd: a circle of British writers who had lived in Paris and in London before arriving in New York, where they collaborated on a magazine called the *Lantern* that held weekly editorial meetings at Windrust's restaurant, near Fulton Street.[19] The *Lantern* crowd were soon followed by another expatriate group who called themselves the Ornithorhynchus Club, after the scientific name of the duck-billed platypus. They met at a restaurant on Spring Street ornamented with a sign depicting a platypus smoking a pipe and drinking a glass of beer, painted by the artist Frank Bellew.[20]

It is little surprise that American bohemianism first emerged in New York City, considering the growing "Parisification of New York," as the journalist Nathaniel Parker Willis put it. At the mid-century mark, the city was rising in prominence as a pleasure destination and drawing the globe's "sweetest voices, most bewildering legs, best players, boldest riders" and "best cooks."[21] The growing number of restaurants and cafés in New York made the city attractive to an American writer, Henry Clapp, who had lived in Paris during the mid-1850s taking part in the bohemian café life along the avenues, then in London where he mingled with British bohemian writers at the Old Cheshire Cheese tavern in Fleet Street, before he returned home to the United States. Clapp was the first American writer to describe himself and his circle of literary friends and acquaintances as bohemians.

A man in "bitter conflict with conventionality" and "reckless of public opinion," Clapp established his new bohemian beachhead at a German beer cellar called Pfaff's, on Broadway, just south of Bleecker.[22] More than two hundred notable writers, artists, and stage performers, male and female, frequented Pfaff's over the next several years.[23] The most famous regular was Walt Whitman, who wrote a fragmentary verse in a notebook from the early 1860s describing evenings at "Pfaff's where the drinkers and laughers meet to eat and drink and carouse." Although he was not a big drinker, Whitman liked watching the young men who gathered for dinners in the beer cellar: "bright eyes of beautiful young men!/Eat what you, having ordered, are pleased to see placed before you – after the work of the day, now, with appetite eat."[24] Whitman's lines captured the Pfaffians' ethos of taking public pleasure in their appetites as a sign of their unconventionality, their independence from the judgment of the bourgeoisie.

Not that they weren't hard-working writers, as well. Many of Whitman's "beautiful young men" worked for Clapp, who in October 1858 launched a new bohemian literary journal, the *Saturday Press*. Clapp leavened the journal's regular fare of book reviews with frequent remarks on gastronomy.[25] The *Saturday Press* defended the pleasures of the table against American reform movements, like Grahamism, that condemned the appetites. A December 1858 article proclaimed that "the human palate being a divine and not a human institution has as much right to be gratified as the human ear or the human eye. Man was not made to live by bread alone, nor by bread and water alone."[26] Take that, Sylvester Graham.

An essay in the same issue, titled "Harmony in the Kitchen," praised the artistry of good cooks, a popular gastronomic theme. Echoing Brillat-Savarin, the author praised the cook as an "analyst, inventor, harmonist. He studies the subtleties of flavor, as the musician studies the subtleties of sound. A grand dinner and a grand opera are kindred compositions."[27] The essay held up French cuisine as the highest expression of the cook's artistry, praising the brilliance that transformed a brace of pheasants or pigeons into *Faisan à la Périgueux* or *Perdrix à la Soubise*.[28]

Pfaff's was more German *Rathskeller* than French restaurant. The menu included calf's liver, tongue, and head, roast venison and beefsteaks, and side dishes of stewed cabbage, boiled potatoes, and potato dumplings.[29] But Pfaff was very well respected for his taste in champagne, and his wine list was top rate.[30] While the food lacked the aphrodisiac associations of the delicate dishes served in *cabinets particuliers*, Pfaff's was subject to sexual rumors because it admitted women customers. "The Germans are not shocked when a woman enters a restaurant," one of Pfaff's regulars explained, but Americans at the time certainly were.[31] And, if the mere presence of women mingling freely among the bohemian crowd at Pfaff's was not shocking enough, the frequent appearance of the notorious writer and actress Ada Clare at Henry Clapp's table sealed the restaurant's disrepute.

Ada Clare, the so-called "queen of Bohemia," was a wealthy young woman from Charleston, South Carolina, who had thrown off the shackles of respectability by openly pursuing a passionate affair with the romantic composer Louis Moreau Gottschalk. She escaped her family's control by stealing money they had raised for a monument to her cousin, proslavery extremist John C. Calhoun, and using it to escape to New York City when she was twenty. Three years later in 1857, unmarried and pregnant, Clare left New York for Paris to give birth to her illegitimate son.[32] Once abroad, she sent letters back to New York for publication in the *New York Musical World* and *Porter's Spirit of the Times*. Clare's letters reporting on Paris's theaters and opera were aflame with the fire of bohemian sensibility. She passionately defended a life of "loving, and grieving, and admiring" against the judgment of "those prophets of bullion, those divinities of the material" who considered the passions to be follies.[33]

Clare was unashamed to be accused of giving way to her own animal sentiments and, after her son Aubrey was born, she was unashamed to acknowledge herself an unwed mother. When she returned to New York in 1858, she was welcomed by Clapp and the crowd at Pfaff's, and she began to contribute articles to the *Saturday Press*. She also hosted frequent bohemian dinner parties at her home on 42nd Street. The writer Getty Gay, another woman who turned up at Clapp's table at Pfaff's, wrote a short piece about Clare's dinners for the *Saturday Press*. "The Royal Bohemian Supper" described the festive mood at Clare's dinner parties, which often ended in performances, when "the champagne baskets and bottles now growing empty, and the Bohemians full, each member of the company gave way to his wildest inspiration."[34]

According to the gossip-filled diaries of Thomas Butler Gunn, an English writer who assiduously chronicled the affairs of the Pfaff's crowd, "the Bohemians had a whispered rumor that the affection between these women was of a Parisian, Sapphic character."[35] Gunn thought the rumors plausible, since both Gay and Clare, in his eyes, were sexually beyond the pale. He described Clare's decision to acknowledge her illegitimate child as her "affecting the Bohemienne," and said she had "self-outlawed from decent womanhood." As for Gay, Gunn heard she "adds direct prostitution to her 'literary' pursuits, taking rides in omnibuses of afternoons and Broadway promenades to pick up $5 with men attached."[36] On the other hand, he acknowledged, rumors of Clare and Gay's Sapphic relationship could have been a "monstrous canard originating in the depraved minds of such men as Clapp or O'Brien." Gunn took the occasion of Gay's unfortunate death at age twenty from consumption to muse in his diary, "were there Bohemians in Sodom and Gomorrah, I wonder?"[37] Bohemian sexual disreputability contained queer possibilities.

Clare's and Gay's appearances at Pfaff's, along with other *bohémiennes*, like the writer Jennie Danforth, and the actress Adah Menken, who had appeared on stage in bare legs strapped to a horse in the play *Mazeppa*, made the restaurant subject to all sorts of rumors. (According to some, Menken inspired the character Irene Adler in Arthur Conan Doyle's story "A Scandal in Bohemia.")[38] Franklin Ottarson, a friend of Clapp's and occasional visitor to the beer cellar, attacked the women as corrupt "Bohemian Aphrodites, whose outward and visible form betrays all of the demon without a shadow of the divinity." Like Gunn, Ottarson also implied that bohemian sexual license went beyond loose relations between men and women. In so many words, Ottarson claimed Pfaff's encouraged illicit relations between men. He condemned the beer cellar for seducing men away from the "domestic attractions and ties that God and nature provide for those who obey physical law."[39] The odd phrasing evoked the so-called "crime against nature," a common euphemism for sex between men in the nineteenth century.

Former regulars at Pfaff's protested Ottarson's slander. Frank Bellew, founder of the Ornithorhynchus Club and a friend of Clapp's, illustrated a diptych comparing the bohemians "as they were said to be" to the bohemians "as they are." The first image pictured a rambunctious mixed crowd of men and women, several clenched in tight embraces, smoking and drinking from foamy steins of lager, nary a pen nor piece of paper in sight. The second showed the Pfaff's crowd far more sedately gathered around a long table, reading papers and conversing spiritedly, while sipping on coffee and champagne. Not only are no women present in the second picture, the men keep a respectable distance from each other.[40]

Frank Bellew diptych showing the "Bohemians as they were said to be by a knight of The Round Table" (top) and "as they are described by one of their own number" (bottom). From Demorest's *New York Illustrated News*, Feb 6, 1864. *Frank Bellew (1828–1888), "'Bohemians as they are declared by one of their own number' and 'As they were said to be by a knight of The Round Table',' Lehigh Library Exhibits, accessed March 12, 2024, https://exhibits.lib.lehigh.edu/items/show/4033*

Although he was not alone in his insinuations, Gunn was unusually direct in linking bohemianism and same-sex sexuality. Nineteenth-century authors typically stuck to euphemism. More than any other author, Walt Whitman can be credited for the queer reputation of New York's early bohemia. It was during his years of frequenting Pfaff's that Whitman wrote his homoerotic "Calamus" poems. Whitman's writings also provide fleeting evidence that Pfaff's was a gathering place for a very early queer subculture in the city: a circle of young bachelors with an inclination toward same-sex intimacy.[41] Whitman affectionately called this small circle of friends the "Fred Gray Association" after their central figure, John Frederick Schiller Gray. Other members of the group, many of them medical students, included Hugo Fritsch, Nathaniel Bloom, Benjamin Knower, Charles Russell, Charles Kingsley, and Charles Chauncey.

During his evenings in the beer cellar, Whitman alternated between sitting at Henry Clapp's table and sharing meals and drinks with the members of the Fred Gray Association. Whitman later told his biographer Horace Traubel that in order to understand the Calamus poems, one had to read his letters with association member Hugo Fritsch, which captured the pleasure that Whitman took in the younger men's company.[42] In 1863, after the Civil War had dispersed their circle and taken the life of handsome Charles Chauncey, Whitman wrote to Fritsch, "I remember . . . the delight of my dear boys' company & their gayety & electricity, their precious friendship, the talk & laughter, the drinks."[43] On Christmas evening in 1888, at Whitman's request, Traubel read the letter out loud to the elderly poet, bringing tears to his eyes. Afterwards, they discussed Whitman's love of men.[44]

By nineteenth-century standards, there was something queer about men who cared too much for food. A passion for the table could easily cross the line from masculine appetite to feminine fussiness. Take, for example, Nathaniel Parker Willis, the highest-paid magazine writer of the 1840s. He made his reputation as a travel writer. His scandalous *Pencillings by the Way*, published in 1834, recounted his adventures in Paris restaurants and his admiration for the city's pretty *dames de comptoir*.[45] Back home in New York, Willis reported on the erotic possibilities to be discovered in the city's eateries, like Florence's Oyster Saloon.[46] He was a staunch defender of "the appetites," a self-declared believer in "eating and living luxuriously."[47] From the very beginning of his career, when he was still in his late teens, Willis cultivated a reputation as a rake. Critics called him "lewd Natty." Female readers fantasized about meeting him. The celebrated Shakespearean actor Edwin Forrest assaulted Willis in Washington Square Park in 1850, beating him with a gutta-percha whip for sleeping with his wife. A published account of the subsequent divorce trial included evidence of a waiter who reported seeing Willis lying on Catharine Forrest.[48]

But despite the excessive and incontrovertible evidence of Willis's womanizing, his epicurean tastes led critics to question his masculinity. The editor of the *Hartford Review* called him "not quite a woman, by no means a man." The smutty journalist William Snelling attacked Willis in a bit of doggerel: "'tis said his sex/Did for a month the neighborhood perplex./('tis doubtful now.)" Others referred to him as "Namby-Pamby Willis" and "a pronoun of the feminine gender." His own sister, the writer Fanny Fern, accused him of "Miss Nancyism," using a common nineteenth-century euphemism for male effeminacy.[49] Willis's refined tastes made him a queer figure by the standards of the nineteenth century. Willis also played a part in defining the queerness of dandyism and epicureanism for nineteenth-century readers.

In an article for the *Home Journal*, Willis described a new American masculine archetype to be found in mid-century New York City: the Fifth-Ave-noodle. Sometimes spelled "avenudle" or "avenoodle," this term referred to a New York dandy. The word "noodle" played on the eighteenth-century dandy stereotype of the macaroni. The macaronis were young British gentlemen who went to the Continent on the Grand Tour to refine their tastes and, while there, picked up a taste for Italian food (macaroni) and possibly Italian sexual indulgence (buggery). The macaroni stereotype was effeminate in dress and sexually suspect.[50] These same characteristics described his nineteenth-century American variant, the Fifth Avenoodle. According to Willis, the avenoodle dressed effeminately: "his pantaloons are so diligently renewed that knee-marks never protuberate. His gloves look like primroses, new-blown with thumb and fingers. His head, smooth from the curling-tongs, sits in his collar like a marigold in a paper holder." The avenoodle desired to be known among the ladies as a "dangerous man," but his flirtations were ineffectual. "He is not, in fact, a dangerous member of society," whatever he might pretend.[51] At least, he wasn't truly dangerous to women, although his indulgence in the pleasures of food, art, and clothes made him dangerous to American masculinity.

There was overlap between avenoodles and bohemians, especially among wealthier bohemians. In his gossipy diaries, Thomas Butler Gunn characterized the writer Robert Pearsall, who hung out at Pfaff's cellar, as a "weak, well-to-do Fifth-Avenoodle." Gunn heard that Pearsall wanted to marry Ada Clare, and he also alleged that Henry Clapp had swindled Pearsall out of thousands of dollars to support the *Saturday Press*.[52] Gunn made similar allegations about Clapp's relationship with Edward Howland, the wealthy scion of a Charleston cotton plantation-owning family and another major supporter of Clapp's journal.[53] "The association of bohemia with stately Fifth Avenue" persisted throughout the nineteenth century, even if the more penurious writers and artists dismissed wealthier visitors to their quarters as "pseudo-bohemians."[54] There was a vanishing line between the "fast" young avenoodles, who queered masculinity with their colorful waistcoats, elongated skirts, and refinement of tastes, and the cash-strapped bohemians who queered masculinity with their long hair, theatrical clothes, and indulgence at the table.

Just as wealthy avenoodles strayed into bohemian restaurants, penurious bohemians sometimes strayed into expensive restaurants. Fitz-James O'Brien hosted dinners at Delmonico's for Clapp and other editor friends, even when he owed hundreds of dollars to his landlords. A fellow Pfaffian described O'Brien's indulgence in fine food while he was deeply in debt as "heavy-swell Bohemianism."[55] A taste for culinary indulgence with flagrant disregard for its costs defined the bohemian ethic. In Murger's very first bohemian sketch, the musician character, Schaunard, orders an expensive dinner and sticks the bourgeois merchant whose portrait he's painting with the bill. According to a popular story that circulated in US newspapers, the writer Alexandre Dumas *fils* once went out with a number of his bohemian companions to the Maison Dorée in Paris, only to discover, when they were handed the bill, that none of them had the wherewithal to pay it. Dumas *fils* hurried across the street to find his writer father, Alexandre Dumas *père*, and beg some money, but he returned to the restaurant with his pockets even emptier. Dumas *fils* had given his last five francs to Dumas *père*, an equally notorious bohemian – and one-time lover of Adah Menken – who needed the money to pay off his own dinner bill.[56] The bohemian tendency for gastronomic indulgence regardless of means was so notorious that conmen used *bohemianism* as an excuse to get out of paying for their dinners. A cynical French author ridiculed "the pretended banker, who invites you to dine at Verey's, and, when the dessert is placed upon the table, has forgotten his purse – Bohemian!"[57]

Beyond New York

Nomadic by nature, New York's self-described bohemians soon transported this new subculture beyond the confines of Manhattan. Ada Clare, Adah Isaacs Menken, Fitz-Hugh Ludlow, and Charles Webb all traveled to San Francisco, where a "self-conscious Bohemia" emerged by the early 1860s.[58] The writer Bret Harte, who grew up on the east coast (his grandfather was a secretary of the New York Stock Exchange), moved to Northern California in the 1850s and began writing a column for the San Francisco *Golden Era* titled "Bohemian Feuilleton," later renamed "Bohemian Papers," describing his outings to the city's cafés and restaurants, which were as central to the identity of west coast bohemians as they had been to the Pfaffians back east.

During his early days in the city, Harte rented a room from a cousin who operated a restaurant out of the ground floor of the house. Harte's cousin was an "epicurean" who had brought a fine cook with him to San Francisco, along with monogrammed silverware. Harte recalled the restaurant as a meeting place for "men of very distinct personality; a few celebrated, and nearly all notorious. They represented a Bohemianism – if such it could be called – less innocent than my later experiences."[59] At that time, Harte couldn't afford to eat at his cousin's high-end establishment. Instead, he ate at inexpensive ethnic restaurants, which were already appearing in the city. For breakfast, he frequented an Italian café at Long Wharf. Harte and his cousin represented the two strains within bohemianism, the monied set and the broke, or as the nineteenth-century Australian writer Marcus Clarke put it, lower Bohemia and lower Bohemia.[60]

There were lots of restaurants and cafés in San Francisco, a surfeit dictated by the surplus population of single men who traveled to the city as a gateway to the gold fields. Not all of the city's eateries were bohemian, but its great number of restaurants gave San Francisco its bohemian reputation. Clarence E. Edwords, author of *Bohemian San Francisco, Its Restaurants and Their Most Famous Recipes*, explained the connection: "San Franciscans, both residential and transient, are a pleasure-loving people, and dining out is a distinctive feature of their pleasure."[61] Edwords insisted that, contrary to rumors, true bohemians were not debaucherous and sexually loose. But he didn't deny that the sexes mingled more freely in bohemian restaurants than in other establishments. "Bohemianism is the protest of naturalism against the too rigid, and, oft-times, absurd restrictions established by society," and those restrictions included the uptight rules against women taking pleasure in public eating.[62] Edwords dedicated his volume to his wife, "the best of all Bohemian comrades." Many of the early restaurants he classified as bohemian had women chefs or women proprietors who mixed convivially with their male customers, and whose company constituted a prime attraction. At Ma Tanta, when the meal ended the French chef *patronesse* would sit at the single long table with her guests over coffee and enter into the conversation.[63]

The first Southern city in the United States associated with bohemianism was New Orleans.[64] The spread of this reputation owed a great deal to the writings of Lafcadio Hearn. Born on an Ionian island to an Irish father and a Greek mother, abandoned by his parents, raised by an aunt in Dublin, then sent to school in France and London before the family money ran out, Hearn traveled to Cincinnati in 1869 as a penniless nineteen-year-old. He began writing sketches of the city's working-class denizens for a local newspaper, but his youthful marriage to a Black woman, Mattie Foley, prompted his dismissal from one newspaper for "deplorable moral habits." The subsequent break-up of that marriage led Hearn to decamp for New Orleans in 1877. His arrival in the Crescent City transformed him into an epicure. Despite his extreme penury, Hearn breakfasted on coffee, donuts and French bread, or figs, corn muffins, cream cheese, and eggs.[65] He also began experimenting with cooking. Hearn wrote to his friend Henry Krehbiel, "I hired myself a room in the northern end of the French Quarter (near the Spanish), bought myself a complete set of cooking utensils and kitchen-ware, and kept house for myself . . . Thus I learned to cook pretty well." In 1878, he opened the 5 Cent Restaurant, also known as the Hard Times Restaurant, which promised customers a good meal for a nickel. "How is that for Bohemianism?" he wrote to Krehbiel.[66] The business was a success, but his partner absconded with the profits after the first month, ending Hearn's career as a restaurateur.[67]

Hearn also regaled Krehbiel with tales of his sexual appetite for New Orleans' mixed-race populace, which he linked to his appetite for the city's cuisine: "I eat and drink and sleep with members of the race you detest like the son of Odin that you are."[68] Hearn's tastes for food and sex broke society's rules governing the discipline of the appetites, and the separation of whites and people of color. Hearn was notorious for visiting brothels in the city's red-light district, Storyville. In 1885, he published a cookbook of New Orleans recipes, *La Cuisine Creole*, which celebrated the charms of the city's Creole people and helped transform the city into a popular tourist destination.[69] Taking a page from Hearn, city boosters in the late nineteenth century celebrated New Orleans' reputation for good food and wicked sex, touting the riverfront city as "the Paris of America."[70] Town fathers encouraged visitors to New Orleans to throw off the shackles of respectability for a weekend, cast aside the judgments of Mrs. Grundy, and indulge their tastes for pleasure.

Wherever they spread, bohemians made restaurants and cafés their headquarters. In Austin, Texas, the bohemian circle that gathered around the writer William Sydney Porter (later to rename himself O. Henry) met at the Bismarck Café, run by a German émigré. In Philadelphia at the turn of the century, the literary bohemian circle drawn to the poet Horace Traubel called themselves the Pepper Pot Club after their favorite restaurant's best-known dish.[71] In Chicago, the writers Sherwood Anderson, Carl Sandburg, and Edgar Lee Masters met at Schlogl's, first founded in 1879, a restaurant and wine room that served up German dishes like hamburger steak, Wiener schnitzel, roast young duck, and apple pancakes. Unlike many German restaurants, Schlogl's forbade women from the ground floor. The bohemian writer John Drury noted the "male camaraderie" that prevailed at Schlogl's, a fact which made it vulnerable to rumors.[72] As bohemia's chronicler Albert Parry put it, Schlogl's regulars pretended to be tough, but that was "no more than a romantic fiction, a characteristic self-adorning touch of the pale long-haired."[73] This questioning of the Schlogl's regulars' masculinity was perhaps unsurprising, considering that Towertown, where it was located, soon became Chicago's first gay neighborhood. The Dill Pickle Club, another bohemian restaurant nearby, even hosted talks on homosexuality by the German sexologist Magnus Hirschfeld.[74]

Manly sympathy

"The attic, the studio, the restaurant, and the café are the accepted symbols of Bohemia," and had been ever since Murger's *Vie de Bohème*, the early twentieth-century writer Arthur Bartlett Maurice explained; what reader "has ever forgotten the Café Momus, where the riotous behavior of Marcel, Schaunard, Rodolphe, and Colline brought the proprietor to the verge of ruin?"[75] By the end of the nineteenth century, Murger's classic might have begun to lose its hold on readers' imaginations, but the publication of George du Maurier's bestselling novel *Trilby* in 1896 refreshed the bohemian fantasy of a life lived out of cafés and restaurants.

Based on his own experiences as a young man, du Maurier's novel tells the story of three British art students living in Paris's Latin Quarter in the 1850s, Little Billee, Taffy, and the Laird, who all fall in love with an Irish-French painter's model and *grisette* named Trilby. When Little Billee, Taffy, and the Laird aren't painting, they're indulging their gastronomic appetites. The novel uses more detail to describe the food the young men eat than the artworks they paint. They frequent an inexpensive bistro, the Restaurant de la Couronne, where for one franc they eat:

> good distending soups, omelets that were only too savory, lentils, red and white beans, meat so dressed and sauced and seasoned that you didn't know whether it were beef or mutton – flesh, fowl, or good red herring – or even bad, for that matter – nor very greatly care. And just the same lettuce, radishes, and cheese of Gruyère or Brie as you got at the Trois Frères Provençaux (but not the same butter!). And to wash it all down, generous wine in wooden "brocs" – that stained a lovely aesthetic blue everything it was spilled over.

When they're feeling more flush, the trio eat omelets at the Café de l'Odéon, near the Jardins Luxembourg, where "the wine isn't blue." Some evenings they cook at home, and Taffy makes a salad with his special recipe. For Christmas, they order a turkey, plum pudding, mince pies, and Stilton from home, and also serve truffled galantines of turkey, tongues, hams, *rillettes de Tours,* pâtés de foie gras, *fromage d'Italie* (which has nothing to do with cheese), *saucissons d'Arles et de Lyon*, with and without garlic, cold jellies peppery and salt – everything that French *charcutiers* and their wives can make out of French pigs, or any other animal whatever, beast, bird, or fowl (even cats and rats) for the supper; and sweet jellies, and cakes, and sweetmeats, and confections of all kinds, from the famous pastry-cook at the corner of the Rue Castiglione.[76]

The novel's lengthy descriptions of meals serve an important purpose. Eve Kosofsky Sedgwick argues that *Trilby*'s bachelor characters work their way through the "homosexual panic" that afflicted men at the turn of the century by both refusing to engage in genital sexuality and by placing "a corresponding emphasis on the pleasures of the other senses" such as taste.[77] Out of loyalty to each other, none of the young men romance Trilby, although she has already had love affairs prior to meeting the English trio and is not a virgin, a detail that was considered shocking at the time. Trilby suffers the consequences of the young men's withholding when she ends up seduced and hypnotized by a sinister German-Jewish musician named Svengali.

Instead of serving up a love story between Trilby and one of the painters, the novel hints at homoerotic dimensions of the trio's friendship. Little Billee's name is taken from a naval ballad written by Thackeray in which two burly sailors demand a younger sailor strip off his chemise and then threaten to eat him up.[78] Similarly erotic are du Maurier's descriptions of Little Billee's intense admiration as he watches the manly Taffy, a powerful athlete, exercise his muscles. The three characters

> share each other's thoughts and purses, and wear each other's clothes, and swear each other's oaths, and smoke each other's pipes, and respect each other's lights o' love, and keep each other's secrets, and tell each other's jokes, and pawn each other's watches and merrymake together on the proceeds, and sit all night by each other's bedsides in sickness, and comfort each other in sorrow and disappointment with silent, manly sympathy.[79]

After Little Billee dies young, Taffy marries his sister, the socially acceptable alternative to his deceased friend.[80]

The publication of *Trilby* reinvigorated the cult of bohemianism for the twentieth century. The novel's characters inspired enthusiastic imitators on both sides of the Atlantic.[81] Arthur Bartlett Maurice wrote of seeing friends dressed as the novel's characters strolling down Fifth Avenue in New York City.[82] In the guest register of Begué's restaurant in New Orleans, where drunk customers wrote their spontaneous verses, three diners in 1902 signed themselves with the names Little Billy, Svengali, and the Laird.[83] As the fantasy of bohemianism was refreshed for the twentieth century, its association with same-sex sexuality became increasingly explicit.

Perhaps no figure was more responsible for tying bohemianism to homosexuality at the turn of the century than Oscar Wilde. An enthusiastic gourmand, the bohemian satirist and playwright peppered his writings with epicurean quips.[84] "Cookery is an art," Wilde opined in an 1885 review of a book titled *Dinners and Dishes*, published in the *Pall Mall Gazette*. He made fun of the moral opprobrium still attached to gastronomy in late Victorian Britain, and attacked the tasteless cooking of British housewives: "the British cook is a foolish woman who should be turned for her iniquities into a pillar of salt which she never knows how to use." Along with French cooking, Wilde praised the New York restaurant Delmonico's, which he said had the best scenery in the United States besides Yosemite.[85] The same light-hearted humor about food suffused his dramatic writings. In *The Importance of Being Earnest* (1895), the titular character jokes about the "reckless extravagance" of a lunch of cucumber sandwiches. Later he and his friend Algernon enter into a hilarious dialogue about the consolation of eating muffins. It was not so funny, however, when the Marquess of Queensberry, the father of Wilde's young lover Alfred "Bosie" Douglas, threatened to turn up at the premier of *The Importance of Being Earnest* carrying a bouquet of rotten vegetables to throw on stage. Tipped off in advance, Wilde had Queensberry banned from the theater.

The Marquess of Queensberry's choice of weapons to escalate his feud with Wilde was only fitting, considering that much of Wilde and Bosie's relationship had taken place in public sight at London's finest restaurants. Wilde was a habitué of the Café Royal, a famous bohemian hangout opened in the 1860s by a bankrupt Frenchman who went by the alias Daniel Nichols. The painter James McNeill Whistler held court there in the 1870s.[86] Wilde first ate at the Café Royal in Whistler's company. After Wilde met Bosie in the summer of 1891, the two frequently dined together in private rooms at the Café Royal. The Irish writer Frank Harris, one of Wilde's first biographers, recalled seeing him with Bosie at the restaurant: "I found Oscar throned in the very corner, between two youths. Even to my short-sighted eyes they appeared quite common; in fact they looked like grooms. In spite of their vulgar appearance, however, one was nice looking in a fresh boyish way; the other seemed merely depraved."

Such scenes enraged Bosie's father, who turned up at Wilde's house and demanded that the writer stop seeing his son. Bosie responded by writing his father a letter informing him "ever since your exhibition at O. W.'s house, I have made a point of appearing with him at many public restaurants, such as the Berkeley, Willis's Rooms, the Café Royal, etc."[87] Queensberry followed by leaving a letter at Wilde's club addressed "For Oscar Wilde, posing sodomite." Wilde then sued Queensberry for libel, which led to the trials that turned up evidence of Wilde's repeated use of restaurant private rooms to meet for sex with his male lovers.[88] Wilde was convicted of gross indecency in May 1895 and sentenced to two years hard labor, only a few of months after the premier of *Earnest*. The trials of Oscar Wilde called enormous public attention to homosexuality and helped fix the link between gay men and bohemian epicureanism in the popular imagination.

"The Nineteenth Century goes out in a blaze of gastronomic glory," the journalist John Bocock announced in his 1901 essay "Dinners in Bohemia and Elsewhere." But the millionaires of the world had grown tired of the fancy French restaurant cooking ascendant throughout the 1800s. Now "the gourmet craves a seat at the table of the poets." In the 1900s, good food would become the purview of the creative classes with their creative approaches to sex and love.[89] And in the new century, women would assert their right to a seat at the table. Claiming their place within the creative classes, Anglo-American women unleashed their appetites and insisted on their right to feed their senses, not simply serve the appetites of men.

SEVEN

Greedy Women

Mary MacLane was not a heroine. The nineteen-year-old writer from Butte, Montana, boasted in her 1902 memoir that she was "charmingly original" and "startlingly bohemian," but in books she read the heroine "falls in love with a man – always with a man, eats things (they are always called 'viands') with a delicate appetite, and on special occasions her voice is full of tears." MacLane, on the other hand, confessed that she was sexually drawn to women as well as men, and "I have never eaten any viands, and my appetite for what I do eat is most excellent." Throwing off the shackles of late Victorian respectability, MacLane fashioned a new female persona for the twentieth century: she was a woman of appetites.[1]

MacLane wanted to call her memoir "I Await the Devil's Coming," but her publisher insisted on the more anodyne title, *The Story of Mary MacLane*.[2] Even without a sensationalist title, the book became an instant bestseller, transforming MacLane into a celebrity. Structured as a diary of her nineteenth year, MacLane's memoir described her sexual longing for her female teacher, professed her desire to meet the devil, and trumpeted her conviction in her own genius. MacLane didn't just hammer a final nail into Victorianism's coffin, she danced on its lid.

In one of her memoir's most erotic chapters, MacLane spends seven pages describing the act of savoring a single green olive. Even before she takes the first bite, the act of holding the olive fills MacLane's mind with images of scantily clad women.

> I take the olive in my fingers, and I contemplate its green oval richness. It makes me think at once of the land where the green citron grows – where the cypress and myrtle are emblems; of the land of the Sun where human beings are delightfully, enchantingly wicked, – where the men are eager and passion-ate, and the women gracefully developed in mind and in body – and their two breasts show round and full and delicately veined beneath thin drapery . . . I set my teeth and my tongue upon the olive, and bite it. It is bitter, salt,

delicious. The saliva rushes to meet it, and my tongue is a happy tongue. As the morsel of olive rests in my mouth and is crunched and squeezed lusciously among my teeth, a quick, temporary change takes place in my character. I think of some adorable lines of the Persian poet: "Give thyself up to Joy."

MacLane's description of the first bite of the olive evokes the act of cunnilingus. As the "salt crisp ravishes [her] tongue," MacLane is overpowered with a "reckless sensuality." The sensation comes on quickly, but it takes a long time to complete her orgasmic account. "Each bite brings with it a recurring wave of sensation" until the final swallow leaves her "entirely satisfied." MacLane's sexual frankness shocked and thrilled readers, as did her refusal to apologize for her appetites. "If this be damnation, damnation let it be! If this be the human fall, then how good it is to be fallen!" MacLane enthused.[3] While few readers may have been brave enough to make the same confession, they were enthralled by reading MacLane's story.[4]

During the first half of the twentieth century, a new wave of women writers, many of them queer or otherwise sexually adventurous, pushed back against Victorian limitations on female appetites and claimed new identities as greedy women. Their writings enthusiastically linked their alimentary appetites and their erotic appetites, flipping the logic that animated Victorian asceticism. Female epicures redefined women's appetites as a positive aspect of selfhood. Through the enjoyment of food and sex, women forged new liberated identities as desiring subjects. To achieve those liberated identities, many found it necessary to leave the United States and its small-minded bourgeois sensibilities. Unsurprisingly, the city they found most copacetic to their hungers was Paris.

The virtue of gluttony

The first Anglo-American to publicly lay claim to the identity of a "greedy woman" was the American journalist, Elizabeth Robins Pennell. Born in 1855 to an upper-class Philadelphia family, Elizabeth Robins was educated in Catholic convent schools where she received a thorough instruction in Victorian norms of femininity, including dietary asceticism. Her school friend Agnes Repplier, who dedicated a memoir of their convent days to Robins, described how they ate their meager meals in silence, and regarded lemonade and hot rolls as rare luxuries. Catholicism inflected the girls' self-denial, as they were taught to regard deprivation as an act of piety. Agnes recalled how "If I ate my bread unbuttered, or drank my tea unsweetened, that was an act." Convent girls would boast about not eating butter for a week.[5]

After leaving school at age seventeen, Robins was rescued from her narrow horizons by her uncle, Charles Godfrey Leland, a bohemian philanthropist who hired her at a public arts school he had founded, introduced her to Walt Whitman, and encouraged her to become a writer. Robins's first article appeared in the *Atlantic* in 1881.[6] In 1882, Leland recommended Robins as a writer for an article to accompany sketches of old Philadelphia landmarks drawn by a young illustrator named Joseph Pennell. Robins and Pennell became friendly. Later that year, each separately met Oscar Wilde during his US tour. Wilde inspired Pennell to travel to Italy. When he returned, he and Robins married with the promise to support each other's careers. They set off together on the first of several bicycle tours of Europe, which they wrote about in popular illustrated volumes that helped make the bicycle a symbol of the New Woman.

In the 1890s, the Pennells settled in London's Bloomsbury neighborhood where they hosted a weekly salon attended by aesthetes like James Whistler. Elizabeth Pennell focused on writing art criticism and began contributing weekly articles on cooking to the *Pall Mall Gazette*. Instead of serving up recipes, Pennell wrote about food from the same aesthetic perspective she applied to art.[7] In 1896, her columns were collected into a volume titled *The Feasts of Autolycus: The Diary of a Greedy Woman*, printed by the avant-garde publisher John Lane. Lane also published *The Yellow Book*, the infamous Decadent-movement magazine, which was first proposed at the Pennells' salon.[8] An advertisement for *The Feasts of Autolycus* appeared in the July 1896 issue of *The Yellow Book*.[9]

The Feasts of Autolycus opened with an essay titled "The Virtue of Gluttony" that served up nothing less than a complete refutation of the anti-alimentary sentiment embedded within Christian ethics. Throwing off the lessons of her convent days, Pennell declared the doctrine that gluttony was a deadly sin to be an outdated "superstition" dating to the Dark Ages of asceticism. Within Catholic thought, "a healthy appetite passed for a snare of the devil, and its gratification meant eternal damnation." Men had long since rejected this superstition, but Pennell argued "it lingered longer among women." For the sake of appearing feminine, women toyed with their food at the table, then later gorged their starved appetites in the pantry. The whole system was "perverted" and led women to "think all too little of the joys of eating." Pennell's goal in *The Feasts of Autolycus* was to enlighten the members of her sex that "the love of good eating gives an object to life." Not only did a love of food make a woman attractive to men (here she quoted Brillat-Savarin), sharing a love of eating created a sensual bond between a man and a woman. "Accept the gospel of good living and the sexual problem will be solved," Pennell declared.[10] By present-day standards, Pennell's writing may appear to barely tiptoe into the erotic, but by the standards of the time her tone was scandalous. As one food historian has put it, Pennell's "gastrofeminism" was "not far removed from sedition or pornography."[11]

Literary scholar Jamie Horrocks has suggested the hint of a "queer element" in Pennell's writings.[12] Pennell introduced *Feasts of Autolycus* by observing that, up to that point, gastronomy had been the exclusive preserve of men. "The kitchen still awaits its Sappho," she noted, placing herself in the tradition of the famed Lesbian poet very much *en vogue* among the circle of same-sex-loving aesthetes with whom the Pennells socialized in 1890s London.[13] Elizabeth Pennell's open embrace of sapphism remained confined to the lyrical tone of her food writing. But another American expatriate who circulated in 1890s London brought food, sex, and queer erotics together more openly.

A generation younger than Pennell, Isadora Duncan was born in California in 1877 to an artistic family. When her mother was pregnant, Duncan wrote in her memoir *My Life*, she could take no food except "oysters and champagne – the food of Aphrodite." This gestational diet, according to Duncan, set her course in life. The famed inventor of modern dance embraced her boundless and interlinked appetites for food and sex, like a true votary of Venus. By the age of twelve, Duncan recalled, she had decided to live an emancipated life, unconfined by marriage laws. Already an accomplished dancer, Duncan toured the United States. In Chicago, she met bohemians and came to see herself as "the spiritual daughter of Walt Whitman." Disenchanted with the vulgar pantomime stage, Duncan set off for London, dreaming of meeting aesthetes like Henry James, George Meredith, and James Whistler.[14] In Bloomsbury, she spent hours in the British Museum studying the figures on Greek vases and bas-reliefs, from which she developed her Neo-Hellenist dance movements. She also dispensed with wearing corsets, stockings, or shoes on stage, risqué innovations that made her notorious.

From London, Duncan traveled to Paris. According to Duncan, she remained a sexual innocent until this time. A would-be lover brought her to a *cabinet particulier* for a champagne dinner, but abandoned his seduction when he discovered that she was a virgin. Finally, during a dance tour in Hungary, a sumptuous meal transformed Duncan into a fully sexual being:

> The first supper that I had ever eaten in company with absolutely care-free and sensual people, the music of the gypsies; the Hungarian goulash, flavored with paprika, and the heavy Hungarian wines – it was, indeed, the first time in my life that I was nourished, over-nourished and stimulated with an abundance of food – all brought about the first awareness of my body as something other than an instrument to express the sacred harmony of music. My breasts, which until then had been hardly perceptible, began to swell softly and astonish me with charming but embarrassing sensations. My hips, which had been like a boy's, took on another undulation, and through my whole being I felt one great surging, longing, unmistakable urge.

Soon after, Duncan lost her virginity to a handsome Hungarian-Jewish actor in the first of countless affairs that defined her life. From that moment forward, in her words, she never ceased to be madly in love.[15]

Duncan took women as lovers as well as men. During an affair with the writer Mercedes de Acosta, Duncan wrote a poem that enthusiastically mixed the erotic and the alimentary: "My kisses like a swarm/of Bees/would find their way/between thy knees/and suck the honey/of thy lips/Embracing thy/too slender hips."[16] Duncan's unrestrained embrace of her appetites transformed her own sylph-like figure over the years. Her growing stoutness led to ridicule. BiB, the caricaturist for Paris's humor magazine, *Le Charivari*, sketched Duncan following her 1923 performance of "La Mort d'Yseult" at the Trocadéro as a ludicrous figure with pendulous breasts, and fat thighs and arms.[17] Duncan made no apologies, believing that "thinness was not equivalent to spirituality." Her favorite photographs of herself were those taken by New York photographer

"Isadora Duncan," photographed by Arnold Genthe during her visit to the
United States, 1916.
*Isadora Duncan photographs, nos. 1–181. Irma Duncan Collection. New York
Public Library*

Arnold Genthe during World War I, when she was already in her late
thirties, her body as soft and fleshy as in BiB's caricature. Genthe, she
thought, captured her very soul.[18]

Duncan's celebration of her curves challenged the strong bias toward
female thinness in Anglo-American culture as well as in French culture.
This ideal had solidified in the United States during the Civil War.
In 1863, a pamphlet titled *A Letter on Corpulence*, written by a British
undertaker named William Banting, triggered "the first dieting craze
in the United States."[19] Banting's advice would be familiar today. He
recommended giving up bread, potatoes, beer, sugar, milk, and butter,
and instead eating large quantities of meat and fish (except pork and
salmon).[20] The novelist Harriet Beecher Stowe complained about the
triumph of the new *belle idéale* in a story from the 1860s:

> We in America have so far got out of the way of a womanhood that has any
> vigor or outline or opulence of physical proportions that, when we see a

woman made as a woman ought to be, she strikes us as a monster. Our wil-lowy girls are afraid of nothing so much as growing stout; and if a young lady begins to round into proportions like the women in Titian's and Giorgione's pictures, she is distressed above measure, and begins to make secret inquiries into reducing diet, and to cling desperately to the strongest corset-lacing as her only hope.[21]

The demand for dieting advice from women soon triggered American imitators of Banting's success.

Susan Dunning Power's beauty column for *Harper's Bazaar* in the 1870s, "The Ugly-Girl Papers," recommended women tailor their diets for their specific compositions. One column advised the stout woman to "eat as little as will satisfy her appetite." That could be very little. Power recalled a time in life when her own appetite had been quite meager and she had lived off "a small saucer of strawberries and one Graham cracker" for her breakfast, "half an orange" for her lunch, and "a handful of cherries" for her dinner. Once a week she supplemented this fruit salad with a beefsteak or soup.[22] Diet advice proliferated in the early twentieth century, justified by a wide range of moral arguments. Reformers argued, among other things, that "teaching people to eat right would keep them away from alcohol and labor unions, and improve their characters and morals." The emerging professional class of home economists who trained in nutrition and diet at American universities believed that pleasure threatened healthy diets because "king palate" would lure home cooks away from following nutritional advice. During World War I, as Arnold Genthe's camera celebrated Isadora Duncan's curves, American women were being called on to support the federal Food Administration's conservation campaign to limit their diets and ration food for the troops.[23] Duncan paid no more attention to these attacks on "the sin of gourmandizing" than she had to earlier messaging.[24]

The Lesbian Left Bank

Duncan's friend and admirer, the Lesbian Left Bank *salonnière* Natalie Clifford Barney, also embraced her voracious appetites for food and sex and followed a similar trajectory from slender to statuesque. Born in 1876, Barney, like Duncan, was raised by an unconventional mother, Alice

Pike, who parted from her conformist alcoholic husband and pursued an independent life as a painter, a decision encouraged by Oscar Wilde, whom she met at a seaside resort, and facilitated by her vast inherited wealth. Barney forswore marriage at a young age, not only because her parents' example illustrated how marriage stifled and restricted women's lives, but because she was exclusively attracted to her own sex. She began pursuing affairs with girls while an adolescent, and by the late 1890s had moved permanently to Paris, or Paris-Lesbos as the city was sometimes called.[25]

At the turn of the twentieth century, Paris had a thriving lesbian subculture, which included cosmopolitan heiresses, famous courtesans, and ordinary working women.[26] In Paris, Barney embraced the life of a libertine. She seduced women in *cabinets particuliers*. She enjoyed a very public affair with the demimondaine Liane de Pougy, which Pougy later fictionalized in her novel *Idylle Saphique*. The relationship soon ended in acrimony. Barney published her first book of Sapphic poetry, *Quelques Portraits-Sonnets de Femmes*, in 1900, the same year that she and her new lover, Renée Vivien (Pauline Tarn), attended one of Isadora Duncan's first performances in Paris, at a salon. By the end of the decade, Barney had inherited her own fortune and launched her own salon at her house in the rue Jacob, in Paris's Left Bank. Barney's salon was celebrated not only for the talented writers and artists it attracted, many of them queer – including Duncan who would sometimes perform a spontaneous dance – but also for the excellence of the food that Barney's cooks prepared. Guests could eat from huge platters of sandwiches, followed by vanilla and chocolate cakes, and French patisseries like meringues and éclairs, all washed down with refreshments ranging from champagne to hot chocolate.[27] At Barney's salon, as one literary guest recalled, "titles and courtesans swayed among the callas, balancing sea urchins or sherbets."[28]

Barney's culinary largesse reflected her appetites as well as her generosity. She had hundreds of lovers throughout her life, and the enjoyment of food played a central role in her affairs. One of Barney's most important affairs, which lasted for most of her life, was with Lily Gramont, the Duchesse de Clermont-Tonnere. The two women met in 1910, and each year they celebrated their "first kiss" with a lunch of half a dozen plover's eggs, considered to be an aphrodisiac.[29] Esther Murphy, a famed raconteuse, once dropped in on Barney and found her enjoying her habitual midday meal, between lunch and tea, of cold ham, hard boiled eggs, pickles, chocolate éclairs, and iced beer, while her friend Alice Robinson read aloud to her from the book *Classic Erotology*, a modern compendium of ancient vices.[30] Barney loved hosting lunches and dinner parties. She organized yearly celebratory meals for the painter Marie Laurencin, the writer Germaine Beaumont, and the bookseller Anacréon, who called themselves the "Scorpion Club," for the astrological sign of their shared birthday, October 31. With each passing year, she grew heavier, dressing in flowing outfits, kimonos, and djellabas.[31]

While few people had appetites quite as voracious as hers, Barney's enthusiasm for the combined pleasures of sex and food was widely shared within the pleasure culture of the Lesbian Left Bank.[32] Gertrude Stein, the lesbian art collector and patron who hosted a Paris salon to rival Barney's, paid equal attention to the food she served.[33] Stein was born in Pittsburgh, in 1874, to a wealthy family that moved to Europe for a year in 1877–8 to expose their five children to high culture. Stein's earliest memory of visiting Paris, at four years old, included having soup and bread for breakfast, and leg of mutton and spinach for lunch.[34] Stein moved back to Paris in 1903 with her brother Leo, and began collecting avant-garde art, which she displayed at her apartment on the rue de Fleurus. In 1907, she met Alice B. Toklas, another American abroad. Toklas soon moved in with Stein and her brother. Later, Leo moved out, taking half their art collection with him, and Stein began hosting salons at the rue de Fleurus, with Toklas in charge of the food.

In their gendered division of roles, Stein claimed the masculine mantle of genius, and Toklas assumed the feminine domestic labor. At their salon, Stein talked with the men and Toklas took care of their wives. The Lost Generation writer Kay Boyle recalled visiting the rue de Fleurus salon once, where "Alice Toklas and I immediately started to talk of cooking, and to exchange recipes." This behavior didn't impress Stein, who declared Boyle "incurably middle-class" and never invited her back.[35] Stein's allotment of domestic tasks to Toklas did not, however, indicate a disinterest in food. Far from it, good eating was a lifetime passion of Stein's. She and Natalie Clifford Barney would go together to Rumpelmayer's, on the rue de Rivoli, and gossip for hours about gastronomy while feasting on the café's legendary desserts.[36] Like Barney, Stein mixed the alimentary and the erotic. In her poem, "Lifting Belly," written soon after meeting Toklas, Stein described the women's erotic relationship in language replete with culinary imagery.[37] "Lifting Belly" followed Pennell's lead in rejecting Victorian proscriptions on women eating and embracing female sensuality in verses like: "oh lifting belly./ What is my another name./Representative./Of what./Of the evils of eating./What are they then./They are sweet and figs."[38] While Stein's modernist grammar is challenging, the use of figs as a symbol of the female sex is clear.

The importance of food in Stein and Toklas's life together served as a central theme in Toklas's "autobiography," written by Stein and published in 1933. In Stein's masquerade, Toklas centered many of her recollections on food. After three short pages of family background, Stein commences Toklas's autobiography with a story about her first visit to the rue de Fleurus for a dinner party prepared by Hélène, the Stein siblings' French cook, who "made a very good soufflé." Moving forward, Stein frames Toklas's observations of the art world through culinary metaphors. She tells the story of a famous banquet that Picasso organized in Montmartre for the primitivist painter Henri Rousseau by focusing on her own role preparing the food with Picasso's lover and muse, Fernande. A passage about Matisse's use of distortion in painting leads to a culinary metaphor about the role of lemon in cooking. "I do inevitably take my comparisons from the kitchen because I like food and cooking," Toklas explains, in Stein's telling. For Stein's Toklas, food is life. To know how to cook is to know how to live.[39]

When Toklas rendered her own life in her own terms, she affirmed her belief in this Steinian apothegm. Invited to write her own memoir of her years with Stein, after Stein's death, Toklas offered up a cookbook. At least, she called her manuscript a cookbook, but it delivered as many, if not more, recollections of her life as her earlier "autobiography" had. Toklas had been considering writing a cookbook as early as 1937.[40] She began work on a memoir-style cookbook in 1944, while she and Stein were waiting out the war in the village of Bilignin. A green-covered lined journal from that year, with the title "We Eat. A Cookbook by Alice Toklas and Gertrude Stein," contains thirty-two scrawling pages of Toklas's childhood food memories from growing up in San Francisco and Seattle, and placeholders for the later insertion of recipes.[41] Most of these childhood memories did not appear in her later published cookbook, which focused instead – like her autobiography – on her life with Stein.

The Alice B. Toklas Cook Book (1954) centers her love for Stein as the animating force behind her cooking. "Before coming to Paris, I was interested in food but not in doing any cooking," she recalls. Raised in a well-to-do merchant family, Toklas came from the class that supervised the kitchen, rather than stirred the pot. But Stein declared that on Sundays, Hélène's day off, they "would have American food" for dinner, and she placed Toklas in charge of preparing the meals. Toklas cooked to Stein's tastes. She started with pie crusts. "When the pie crust received Gertrude Stein's critical approval," she moved on to Thanksgiving dressing. Stein liked mushrooms, chestnuts, and oysters, so Toklas developed a recipe that combined all three.[42]

Toklas cooked as an act of queer devotion and as self-expression. "Some of us, who consider cooking an art, feel that a way of cooking can produce something that approaches an aesthetic emotion," she explains in a chapter titled "Treasures" that begins with her earliest food memories. Toklas's most treasured recipes share an aesthetic of excess. She begins a recipe with the instruction to "marinate for an hour 100 frogs' legs." Her recipe for "Steamed Chicken Mère Fillioux" instructs readers to fill a chicken with truffles. Her recipe for Alexandre Dumas *fils*'s Françillon Salad mixes two pounds of potatoes, and three quarts of mussels, with as many truffles as the budget permits. Her *truites en chemise* are baked "in enough melted butter to float them." The recipe for chicken sauté aux Ducs de Bourgogne includes three-quarters of a cup of port, half a cup of brandy, a quarter cup of whiskey, and a quarter cup of kirsch, to flavor a single bird. These are recipes that, in words taken from her infamous hashish fudge recipe, should induce eaters to feel "ravished."[43] Toklas's ethic of sensual indulgence has led many to view hers as the first queer cookbook published in English.[44]

Literary critic Elspeth Probyn argues that Toklas's cookbook fits into a "queer mode of eating" that intermixes the alimentary and the erotic in a challenge to normative restrictions.[45] Certainly, Stein's and Toklas's enthusiasm for the intermixed pleasures of food and sex were widely shared in the Lesbian Left Bank. Sylvia Beach, the American expatriate who owned the English-language bookstore Shakespeare and Company and published the first edition of James Joyce's *Ulysses*, shared an alimentary–erotic bond with her lover, Adrienne Monnier, which echoed Stein's with Toklas. Beach, born in 1887, spent part of her adolescence in Paris, where her father served as the assistant minister at the American Church. She returned to Paris in 1917 and began attending readings of modernist French literature at a bookstore owned by Monnier, who soon became her lover. In 1919, Beach opened her own bookstore near Monnier's, decorating the walls with pictures and letters of Whitman and Wilde, and stocking the shelves with the writings of Joyce, T. S. Eliot, and other modernists. She soon became friends with Stein and Toklas, although their relationship had its ups and downs. She was also friendly with Barney and praised the chocolate cake served at her salon.[46]

Beach both appreciated good food and, like Stein, shared her alimentary appetite with her lover. Adrienne Monnier matched Pennell and Duncan in the lists of greedy women. She heartily laid claim to her own *gourmandise*, a challenging term to translate. As the French historian Brigitte Mahuzier put it, "What is more essentially French and feminine than 'gourmandise,' a term for which there is no equivalent in the English language? Combine food and sex in a large bowl, add language, and you have something essentially French."[47] French–English dictionaries define *gourmandise* as the "love of food," with connotations of "greed" and sinful excess.[48] By laying claim to her own *gourmandise*, Monnier was embracing a sexualized identity as a greedy woman. Not a fan of "elaborate dishes," she delighted in preparing simple French dishes accompanied by rich butter sauces or mayonnaises. Monnier told friends, "I loved fats; I was not afraid of becoming fat." Pictures from the 1920s until her death in the 1950s show the roundness of her figure. The lesbian writer Janet Flanner said Monnier was "buxom as a handsome abbess."[49] Monnier boasted that her fatness helped her survive the austerity of life in Paris during the Nazi occupation.[50]

In addition to cooking for Beach, Monnier prepared dinners for the couple's literary friends. When F. Scott Fitzgerald wanted to meet James Joyce, Beach invited them both over with their wives for a French meal cooked by Adrienne Monnier. Fitzgerald memorialized the dinner party in a sketch in Beach's copy of *The Great Gatsby*.[51] When T. S. Eliot visited Paris, Monnier and Beach had him "to dinner at our place," along with André Gide and Paul Valéry.[52] In 1929, Monnier commemorated her publication of a French translation of *Ulysses* by hosting a "Déjeuner Ulysses" at the Hôtel Léopold near Versailles. The meal began with a "Paté Léopold," before moving on to *quenelles de veau, poulet de Bresse*, potatoes, salad, cheese, and a strawberry tart. Monnier kept the menu as a souvenir.[53]

In 1942, when the German occupying forces interned Sylvia Beach at the Vittel concentration camp, Monnier scrambled to send Beach care packages filled with food. The women's correspondence during her seven-month internment is almost entirely taken up with discussions of food. Beach thanked Monnier repeatedly for the fruit, honey, nuts, and canned chicken that she sent, as well as the homemade cookies and ginger cake. Her letters repeatedly described *le plaisir*, or the pleasure, that Monnier's food brought her in the midst of the horrors of war.[54] Writing to an influential friend, Monnier poured out her anxieties that Beach wouldn't be able to stick to the strict diet that controlled her migraines.[55] In fact, Beach's migraines were so bad she spent her first month at Vittel in the camp hospital. But her letters to Monnier speak little of her health, nor do they give an accurate accounting of the rations in Vittel, which she described, after her release, as a daily "soup" of hot water with potatoes and cabbage served in little bowls that "sufficed" because "the smell of that soup took away all desire for it," accompanied by a weekly round loaf of black bread. These starvation rations were complemented, thankfully, by Red Cross packages containing milk, sugar, coffee, prunes, chocolate, and cigarettes.[56]

Beach served as a beacon of the American expatriate literary community in Paris during the interwar period, and particularly of the American expatriate lesbian literary community. Newcomers came to Shakespeare and Company hoping Beach could introduce them to fellow writers abroad. Janet Flanner, who wrote a Paris letter for the *New Yorker* from 1925 to 1939, described Shakespeare and Company as "the hearth and home" of the community. Flanner's own first memories of arriving in France were dominated by alimentary nostalgia. "Eating in France was a new body experience," she wrote in the introduction to *Paris Was Yesterday*, a collection of her *New Yorker* columns: "with my palate even now able to recall the sudden pleasure of drinking a tumbler of more than ordinary red or white French wine, I can relive the sensual satisfaction of first chewing a bite of meat and a crust of fresh French bread and then the following swallow of the wine itself." She soon had her favorite bistro, which specialized in the food of the Jura region, and a circle of friends and lovers with whom to share meals.[57]

One of those friends was the celebrated French writer and actress Colette, author of the four *Claudine* novels and one of the great loves of Natalie Barney's life. Colette's 1932 book *The Pure and the Impure*, initially titled *Ces plaisirs*, took the form of a series of conversations about sexuality that captured a snapshot of lesbian Paris in the interwar era. According to Flanner, Colette was very much a "gourmet and a good cook."[58] The socialite and author Violet Trefusis said Colette "loved mixing the *sauce vinaigrette* that accompanied her home-grown salad," and "disliked women whose conversation was as skimpy as their diet."[59] After a youthful open marriage to a Svengali-like writer and publisher who encouraged her to pursue lesbian affairs, she paired off for six years with the Marquise de Belbeuf (Morny), born Mathilde, who dressed in male clothes and went by Max.[60] Colette and Max shared a domesticity that centered on good food. Colette's "household always included an excellent devoted cook."[61] In the decades that followed, she remarried several times and had countless affairs with women as well as men. All the while, her "infamous *gourmandise*" remained central to her celebrity.[62] Adrienne Monnier wrote rapturously about a meal they shared together in 1942 when Colette was sixty-nine, bedridden and obese, her weight a constant source of ridicule in newspapers.[63]

Flanner also counted Alice B. Toklas as a dear friend. It was Flanner who organized the donations that kept Toklas housed and fed in her final years.[64] When Toklas was persuaded in 1958 to co-author a cookbook with Poppy Cannon, author of the infamous 1952 *Can-Opener Cookbook*, Flanner reacted with horror. In Cannon's preface to *Aromas and Flavors of the Past*, she described how she had struggled to persuade Toklas that "it is possible to be an epicure, even a cook-epicure, in a hurry" by using frozen and canned foods.[65] Flanner's savage review of the book for the *New Republic* said that Cannon's annotations to Toklas's recipes would "help the American kitchenette gourmet to avoid the bother of cooking anything like as well as Miss Toklas."[66] Toklas expressed a certain openness to the cooking innovations of the postwar era. She was particularly enamored of a blender that Poppy Cannon gifted her, saying it "revolutionized kitchen work" and was a "life saver," and she assured Cannon that the blender was a perfect centerpiece on her Tuscan Renaissance table.[67] To Flanner, on the other hand, Poppy Cannon, the food editor of *House Beautiful*, epitomized the gauche American approach to eating and culture that she and her Left Bank circle had moved to Paris to escape.[68]

In Flanner's estimation, the "most important woman writer" in the literary Left Bank was Djuna Barnes, author of the classic lesbian novel, *Nightwood*, about her stormy affair with the silverpoint artist Thelma Wood.[69] The relationship between the two women never settled into an easy domesticity centered on shared meals; instead, the conflation of the erotic and the alimentary in their relationship remained a matter of linked hungers. Djuna Barnes found Thelma Wood so desirable, she literally wanted to devour her. In *Nightwood*, Barnes described the character based on Wood, Robin Vote, as smelling of fungi, and wrote "we feel that we could eat her."[70] Unlike many of her compatriots, Barnes left Paris in the early 1930s, long before the Nazis broke up the party. In 1940, after the German occupation, *Town & Country* commissioned Barnes to write an essay about the city. In "Lament for the Left Bank," Barnes opened her elegy with her longing to be back in Paris as it was, "sitting at a bistro table with its iron legs in the sawdust from the escargot baskets, the cheap, badly-pressed cotton napkin coming off all over my best cloak . . . a carafe of vin ordinaire before me, an oval dish of salade de tomate, a bowl of cress soup, a blanquette de veau, [and] green almonds."[71] Barnes couldn't boil an egg, but she could write about food with the best of them.

As for Wood, she was an excellent cook with a taste for French food. After her affair with Barnes ended, she ran a gourmet catering business in Connecticut, and later launched a business selling herbs and exotic foods (both businesses were undermined by her alcoholism).[72] On her death, Wood left behind a dog-eared copy of Samuel Chamberlain's cookbook *Bouquet de France*, with pages marked at recipes for Boeuf Rôti à la Bordelaise, Boeuf Bouilli à la Bordelaise, Gâteau de Foies de Poularde, Sauce d'Ecrevisses, Canard à la Solognotte, Culotte de Boeuf à la Beauceronne, Sole Marguery, and Langoustine Newberg.[73] The last recipe harkened back to a line in Barnes's *Nightwood*, where a character described Lobster Newburg as the epitome of "going to the limit."[74] The dish, invented by chef Charles Ranhofer at Delmonico's in New

York City called for the lobster to be cooked in a cream and sherry sauce.[75] It represented the American ideal of French cooking as a sensual indulgence.[76]

French food's association not simply with sensuality, but with illicit sexuality, made expressing a taste for rich sauces, truffles, oysters, and champagne a way for women to signal their erotic orientation toward other women in the first decades of the twentieth century. As urbanization and industrialization led to expanding numbers of women living independently of their families, opportunities arose for women who identified as lesbians to gather together in urban neighborhoods, like the Left Bank or Greenwich Village, and develop their own cultural expressions that marked them off from the mainstream.[77] The Anglo-American expatriates and their French friends and lovers who concentrated in Paris's Left Bank during these years were creating one of the first lesbian subcultures in the modern world. This subculture grew out of a new understanding of sex and sexuality that regarded lesbians and gay men as distinct types of people, with divergent characteristics, including gender, which differentiated them from straight people.[78] Books by Barnes, Colette, and many other women in their Left Bank circles – most importantly Radclyffe Hall – participated in the construction of this new lesbian taxonomy.[79] Celebrating *gourmandise*, like wearing a man's jacket and a monocle, became a signifier of lesbianism.[80]

Like the bohemians of the nineteenth century, lesbians of the Left Bank demonstrated their rejection of normative expectations by refusing to be bound by restrictions on the female appetite. Embracing an alimentary ethic of sensual indulgence signified their orientation to a pleasure-centered sexuality, rather than the reproductive sexuality of the respectable married woman. Refusing to confine their appetites within accepted limits, women like Stein and Monnier did not apologize for their abundance of flesh. Colette turned the tables by voicing her dislike for women who limited themselves to skimpy diets. Of course, a taste for good food did not necessarily find expression in the body. Toklas and Beach were far scrawnier than their lovers. In her early unpublished novella *Q.E.D.*, Stein observed that, contrary to assumptions, "the body of a coquette often encloses the soul of a prude and the angular form of a spinster is possessed by a nature of the tropics."[81] You couldn't judge a woman's sexuality solely from appearances, even given the monocle trend, but you could maybe judge her sexuality from what, and how much, she ate.

A rapture for cooking

Maybe, but only maybe. The bohemian women expatriates who flocked to Paris in the 1920s, enticed by high exchange rates, legal alcohol, and the city's sexually freewheeling reputation, often shared a fondness for French food whether they slept with other women or not. Sara Murphy, one half of the most glamorous golden couple of the Lost Generation, matched any of her queer friends in her love of good food. Best known as the inspirations for Nicole and Dick Diver, the main characters in F. Scott Fitzgerald's 1934 novel *Tender Is the Night*, Sara and Gerald Murphy were a wealthy American couple who moved to France in 1921 and soon became central figures on the expatriate scene, known for hosting fabulous dinner parties. The dedication of *Tender Is the Night* reads "to Gerald and Sara, Many Fêtes."[82]

Gerald was an accomplished modernist painter, which gained the couple entrée to artistic circles. In spring 1923, they threw their first important Paris dinner party, a fundraiser for a Moscow theater troupe, hanging their apartment with found sculptures made by their friend Fernand Léger, and serving mountains of couscous, and a "fruit and chocolate mousse, molded into a suggestive shape and cloaked in *crème Chantilly*, called *négresse en chemise*." Even more legendary was the dinner party they hosted that summer to celebrate Stravinsky's new ballet, *Les Noces*, for which Gerald had helped to paint the sets. They held the party on a rented barge on the Seine. Sara filled it with cheap toys from a Montparnasse bazaar, which Picasso arranged into an enormous sculpture. The champagne flowed without cease.[83]

The guest list was only one of the attractions at the Murphys' dinner parties. The food, which Sara organized, and often cooked, held equal billing. In *Tender Is the Night*, Fitzgerald famously describes Nicole Diver lounging on a beach along the French Riviera, wearing pearls and a deep suntan, while "looking through a recipe book for chicken Maryland."[84] The Murphys began visiting the Riviera in 1923 and purchased a home in Antibes, which they called the Villa America, where they hosted elaborate dinners. Guests recalled:

the delicious food that always seemed to appear, exquisitely prepared and served, at the precise moment and under the precise circumstances needed to bring out its best qualities (Provençal dishes, for the most part, with vegetables and fruits from the Murphys' garden, though there was often a typically American dish, such as poached eggs on a bed of creamed corn).[85]

Gerald would prepare the cocktails on the flagged terrace beneath a giant linden tree. Sara wrote out the menus for guests.[86]

Sara's thick collection of recipes and menus collected over her lifetime of hostessing show her love of French and Mediterranean cooking, as well as the friends she made during her years in France. Her souvenirs include instructions for how to pronounce ratatouille ("ratatoo-ee"), a French recipe for risotto from the "Inauguration de l'Hôtel Cap d'Antibes," a *côte de boeuf* recipe from Jeanne Leger, and Katy Dos Passos's recipe for "Mustache Sandwiches" (mustard greens with mayonnaise) with the note that "they are peppery + delicious." Even after returning to the United States, Sara continued to prepare French feasts. For the writer Dawn Powell, Sara cooked a meal of *rouget Americain, sauce mousseline, selle d'agneau printanière, purée de petit pois, pomme paillasson, carrée de bric*, and *la brioche glacé au jus de fraises* (fish with a champagne sauce, spring lamb, peas, potato cake, pastry, and a brioche glazed with strawberry juice). Alongside the French recipes are countless recipes for American classics, such as a full page of classic corn dishes, including corn muffins, corn dodgers, Kentucky corn pone, and thin cornbread. Later, the Murphys' daughter Honoria tried to publish a cookbook from Sara's archive, titled "The Villa America Cookbook," filled with photos and the recipes of the Murphys and their famous friends from the 1920s onwards. Sara's archive reveals the central role that epicureanism played in bohemian visions of the good life during the early twentieth century.[87]

In Honoria's words, the Murphys presented a "formula for living" that inspired their friends. This formula combined a love of good food with an atmosphere of sexual hedonism. Sara and Gerald were devoted, but not necessarily exclusive, partners. Gerald was primarily attracted to men.[88] Sara was rumored to have had an affair with Picasso. He sketched her naked on the beach at La Garoupe dressed only in her rope of pearls. F. Scott Fitzgerald was in love with Sara, who didn't return the regard.

She called him a "masher," explaining that he was the type who would "try to kiss you in taxis and things like that. But what's a little kiss between friends?"[89] Sara was also rumored to have had a brief passionate affair with Hemingway during a solo visit to Key West in 1936, when Sara and Gerald's sexual relationship had fizzled out.[90] Just to complicate matters, readers have noted the homoerotic tensions in Hemingway and Fitzgerald's relationship, and Fitzgerald and Hemingway both had ambivalent responses to Gerald's homosexuality.[91]

The American expatriate writer Kay Boyle also combined an appetite for food and sex. It was Boyle who spent her one and only visit to Gertrude Stein's salon chatting with Alice B. Toklas about recipes, and was pointedly told not to come back. Janet Flanner described Boyle as having a "rare domestic center" for a writer.[92] Boyle had "a rapture for cooking," as she put it, and she had six children over her lifetime, but her domesticity didn't extend to monogamy (her six children were from three different relationships, five with two of her three husbands, the sixth with a lover). Boyle moved to France in 1923 with her first husband, a French exchange student named Richard Brault. She had already begun cooking for literary friends in New York. Brault's sister taught her the elements of French cooking, like "how to make mayonnaise by beating oil with a fork into the yolks of eggs cracked into a deep, narrow bowl." Her memoir of her years in France is filled with food memories: picking mussels from the shore at Le Havre and steaming them in butter, parsley, onion, and white wine; drowning squabs in water to cook them for dinner; chasing fresh crabs around her apartment.[93] As men in Boyle's life came and went, her love of cooking remained a constant.[94]

Boyle may not have confined her romances to men. The close relationship between Boyle and the socialite/publisher Caresse Crosby sparked rumors that the two were lovers, or that Boyle may have been involved in a polyamorous relationship with Caresse and husband Harry Crosby, a notorious philanderer.[95] Harry and Caresse were so devoted to their lives of hedonism that they hosted dinner parties from bed in their rented apartment on the rue de Lille. Taking a page from the Murphys, the Crosbys served French indulgences like champagne, caviar, and oysters, complemented with American touches, like cornbread or fish chowder. The poet Archibald MacLeish and his wife were "not much beguiled by the Crosbys' custom of entertaining friends at dinner from their bed."

Other dinner parties may not have started in bed, but ended there. A supper party catered by Rumpelmayer's that the Crosbys threw for the infamous Quat'z'Arts ball, a yearly bacchanal of Parisian arts students, included an enormous bowl of brandy, and culminated the next morning with six in the bed and a strange man in a pale blue undershirt playing the song "Paris C'est une Blonde" over and over again on their gramophone. According to Harry Crosby's biographer Geoffrey Woolf, these acts of sexual and alimentary excess were committed "not only in the service of pleasure but against self-government."[96] Harry didn't particularly care for food, and Caresse did not necessarily enjoy orgies, but both were committed to repudiating any limits on their appetites.

Sara Murphy, Kay Boyle, and Caresse Crosby shared with their queer friends an identity as greedy women, hungry for life. For women to express unleashed hunger remained shocking well into the twentieth century. Their greed offended the sensibilities not only of polite bourgeois society but of bohemian men in their circles. John Glassco, a bisexual poet who traveled to the Left Bank with his boyfriend, Graeme Taylor, in the late 1920s, socialized with Boyle, Crosby, and many of the other women in their circles. According to Glassco, he even slept with several of them, but he still found their unrestrained appetites repellent and corrupting. Describing a night he spent with Kay Boyle, Djuna Barnes, and Thelma Wood at the Falstaff bar in Montparnasse, Glassco wrote "there is nothing, I have found, more dangerous to young people than middle-aged women who have renounced all pretension to coquetry, for the sheer force of their desires is channelled into a cannibalistic selfishness, an appetite that has engrossed all the resources of their charms, brains, and conscious appeal as human beings." Barnes was thirty-five at the time, Wood twenty-seven, and Boyle twenty-five. They were hardly middle-aged, but they were expressive of their appetites.[97]

Naturally, Glassco didn't find men's appetites to be appalling. His memoir of Montparnasse is crowded with recollections of the meals he ate. From the hindsight of his fifties, Glassco wrote "I am persuaded half of man's miseries result from an insufficiency of leisure, gormandise [sic] and sexual gratification during the years from seventeen to twenty."[98] What was not good for the goose was very good for the gander. The greedy women of the early twentieth century pushed back against the outdated Victorian limits on the female appetite that still held Anglo-American society in thrall, but they did so, for the most part, from the safe remove of Paris. Soon they were followed by a younger cohort who tried to build lives as greedy women back home.

EIGHT

Mistresses of Gastropornography

Good women didn't indulge their appetites, but Elizabeth Gwynne wasn't a good woman. She had abandoned her upper-class Tory upbringing in Sussex and run away in her twenties with a married Jewish actor who was trying to escape the draft. Together they boated down France's waterways, stopping for six months in Antibes, where she fell in love with a notorious old pederast. Eventually, Gwynne and her actor lover sailed on to Italy, and were briefly imprisoned following Britain's entry into World War II. After their release, the two traveled to Greece before they were forced to flee before the German invasion. Gwynne continued to Egypt for the remainder of the war. In Cairo, she had a series of affairs, and married a good-looking soldier named Tony David and traveled with him to India, then returned alone to England, where in the winter of 1946–7 she washed up in Ross-on-Wye, mourning the end of an affair with a different lover from her Egypt days. Depressed by the horrible rationing cuisine served at the hotel, she put pen to paper and poured out her longing for the flavors of the Mediterranean, while sitting at a desk on which she had set a frail white jug imprinted with the face of John Wesley, the founder of Methodism and a proselytizer for abstemious diets.[1]

Elizabeth David's impassioned *cri de coeur* became the basis of her first cookbook, *A Book of Mediterranean Food* (1950), which many credit with transforming postwar British cuisine. David said the book was so successful "because it was immoral."[2] At the time, lemons and apricots were dirty words in Britain. Unsurprisingly, David has always had her critics as well as her fans. Half a century later, well after David's death, the food writer Adrian Gill described David's ingredients list in *Mediterranean Food* as "the first purple beginnings of food pornography."[3] It seems that even in the Britain of the early 2000s, lemons and apricots remained dirty words when they came from a woman's pen.

Beginning in the late 1930s, a new generation of Anglo-American women food writers emerged who embraced food as a sensual pleasure.

Many of them discovered good food on visits to France, then carried that love with them back home, where they crafted professional identities as greedy women, or epicures. Their writings found enthusiastic readers but also sparked angry reactions. Conservative critics objected to the immorality of women writing about their pleasure. Male gastronomes demeaned women authors who had the temerity to trespass into their territory. By claiming identities as gourmands, women authors threatened the seriousness and value of gastronomy. Male anxieties about the feminization of epicureanism inspired attacks on women food writers as purveyors of food porn, or gastropornography. The association between good food and illicit sexuality continued to shape perceptions of female epicures through the end of the twentieth century.

Across Britain, the United States, and France, the history of gender and food writing followed similar trajectories. In broad brushstrokes: the earliest published cookbooks in the sixteenth and seventeenth centuries tended to be written by professional male chefs for an audience of professional chefs. In the eighteenth century, the first cookbooks written by women were published, emphasizing frugality and other domestic virtues that typified the home kitchen. At the turn of the nineteenth century, a new genre of gastronomic literature authored by men emerged, which focused on the sensual pleasures of the table. Women's cookbooks grew in number during the nineteenth century, but remained largely pragmatic and only tangentially concerned with pleasure. At the end of the nineteenth century, women authors began trying their hand at gastronomic writing. But moral injunctions against women indulging their alimentary appetites remained in place into the twentieth century.[4]

The pleasures of French food

The cohort of Anglo-American women food writers who began publishing in the mid-twentieth century all shared a common experience of being taught when growing up that good food was morally suspect.

M. F. K. Fisher, who was born in Southern California in 1908, recalled that "American Anglo-Saxon children" were "taught when we were young not to mention food or enjoy it publicly" because such a display was "unseemly."[5] Her grandmother, a frequent visitor at John Harvey Kellogg's Battle Creek Sanitarium, ruled the cooking at Fisher's family table, and she fully subscribed to the Seventh-Day Adventist belief that flavorful foods generated carnal desires, and thus were to be avoided.[6] Elizabeth David, born in 1913 to an upper-class family and raised in a manor house, recalled a nursery regime of "abominable" and "repulsive" food: plain mutton, watery vegetable marrows, slippery and slimy puddings. Luxurious foods were regarded as corrupting, and discussions of food were forbidden as vulgar. The only break in this regime came from a nanny who taught David and her sisters how to cook wild mushrooms in the nursery fireplace. This "illicit cooking" made good food into a naughty secret.[7] Julia Child's editor at Knopf, Judith Jones, who was born in 1924, said that in her white upper-class upbringing, talking about food "was considered crude, like talking about sex."[8] The food historian Betty Fussell, born in 1927, learned from her grandparents, evangelical Midwesterners who cooked everything in a pressure cooker, that it was God's plan "that all food tasted like dishwater."[9] Only libertines enjoyed food. "Eating for fun was wicked."[10]

Each woman experienced a gastronomic awakening when they left home for France. Fisher arrived there in September 1929, along with her new husband, Al Fisher, who was studying for a doctorate in literature in Dijon. Stopping first in Paris at "a little hotel on the left bank," Fisher went out for "the most wonderful dinner I ever ate."[11] The food in Dijon proved even more revelatory. In October, she and Al enjoyed their first meal at Aux Trois Faisans, one of the most celebrated restaurants in France. Fisher wrote to her family that the *prix fixe* dinner cost US$1.00 each, which included "eight kinds of hors-d'oeuvres, a cream soup, a sole, a filet mignon with shoestring potatoes and artichoke hearts stuffed with tomatoes, a capon, cheeses, a dessert of baked apples and méringues in rum, fruits, coffee, and little cakes all with the most perfect wine sauces, piping hot and beautifully served."[12] She had never eaten so much, or so well, in her life. "I like French cooking – everything is so rich and yet fresh and juicy, and there are so many vegetables," she reported in a follow-up letter the next day.[13] Her appetites had been awakened, but her powers of description had not yet quite caught up.

Elizabeth David arrived in Paris the following year, aged sixteen, to study at the Sorbonne. She lodged in the wealthy Right Bank neighborhood of Passy with a bourgeois family who took food extremely seriously. The Robertots, as David called them, "were both exceptionally greedy and exceptionally well fed." Their daughter, Denise, "was the greediest girl I had ever seen." Their cook prepared dishes previously unknown to David, like *rôti de veau*, purée of sorrel, and *pommes mousseline* – or mashed potatoes made with heavy cream, a far cry from the dry riced boiled potatoes that David ate in the nursery growing up. David forgot the lessons in Racine and cathedral architecture she received at the Sorbonne. "What had stuck was the taste for a kind of food quite ideally unlike anything I had known before." Looking back on this early gastronomic experience three decades later, David reflected "ever since, I have been trying to catch up with those lost days." Like for Proust, taste and memory were inextricably intertwined for David.[14]

After Paris, and a six-month stay with aristocratic friends in Munich, David returned to Britain and tried to become an actress. She failed at acting but succeeded at throwing off the manor-house expectations of her upbringing. She bought her first cookbooks and had her first love affairs, including a stormy relationship with a married Jewish actor-director and reprobate named Charles Gibson Cowan. In 1938, David and Cowan bought a small boat, and the next summer they sailed for Le Havre. David packed a trunk of cookbooks and travel books.[15] From Le Havre, they traveled the Seine to Paris and then along the canal system, stopping for dinner at Aux Trois Faisans in Dijon, before arriving at the Mediterranean port of Marseille in September 1939, just as Germany invaded Poland. They continued along the coast until they docked at Antibes, where David met the man who would have the greatest influence of her life on her philosophy of food and sex: the seventy-two-year-old writer Norman Douglas.[16]

Douglas was the author of a bestselling 1917 novel, *South Wind*, which did as much to shatter Victorian sexual norms as any other contemporary work of fiction or scholarship. *South Wind*'s influence on a generation of writers has been largely forgotten because Douglas's sexual notoriety made him impossible to memorialize. An unrepentant pederast, he was living in Antibes to escape arrest in his adopted country of Italy for the sexual abuse of a pre-pubescent girl, an exception to his usual fondness for thirteen-year-old boys.[17] Douglas and David struck up a friendship in Antibes, taking long walks together and sharing lunches of bouillabaisse. In later essays, David described how she learned from Douglas "the importance of the relationship between the enjoyment of food and wine and the conduct of love affairs." He gave her a copy of his early book *Old Calabria*, with an inscription in the front cover to "always do as you please, and send everybody to Hell, and take the consequences. Damned good rule of life." David took Douglas's advice to heart.[18]

Douglas also had tremendous influence on another postwar woman food writer who absorbed his philosophy of food and sex, the Irish cookbook author Theodora FitzGibbon. Born in London's East End in 1916, FitzGibbon was an aspiring actress, like David, who lived in Paris in the late 1930s, mixing with artists, and enjoying the city's erotic and gastronomic pleasures. When the war broke out, she returned to Britain where she met Douglas, who (following an interlude in Portugal living with Elizabeth David's cousin) had been allowed to return to the country in 1942, after a twenty-five-year self-imposed exile to escape prosecution for sexually abusing a teenage boy. FitzGibbon and Douglas took long walks together across Hampstead Heath. His combination of classical learning and bawdy humor made him, in FitzGibbon's estimation, "perhaps the most interesting person I have ever met." He would sit in her kitchen while she cooked, giving her tips, most of them impossible to carry out for lack of ingredients. After the war, FitzGibbon and her husband, Constantine FitzGibbon, moved to Capri, in the Bay of Naples, where Douglas had returned to live out his final years. Constantine had a contract to write Douglas's biography. The biography failed (Constantine was unable to surmount the challenge of writing about Douglas's pederasty), but a publisher offered Theodora a contract to write about cookery. At the time, as FitzGibbon reflected, there were very few cookery books being written by women in Britain. She took inspiration from Elizabeth David.[19]

After World War II, Paris filled once again with British and American visitors, and a new cohort of women underwent alimentary and erotic awakenings that would lead them to careers as food writers. Julia Child, born in 1912, moved to France in 1948 with her new husband, Paul, whom she had met in Ceylon (Sri Lanka) during the war while both were working for the Office of Strategic Services (OSS). They were transferred to China, where they courted over delicious Chinese food. But Child's true gastronomic awakening came in 1948 when Paul was posted by the State Department to the American Embassy in Paris. En route from Le Havre to Paris, the Childs stopped in Rouen at the Restaurant La Couronne.

Their lunch of oysters, Dover sole with a butter and parsley sauce, green salad, baguette and creamy fresh cheese, washed down with a bottle of Pouilly-Fumé and coffee, "was the most exciting meal of my life." That Child's discovery of good food was intertwined with sexual discovery is clear from a gloating letter that Paul wrote to his twin brother from Paris: "Lipstick on my belly button and music in the air – that's Paris." Child signed up for cooking classes at Le Cordon Bleu to learn to recreate the meals they were enjoying at restaurants.[20] Soon, she was teaching other American women how to cook French food, and working with Simone Beck and Louisette Bertholle on the first volume of *Mastering the Art of French Cooking*.

Child's future editor, Judith Jones, was undergoing a similar experience of alimentary and sexual discovery in Paris at the same time. As a young editor, she sailed to Europe in the summer of 1948, armed with introductions to Sartre, Camus, and André Malraux. Already an aspiring gastronome, the reputed "pleasures of French food" drew Jones as surely as the literary scene. She settled on the Left Bank and plunged into the world of bistros and love affairs. "My appetite is fantastic," she wrote home to her parents. "Another thing I find happy is that almost all Frenchmen are bachelors until well into their thirties, and have a good time until they are well established before getting married. So there is a fortunate number of gents about, gay and attractive." She began an affair with a journalist named Pierre Ceria, who "took great pleasure in cooking." Following in the footsteps of the greedy women of the interwar years, Jones delighted in female *gourmandise*. She wrote to her mother, a woman who disdained garlic as too flavorful until her dying day, gushing about a cook she had met who "is a lovely, gross woman who has dedicated her whole life to the art of eating in its finest forms." She even began hosting a supper club with a young American friend, hiring Ceria as their cook, before finding a publishing job working for a new magazine whose married editor, Evan Jones, another epicure, soon became her lover and, ultimately, husband.[21]

The first time that food historian Betty Fussell's "cooking horizons" expanded beyond spaghetti and brownies was in 1952, when she and her husband, a literature scholar named Paul Fussell, sailed to France. "I fell in love with France at first bite – into one of the crusty rolls baked on the *Liberté* and served fresh at every meal." But this discovery didn't translate into her home cooking until 1961, when Julia Child's *Mastering the Art of French Cooking* hit the shelves. And she didn't feel good about her choice to devote herself to gastronomy until 1964, when she finally read M. F. K. Fisher's *The Art of Eating*, an omnibus of her first five books. Fisher wrote about "human need and the hunger for sex, love, warmth and cherishing" in terms that reshaped Fussell's moral universe.[22]

The generation of American and British women food writers born in the first decades of the twentieth century shared experiences of gastronomic and erotic awakenings in France that would not have been entirely unfamiliar to the nineteenth-century women travelers who preceded them, but the products of those awakenings broke new ground. The new cohort of female epicureans brought their erotic and their alimentary appetites together in their gastronomic writing, a combination forbidden to earlier generations of women writers. Their writings had transformative effects on the lives of many women readers.

Writing about love and the hunger for it

M. F. K. Fisher is often credited as the first woman to write sensually about food for an American audience. As with all claims to firsts, the case for Fisher's primacy is debatable. Elizabeth Robins Pennell's *The Feasts of Autolycus* (1896) preceded Fisher's first book, *Serve It Forth* (1937), by four decades. More immediately, Fisher was preceded by a once prominent but now mostly forgotten journalist named Sheila Hibben.[23]

Born in Alabama in 1884, Hibben bridged the older generation of greedy women to the younger generation of women food writers.[24] Biographical details about Hibben are scarce. She lived an "unconventional life," as one account discreetly put it. Named Cecile Craik at birth, she was born into a socially prominent but freethinking family. In her youth, she was friendly with Sylvia Beach, and they traveled together in Italy. A letter from Beach describes how they shared a thermos of hot chocolate on a hike in Pistoia.[25] In 1914, Craik volunteered with the Red Cross Ambulance Service, and was awarded the Croix de Guerre from France for her service.[26] During the war, she married a radical diplomat and journalist named Paxton Hibben. After living together in Russia, France, and Scotland, they moved to Greenwich Village, mixing with the neighborhood's radical bohemian crowd. When Paxton died in

1928, Hibben needed to earn a living. Having written journalism since her youth, she turned to the pen and cooking, the two things she knew best.[27] Her first gastronomic effort, "Food Is to Eat" appeared in the *Independent and Outlook* in March 1929.[28] Hibben published her first cookbook, about American regional cuisine, in 1932.[29] And in 1934 she became the first food critic for the *New Yorker*, writing over one hundred columns for the magazine before her death in 1964.[30] She also contributed to *House Beautiful, Vogue*, and other women's magazines.

From the outset, Hibben approached food from a gastronomic and sensualist – even risqué – perspective. In "Food Is to Eat," Hibben attacked the dainty decorative cooking encouraged in women's magazines and positioned herself on the side of male eaters who, she argued, had more appreciation of food than women. At the essay's end, she quoted a male friend who had "an interesting theory that no virgin can cook really well." If a mother he knew prepared a "gorgeous bouillabaisse" he would say "You see!"; and if a debutante made a perfect omelet, he would murmur "I thought so."[31] The anecdote could have come out of Brillat-Savarin.

Hibben's writing expressed her love for all types of food. She had a breezy familiarity with European restaurants and products, tossing off comments about her favorite shop in the rue de Varenne that sold *petits coeurs* cookies, or a meal she ate at a "delightful little Parisian restaurant." But she also advised readers how to use a European product like mozzarella cheese for an American dish like *chiles rellenos,* and she heaped praise on the good cheeses coming out of Wisconsin.[32] Her cooking instructions were unabashedly physical and sensual. Young chicken, she wrote, "should be massaged well with butter."[33] On a rare occasion when she slipped into memoir, Hibben recalled her "earliest memory of intense pleasure in eating," when her mother snuck her a glass of hot whiskey punch and a piece of Edam cheese during a party. Decades later, she still remembered the flavors of this midnight meal: "the hot punch tasted of cloves and lemons and tangerine peel and a delightful, unfamiliar smokiness." Distraught when she finished her own cheese, she begged for her sister's piece and "nibbled it all away between voluptuous little sips of the warm drink."[34] Hibben embraced her appetites in her food writing, freely acknowledging her "gourmandise" or "gluttony," and setting the stage for the better remembered writers who followed in her tracks.[35]

M. F. K. Fisher's celebrity may overshadow Hibben's legacy, but in the 1930s and 1940s, Fisher was one of Hibben's biggest fans.[36] Fisher embarked on her own professional writing career when, like Hibben, she had returned to the United States from Europe and her first marriage was coming to its end (by divorce, not widowhood). Despite Hibben's inroads, it's more than fair to say that at the time Fisher's first book came out, sensualist food writing remained very much a male preserve. The British horticulturalist Edward Bunyard wrote in *The Epicure's Companion*, published the same year as *Serve It Forth*, that "to the average middle-class English woman food is of the nature of sin, and in her domestic economy the crime and the punishment are swallowed together."[37] Fisher did not accept this dictum. She acknowledged the widespread attitude – in one story from *Serve It Forth*, a man watches Fisher enjoying a steak and says "She likes it, she likes good food! . . . She cannot be a real woman!"[38] – but she refused to conform to proscriptions on her carnal appetites.

By 1937, Fisher had abandoned whatever attachment to sexual respectability and alimentary restraint she'd imbibed growing up. After Al completed his PhD, they had moved back to Southern California, where she started an affair with a married writer and illustrator named Dillwyn Parrish. Fisher started writing, with Parrish's encouragement, and by 1937 both their marriages had broken up and the two were living together in Switzerland.[39] In the very first sentence of *Serve It Forth*, Fisher invoked the godfather of gastronomy, Brillat-Savarin, announcing to readers that her book would not follow conventions that limited women to writing about domestic economy, and reserved the domain of pleasure to men. After this introduction, Fisher turned immediately to the topic of food as a "sensuous passion."[40] Readers beware.

Despite her use of initials in place of her given name, Fisher did not try to disguise her sex. The book's first essay, "When a Man Is Small," includes recollections of her years as a co-ed, going out to dinner dates with men, and showing off her *gourmandise*. The next two essays discussed the history of food writing, from ancient China to modern times, and tackled women's reputation as anti-epicureans who cooked from necessity and had no taste. As if to refute this slander, the next essay discussed potatoes, not as a boring domestic staple but as a romantic symbol that had once been considered "strongly aphrodisiac." Potatoes could be a "gastronomic pleasure" when cooked well. Fisher took the essay's title, "Let the Sky Rain Potatoes," from *The Merry Wives of Windsor*. From Shakespeare's most ribald female characters, Fisher turned next to Colette's erotic heroine Claudine, who took secret pleasure from toasting chocolate on a hatpin, to introduce an essay describing her own pleasure toasting sections of tangerine on a radiator. "My pleasure in them is subtle and voluptuous" Fisher wrote, transported back to the present tense by the power of her food memory. A later essay in the collection described returning to a restaurant where she'd eaten with her husband, Aux Trois Faisans, this time in the company of her lover. During their visit, the adulterous couple watched "two Lesbians" drinking wine at a nearby table.[41] Fisher's openness about sexuality, and her own sensual appetites, raised eyebrows. A reviewer for the *New York Times* claimed to be "charmed and shocked and entertained" by the book.[42]

If *Serve It Forth* challenged conventions against women writing about food and sex, Fisher's next book, *Consider the Oyster* (1941), shattered them entirely. Some could not believe that a woman had written the volume of essays about the food most commonly attributed with aphrodisiac powers in the gastronomical tradition. The reviewer for the *New York Times* even referred to the book's author as "Mr. Fisher."[43] *Consider the Oyster* can be read as a love song for Fisher's second husband, Dillwyn Parrish, who committed suicide in 1941 after developing a painful blood-clotting disorder. From the book's first chapter, "Love and Death among the Molluscs," Fisher focused on the oyster's erotic associations. She didn't miss the chance to give the Latin name of the slipper shell oysters found on the Pacific coast: *Crepidula fornicata*. Amid recipes for oyster stew, Hang Town fry, and oyster gumbo, she dwelled on the oyster as a sensual experience, or in the words of another chapter title, "A Lusty Bit of Nourishment." Fisher entertained readers with the story of a man she met in Mississippi "who swears he has cured seven frigid virgins by the judicious feeding of long brownish buck-oysters from near-by bayous."[44] Such overt writing about the connection between food and sex by a woman writing under her own name broke new ground.

However shocking some readers found *Consider the Oyster*, none of its essays were as personal and erotic as the chapter on oysters that Fisher included in her 1943 memoir, *The Gastronomical Me*. On the book's opening page, Fisher had laid her cards on the table: "when I write of hunger, I am really writing about love and the hunger for it."[45] In nineteenth-century fiction, descriptions of eating had often served as stand-ins for descriptions of sex, which couldn't be written about. Even in the 1940s, fairly strict censorship governed descriptions of sex and sexuality in published books. Fisher's memoir challenged the boundaries of respectability, regardless of her gender.

In "The First Oyster," she described her sexual awakening as a sixteen-year-old student enrolled at "Huntingdon's School for Girls" (actually, the Bishop's School – Fisher liked to change names). The chapter opens with a story about the lesbian culture of the schoolteachers at Huntingdon's. The arrival of a new gym teacher who "had the most adorable little cracked voice, almost like a boy's" and a "short and boyish" haircut, leads to an outpouring of "passionate notes to her" from the other teachers. Fisher is forthright about the teachers' sexuality, even calling one of them "a skin-and-bones edition of Krafft-Ebing," referring to the famous sexologist who recorded many stories of boarding-school lesbianism in his classic *Psychopathia Sexualis*.[46] The homoerotic culture at Huntingdon's was widespread in boarding schools from the mid-nineteenth through early twentieth centuries. Crushes between students, between teachers, and between students and teachers were a familiar theme in fiction.[47] The "First Oyster" describes Fisher's own initiation into that culture.

At the annual Christmas party during her sophomore year, all the students dress up in evening gowns, the seniors wearing the most recent flapper fashion of "firmly flattened young breasts" under sheer silk. When the waiters serve raw oysters, Fisher is daunted. The sophisticated older girls seated on either side of her swallow first, then dare Fisher to follow their lead, saying "Try one, Baby-Face." Fisher lifts an oyster to her lips, sucks it into her mouth, but cannot swallow. The senior seated on her left, "the most wonderful girl in the whole school," pulls Fisher from her seat for the first dance, and when "Olmstead put her thin hand on my shoulder blades, I swallowed once, and felt light and attractive and daring, to know what I had done." She is speechless with pleasure at dancing with Olmstead, but feels repelled when the junior seated on her right, Inez, asks her to dance next. Inez promises "there are a couple of things boys can do I can't, but I can dance with you a damn sight better than that bitch Olmstead." Inez presses Fisher close and coos into her ear. "She was getting a crush on me," Fisher realizes.

"Relax, kid," Inez instructs, "just pretend . . ." Before Inez can finish her sentence, Fisher runs into the kitchen. "I had to escape from her and the delightful taste of oyster in my mouth, my new-born gourmandise, sent me toward an unknown rather than a known sensuality," she explains. But in the kitchen, Fisher witnesses a sexually disturbing scene of the school's female cook feeding oysters to the school's female nurse. The sight prompts her to reject lesbian sexuality: "If I could still taste my first oyster, if my tongue still felt fresh and excited, it was perhaps too bad. Although things are different now, I hoped, then, suddenly and violently, that I would never see one again."[48] At least, that's how Fisher ended her chapter. Memoirs often diverge from real life.

In actuality, Fisher did not run away from her first erotic attraction to another student. When she developed a crush on Eda Lord, a wild girl with a bob, Fisher chased after her with passionate intent. Writing to Lord years later, Fisher said she believed "you were the most dazzling exciting human being I had ever met."[49] Fisher was notoriously cagey about her sexual partners. She never even told her daughter Anna who her father was. Whether or not Fisher and Lord consummated their mutual attraction, the women remained lifelong friends and both went on to have many erotic relationships with women during their lifetimes.[50]

Following another short-lived marriage, to editor Donald Friede, Fisher had relationships primarily with women during the later years of her life.[51] As she explained,

> I like people who are different from me sexually . . . Most of all I think I like men, who think of themselves as men, inert and unquestioned *men*. But I also like people who are not settled in one sex or another. Here I am not quibbling, for my approach is still direct. I make a lot of people turn away, or at least off, from me, by being so open in my assertion that I like people, men or, women or, this or that or.[52]

After a short marriage, Eda Lord, who also became a writer, had relationships exclusively with women, including with the German–British food writer Sybille Bedford, whom she introduced to Fisher.

Born near Berlin in 1911, Sybille Aleid Elsa von Schoenebeck acquired her English last name from a *mariage blanc* to a gay man in London in the mid-1930s in a bid to escape being deported to Nazi Germany. She acquired an early education in gastronomy from her father, a wine and antiques collector who had grown up speaking French at home in Bavaria, and whose own father was an accomplished cook. Bedford's mother was Jewish, a noted beauty and intellect, who soon abandoned her husband and daughter. When Bedford's father died in 1925, Bedford briefly joined her mother and her much younger Italian stepfather on an Italian tour, where she enjoyed meals of *mozzarella di bufala*, figs, and calamari. At fifteen, she was sent off to school in England, where she was first exposed to the horror of "sodden vegetables."[53] This education in British cookery didn't take, but Bedford did learn to speak English like she'd grown up in Oxford, and it became the language she wrote in. Later, she rejoined her mother and stepfather in Sanary-sur-Mer, a seaside village in Provence, where she became friends with Aldous Huxley and other expatriate writers and painters who lived in the artists' colony.[54]

Bedford credited Renée Kisling, the bisexual wife of the painter Moïse Kisling whom she met in Sanary, with influencing her love of cooking.[55] Renée Kisling was also Bedford's first lover. Another of her early lovers in Sanary was Maria Nys Huxley, wife of the writer Aldous Huxley, who inspired Bedford's desire to become a writer. Whereas Aldous Huxley balanced his extensive womanizing with literary productivity by cutting out all courtship, leaving Maria to take care of cultivating his mistresses, Bedford's appetites for food and sex got in the way of her writing. She frequently complained to her former lover Allanah Harper about her tendency to let "the rut of endless cooking and shopping" get in the way of writing.[56]

In 1946, Bedford attempted to put her love of food to good use by writing a cookbook, but she could not find a publisher for her manuscript, which was judged "not suitable" for the English market.[57] Bedford's on-again, off-again lover Esther Murphy – the sister of Gerald Murphy, who with his wife Sara hosted Lost Generation writers at their Villa America – gave the book to her sister-in-law Noel Murphy, who "seized on it avidly" and was "most impressed."[58] But the Mediterranean ingredients and dishes that Bedford loved to cook were still, in the years before Elizabeth David's *Mediterranean Food*, too risqué for the flavor-averse Anglo-American market.[59] In 1947, Bedford visited Norman Douglas, an old friend, in Capri and helped him write the recipes for an aphrodisiac cookbook, *Venus in the Kitchen*, which became his final posthumous work, published in 1952.[60]

In 1953, Bedford finally published her first book under her own name, a Mexican travelogue titled *The Sudden View*, later reissued as *A Visit to Don Ottavio*. The book included several long passages about food, including a description of a picnic Bedford packed for the train and consumed with the aid of the French zigzag corkscrew, silver clasp knife, and pepper mill that she always kept on hand. Bedford later faulted this passage for its "gastronomic self-posing" and banality.[61] The love of good food, however, proved too integral to Bedford's identity to be abandoned. Over the following decades, she published a mix of fiction, journalism, and memoir, in which descriptions of food played a recurring theme.[62] "Lobsters, olives, figs, truffles, trussed birds and bread are passionately consumed and portrayed on every other page" in her books, as one critic wrote with only minor exaggeration.[63]

In later years, Bedford also contributed many articles about food and wine for epicurean publications and was widely known as a food writer. Still, she published less than she thought she should, telling an interviewer "I wish I'd written more books and spent less time being in love."[64] After splitting from Esther Murphy, who lived off alcohol and was largely indifferent to what she ate, Bedford fell in love with a young American she met in Rome named Evelyn Gendel, who shared her love of food.[65] The two women co-authored four articles about cookery for the American magazine *House Beautiful*. They lived together for three years before Gendel returned to the United States where she became an editor at Bobbs-Merrill, the publisher of the *Joy of Cooking*, and went on to write her own cookbooks, including *Soup!* and *Pasta!*, drawing on what she'd learned from her years living in Rome with Bedford.[66]

Too sexually voracious to remain committed to one woman for long, Bedford ended her relationship with Gendel so that she could pursue a love affair with Eda Lord, M. F. K. Fisher's friend from her school days. Bedford and Lord had first met in 1932, and their sexual histories intersected at multiple points (they shared exes), which was fairly common in the incestuous world of mid-century lesbian writers. After more than twenty years of acquaintance, they fell in love in 1957. Like Gendel, Lord was a fine cook – although not as good a cook as the professional-level

Bedford. When the women were apart from each other, Bedford wrote Lord letters filled with detailed accounts of her meals.[67]

In 1959, Lord introduced Bedford to M. F. K. Fisher.[68] A few years later, Bedford forged a friendship with Elizabeth David. According to Bedford, they first met briefly at a party in the 1950s, when Bedford had complimented *Mediterranean Food*.[69] Then, in 1963, Bedford sent David a fan letter, praising an article she had written about food markets in Venice.[70] David responded warmly, telling Bedford she was a great fan of her writing, especially a passage about a meal of *loup-de-mer* in her first novel *A Legacy*, which she likened to Lawrence Durrell's description of black olives in one of his novels.[71] The two women met in 1964, and Bedford published a profile of David in the *Sunday Times* in 1966.[72] Early the next year, she met Julia Child in Provence, where both women frequently spent time – Bedford at Les Bastides, a property owned by her friend Allanah Harper, and Julia Child at her house La Pitchoune, on the property of her friend Simone Beck.[73] Julia Child had been following both Bedford's and Fisher's food writing with interest since the 1960s.[74] Child also met Fisher in the summer of 1966 in Cambridge, Massachusetts, after Fisher came back from a trip to Provence where she had spent time with a friend who was renting La Pitchoune.[75] But David refused to be introduced to Fisher, whose writing she disliked.[76]

From the mid-1960s onwards, Bedford, David, Fisher, and Child established a complex network of friendships and enmities, shared meals and gossip. The press took notice, frequently comparing the women authors, for good or ill. Food journalist Christopher Driver saw "Fisher, Bedford, and David [as] survivors of a remarkable generation."[77] James Beard wrote about Child and David as outstanding French cooks.[78] But an article praising Elizabeth David said she was "nothing like her ebullient American counterparts. If they are unabashed country hams, then she is a slice of prosciutto, and a thin one at that."[79] Sybille Bedford concurred that there was no comparison between Child and David. "It's a Hovis advertisement against a Chardin," she wrote, comparing Child to mass-produced brown bread and David to a still life by the eighteenth-century French master Jean Siméon Chardin.[80]

Rapturous food porn

If each author had her partisans and detractors, collectively their cook-books, novels, food writing, and television appearances played a profound role ushering in a new enthusiasm for good food in Anglo-American popular culture during the 1960s and 1970s.[81] Well after World War II, the association between good food and illicit sexuality still lingered. The California food writer Helen Evans Brown wrote to her friend James Beard that when she mentioned the word "gastronomy" at a food indus-try luncheon in 1958, "there were a couple of giggles as if I had said something mildly dirty and then awful silence."[82] Claudia Roden, the cookbook author, recalled the same attitude prevailing in London in the late 1950s and early 1960s, where talking about food was like talking about sex.[83] Bedford, David, Fisher, and Child's popularity changed Anglo-American attitudes toward eating and cooking, but their writings didn't break the imagined connection between food and sex. Far from it, their sensualist approaches to cooking became popular in the context of an emerging sexual revolution on both sides of the Atlantic.

Betty Fussell described this interlinked social transformation in her memoir. In the early 1960s, she was living in Princeton with her husband Paul when their "Puritan" milieu was swept by a wave of epicureanism and adultery. "In food as in sex," Fussell recalled, "Europe beckoned. . . . Food was an index of how far we'd moved into the fleshpots of Dionysus." From hot dogs on the grill, they graduated to "butterflied legs of lamb, marinating them in olive oil scented with herbs from Provence," a recipe straight out of Elizabeth David. Unhappy in her marriage, she and her first lover met for picnics and sex alfresco. "We were discovering what the French had known forever, that food was like literature and art, and that sex was above all like food." Fussell and her friends read M. F. K. Fisher and James Beard, and with the help of Julia Child's *Mastering the Art of French Cooking*, she and all the women she knew gave up Irish stew and began cooking *boeuf bourguignon* and *boeuf en daube* in French cookware they bought from Elizabeth David's shop in London.[84] Eventually, her marriage ended, and Fussell became a food writer, fol-lowing in the footsteps of the women who inspired her awakening.[85]

In 1973, the Wine & Food Society gave Elizabeth David the first ever André Simon Memorial Prize, named for the organization's founder. In a press release, the Society declared that "the Puritan attitude to eating and drinking has today largely gone: the enjoyment of our meals is now widely recognized as an important part of the art of living."[86] Like many press releases, its claims were rather exaggerated. The alimentary-sexual regime that regarded a taste for good food as deeply suspicious, especially when voiced by someone female, lingered well into the women's final years.[87] Against their tottering stacks of awards could be placed an equally high stack of critiques.

"I get pretty peeved about being called things like 'past mistress of gastronomical pornography' and so on," Fisher complained in a 1971 interview. Yes, eating well was a sensuous experience, but it was "Puritanical rubbish to say that the enjoyment of freshly picked green peas cooked over hot coals on a hillside is 'pornographic.'"[88] Fisher made similar complaints privately, writing to her friend Eleanor Friede about how the "Fisher as pornographer" narrative annoyed her. "I just wish my fellow-countrymen were more relaxed. They have been conditioned to believe that there is something basically EVIL about physical and moral sensuality."[89] Admirers as well as critics were apt to characterize Fisher's writing with this language. Betty Fussell described Fisher's account of eating mashed potatoes with ketchup as like "a pornographic rite."[90] Fussell, who had traveled all the way to Sonoma County to meet Fisher at her "Last House" for an interview, meant this in the best possible way. Fisher no doubt gritted her teeth when she read the passage. Despite her frustration, Fisher could never shake off the narrative, which lingered long after her death. Anthony Bourdain described her books as "rapturous food porn" in 2013.[91]

Elizabeth David endured similar treatment. The feminist writer Rosalind Coward described David's work as "erotica" in a 1982 article, "Naughty but Nice: Food Pornography."[92] Unlike Fisher, David did not write overtly about eroticism, hiding her sexually unconventional life behind a frosty hauteur. She dismissed questions from a profile editor for *Wine & Food*, as she dismissed so many inquiries, saying "why should anyone want to know about me?"[93] But David's personal reserve did not dissuade attacks on her writing as "light gastroporn," and characterizations of her as "the first modern food porn writer."[94] Julia Child was subject to similar critiques. "She brought food porn to the people," read the headline of a 1997 profile in Canada's *The Globe and Mail*.[95] Film reviewer Lisa Rosman agreed that we "have Julia to thank for the glut of food porn." Close-up shots of Child's hands massaging the bare flesh of chickens with butter, and making sexual double-entendres like calling a stewing chicken "beyond the age of consent," fueled these attacks.[96]

From its origins, the gastronomic tradition of food writing had incorporated references to sensuality. Brillat-Savarin wrote about the aphrodisiac properties of truffles. Grimod de La Reynière wrote that blondes went better than brunettes with food. That tradition persisted into the twentieth century. The *New Yorker* journalist A. J. Liebling, a famous gourmand and sexual hedonist, compared dishes on a menu to women's body parts, observing that no single woman or menu was entirely comprised of perfect pieces.[97] And yet Brillat-Savarin, La Reynière, and Liebling weren't described as pornographers, not because their writings were less sexual than those of their female counterparts but because they were male. In fact, Liebling's food writing has been described as the antithesis of food porn in a 2018 article that likewise praises a passage written by Jim Harrison about seeing a hot woman in the cheese section of a grocery store and making "an involuntary humping motion."[98] Not pornographic. But Elizabeth David writing about the toothsomeness of cassoulet, on the other hand . . .

NINE

Gay Gourmets

Before he became the reigning gourmet of interwar London, X. Marcel Boulestin was an aspiring gay novelist and journalist. Born in Poitiers, France, in 1878, Boulestin moved to Paris as a young man, drawn to the city by the works of the French Decadents and queer authors like Pierre Louÿs, André Gide, and Joris-Karl Huysmans.[1] In Paris, he worked as a secretary and ghostwriter for Henry Gauthier-Villars, better known by the mononym Willy, the husband of the French writer Colette. Soon Colette and Boulestin became close companions. They shared alimentary appetites – Boulestin remembered one "quiet greedy supper with pounds of beautiful truffles, quite plain, cooked under the ashes, of which Colette and myself ate an enormous amount" – but they didn't share sexual appetites.[2] As Willy put it, "Ce Marcel était un peu filou et énormément pédéraste," or in other words, Boulestin was a little scamp and enormously homosexual.[3] He was also an enormous Anglophile. He made his first visit to London in the early 1900s, where he fell in love with the men's tailoring, the fog, and the cozy Englishness of it all. Returning to France, he took vacations in Dieppe, a resort town on the Channel that drew many English visitors. He lived in the same building as the queer English writers Reggie Turner and Max Beerbohm, both of whom had been loyal friends to Oscar Wilde. They encouraged Boulestin's literary aspirations.[4]

When Colette's performance at the Moulin Rouge with her lover the Marquise de Belbeuf swept Boulestin into a public scandal, he left Paris for a new life in London. That new life proved even queerer. Along with resuming his friendships with Turner and Beerbohm, Boulestin made new friendships with additional gay writers, including Robbie Ross, Ronald Firbank, Vyvyan Holland (Oscar Wilde's son), and Adolf de Meyer.[5] In 1911, he published a book set in London, *Les Fréquentations de Maurice*, which has been described as "a brilliantly chatty gay novel whose central character is an androgynous dandy and man about town."[6]

Having used a nom de plume, Sidney Place, for the novel Boulestin then reviewed the book under his own name in the pages of the *Cambridge Magazine*, tut-tutting the dissolute characters and warning that the novel was not to be read by young girls.[7] The joke typified the campy persona he had crafted in two countries.

Boulestin frequently remarked on the prudery of English culture and its restrictive approach to pleasure. After serving in France for the entirety of World War I, Boulestin returned to London broke and desperate to restart his writing career. During a meeting with a publisher, he said, "By the way, you would not be interested in a cookery book, would you?"[8] Boulestin's first cookbook, *Simple French Cooking for English Homes*, came out in 1923 and was such an immediate hit that he published five more cookbooks over the next decade, along with food columns in *Vogue*, the *Spectator*, the *Daily Express*, and numerous other magazines and newspapers.[9] Boulestin's food writing went beyond recipes. He aimed to translate the French approach to food and pleasure for English readers. "The English habit of not talking about food strikes the foreigner, however long he may have stayed in England, as a very queer one – indeed, as a quite unnatural custom," Boulestin wrote. With his typical campy wit, Boulestin flipped the script on Anglo-American prudery, calling its aversion to alimentary pleasure "queer" and "unnatural," terms often used for gay men. Boulestin encouraged readers to break free from this pleasure-denying tradition. "One should talk about food and wine; they taste better if you do."[10] Indifference to what one ate should not be treated as a virtue.[11]

At the same time that Boulestin was finding success as a food writer, he was also making a name as a restaurateur. After the war, when he was trying to scrape together enough money to survive, he had started cooking for people for pay. Luckily, he knew the right people. Aldous Huxley introduced him to Dorothy Todd, the "alarmingly butch" lesbian editor of *Vogue* magazine, who hired Boulestin to cook a lunch for Virginia Woolf, whom she was trying to cultivate as a writer. Woolf didn't like eating in restaurants. The lunch proved such a success that afterwards the guests encouraged Boulestin to open a restaurant.[12] Together with his lover, Robin Adair, in May 1925 Boulestin opened his first restaurant, which was decorated by Bloomsbury artists Vanessa Bell (Woolf's sister), her bisexual lover Duncan Grant, and the painter Alan Walton. For the next decade and a half, until the start of World War II, Restaurant Boulestin was the chicest and supposedly most expensive restaurant in London.[13] Woolf even deigned to eat out there.[14]

Boulestin's success with the Bloomsbury set spoke to the ongoing centrality of pleasure-oriented approaches to food and sex within bohemianism. Bloomsbury's bisexuality, open marriages, and polyamorous arrangements are well known. Less attention has been paid to their cooking. Virginia Woolf wrote that when she and Leonard Woolf, her husband, moved to Bloomsbury in 1904, "We were full of experiments and reforms. We were going to do without table napkins, we were to have Bromo instead; we were going to paint; to write; to have coffee after dinner instead of tea at nine o'clock. Everything was going to be new, everything was going to be different. Everything was going on trial."[15] At the top of the list of conventions to be challenged was the English diet which, according to E. M. Forster, was guided by a "spirit of gastronomic joylessness." English menus, he sniffed, "eschew pleasure and consider delicacy immoral."[16] The Bloomsbury set took their culinary inspiration from France, as helpfully translated by Boulestin. Roger Fry loved to cook in his Provençal *diable* pot. Quentin Bell adopted the French way to make salad dressing: mixing vinaigrette at the bottom of a wooden bowl, topping it with a piece of bread rubbed with garlic (the *chapon*), piling the greens on top, and tossing it all together when ready to serve. Virginia Woolf filled the pages of her novels with dinner party scenes, including the famous *boeuf en daube* in *To the Lighthouse* (1927).[17]

By the 1930s, as Boulestin hit the peak of his success, centering pleasure in one's approach to food and sex had become not simply a signifier of bohemianism, but of homosexuality in particular. His restaurant attracted a notably queer crowd. For example, the restaurant was frequented by "Lord C. W." who was "notorious for certain tastes" and was known among the Chelsea Guardsmen as "the terror of the district." One afternoon at lunch, Boulestin witnessed Lord C. W. ask a handsome young waiter whether the steak was tender, and receiving affirmation, follow up with: "And you – are you tender?" He didn't seem to care whether anyone was listening, Boulestin noted. You could get away with such behavior at Restaurant Boulestin, whose proprietor himself enjoyed rough trade like Chelsea guardsmen.[18]

Boulestin's campy persona and wild success affirmed a growing popular association between gay men and good food. While only the wealthy could afford his restaurant, Boulestin's writing influenced a wide audience, including the British food writers who came after him.[19] Elizabeth David described him as one of the chief influences on her cooking, praising his non-pretentious, creative, and authentic approach to food.[20] She even used an illustrator for her cookbooks, Arthur Lett-Haines, who was a friend of Boulestin's and the lover of Boulestin's illustrator, the painter Cedric Morris. (Lett-Haines and Morris ran a painting school together where Lett-Haines cooked delicious garlic-laden French meals.[21]) Along with his books and journalism, Boulestin endorsed food products, gave in-person cooking demonstrations at shops, and appeared in the first cooking demonstration ever aired on British television, in 1937. Reviews of his TV appearances at the time slyly winked at his queerness, noting for example the "delicate pinky-white powder" he wore on his face.[22]

By the 1930s, men who showed an interest in fine cooking were seen as "effete," "homosexual," or "light in their loafers."[23] This stereotype held more than a grain of truth. In fact, during the middle decades of the twentieth century, many of the most influential authorities in the Anglo-American food world were gay men. Marcel Boulestin represented what became a familiar type: the urbane, witty, campy, professional, gay gourmet. Multiple explanations have been offered for the preponderance of gay men in gourmet cooking. Early twentieth-century psychologists attributed the pattern to gay men's supposed gender inversion. The 1936 Terman–Miles Masculinity and Femininity Test, a diagnostic tool used by organizations like government agencies and corporations to identify the homosexuals in their midst, scored a male interest in cooking as a sign of homosexuality. The Terman–Miles Test assessed answers to 455 questions and prompts to determine degrees of gender conformity. Men who scored as highly feminine and women who scored as highly masculine were determined to be likely sexual inverts, attracted to their own sex. According to the answer key, "the typical male invert" preferred "appliances such as food choppers" to tools that required physical force. Inverts could define a buffet, while straight men appreciated "things cooked in grease." In short, homosexuals were feminine men who craved penetration and enjoyed activities associated with femininity, like cooking.[24]

These assumptions filtered into popular culture. Magazines and advertisements in the 1940s and 1950s attacked "sissy foods" that were too delicate or refined for masculine tastes. "Give a Man Man's Food," a 1941 *Good Housekeeping* article instructed its women readers. "Men get tired of sissy food. They like dishes they can sink their teeth into."[25] The article followed with a recipe for boiled beef and horseradish. *House and Garden* warned wives in 1944 that omelets and soufflés were too "sissy" for men, who needed their eggs augmented "with the lusty presence of minced onions and ground meat."[26] The advice reflected the longstanding American belief that a taste for French cooking was effete.[27] Real men ate beef, the protein most associated with masculinity in Anglo-American culture. Light and delicate foods like salad, or ice cream, were effeminate, which by the 1940s, and the concretization of the hetero/homo binary, had become a euphemism for homosexual.[28]

Gender-determinist analyses of homosexuality were challenged by the gay rights movement in the 1960s and 1970s, which protested the treatment of homosexuality as a mental illness, and fought against effeminate stereotypes of gay men. The association between gay men and gourmet cooking, however, didn't go away. After the 1970s, gay men's supposed gourmet proclivities became something to celebrate rather than stigmatize. New positive explanations attributed gay men's gourmet tendencies to their innate creativity, or to their shared belief in taking pleasure seriously.[29] But any explanation for the rise of the gay gourmet that depends on the supposedly inherent qualities of queer men, whether negative or admirable, cannot withstand historical scrutiny. A historical explanation for the rise of the gay gourmet must attend to timing.

Gourmet tastes became a significant aspect of gay male subculture in the twentieth century. The elevation of epicureanism within queer culture probably originated with the aesthetic Decadent movement of the 1890s. Oscar Wilde, whose turn-of-the-century celebrity played such a prominent role in shaping queer aesthetics, was a well-known epicure who frequently held court in London's best restaurants. Since the mid-nineteenth century, bohemians had indulged their alimentary appetites as a way of rejecting bourgeois respectability. In the early 1900s, gay aesthetes in London, New York, and other cities, made a taste for fine food into a defining aspect of queer subculture. Cooking's feminine associations played a part, not because gay men were inherently feminine but because femininity served as an important way to signal same-sex desires, and because queer male subcultures included many people on the trans feminine spectrum. Shared tastes in good food proved a way of creating community. Across time and space, eating together, or eating the same diet, has served as a primary way to forge community. Food served this purpose as queer subcultures took shape in the early 1900s. By the 1970s, the significance of gourmet food to queer culture went well beyond the prominence of gay men in the food business. A whole queer food culture took shape, of gay and lesbian restaurants, gourmet societies, favorite dishes, and countless cookbooks, from the tongue-in-cheek to the heartrendingly earnest.

The brotherhood of bachelor cooks

Although he disliked the word "gourmet," James Beard probably did as much to fix the association between queer men and gourmet food in the United States as Marcel Boulestin had in Britain.[30] Like Boulestin, Beard was a true food celebrity: a food writer, cooking teacher, television performer, and widely recognized personality. Born in Portland, Oregon, in 1903, Beard was noted for his *gourmandise* from a very young age. His mother, Elizabeth, ran a boarding house known for its good food. Raised in England on the dietary principle that virtue demanded the rejection of flavor, the strikingly independent Elizabeth rejected her upbringing, left home, and settled in Portland in part because of the excellent ingredients available there. As one Beard biographer points out, her "unconventional attitudes to food" mirrored those of the original greedy woman, Elizabeth Robins Pennell.[31] Oriented erotically to women, and frank and funny in her sexual conversation, Elizabeth's social circles included many sexual nonconformists.[32] She liked to bring her son along with her to Portland's racy French restaurants such as Falt's Quelle, a "gay" joint frequented by "travelling men" and their escorts.[33] When Beard was only five, she brought him to the most notorious French restaurant in Portland, the Louvre, which had private rooms for sex and was particularly popular among the city's gay men. They ate oysters and drank champagne. A few years later, the Louvre was busted in "the vice clique scandal," a crackdown on gay sex in the city.[34]

In 1922, Beard was caught up in a gay sex scandal of his own when he was expelled from Reed College for having an affair with a male professor. He had done little to disguise his sexuality, showing up to the freshman Halloween party in full drag, drawing attention with his witty repartee, and pursuing male students.[35] Driven out of Oregon, Beard traveled to London and Paris where he trained as an opera singer, ate in countless restaurants, and enjoyed both cities' gay life. He returned to the United States in 1924, moving around the country as he tried and failed to launch a theatrical career. But at 6 ft 3 in and 250–300 lbs, he had a hard time getting cast. In 1937, he returned to New York City. Short on funds, Beard, like Boulestin had, began hiring himself out to cook for friends' parties. His mother had cooked for paying guests at their summer cottage on the Oregon shore, and Beard had made money this way at numerous points over the years.[36] One of the first parties he catered in New York was for the lesbian theater producer Cheryl Crawford, whose partner Ruth Norman would become a good friend of Beard's, and later write her own cookbook and open a restaurant.[37] Soon Beard moved in with a wealthy queer friend, Jim Cullum, to serve as his major-domo of sorts, handling the food at the parties he liked to throw. At one of Cullum's parties, Beard met a strikingly handsome man named Bill Rhode who shared his love of food and had an idea for how to make it pay. Rhode had just published a cookbook, and his sister Irma claimed to have been trained to cook by the "Grand Duchess of Baden."[38] In January 1939, they collaborated on launching a storefront catering company they called Hors d'Oeuvre, Inc., funded by Cullum.

Beard's and Rhode's connections in New York's queer circles helped make the business an immediate success. The syndicated journalist Lucius Beebe, an effete dandy who wrote about goings-on within the city's "café society," praised the business in a May column.[39] Beebe had a thing for Rhode, who was straight but a willing flirt. Sheila Hibben wrote them up in her Markets and Menus column for the *New Yorker*.[40] Jeanne Owen, the president and secretary of the New York chapter of the International Wine & Food Society, invited Hors d'Oeuvre, Inc. to cater a reception and befriended Beard, introducing him to the queer epicurean men she collected as friends. Owen also encouraged Beard to publish his own cookbook. Beard's *Hors d'Oeuvre and Canapés*, which came out in 1940, made no mention of the fact that many of the recipes originated with the Rhodes. (One of the biggest disputes concerned the origins of the company's famous onion sandwich, which Beard claimed his mother invented, and which Bill Rhode said he had adopted from a Parisian bordello.[41]) Rhode and Beard's business partnership dissolved. Bill Rhode died shortly after the war, and soon passed from popular memory.[42] In 1962, Beard finally acknowledged the Rhodes in his introduction to a new edition of the book.[43] By that time, Beard's celebrity shined brightly enough to go undimmed by sharing a little credit.

From the 1940s through the 1980s, Beard's life was a whirlwind of work in the food industry. At any one moment, he was working at least three jobs to generate enough income to support his extravagant hospitality. Guests described bathtubs of champagne in his West Village apartments. Beard wrote countless newspaper recipe columns and cookbooks, or, more accurately, he put his name on countless columns and cookbooks compiled from his notes by secretaries and ghostwriters who had a more disciplined approach to punctuation and grammar than he had. He appeared on television, hosting one of the earliest American cooking shows, *I Love to Eat*, on NBC. He started a cooking school, frequently teaching classes out of his apartment but also taking to the road to give classes around the country. He shilled corporate products like Omaha Steaks and Green Giant Corn Niblets. He went on publicity junkets. He judged cooking competitions. He did speaking engagements for industry groups. By the time Beard died in 1985, "his was the most famous food name in America."[44] Beard personified American cooking.

Beard's sexuality was never a secret to his friends, but how queer was his public reputation? At the very beginning of his culinary career, in 1940, Jeanne Owen referred to him in her book *A Wine Lover's Cookbook* as "one of the brotherhood of bachelor cooks."[45] At a time when it was considered libelous to refer to someone as homosexual in print, the term "bachelor" was often used as a euphemistic synonym. Many readers might have guessed from Owen's wording that Beard was a gay man. The word "bachelor" turned up repeatedly in descriptions of Beard.[46] His most recent biographer, John Birdsall, argues that he cultivated a public persona as avuncular and asexual.[47] But Beard's gleeful embrace of embodied pleasure, the signs of gluttony that he forever carried on his large body – he was, indeed, a man who would eat a large meal at a restaurant, then order it again and eat it a second time – would not have read as asexual to many people.[48] Quite the opposite. Skinniness was associated with asexuality. Spinsters were skinny. Dietary restrictions tempered sexual appetites. Fatness signified a person with large appetites, both alimentary and sexual. Like Falstaff. Betty Fussell described Beard's persona as a cross between "Bacchus and Sydney Greenstreet," the God of revelry and the mid-century actor famous for playing "the Fat Man" in *The Maltese Falcon*.[49]

Forever appearing on television, at county fairs, and at industry events, James Beard interacted constantly with fans over the course of his fifty-year career in the food industry. Countless people had the chance to judge his personal affect, and that affect struck a lot of people as queer. At the beginning of his career, the publisher of *Gourmet* blacklisted Beard for being "too brazenly queer." His writing incorporated gay slang like "chi-chi" and "doodaddery."[50] He lived in the Village, which even stuffy straight people knew was a gay neighborhood.[51] Beard was dramatic. He wore eccentric clothes, mixing polka dots and plaids. He filled his house with bric-a-brac. He was catty and backbiting. He enthralled audiences with gossip.[52] His language was often "salty." "Now eggplant, that's a very sexy dish," he would say.[53] He cooked for a summer at a restaurant called Lucky Pierre, a slang term for a man who took the middle position in a queer daisy chain.[54] He described himself as "the world's great gastronomic whore," words that it's hard to imagine coming from the mouth of a straight man in the mid-twentieth century.[55] Beard also had a tendency to expose himself to good-looking young men, a habit that left the unfortunate victims with little doubt about his tastes.[56] In sum, his sexuality was obvious to anybody with eyes to see it and plausibly deniable to anybody who didn't want to know.

If Beard's celebrity alone was not enough to fix the association between gourmet food and homosexuality in mid-century American culture, the rise of Craig Claiborne helped seal the deal. "There is not and never has been any question in my mind that it was Craig Claiborne, not James Beard or Julia Child, who first introduced Americans to the glories of good cooking and fine dining," the cookbook author and food editor James Villas wrote.[57] After a short stint writing for *Gourmet* magazine, Claiborne was hired in 1957 as the first male food editor at the *New York Times*. In that role, he invented the modern restaurant review and authored a series of bestselling cookbooks that reshaped American tastes in the post-World War II era. Like Beard, he was a gay man whose sexuality was never a secret to the people who knew him. His conversation went beyond "salty." The *Times* editor Arthur Gelb said Claiborne "talked about sex compulsively" and was "over the top."[58] Villas described how the first time he met Claiborne, they "camped like two old queens who'd known each other for years."[59] Gael Greene, the restaurant reviewer for *New York* magazine, said Claiborne frequently boasted about how many straight men he had fellated, leaving no doubt about how many he must have propositioned.[60] In short, Claiborne was as out of the closet as a gay man could be in mid-century America and still keep his job.[61] As with Beard, Claiborne was often euphemistically described in print as "a bachelor."[62]

Although Claiborne didn't have the same level of personal celebrity as Beard, he was widely read and widely known in the United States. He was a public character, not simply a writer and editor. His hiring at the *New York Times* had itself been newsworthy. "Revolutionary News!" one newspaper announced, the *Times* food department had been taken over by "a MAN!"[63] Before Claiborne, the newspaper food beat had been considered a female preserve; the section of the newspaper in which food writing appeared was known as the "women's page." After World War II, there was a big boom in food journalism. In 1950, *Editor & Publisher* reported that the number of food editors had more than doubled in a single year from 240 to 561. Many of the most important women in food journalism lived in New York City, including Jane Nickerson, food editor at the *New York Times*, and Cecily Brownstone, the Associate Press editor who invented green bean casserole as a Thanksgiving dish.[64] When Nickerson decided to move to Florida, James Beard put forward his friend Helen Evans Brown for the job.[65] They assumed that Nickerson's replacement would be a woman. Both Beard and Brown were surprised to discover that Claiborne had got the job. "Isn't that awful?" Brown wrote to Beard, dismissing Claiborne as a "phoney."[66] She probably meant this put-down as a reference to Claiborne's effeminacy. Brown disliked it when men were "too swishy."[67] Claiborne, who had been outed as a "sissy" by his gym teacher when he was a child in Mississippi and then tormented by other students for the rest of his school years, fit that definition to a tee.[68]

Claiborne was always more open about his sexuality than Beard. He made no attempt to extricate his sexual identity from his food writing.

He self-consciously situated himself within the long tradition of queer gastronomical writing, especially in his 1965 *A Cookbook for Booksellers*. This small volume, only thirty-six pages long, matched portraits of authors and quotations from their works with recipes. Most of the eleven authors Claiborne included were queer men. Any gay man steeped in queer subculture who picked up the volume would have recognized the roster, and understood Claiborne as a fellow traveler. The book opened with a romantic profile of Lord Byron and a quote from his most sexually disreputable poem, *Don Juan*: "'An oyster may be cross'd in love,' – and why? Because he mopeth idly in his shell." Opening with oysters set the sexual tone for what was to follow. Along with Byron, Claiborne included Marcel Boulestin, Norman Douglas, Marcel Proust, Henry James, and Osbert Sitwell. He also included Tobias Smollet, whose character Earl Strutwell, from his 1748 novel *Roderick Random*, is considered to be one of the first gay characters in British literature, and William Makepeace Thackeray, whom the critic Joseph Litvak uses to illustrate his theory that sophisticated tastes are always read in the English literary tradition as sexually impure or gay.[69]

Borrowing a phrase from Proust, Litvak argues that "*every* gourmet is a strange gourmet," or in other words, that the excessive tastes of the sophisticate are viewed as "inherently gay."[70] This cultural precept made it impossible for Beard and Claiborne to entirely hide their sexualities from their audiences, whether they wished to or not. Beard relaxed his efforts to hide his sexuality at the end of his life. He acquired jeans, a nail-studded belt, and "the whole Village outfit," and went out with friends to hustler bars, prompting one of his assistants to complain in 1975 that he was "losing all sense of dignity and decency."[71] His 1964 memoir had slyly alluded to discovering that the "gay life was for me" when he was a child, but an unpublished memoir he began working on in the early 1980s stated plainly that he knew he was gay by the time he was seven and that it was "time to talk about that now."[72] Claiborne publicly outed himself in his 1982 memoir, which shocked readers not because he disclosed his homosexuality, but because he opened the book with an affectionate memory about the incestuous boyhood encounters he had with his father.[73] Beard's efforts to blend in with so-called 1970s "clone" culture and Claiborne's lusty accounts of his father's penis brought their sexuality to the foreground in ways that couldn't be obscured by the fiction of the "open secret."[74] But their self-disclosures only elaborated what had always been implicit knowledge.

The strong association between gay men and gourmet cooking in the postwar era led to suspicions that straight men in the food world were closeted homosexuals. Rumors swirled around Julia Child's aesthete husband Paul Child, who introduced her to fine French cooking and who was regarded by some as the Svengali in control of her career. In April 1955, when Paul Child had a State Department posting in Plittersdorf, Germany, he received a summons recalling him to Washington, DC. He and Julia hoped that he was finally getting promoted. Instead, it turned out he was being investigated. Two FBI agents reading from a foot-high dossier grilled Child about his leftist connections before shifting gears to his sexuality. Someone had reported that Child was a homosexual, a charge seemingly generated by his gourmet reputation. The agents demanded that he drop his pants. Child angrily refused. Shortly afterwards, he retired from the government and the couple moved back to the United States.[75]

Evan Jones, the husband of Julia Child's editor Judith Jones, also suffered a McCarthyite interrogation into his politics and sexuality. In 1957, the Joneses were living in Alstead, New Hampshire, where Judith was working as a substitute teacher while Evan worked on a book. One day, a member of the local school board came to ask questions: Why did Judith wear her hair loose? Why did Evan have a beard? Just as the school board member was leaving, "he shot one last remark at Evan: 'I hear you like to cook, too.'" Evan Jones's reputation as a gourmet, like Paul Child's, had provoked suspicions that he was homosexual, and ergo, by the logic of the Red/Lavender Scare, a communist.[76] This interrogation prompted the Joneses to leave New England for New York City, where Judith was hired as an editor at Knopf and became the acquiring editor for Julia Child's *Mastering the Art of French Cooking*, after she and Evans cooked the manuscript's boeuf bourguignon recipe and declared it the best they had tasted since leaving France.

Julia Child's experience of having Paul investigated for homosexuality did not turn her into a crusader for gay rights. She used homophobic slurs like "pedalo," "fairy," and "faggot," both in conversation and in her correspondence. Despite her close friendship with James Beard, and her support for other talented gay chefs she knew, Child voiced resentment about the predominance of gay men in the food world. "I wish all the men in OUR profession in the USA were not *pedals!*" she wrote to her French collaborator Simca, yearning for a culinary culture more like that in France, which was dominated by straight men. She worried that the growing number of gay men in the industry would chase away straight men who might consider cooking. "It is like the ballet filled with homosexuals, so no one else wants to go into it," she wrote, and she "urged a few close friends in the food world to encourage the 'de-fagification' of cooking."[77] This nasty fantasy was not attached to any programmatic agenda, but Child was sued for discrimination, late in life, by a gay candidate who was rejected for a position at the American Institute of Wine and Food, which she established with Robert Mondavi and Richard Graff.[78]

The rise of the gay food world

The predominance of gay men in the postwar Anglo-American food world sparked gossip and homophobic reaction, even from liberal do-gooders with close gay friends, like Julia Child. All the same, the food industry was a far more welcoming professional space for queer men in the 1950s, 1960s, and 1970s than the corporate world or government. In the wake of Boulestin, Beard, and Claiborne, a gay gourmet food world took shape that extended beyond writers to food merchants, hoteliers, and restaurateurs.

After the death of Marcel Boulestin in France in 1943, Robert Carrier, a "dark, handsome, affable bachelor" (actually, a gay man with a life partner) took his place in postwar Britain, publishing cookbooks and recipe cards, running restaurants and hotels, and hosting a campy television cooking show. Carrier had grown up in the United States but learned to cook from his French grandmother and from a stint at a restaurant called Chez Fifine in St. Tropez. Like Boulestin and Beard, he made his entrée to the food industry via dinner parties, which he hosted while living in London in the 1950s. An editor at *Harper's Bazaar* who attended one of his dinners was so impressed that she hired him as a food writer, launching his career. His recipes, like Boulestin's, embraced pleasurable excess, calling for large amounts of cream, butter, brandy, and garlic at a time when British eaters still regarded garlic with deep suspicion.[79] Not that cream and butter were entirely free from suspicion. In a 1973 cook-book, the English writer Jane Grigson said that many of her countrymen regarded cream and butter as "a sexual perversion."[80]

Another bright light in the London gay gourmet world of the 1950s was Le Matelot, a restaurant on Elizabeth Street, in Kensington, run by a psychiatrist named Hillary James, and inspired by the recipes of Elizabeth David, as well as by James's travels in the south of France. Le Matelot, a French word meaning sailor, had campy ashtrays, blue-rimmed white ceramic with a picture in the center, drawn in the style of Tom of Finland, depicting three hunky sailors dressed in tight-fitting clothing that emphasized all their bulges. The food writer and television host Fanny Craddock, who looked like a drag queen but was in fact a married woman, reviewed the restaurant in a 1955 restaurant guidebook and described the waitstaff at Le Matelot as "young, gay, inconsequential and yet highly efficient." If that didn't send a clear enough message to readers, her closing paragraph left no confusion: "It is a delightfully uninhibited, scatty little place, canopied with fish-nets, discreetly lit and gay, gay, gay, in our stuffed shirt old town."[81] Le Matelot wasn't simply a restaurant run by a gay man, it was a gay restaurant, with a gay staff, gay decor, and a gay clientele.[82]

Le Matelot was not London's only gay restaurant. The Lyons' Coventry Street Corner House in the 1950s was well known for its "flamboyantly queer" waiters. Since the 1920s, queer men in London had frequented many of the Lyons' tea houses in London. While Lyons' outposts were typically genteel, gay men also socialized in rougher places, like Harry's Restaurant and Sam's Café, both of which attracted a mixture of female and male prostitutes as well as criminals. Most queer restaurants, how-ever, were not underworld resorts. The Café Royal attracted an elite queer crowd from Oscar Wilde's day onwards. Middle-class gay men socialized in a shifting range of restaurants whose proprietors and waiters either turned a blind eye to their clientele or actively recruited them. Literary types gathered at Gennaro's in New Compton Street as early as the 1930s. Queer men also clustered in Soho cafés like the Little Hut on Greek Street, the Alexandra on Rathbone Place, and the Bar-B-Q on Frith Street.[83]

Cafeterias and low-priced automats in New York were also frequented by gay men beginning in the 1920s and 1930s. Numerous outposts of

An ashtray from "Le Matelot," a 1950s restaurant run by London psychiatrist Hillary James. The blue-rimmed oval dish features three muscly sailors wearing tight clothes that feature all their bulges.
The Queerseum

the Childs' coffee shop chain attracted raucous gay crowds.[84] Finer restaurants catered to gay clienteles as well. In New York City, an antiques dealer named Johnny Nicholson and his romantic partner Karl Bissinger opened a restaurant in 1948 in the back garden of their antique shop in the shadow of the Queensboro Bridge. The "Café Nicholson" had an overstuffed aesthetic that Nicholson described as *"fin de siècle* Caribbean of Cuba style." Multiple revolving fans blew over white marble nudes, a bronze slave boy, Tiffany lamps, decorative wall tiles, gilt mirrors, and potted palms, all overseen by a parrot named Lolita. In the kitchen,

Nicholson's fifty–fifty partner in the business, a Black labor activist named Edna Lewis, cooked up a simple menu of gazpacho, roast chicken with herbs, steak with béarnaise sauce, and either chocolate soufflé or a ripe pear with Stilton for dessert. The combination of rococo decor and French cuisine drew a creative queer crowd.

In 1949, Bissinger shot a photo at the restaurant for a magazine article titled "The New Bohemians." Around a table in the garden sat the gay writers Tennessee Williams, who had just won the Pulitzer Prize for *A Streetcar Named Desire*, Gore Vidal, who had just published *The City and the Pillar*, the first postwar queer novel not to kill off its main character, and Donald Windham, who was working on his own gay novel, *The Dog Star*, which would be published the following year. They were joined at the table by the bisexual painter Buffie Johnson, a former lover of Patricia Highsmith, and by the ballerina Tanaquil Le Clercq. Waiting on this lively lunch was the café's waitress, a Black woman named Virginia Reed who was renowned for her quick wit and bawdy sense of humor.[85] The restaurant became a hit among gay men, which Craig Claiborne acknowledged in euphemistic language when he reviewed the restaurant, calling attention to its "whimsy."[86]

Claiborne was also an enthusiastic supporter of another early queer restaurateur, Christopher Blake, based in New Orleans. Blake was a World War II veteran who described himself as the last protégé of Gertrude Stein, although it might be fairer to call him the last protégé of Alice B. Toklas. Posted in Paris at the end of World War II, Blake befriended the two women as Stein was dying from stomach cancer. Toklas cooked meals for the hungry young GI and taught him to make mayonnaise and hollandaise sauce. Blake remained in Paris until the early 1950s. "Six formative years in Paris tend to orient one's interest toward sex or cuisine," Blake later reflected in a cookbook.[87] In his case, the city did both.

After leaving France, Blake moved to New Orleans and began hosting dinner parties for friends in his Faubourg Marigny house on Chartres Street. Claiborne wrote about these dinner parties in the *New York Times* in 1965, giving Blake the encouragement he needed to open his eponymous restaurant in the Swoop-Duggins house in the Upper Central Business District, previously home to one of the longest-running brothels in the city.[88] During its heyday, Christopher Blake's earned a reputation for debauchery, including hosting "bath parties where they would fill the bath tubs with Bloody Mary's."[89] A 1970 review mentions customers staggering from the unlimited Bloody Marys served at brunch.[90]

By the early 1960s, when gay bar owner Bob Damron began publishing guidebooks to queer-friendly establishments in the United States, there were restaurants all over the country that catered to a gay clientele: The Brass Rail in Detroit; The Bleecker Restaurant in Albany; The Candlelight in Miami; Carroll's Tavern in Washington, DC; Chances in Witchita; The Copper Lantern in Miami; The Crown Hotel Coffee Shop in Providence; Diamond Lil's in Phoenix; Drury Lane in Philadelphia; Entre Nous in Los Angeles; Fedora in Manhattan; Flame in Ann Arbor; The Golden Gate in St. Louis; Hoot Mon in Charlotte; Huddle Restaurant in Indianapolis; Jorge's in Cincinnati; Kiri Café in Columbus; Mammy's Pancake House in Birmingham; Mena Café in Evansville; Oceana in Long Beach; Pier 16 in Sausalito; Pink Adobe in Santa Fe; Pizza Palace in Chattanooga; Pub Restaurant in New Haven; Quarrier Diner in Charlestown; Swiss Chalet in Kailua; Town & Country in Rochester; Twelve Carver in Boston; University Grille in Pittsburgh. This list is just a sampling of restaurants included in Damron's 1965 edition.[91]

After Stonewall, queer restaurants came out of the closet. While Café Nicholson and Christopher Blake's manifested a queer culinary aesthetic, they were succeeded a decade later by restaurants that loudly broadcast their gayness. In the late 1970s, lovers Paul Doll and Tom Struve opened Flamingo's Café & Bar in New Orleans less than a mile from Christopher Blake's, becoming the first openly gay business in the neighborhood. The restaurant was decorated with pink flamingos, the chef was a drag queen named Mina, and the menu was filled with campy puns. A cocktail named "The Stinger 'Struve'" was advertised as a drink "that separates the boys from the other boys." The "Flamingo" cocktail was nicknamed the "butch man's downfall." Customers who ordered the eggplant sticks were told to send them back to the kitchen if they were limp. Naturally, the restaurant specialized in quiche. In a 1979 review, Tom FitzMorris called the place a "screaming queen-themed restaurant," a description he borrowed from the owners.[92]

By the 1980s, gay gourmet culture had escaped the confines of camp and the closet. Gay men didn't have to look in the pages of Damron's guides to find a queer restaurant in most large cities. They could look through the windows. A 1980 article in the Toronto gay newspaper *Body Politic* described "gay eateries" as "by-products of liberation."[93] San Francisco had a particularly notable gay restaurant scene. A humor piece published in the *Bay Area Reporter* in 1982 offered instructions in how to determine whether a restaurant was gay, from reading the menu (quiche was gay, scrambled eggs were not) to assessing the waiters' dress code (Levi's 501s and a tight tee-shirt were gay, a blue polyester dress was not, unless a man was wearing it).[94] Some of the city's best restaurants were uninhibited gay spaces, like the Zuni Café, opened by Billy West in 1979. The innovative Southwestern cooking kept the tables full. Elizabeth David ate there in 1981, after which it became her favorite restaurant in San Francisco. "Ask for Billy. Say I sent you," David told a friend planning a visit to the city.[95]

The expansion of the gay restaurant scene went hand in hand with the expansion of an interest in cooking among gay men. To service the growing focus on fine food in gay male culture, aspiring gourmets could turn to the large number of high-end grocery, wine, and kitchenware stores run by gay men. Bob Balzer, whose family ran a gourmet food store in Los Angeles, took over as the wine buyer at his family's store during his late twenties. He published the first important book on California wines in 1941, and then served as wine editor for the *LA Times*. In 1963, he and his lover James Willett opened an incredibly expensive destination restaurant called the Tirol, in the mountains outside of Palm Springs. He also sold expensive gourmet groceries at the site. In the mid-1960s, the Tirol was known as the most beautiful restaurant in California, and it was frequented by movie stars and politicians, as well as by the gay men who had begun to settle in Palm Springs. When financial problems forced Balzer to close the Tirol, he opened new restaurants and continued his career as the preeminent wine journalist covering California's growing industry.[96]

Perhaps Balzer's greatest competitor in the world of California wine journalism was also a gay man, Gerald Asher, who had grown up in Britain and worked as a wine merchant in London before relocating to San Francisco. Asher was the wine editor for *Gourmet* magazine.[97] Another looming figure in the California gay gourmet world was Chuck Williams, who began selling French cookware in Sonoma, California in the 1950s, and built an empire of hundreds of stores. He also published more than two hundred cookbooks, which sold millions of copies.[98] James Beard, who knew both men, introduced Asher to Williams during a visit to San Francisco in the 1970s.[99] Williams was also friends with Elizabeth David, who wrote articles for the Williams-Sonoma newsletter.[100] Many of David's close friends throughout her life were gay men, including a number who worked in the food business in the United States and Britain.[101]

Gay men established prominent gourmet dry goods, catering, and wine shops on the US east coast as well. In 1966, lovers Bert Greene and Denis Vaughan co-founded The Store in Amagansett, at the eastern tip of Long Island, a high-end takeout shop that specialized in pâtés and lemon mousse and other French dishes. Greene and Vaughan wrote a cookbook together in 1974 that was filled with gossipy asides about French gastronomy, the demi-monde, and queer history. They named a recipe "Eggs Buckingham" after George Villiers, the first Duke of Buckingham, who was notorious for being the lover of King James I, a reputation which – along with his corruption – got him exiled and eventually assassinated.[102] In the eighties, Greene became the food columnist for the *Daily News*, assisted in his writing by a subsequent lover, Phillip Schultz. The founders of the gourmet chain Dean & DeLuca, which eventually expanded to over forty stores, were cheesemonger Giorgio DeLuca, who liked to shock the old women who visited his shop by comparing the flavor of his cheeses to "angel's cum," and business manager Joel Dean, whose boyfriend (and business partner) Jack Ceglic designed the store's much-copied look.[103] Dean & DeLuca also sold prepared food cooked by James Beard's protégé (boyfriend) Felipe Rojas-Lombardi.

Other Beard love interest/protégés became prominent in the New York food world. One of his earliest students, John Clancy, wrote influential cookbooks and ran a beloved Greenwich Village restaurant, which claimed to be the first on the east coast to grill food over mesquite wood (the two later had a falling out and became estranged). Gino Cofacci, one of Beard's earliest serious lovers, was sent by Beard to pastry school in Paris and became a successful New York City pastry chef and food writer.[104] Carl Jerome, one of Beard's last protégés, took control of his cooking school and authored cookbooks. Beard also promoted the careers of gay men in the business who had not started as his protégés. He was an early booster of Richard Olney, an American expatriate painter in France and friend of James Baldwin, who began publishing food journalism in his adopted country in the 1960s, and whose influential *The French Menu Cookbook*, published in 1970, immediately elevated him to the stratosphere of the American cooking establishment.[105] Gay men were not the only recipients of Beard's imprimatur. He also promoted many women friends' careers. Beard had "an enormous number of friends, acquaintances, and hangers-on," in the words of one of his self-described hangers-on.[106]

But if the postwar Anglo-American food world was defined by tangled networks of relationships in which gay men figured in high numbers, it wasn't all rainbows and unicorns. Everybody knew everybody, and everybody talked about everybody behind their backs. This gossip often had a sexual edge, whether it originated from queer or straight people. James Beard was an unrepentant kibitzer who always had "some delicious gossip of the food world." Stephen Spector, Cecily Brownstone, Helen McCully, and many of his other friends all claimed to get daily phone calls from Beard with the most recent updates.[107] Beard joyfully recounted a "rather riotous" food industry party in 1966 with a guest list that "included all the *prime donne* of the business . . . It was like a great party backstage at the opera – everyone complimenting everyone else and then picking flaws behind backs."[108] One of the food world's great appeals, for Beard, was that it offered the same opportunities for bitchiness as the theater world.

When Beard reviewed Richard Olney's first book enthusiastically, Olney wrote to thank him since "the tight little world of American gastronomic journalism is, as I understand it, highly competitive and newcomers are not always welcomed."[109] But Olney's memoir, which drew on his letters, was a masterclass in backbiting. Olney accused Beard of plagiarizing recipes and said "his selfishness and his willingness to use friends dishonestly knew no bounds and prompted no remorse." Olney described M. F. K. Fisher as "essentially empty-headed" with "no palate," and wrote she "eats practically nothing and drinks tumblers-full of sweet vermouth all day and her writing is silly, pretentious drivel."[110] Fisher wasn't above pointing out people's drinking habits, saying that Michael Field "drank a lot of vodka and preferred to eat deli sandwiches over any pâté en croûte."[111] Olney also called the Childs bitter, destructive, and anti-French, and said Julia had a "sugar-coated barbed tongue."[112] Julia Child's letters show her own participation in this network. "Let me know any news and gossip, SVP," she wrote to Beard when they first became friends. Beard and Child gossiped about Craig Claiborne. He was "bitter and destructive and rather disagreeable," Beard wrote; Child agreed that Claiborne had "gotten a little sour." She also called Michael Field a publicity hog, Narcisse Chamberlain a people-eater, and described her collaborator Simca Beck as hell to work with. Child wasn't above passing on second-hand gossip either, like the fact that Sybille Bedford said her old lover Evelyn Gendel was a bad cook.[113]

The gossipy quality of the postwar food world read as peculiarly gay to many of its participants. The "gay gossip" was a cliché on both sides of the Atlantic. Gossip, which had historically been regarded as a malicious feminine behavior, came to be associated with supposedly effeminate gay men in the twentieth century. This association reflected the stigmatization of homosexuality, but as one historian points out, gossip also "drew upon concepts and logics with close ties to queer identity before the decriminalisation of homosexual acts: exposure, revelation and self-deception."[114] The link between gayness and gossip, in short, was not wholly imaginary. In fact, gossip was a constitutive element of queer camp culture in the postwar era, especially within artistic circles.[115]

During the early 1960s, same-sex sexuality escaped the confines of gossip and became increasingly a matter of public discussion, a shift reflected in sensationalistic headlines in mainstream periodicals and newspapers. "Growth of Overt Homosexuality in City Provokes Wide Concern," screamed a 1963 *New York Times* headline. The second paragraph singled out the Heights Supper Club in Brooklyn, on Montague Street, as an example of this disturbing trend.[116] *Time* magazine's 1966 exposé "The Homosexual in America" complained about the queer double entendres in Rock Hudson movies, and called out Doubleday Book Shops for running "smirking ads for *The Gay Cookbook*."[117] Gay food culture was coming out of the closet, moving from an open secret to open knowledge.

Queer cookbooks

Published in 1965, *The Gay Cookbook*, written by Lou Rand Hogan, a former steward and cook for the Matson Cruise Line, was the first expressly queer cookbook. The front cover pictured a slim man in a ribboned apron holding a steak by one limp-wristed hand over an outdoor grill, besides which were printed the words: "The complete compendium of campy cuisine and menus for men . . . or what have you." From its front matter – which announced "all rights reserved, Mary" – through its chapter titles – like "In Your Oven!" – *The Gay Cookbook* embraced camp. In the introduction, Hogan explained that with the expansion in new cookbook titles to fill every marketing niche, a "mad, mad, mad Editor" suggested to him "why don't you people have a cookbook? After all, you're supposed to be 'one-in-six,' and that's a lot of cooking!" The one-in-six figure, taken from the 1948 Kinsey Report, highlights the earnest context behind this humorous title. Since the Kinsey Report had revealed the high percentage of US men with same-sex sexual experiences, the cone of silence surrounding the subject of homosexuality had undergone a gradual shattering, to the point that a "gay cookbook" could be published and even sold in one of the country's largest bookstore chains.[118]

As groundbreaking as Hogan's cookbook was, its sexual ribaldry paled in comparison to another queer cookbook published a mere five years later, in the wake of Stonewall. In 1970, the writer Gore Vidal's lover, Howard Austen, published *The Myra Breckinridge Cookbook* in tribute to the transsexual anti-heroine of Vidal's 1968 novel, *Myra Breckinridge*, which had been adapted into a 1970 film starring Raquel Welch. "Anybody who likes sex and food can't be all bad," announced the epigraph. The cookbook topped Hogan's in campiness, including recipes like "Cumin Covered Cock," "Flaming Faggot Trout," and "Bearded Oysters." Sexual puns also appeared throughout the text introducing the recipes, in Breckinridge's voice. A section on quick seductions instructed readers that "your door's peephole can well be the glory hole of your future," and advised readers to always be prepared "even if it is only a jar of peanut butter or a tube of jelly." The cookbook was also chockablock with references to queer icons, including Queen Christina of Sweden, Rudolph Valentino, and Alice B. Toklas. But, as in *The Gay Cookbook*, the campiness couldn't fully disguise a more earnest message. "There are those who frown upon eating and even upon sex as belonging to a decadent society," but eating and sex should be regarded as arts, Austen argued. Those who denied themselves the pleasures were "incapable of taking their seat at the table of life's banquet." Austen's cookbook sought to liberate readers to embrace their appetites.[119]

In the 1980s, the genre of gay cookbooks took off. There were political cookbooks, like *The Political Palate: A Feminist Vegetarian Cookbook* (1980) published by the lesbian collective that ran the famous Bloodroot Restaurant in Westport, Connecticut, which argued that the raising and slaughtering of animals was part of a patriarchal system that also included the control of women's bodies. There were romantic cookbooks like *Dinner for Two: A Gay Sunshine Cookbook* (1981), which built on the author's discovery that "lots of gay men could cook," while acknowledging that most did not have the families of four or five that most cookbooks anticipated in their recipes. There were fine-dining cookbooks, like *The Gay Gourmet Cookbook* (1980), advertised for mail order in gay newspapers. There were fundraising cookbooks, like *The Whoever Said Dykes Can't Cook Cookbook* (1983), which solicited recipes from readers of lesbian magazines, and offered proportions suitable for "those sensual magnificent feasts: lesbian potlucks." There were health food cookbooks, like *Red Beans & Rice: Recipes for Lesbian Health and Wisdom* (1986), which offered dubious nutritional advice, or in the words of the back cover, "a full course dinner of slightly wacked-out, politically and spiritually conscious Lesbian thought." And there were campy cookbooks, like the *You've Had Worse Things in Your Mouth Cookbook* (1985), filled with salacious jokes, and promises like "this recipe will snatch a faggot away from a Judy Garland movie."[120] By the 1980s, the gay food world contained multitudes.

As *The Whoever Said Dykes Can't Cook Cookbook* had suggested, during the post-Stonewall era potlucks, collective meals where everyone brought a dish to share, became a central signifier of lesbian subculture. Just as a taste for gourmet food marked a man as gay in the postwar era, an appetite for tofu and lentil potluck dishes marked a woman as a lesbian in the 1970s and 1980s. The humor writer Gail Sausser devoted a chapter of her 1986 book *Lesbian Etiquette* to potlucks, which had "played an important role in lesbian history." She traced this tradition back to the Paris Left Bank lesbian gatherings of the 1920s ("what was then called a salon but what we now know was a potluck"). Sausser had been to so many potlucks since coming out that she "once threatened to write a cookbook called '1,001 Things to Make for a Lesbian Potluck.'"[121]

In a more serious vein, the lesbian potluck tradition can be traced to an anti-capitalist political tradition emerging out of the gay liberation movement in the late 1960s. Lesbian-feminist newsletters and periodicals from the 1970s are filled with notices of upcoming potlucks.[122] At potlucks, lesbian-feminists asserted identities that rejected mainstream meat-eating, patriarchal, market-oriented culture. As one student of the tradition summarized:

> Lesbians consider potlucks not only distinctly lesbian forms of expressive behavior but perhaps even the quintessential lesbian food event. The kind of food prepared, the way the food is displayed, and the way preparation tasks are allotted all express core values of this folk group, promoting a sense of collaboration and eliminating opportunities for competition between participants. Additionally, the potluck participants use the event as an opportunity to extend the scope of their alternative families and to reassert existing ties between community members.[123]

The tofu, nutloaf, and brown rice potluck tradition has often been castigated as anti-hedonic, a sort of mirror image of gay male culture during the 1970s and 1980s. But the divide between gay male food culture and lesbian food culture may have been less sharp than the stereotypes suggest. Lesbian writers, including lesbian cookbook authors, emphasized the sensual quality of these shared meals, while queer men also turned to the potluck for community building. In the Bay Area, Nikos Diaman, a member of the Gay Liberation Front, began organizing "Hyacinthus Potlucks" in the mid-1970s for gay men and lesbians of Greek ancestry. A decade later, Diamon expanded his efforts, establishing a San Francisco group called "Epicures Unlimited" that organized bimonthly "gay gourmet potlucks" for men and women. The invitation for women may have been mostly aspirational; a sign-up sheet for a September 1987 potluck included only male names. The dishes served at these Gay Gourmet potlucks didn't stick to the vegetarian format of their lesbian counterparts.

One eager participant wrote to the organizer describing his repertoire of chicken and beef curries. Other dishes served up included buzzy ingredients from the hot restaurants of the day, like "corn meal-cream cheese pastry shells filled with green salsa and fresh corn," which would have fit perfectly on the menu at the very hip – and very gay – Zuni Café on Market Street.[124]

Diaman's were not the only potlucks oriented to gay men in San Francisco in the 1980s. The group Professionals Over Thirty also held regular potluck dinners. Advertisements for a "Gay Gourmet Group" began appearing in the *Bay Area Reporter* in 1987.[125] The tradition spread outside the Bay Area as well. Gay men in Toronto organized a "Gay Gourmet" dining club for men with an interest in cooking and restaurants in the early 1980s.[126] The Bisexual Forum, the first specifically bisexual identity advocacy group, hosted an "erotic food partie" to recruit new members in New York City in the late 1970s.[127] For queer men, as well as women, eating food together served important community-building functions, in addition to feeding the appetites.

All the waiters are dead

The community-serving function of the gay food world became all too necessary in the early 1980s, when the AIDS epidemic began to claim the lives of large numbers of gay men. Zuni Café in San Francisco was one of the first queer restaurants to be hit hard. By 1982, its founder Billy West was sick from HIV, the virus that causes AIDS. Many of the restaurant's waiters soon sickened as well.[128] Zuni, which had participated in the city's gay political activism from its opening, began to host memorial services and fundraisers for people with AIDS.[129]

HIV/AIDS tore through the gay food community with the same cruelty with which it decimated other gay artistic communities. Waiting tables was a profession that had long attracted gay men, and entire fronts of house were wiped out by AIDS-related illnesses. Another article in the *Bay Reporter*, from 1981, noted how many of the waiters and managers even at the city's straight restaurants were gay.[130] The author of the cheeky *Bay Area Reporter* article on how to identify gay restaurants, Mike Hippler, worked as a popular waiter at Vanelli's Seafood Restaurant on Pier 39 for seven years before he succumbed to AIDS in 1991.[131]

Waitstaff were also hit hard in America's leading restaurant city. In a 1993 interview, the actor Matthew Modine recalled that "When I moved to New York, I was a chef in a restaurant, and to the best of my knowledge all the waiters are dead. They were some of the first to go before they called it gay-related immune deficiency. They died of colds? That was in '79–'80–'81."[132] People told similar stories about restaurants across the country that lost large numbers of waiters and managers to the virus, like the Coventry and the King Lear in Washington, DC and Pesca in New York City.[133]

Chefs and food writers were also hit hard by the virus, although it can be difficult to judge from the listed causes of death in the men's obituaries. The likely casualties included men within James Beard's circle. Stephen Spector, a former art dealer whose restaurant Le Plaisir on the Upper East Side brought nouvelle cuisine to Manhattan, and who gossiped with Beard on the phone most every morning, died in 1985 at the age of forty-nine from a "long illness."[134] Felipe Rojas-Lombardi, who had progressed from Beard's assistant to become the founding chef of Dean & DeLuca, and who is often credited with bringing tapas to the United States, died in 1991 of "degenerative osteoperosis" at age forty-six.[135] Richard Sax, creator of the test kitchen for *Food & Wine*, who worked with Richard Olney on his Time-Life cookbook series and authored four cookbooks of his own, died at age forty-six of "lung cancer" in 1995.[136] Obituaries of Bill Neal, founder of Crook's Corner in Chapel Hill, North Carolina, a restaurant often cited as launching the new Southern cuisine, said he died of "pneumonia" in 1991, although posthumous biographies have since clarified that he died from AIDS.[137] Ernest Matthew Mickler, author of the bestselling 1986 cookbook *White Trash Cooking*, did not hide his AIDS diagnosis, but his family still listed the cause of death in his 1988 obituary as "bone cancer."[138]

Some chefs with AIDS were more public about the origin of their illnesses. When Herb Finger, a restaurant owner and caterer in Fair Oaks, California who was at the center of a circle of "gay gourmand friends," died in 1987, his lover Dirk Fullmer published an obituary in a local queer paper that stated the cause was AIDS.[139] Mark Early, a New York City chef who cooked meals for people with AIDS, was also publicly acknowledged as a casualty of the epidemic when he died in 1987.[140] Likewise, obituaries of Ronald Ross Huber, a prominent

Chicago chef and AIDS activist, clearly stated his cause of death in 1993.[141]

Restaurant owners had practical reasons to hide their chefs' and staffs' deaths from AIDS-related illnesses. Rumors about sick employees could destroy a business, as paranoid customers avoided eating there.[142] Customers shunned Herb Finger's restaurant when news of his health status became public, and he lost a job catering Governor Deukmejian's social functions.[143] A street preacher in Chattanooga, Tennessee, offered a bounty of US$100 for each person who identified a gay waiter, arguing they were a threat to public health.[144] Some states tried to pass laws banning gay men, or people with AIDS, from working in restaurants. Right-wing activists in California in the mid-1980s warned that passage of an employment discrimination statute protecting gay men and lesbians would prevent the passage of a law banning gay men with AIDS from working in restaurants in the state.[145] Republicans in Oklahoma added a plank to their 1987 party platform calling for a law banning all gay people from working in restaurants.[146]

While restaurants were frequent sites of death and discrimination during the first decade of the AIDS epidemic, they also played key roles in fundraising for HIV research and for social programs to help people with AIDS. The first big glitzy fundraiser held in San Francisco to support AIDS research, in early 1985, started with a musical event at the opera and closed with an afterparty at Stars, the chic restaurant operated by the gay chef Jeremiah Tower. Stars had already lost two of its staff to AIDS the previous year, and Tower's former boss at Chez Panisse, Tom Guernsey, would die from the disease within years. The 1985 event proved the first of many Tower took part in, raising thousands of dollars, as well as criticisms from those who saw him as a self-promoter.[147] Gay newspapers from the late 1980s are filled with notices of AIDS fundraisers held at restaurants, particularly in hard-hit cities like San Francisco. Chefs also contributed to AIDS service organizations that provided meals for sick and homebound people, like Project Open Hand and God's Love We Deliver.[148]

The AIDS epidemic sparked the emergence of its own category of queer cookbooks, published as fundraisers to care for the sick and dying. Congregation Sha'ar Zahav in San Francisco published *Out of Our Kitchen Closets: San Francisco Gay Jewish Cooking* in 1987, mixing endless kugel recipes with Zunified touches, like "latkes nouvelle California" which called for blue corn tortilla crumbs, and suggested garnishes of sushi, kiwi, or wild raspberry chutney.[149] The city's inclusive Metropolitan Community Church followed Sha'ar Zahav's example, dedicating its fundraising cookbook published in the 1990s to those lost to AIDS.[150] Robert Lehmann, who was the chef at Philadelphia's Metropolitan AIDS Neighborhood Nutrition Alliance (MANNA), providing meals to homebound people with AIDS, published *Cooking for Life: A Guide to Nutrition and Food Safety for the HIV-Positive Community*, revealing a trend in gay food culture away from gastronomic excess toward a focus on nutrition.[151] Some have treated this shift as a betrayal of the spirit of queer food.[152] But even at the nadir of despair, gay gourmets found room for sexy, campy humor. In his AIDS humor zine *Diseased Pariah News*, the satirist Beowulf Thorne published a column titled "Get Fat, Don't Die," from 1990 until his death in 1999. His column included recipes for dishes to counter the effect of AIDS wasting syndrome, like shakes made from Ovaltine, protein powder, and ice cream, and bowls of cereal with extra whipped cream. The zine also published cheesecake photos of Thorne and his fellow editors, skeletal figures in full view.[153] Ultimately, HIV/AIDS destroyed countless lives, but even at the nadir of the epidemic, gay gourmet culture survived to entertain the appetites.

TEN

Foodies

Investigative reporter Frank Lalli broke a lot of stories for *Forbes*; only one of those stories resulted in a full-page advertisement promoting his work in the *New York Times*. In March 1976, Lalli made a bold announcement in a special food-themed issue of the stalwart financial magazine: "If you cook, you are no longer a sissy; you are sexy." With alliterative elegance, Lalli announced a swelling sea change in Anglo-American food culture. On both sides of the Atlantic, straight people were reclaiming gourmet cooking and fine dining as heterosexual enthusiasms. The fact that Lalli credited this cultural shift in large part to Craig Claiborne, a self-described sissy, didn't appear to provoke any cognitive dissonance.[1] The magazine was so enthusiastic about his article that it celebrated his accomplishment in the *New York Times* with an ad featuring a large photograph of Lalli pouring wine into a saucepan held above a cutting board crowded with prawns and artichokes – foods traditionally regarded as aphrodisiacs – and a caption in bold type reading: "Sexpot." Small print touted Lalli's article as typifying *Forbes*'s cutting-edge coverage of trends that interested American businessmen. The straightening of gourmet food culture would prove to be big business in the decades to follow.[2]

Lalli's article signified a tipping point in a decades-long process. With the rise of sexual liberalism in the 1950s and 1960s, a new wave of food media, from cookbooks to memoirs to television shows and films, celebrated good food as a sexy aspect of straight life. These sources pushed back against cultural norms that treated men's gourmet inclinations as queer and women's alimentary appetites as promiscuous. By the 1970s, these attitudes were outdated. The world of singles bars and zipless fucks had moved beyond treating good food as a perversion. "The beginning of America's love affair with food coincided with the start of the sexual revolution," explained one rosy-eyed chronicler of the so-called food revolution. "By the time the mid-1980s rolled around, it looked like casual sex was becoming the national pastime," and the "appetite was no longer experienced as something sinful or threatening."[3] But this cultural reboot couldn't rescue the word "gourmet" from a generation of negative associations. The word "foodie" arose to take its place.

Both Gael Greene, a restaurant reviewer for *New York* magazine, and Paul Levy, the food and wine editor for the *Observer* in the United Kingdom, claimed to have coined the term.[4] It didn't matter who said it first. The important point was that foodies could be male or female, straight or gay, married or single – as long as they had money to spend on the most recent trendy food products, kitchen tools, and fancy restaurants. The word foodie helped businesses harvest the enormous profits that *Forbes* had promised its readers were ripe for the picking. It's no wonder that some of the gay men and greedy women who had led the revolt against Anglo-American food puritanism in the postwar era hated the word. When Elizabeth David wrote to her cousin Neil Hogg that she despised the word "foodie" and was contemplating writing an essay to that effect, he offered his wholehearted support. "I have never learnt what a 'Foodie' is, but the name is so revolting that I hope you damned them all to eternity," Hogg replied.[5]

The strenuous disapproval from one of their greatest icons could hardly hold back the foodie tide. Foodie culture flourished at the end of the twentieth century. Macho celebrity chefs rose to take the place of the aesthete dandies who had personified gourmet culture. Food companies advertised their products as dude food for macho men. Gradually, good food shed its associations with queerness. By the time of the #MeToo movement, professional kitchens had become far more closely linked to sexual harassment of women, a red flag that the revolution in attitudes toward females in the food world remained incomplete. While the social stigma against women's expression of their alimentary appetites lessened, television shows led by female chefs and food blogs produced by women were routinely dismissed as "food porn." This term, which first emerged in attacks on the writings of Elizabeth David and M. F. K. Fisher, spread to encompass female foodies more broadly. Male foodies liberally threw around the term "food porn" to separate their own epicureanism – recently rescued from the stigma of queerness – from association with the taint of femininity. At the beginning of the twenty-first century, the relationship between food and sex in the Anglo-American imagination remained troubled when it came to women.

Recipes for seduction

The commercial impulse to cash in on food's place in heterosexual romance can be traced back to the early decades of the twentieth century, when publishers, business associations, and food-industry companies began producing cookbooks for new brides. These cookbooks followed in the wake of nineteenth-century cookbooks aimed at women, with their emphasis on managing the household, rather than a focus on hedonic pleasure. One of the earliest, *The Bride's Cook Book* (1908) by Laura Davenport, included sophisticated recipes for lobster timbales, but most were simpler.[6] Another book by the same title, published in San Francisco in 1909, included plain recipes along with encomia on the role that cooking played in marital bliss.[7] Louise Bennett Weaver and Helen Cowles LeCron's *A Thousand Ways to Please a Husband: With Bettina's Best Recipes* (1917) pitched itself to June brides, with a series of chapters that alternated stories of a couple's first year of marriage with suitable recipes. An illustration showed a young white couple, the woman wearing a house dress and bonnet, the man in a sharp business suit, clinched together. The woman holds a baking tray, the man holds a cookie with one bite missing. His eyes are closed in bliss. Underneath a short poem reads: "No, you cannot live on kisses,/Though the honeymoon is sweet,/ Harken, brides, a true word this is,–/Even lovers have to eat." In the foreground, two aproned and toqued putti serve a freshly baked pie. The text kept with nineteenth-century tradition by emphasizing frugality as a domestic virtue, but the title and illustrations, rife with putti, centered romantic love as the genius of the kitchen.[8]

As the booming early twentieth-century advertising industry discovered how effectively romantic love worked as a marketing device, businesses began producing newlywed cookbooks to promote their products. Oftentimes, these booklets were given away in government offices to couples applying for marriage licenses. The front cover of the 1912 *The Bride's Cook Book*, published in San Francisco, sandwiched the gilt-lettered title between advertisements for packed sardines, silver polish, and a jewelry store.[9] The *For the Bride* cookbook distributed in Memphis, Tennessee, included recipes for regional cuisine, like crab gumbo, along with advertisements for local businesses.[10] City-specific editions of *The Bride's Cook Book: A Gift from the Merchant*, distributed

JUNE.

No, you cannot live on kisses,
Though the honeymoon is sweet,
Harken, brides, a true word this is,—
Even lovers have to eat.

An illustration from the opening pages of Louise Bennett Weaver and Helen Cowles LeCron's *A Thousand Ways to Please a Husband* (1917) features a young white couple standing clinched together. The bride is dressed in a bonnet and house dress, and holds a tray of freshly baked cookies. The husband holds one of the cookies in his hand, a bite is missing, his eyes are closed in domestic bliss.

in Los Angeles, San Francisco, Portland, and Seattle, framed the recipes within advertisements for local businesses like milliners, hardware companies, umbrella stores, and pharmacies.[11] A letter from the United States Food Administration tucked inside a 1918 *Bride's Cook Book* informed women that following the cookbook's wheatless and sugarless recipes would support US allies and armies abroad.[12] The 1929 *Cupid's Book* opened with a fillable "Marriage Record" with blank lines for the spouses' names, and the date, time, and place of their ceremony, and included coupons.[13] Eventually, advertisement- and coupon-filled cookbooks fell out of favor, but the genre of cookbooks aimed specifically at brides resurged after World War II, with new contributions like Poppy Cannon's *The Bride's Cookbook* (1954) – a paean to processed food – and Myra Waldo's *1001 Ways to Please a Husband* (1958), which included a series of saccharine dialogues between "Peter" and "Jane," tracing Jane's progress from inexperienced cook to budding gourmet.[14]

While brides' cookbooks never vanished, a new genre of erotic cookbooks emerged in the 1950s that presented cooking as a strategy of courtship, or seduction, rather than as an ingredient of marital harmony. Robert H. Loeb, Jr., the food and drinks editor at *Esquire* and author of the magazine's "Man in the Kitchenette" column, published a trio of seduction cookbooks aimed at men, women, and youth: *Wolf in Chef's Clothing* (1950), *She Cooks to Conquer* (1952), and *Date Bait* (1952). Loeb's authorial voice was far more risqué than the sentimental tone typical of brides' cookbooks. "The art of cooking, like the art of love-making, depends more on the proper use of ingredients than on their exact qualitative measurements," Loeb advised in *Wolf in Chef's Clothing*.[15] Wink, wink. Loeb's cookbook for men marks the emergence of a counter-discourse linking good cooking to heterosexuality that would eventually overpower the stereotype of the gay gourmet.

Loeb's instructions for men included different menus for different varieties of women: the indoor type, the intellectual type, and the 3-B type (brains, bonds, and beauty). For women, Loeb offered parallel advice, dividing men into three types: the somatotonic, the viscerotonic, and the cerebrotonic, or in other words, the muscle man, the gourmand, and the lean and thin type who was "more apt to be a Casanova." Of this final type, Loeb promised, "his taste-buds should be subtly titillated, but once aroused are rewarding." For the sake of appearances, Loeb pitched his seduction advice for women as designed to bag a husband, but he slyly added the caveat "that neither the author, the illustrator, nor the publisher assumes any responsibility for the order in which this book may be used."[16] Another wink, wink. Finally, Loeb's book for teens presented cooking as a seduction tool to be used by youth of either sex. In a double-page illustration, two boys lurk behind a tree, one mixing a salad dressing while reading a cookbook, the other holding a string that leads to a stick holding up a box under which have been set a cake and a pitcher, setting a trap for two young women walking up a path toward them. On the book's cover, the scene of the boys behind the tree is repeated, and the girls are depicted behind their own tree with an identical set-up.[17]

In 1954, Hugh Hefner's new bachelor lifestyle magazine, *Playboy*, followed *Esquire*'s lead and launched a cooking column.[18] Its author, Sidney Aptekar, was a happily married World War II veteran who had grown up in Pennsylvania, the child of grocers, and worked as an executive chef at a gentlemen's club in New York during the 1930s, an experience he wrote about in a *roman-à-clef, The Face in the Aspic* (1944), under the pen name Thomas Mario.[19] The old-fashioned club excluded women from its premises. One chapter of the novel described the collective shock when the club opened its doors to female relatives and friends for one day (the women ended up drinking all the scotch).[20] When Aptekar returned from his military service, he found a changed world. Restaurants in the United States were opening their doors to women, and commensality was becoming increasingly central to heterosexual dating culture.

After seeing the first issue of *Playboy* on the newsstand in December 1953, and noticing its attention to writing, Aptekar pitched an article about the "Pleasures of the Oyster" to Hugh Hefner. He figured that the mollusc's sexual associations would titillate the magazine's readership.[21] Hefner responded positively, so Aptekar followed by volunteering a series of columns that would appeal to "the male appetite" and focus "on the pleasures of eating," as well offering "practical tips as to how a young bachelor and his girlfriend could cook together more easily and delightfully." Hefner agreed, and Aptekar (using the pen name Thomas Mario) worked as *Playboy*'s food and drinks editor for the next twenty years.[22] Aptekar's use of a pen name led many readers, including Craig Claiborne and James Beard, to believe that he must really be a woman. He couldn't possibly be a straight man.

From Aptekar's perspective, having worked in grocery stores and restaurants since the beginning of the century, the early 1950s were a moment of profound change when interest in cooking suddenly became a sign of sophistication for a "young bachelor," like having superior taste in music.[23] Although the gay gourmet reigned supreme, he was beginning to have competition. In his first appearance, in the 1953 novel *Casino Royale*, Ian Fleming's spy hero James Bond modeled the new straight, single, gourmand ideal by explaining to his love interest Vesper Lynd over a gourmet French dinner: "I take ridiculous pleasure in what I eat and drink. It comes partly from being a bachelor." Bond apologizes to Lynd that his epicureanism is "old-maidish really," but as Fleming describes Lynd's growing sexual desire for the handsome Bond during their meal together, the image of the old-maidish (or queer) gourmet is supplanted by a new persona: the seductive epicure.[24]

If James Bond symbolized the masculine ideal that readers of *Playboy* strove to embody, Thomas Mario's columns helped them achieve a connoisseur's knowledge of food and drink. Letters from readers testified to the important role that *Playboy* played in training their palates. "Where else could a small-town yokel like me learn a little about wine and food selection as well as accepted methods of dealing with the fairer sex," wrote a reader from Florida.[25] Aptekar's initial columns in the 1950s included a lot of sexual content to reassure readers that cooking good food – which often meant French food – could be a straight man's hobby.

In "Playboy at the Chafing Dish," from September 1954, Aptekar promised readers "it is possible to have a woman eating out of your hand without ever laying that hand on her, by simply catching her eye with the romantic blue flame of a chafing dish."[26] His Christmas column in 1954 recommended gifting a love interest a bottle of Dutch apricot brandy which "will set her a-tingle." Drinking the brandy would lead her to "forget the pawing and fumbling in the taxicab and the jiujitsu you had to use to extract the first kiss" and "the solid core of her resistance will, of course, liquefy completely. At this point, you stop pouring."[27] In this column, and in others about drinks, Aptekar celebrated alcohol's inhibition-lowering properties while always instructing readers to stop serving before their dates became incapacitated. The goal was to cultivate a mood of enthusiastic mutuality.

In a 1955 column on cheese, Aptekar celebrated women with sexual experience for their superior alimentary tastes: "It's almost impossible to imagine a virgin eating a sharp Roquefort cheese . . . A woman must have heard and told an off-color bon mot or two before she is sufficiently discriminating to see that Italian Ricotta is superior to the cottage cheese salad she ate in the Women's Exchange Tea Room."[28] Even columns that made no references to dating or seduction would use sexual metaphors just to keep the content aggressively straight. The omelet, Aptekar wrote in a 1958 column, was "as luscious as a Renoir nude." A photo illustrating the column pictured a beautiful young woman leaning her head on the shoulder of a man wearing a tux, gazing at him dreamily as he cooks an omelet.[29] The image later appeared on the cover of *The Playboy Gourmet*, a 1961 cookbook. The couple mirror the young marrieds pictured in the opening pages of *A Thousand Ways to Please a Husband*, while flipping the gender roles. Notably, however, the woman in the latter couple isn't eating, as is the man in the earlier couple, and the man in the latter couple is dressed dashingly in a tuxedo, instead of in a domestic apron.

Alongside extracts from Aptekar's columns, *The Playboy Gourmet* was punctuated with pen-and-ink illustrations of Playboy bunnies reclining in martini glasses, sitting on plates, and bursting from beer steins. Just in case readers didn't get the message, Hefner's introduction promised that the recipes weren't for "finicky-fussy" epicures, but were delivered "with a hearty, masculine tang, a well-spiced wit, a refreshingly Rabelaisian sprinkling of exotic and toothsome tidbits from gastronomic lore, and above all with a full-bodied and unabashed appreciation of the sheer sensual pleasure of eating and drinking well."[30] The book was a great success, but Aptekar gradually moved away from the use of sexual allusions in his columns and let the recipes speak for themselves. Perhaps by then it was no longer necessary to play defense against gourmet food's association with gay men. Or maybe Aptekar, a devoted husband since 1934, couldn't be bothered to pretend to be a playboy any longer.[31]

The rise of sexual liberalism during the 1950s, which gave birth to *Playboy*, also led to the publication of magazines and books aimed at single women who enjoyed sex and dating. A specialized genre of food writing aimed at this liberated female audience emerged during the 1960s. Helen Gurley Brown led the way with the publication in 1962 of her advice book *Sex and the Single Girl*, celebrating single women's capacity

The front cover of *The Playboy Gourmet* (1961) promoted a new ideal of the straight male gourmet, which would eventually supplant the dominant stereotype of the gay gourmet.

for a satisfying sex life based on personal desire rather than marital duty. The book ranged widely over topics including where to meet men, how to furnish an apartment, how to dress, how to manage money, and how to entertain. Brown complained that magazine articles aimed at women didn't include color spreads on hosting "seductive little suppers." They were too focused on cooking for households. But Brown recognized that cooking dinner was an effective way to woo a man. She offered readers practical advice, such as creating a "sexy kitchen" by having an extravagant spice shelf that would appeal to men who liked to cook.[32]

Sex and the Single Girl was a runaway bestseller. In 1965, the Hearst Corporation hired Brown to take over the editorship of the failing *Cosmopolitan* magazine. She rescued it from insolvency by refocusing its articles to fit the interests of the growing number of single women embracing their social and economic independence.[33] Under her leadership, *Cosmopolitan* stuck to a formula of short fiction and non-fiction articles that included frank discussions of sex and money. She also included food and drinks coverage focused on two primary aims: delivering recipes that would aid in the seduction of men, and recipes that would keep the single girl's figure trim and enticing.

In 1969, Brown collected her recipes in the *Single Girl's Cookbook*, which promised "entertaining advice on how to stir up a little seduction in the kitchen." Unfortunately, Brown was not the cook that Sidney Aptekar was. More unfortunately, the social anathema on women's appetite had not vanished overnight, resulting in recipes that often prioritized low caloric intake over alimentary pleasure. If you were cooking for a man, Brown advised using cream, butter, brandy, and even sugar; "let him get skinny at somebody else's house; you're out to be remembered for your delicious food." But for solitary breakfasts, Brown included a recipe for a shake made with yeast-liver mix, the less said about the taste the better. Not that women were the only sex who sometimes had to suffer at the table. Brown also included a recipe for shaking off a man when you were done with an affair, which involved mixing stale chips with "any other revolting, but essentially edible" items in your refrigerator or pantry, such as dried-out cheese cubes, the last of a can of deviled ham, and a cold raw frankfurter.[34]

Brown's spirited advice for single girls inspired many imitators. One of the most popular was Jinx Kragen and Judy Perry's *Saucepans and the Single Girl*, a cookbook published in 1965 by two twenty-something roommates who shared the goal of cooking for a man to lure him into marriage. Kragen and Perry followed Loeb's model of organizing recipes for different types of men: Man in a Brooks Brothers Suit, Man's Man, Man in a Garrett, Lover with a Leica, etc. But they fell short of Brown's full-throated defense of single women's right to enjoy sex for its own sake. They weren't even comfortable advising women to embrace their love of eating. "One of the most closely guarded secrets of the single girl is that she can out-eat any man," they confessed. Instead of bucking this social norm by advising women to eat however much they wanted in front of men, Kragen and Perry suggested hosting other women for dinner and flexing their true appetites in single-sex company.[35] The authors closed the book by announcing their own recent marriages – one to a downstairs neighbor, the other to a dashing young executive – and followed their first cookbook with a 1968 sequel, *The How to Keep Him (After You've Caught Him) Cookbook*, which followed in the spirit of earlier newlywed cookbooks.[36]

Far more in keeping with the spirit of Helen Gurley Brown was Mimi Sheraton's 1963 *The Seducer's Cookbook,* excerpts of which later appeared in *Cosmopolitan*.[37] While Sheraton dedicated it to her husband, the cookbook was far more sexually frank and far less domestic than *Saucepans and the Single Girl*. "To guard against buying this book under false pretenses, I must tell you at the start that the kind of seduction dealt with here is purely, exclusively sexual," Sheraton warned in the book's introduction. She defined seduction as getting someone to do something that they might not want to do. For men, that meant getting women to say yes; for women, that meant having more reason to say yes. Cooking for a lover was a way to achieve those ends because "the urge to eat and the urge to procreate are basic, natural, and deliciously intertwined." Sheraton confessed that she herself had first been persuaded to neck by the gift of a frozen Milky Way bar. Quoting from Alexandre Dumas *père*, Grimod de La Reynière, Brillat-Savarin, Norman Douglas, and Colette, Sheraton updated the gastronomic-sexual tradition for the 1960s, a period when "women have had equal rights for some time now." Traces of the old order lingered on. Sheraton acknowledged that the innocent girl next door "may blush when you suggest going to a French restaurant." The old frisson of the *cabinet particulier* had not been entirely forgotten. On the other hand, Sheraton warned, the innocent girl-next-door shtick was probably just an act, designed to hook a husband.[38]

By the 1970s, both women and men were ready to give up the act. Dating, seduction, and newlywed cookbooks gave way to pornographic cookbooks. Sidney Aptekar published several more *Playboy* cookbooks on the themes of wine and spirits and parties, but they seemed tame in comparison to Pierre Le Poste and David Thorpe's *Rude Food* (1978), which was illustrated with *Penthouse*-style photographs of naked women's bodies tastefully adorned with food. Aptekar's opening sentence from his first *Playboy* article – "You cannot talk about oysters and leave out sex" – was positively prudish compared to Thorpe's image of an oyster arranged over a woman's naked vulva. Other photographs showed spaghetti arranged as bondage ropes around a woman's wrists, a woman licking a banana, a woman holding artichokes in front of her breasts, and in the interests of gender equity (if not racial equity), a bare-torsoed Black man holding chopped meat cradling a raw egg yolk.[39] The book's success led to follow-ups, *Vin Rude* (1980), *Rude Cocktails* (1983), and *More Rude Food* (1984), all similarly illustrated with Thorpe's pornographic photography.[40]

Ron Stieglitz and Sandy Lesberg took a more classic approach to their 1977 pornographic cookbook, *Saucy Ladies*, illustrating the recipes with nineteenth-century photographs of undressed women, some wearing strappy Grecian sandals, arranged in art photography poses, playing badminton, standing alongside a donkey, and leaning on a stone column.[41] Lesberg was also the author of *The Cookbook for Swinging Singles* (1976), which served up seduction advice along with recipes heavy on cottage cheese and MSG, but left out the dirty photos.[42] Jon Paul Frascone and Mark Allen David's *Aphrodisiac Cook Book* (1975) incorporated a mix of pornographic imagery, including pen and ink drawings, and photos of classical sculptures and Hindu erotic statuary. The imagery shared a common tendency toward large-breasted women, not unusual in the genre. Frascone and David also supplemented the text with sexy anecdotes about female historical figures like Nell Gwyn, mistress of King Charles II, Maria Luisa, the "harlot queen" of King Carlos IV, and Pocahontas, John Smith's supposed rescuer.[43]

Women also contributed to the genre of pornographic cookbooks. Billie Young, who had been hired to pose as Penelope Ashe, the fictive author of a bestselling sexually explicit trashy novel titled *Naked Came the Stranger* (1969) that was actually a literary hoax written by twenty-four male and female journalists, cashed in on her moment of fame by publishing *The Naked Chef: An Aphrodisiac Cookbook* (1971). The front cover had an illustration of a cleft pear that resembled the woman's backside on the cover of *Naked Came the Stranger*, with a snake wearing a toque licking the fruit. Young dedicated the book "to my inflammable bedmate, his thirsty libido, and to my Mother and Father who had the foresight to provide me with ancestors whose seething, spicy, savage bedside appetite I so luckily inherited!" A series of erotic sketches, photographs, and anecdotes illustrated the recipes.[44]

Louise Woolf and Susan Sky's *The X-Rated Cookbook* (1977) had two women reclining naked in a bubble bath on the front cover, and more nude photos inside. The front cover of a later edition had a cartoon of a woman bending over a hot stove wearing an ass cheek-baring negligee.[45] A copy of the cookbook signed by Sky for Helen Wolff, owner of the Come Again sex shop in midtown Manhattan, suggests a relationship between shop owner and author.[46]

Many of the pornographic cookbooks published in the 1970s were expressly funny. One of the most unusual was *Bridget's Diet Cookbook*, from 1972, illustrated with full-page color photographs of a fat, naked model in funny poses. On the front cover, she's swigging from a bottle of olive oil, dressed only in a toque and an apron. The text matches the humor of the photos. A recipe for "Braised Sardine Spleens" begins with the instruction to find a can of sardines where the sardines appear to be smiling because that indicates a healthy outlook on life, then remove the sardines' spleens with a tweezer, spear them with barbeque skewers, and grill them over a candle flame for 15 seconds. A photograph on the facing page shows Bridget, dressed again only in her toque and apron, grinding pepper over an empty frying pan, with a caption reading "Pepper your Sardine Spleens judiciously." Other recipes in the book include stuffed grape seeds, peanut shell casserole, and ice cube soufflé. In all the photos, Bridget is clowning joyously, seemingly entirely at ease naked in front of the camera, mocking diet culture.[47] The authors later followed up with two additional titles featuring the same naked model, *Bridget's Organic Cookbook* (1973) and *Bridget's Basic Sex* (1973).[48]

Suiting the spirit of the decade, the genre of erotic cookbooks expanded in the 1970s into a free-for-all. There were aphrodisiac cookbooks, which often took a self-serious tone despite the total hokum of their subject matter.[49] There were seduction cookbooks for men and for women.[50] There were special-topic sex cookbooks for people who hosted orgies, for people into astrology, for witches, and for adulterers.[51] There were artistic cookbooks put together by art schools, or prominent artists.[52] There were

The front cover of *Bridget's Diet Cookbook* (1972), which satirizes American diet culture and restrictions on female appetites, features a naked heavy-set model swigging olive oil directly from the bottle, while dressed only in a toque and apron.

celebrity cookbooks, like Sophia Loren's *In the Kitchen with Love*, with serious recipes that just happened to be illustrated with lusty photographs of Loren's remarkable cleavage.[53] There were even cookbooks designed as marriage aids.[54] What all these cookbooks shared in common was a level of sexual explicitness, in their texts and their illustrations, which far exceeded anything that had come before.

As sexual liberalism broadened the conversation about food and sex, straight male authors laid claim to the masculinity of gourmet cooking. "There is not a damn thing effeminate about preparing good food," Cory Kilvert wrote in the introduction to *The Male Chauvinist's Cookbook* (1974), the front cover of which had a picture of a hairy-chested man dressed only in an apron dangling an apple in his left hand over the mouth of a naked, blonde-haired woman kneeling on the kitchen floor. The back cover carried over the illustration, with the man's oven-gloved right hand extended toward a naked, brown-haired woman kneeling beneath him in supplication. "The man who is truly confident of his virility will not give a second thought to donning an apron," Kilvert insisted, but the book jacket suggests overcompensation.[55]

Perhaps the most remarkable example of a 1970s sex-themed cookbook reclaiming gastronomy for the heterosexual male was Lionel H. Braun and William Adams's *Fanny Hill's Cook Book* (1971), with illustrations by Brian Forbes, a cartoonist for *Penthouse* magazine. The title pages were illustrated with an image of a naked, busty woman reclining on a daybed, while a bald-headed heavy-set man looking very much like James Beard crouched at the end, licking the sole of one daintily extended foot. In 1971, James Beard was the most visually recognizable male figure in the American food world; the resemblance could hardly have been unintentional. Titled after the whore-heroine of the first pornographic novel written in English, John Cleland's *Memoirs of a Woman of Pleasure* (1748–9), the cookbook includes sexual puns like "Whores d'Oeuvres" and "Marquise d'Salade with Crafty Ebbing Undressing." Carrying through on its mission of straightening American gourmet culture, the book included a recipe for "Rump Roast or Backside Entree" that alluded to the ancient Greeks – in other words, to the history of pederastic anal sex – but Braun and Adams erased queerness from the classical tradition. "The Greeks had a word for it, but they backed into it," the recipe started. An accompanying illustration depicted a naked woman lying in a serving

The title pages for Lionel H. Braun and William Adams's *Fanny Hill's Cook Book* (1971) reclaimed good food for straight men by depicting a man looking much like James Beard licking the naked body of a buxom woman named for the whore-heroine of John Cleland's early pornographic novel, *Memoirs of a Woman of Pleasure* (1748-49).

bowl on her stomach with her buttocks raised up.[56] *Fanny Hill's Cook Book* not only reimagined James Beard as a toe-licking straight man, but it redefined Greek anality as oriented toward women.

Straight food

By the early 1980s, the association between gay men and gourmet culture had become a joke in Anglo-American culture, no longer a belief intended to be taken seriously. Take, for example, Bruce Feirstein's May 1982 *Playboy* article, "Real Men Don't Eat Quiche," which he later expanded into a bestselling book by the same title.[57] Feirstein could not have chosen a better metonym for gay gourmet culture than quiche. The dish had been relatively unknown in the United States before the 1940s. James Beard claimed he was "the one who introduced quiche to

America" after he tried it at the Swiss Pavilion at the New York World's Fair in 1939. He began serving the "cheese tartlets" at parties catered by Hors d'Oeuvre Inc, and included the recipe in his appetizer cookbook.[58] In the 1950s, Craig Claiborne popularized the recipe in his recipe column in the *New York Times*.[59] By the 1970s, quiche had become known as a quintessentially gay dish, served up at that most quintessentially gay meal, the weekend brunch. A reporter writing for a gay newspaper in 1981 described a brunch spot in New York City where Warhols hung on the walls, quiche curled on the hot trays, and glossy copies of *The Joy of Gay Sex* lay bookmarked on diners' tables.[60] The dish's very name sealed the deal, both in its Frenchness that registered as effete to Americans, and in its alliterative link to the word queer.[61]

Quiche made the perfect punchline for Feirstein's article mocking the tensions between the reformed "new man," who emerged in the wake of the second-wave feminist movement, and the unreformed "real man" who disdained all challenges to traditional masculinity. The article is set at a truck-stop lunch counter, where the narrator, a wimpy stand-in for Feirstein, sits down next to a he-man named Flex Crush who lays out the rules for what real men eat: a diet of meat, junk food, and absolutely nothing French. The article hit a nerve and led swiftly to a book contract, followed by international adaptations, translations, and even a cookbook, *Real Men Don't Cook Quiche*, which ironically included a fair number of French recipes by the classically trained chef who stepped in as Feirstein's co-author. Although Feirstein's title became the clarion call of gender reactionaries like Phyllis Schlafly, who delivered quiches to US senators who supported the Equal Rights Amendment, the article and the book were steeped in irony, making equal fun of "real men" and "new men." Feirstein, a nerdy Jewish writer, was ridiculing the idea that a taste for gourmet food made you gay when he had Flex Crush complain that "we've become a nation of wimps. Pansies. Quiche eaters." To Feirstein, it was all a big joke.[62]

In the 1980s, good food, which often still meant French food, had become a defining element of straight single life. A new archetype emerged that didn't carry the queer resonances of the gourmet: the foodie. British journalists Ann Barr and Paul Levy (who was American-born but working in the United Kingdom) defined the term in their 1984 bestseller *The Official Foodie Handbook*:

What is new about an interest in food? Everyone knows some older person who was called a "gourmet" before the term "Foodie" arrived (Foodies and Foodism were christened by *Harpers & Queen* in August 1982). But Foodies *are* new, children of the consumer boom. The gourmet was typically a rich male amateur to whom food was a passion. Foodies are typically an aspiring professional couple to whom food is a fashion.

Gourmets had been effete men. Foodies were yuppie couples, straight or gay – "but that doesn't matter among foodies" – who spent all their disposable income on kitchen-related items. Barr and Levy included a timeline in their guidebook that traced the foodie's genealogy from the originating moments of French gastronomy, such as the opening of Beauvilliers' Le Grande Taverne de Londres in Paris and the publication of Grimod de La Reynière's *Almanach des Gourmands*, through the rise of greedy women and gay gourmets like Elizabeth David and Craig Claiborne, to the ground-zero event in the foodie revolution, the opening of Alice Waters's restaurant Chez Panisse in Berkeley, California in 1971.[63]

Histories of the foodie revolution frequently point to the opening of Chez Panisse as a landmark event that launched a new era of American gastronomy.[64] While Alice Waters was not single-handedly responsible for the foodie revolution, her influential restaurant signaled the emergence, in Paul Freedman's words, of "a radically new aesthetic of pleasure" in Anglo-American cuisine. This aesthetic owed a debt to "changes in gender attitudes and sexuality," even if there seems to be little connection between goat cheese salad and gay rights or feminism.[65] Waters very self-consciously situated herself in a lineage of greedy women and gay gourmets who had come before her (and, like Elizabeth David, she claimed to hate the word "foodie").[66]

James Beard first ate at Chez Panisse in 1974. His syndicated column, praising the "perfectly cooked duck with green peppercorns," put Chez Panisse on the gastronomic map and initiated a lasting friendship between Waters and Beard.[67] Waters had taught herself to cook by working her way through Elizabeth David's recipes, and meeting David was her "most cherished dream." She wrote to David in 1976, and in 1977 Richard Olney introduced the two women, serving them a "light truffle lunch" that Olney described as the essence of "simplicity," but which involved a starter of scrambled eggs with truffles, followed by truffled and pistachioed sausages poached in white wine, and then a cheese plate with white truffles accompanied by a 1973 Bollinger, a 1975 Montrachet, a 1974 Hubert de Montille Volnay Champans, and a 1953 Domaine de la Romanée-Conti Grands Échézeaux to wash the meal down.[68] After this lunch, Waters kept up a correspondence with David, cooked for her at Chez Panisse during the Englishwoman's visit to California, and packed her a picnic in caviar tins for her return flight.[69] Waters also wrote to M. F. K. Fisher who lived nearby in Glen Ellen, inviting her to a celebratory seventieth-birthday meal in July 1978.[70] The menu started with a course titled "Consider the Oyster," oysters on the half-shell accompanied by a magnum of French champagne, which was followed by escargot, rock fish, pheasant, bitter greens with goat cheese croutons, and a three-plum sorbet. The two women connected over their shared appetites. Waters would send Fisher salacious postcards, and Fisher wrote back calling her "my girl" and inquiring about her "romantic rendez-vous."[71]

Of romantic rendezvous, there were many. During its first decades, Chez Panisse was notorious for its bacchanalian culture. The restaurant's early alumni included Willy Bishop, an artist who painted "wild watercolors of guys jerking off and cum flying all over the place," and Jeremiah Tower, who had a "pansexual appeal" and slept with everyone, including Alice Waters and Richard Olney. Waters was totally committed to the program of sexual liberation. After the restaurant closed, the staff would break out the wine and drugs, for those who partook, and "Alice would get drunk, her incisors would show, and she would attack some poor innocent person and bed them." The "Caligulan" atmosphere at Chez Panisse signified the foodie ethos of sexual liberation; it might include same-sex sexual expression, but it wasn't defined by it. The restaurant's sexual atmosphere wasn't limited to the back of house. Chez Panisse's promotional materials mixed food and sex in provocative and joyful ways. Jeremiah Tower cooked menus inspired by Alice B. Toklas's cookbook and by Salvador Dalí's cookbook, which included a lamb dish called "l'entre-plat drogue et sodomise."[72] The graphic artist David Lance Goines, Waters's ex-boyfriend, designed posters for the restaurant that evoked "the flesh pots of Berkeley," in his words, and were illustrated with naked women.[73]

The fleshpots of Berkeley were also the proving ground of another critical figure in the foodie revolution, the food writer Ruth Reichl. In the mid-1970s, Reichl was living in a hippie commune in Berkeley and working as a cook at The Swallow. Once a year, she and her husband, the sculptor Doug Hollis, would go to Chez Panisse to celebrate. Reichl recalled seeing Alice Waters around Berkeley, "a petite, pretty woman who swept through town trailing disappointed men in her wake." Reichl was awed by Waters, and jealous of her reputation. Within a few years, however, she'd be carving her own parallel path.

A job offer to become a restaurant reviewer allowed Reichl to leave behind the anti-materialism of her twenties and plunge herself into hedonistic excess. Her editor Colman Andrews seduced her with a meal of caviar, oysters, and champagne, and the two soon plunged into a heady affair. Over a meal together at Le Tour d'Argent in Paris, the foie gras was so delicious that Reichl felt the thrill all the way down to her fingertips, and she "understood for the first time ever, why those turn-of-the century restaurants had private rooms with velvet couches. I would have liked a couch." Eventually, her affair with Andrews ended, and she began a new affair with a radical journalist named Michael Singer. Reichl took Singer to meet M. F. K. Fisher, who gave her blessing to the couple by packing them a picnic and sending them on a hike to a nearby waterfall, where Reichl and Singer had sex alfresco. Eventually, Reichl and her husband each confessed their affairs to each other (he'd had many more than her), their marriage dissolved, and Reichl went on to become the restaurant reviewer at the *New York Times*, then the editor of *Gourmet* magazine, and finally a bestselling food memoirist.[74]

Reichl's rival restaurant reviewer at *New York* magazine, Gael Greene, challenged Levy and Barr's claim to have originated the term "foodie," and she matched Waters and Reichl in combining the twinned pleasures of food and sex in her life and in her writing. Greene began her career as a journalist in the mid-1950s, interviewing Elvis in his hotel room as a twenty-one-year-old cub reporter, after which she joined him in bed then ordered him a fried egg sandwich from room service on her way out the door. After a period at the *New York Post*, she was hired by *New York* magazine in 1968 as its first restaurant critic and stayed for the next thirty years.

Greene devoted her life in equal measure to the pursuits of food and sex, although she valued the latter over the former, writing in her memoir "I have read restaurant critics who claimed to have tasted chocolate ice cream that was better than sex. I have never eaten anything that was better than sex; *almost* as good as great sex perhaps, but never better." She boasted of having affairs with sex symbols Clint Eastwood and Burt Reynolds, the three-Michelin-starred chef Jean Troisgros, and the hardcore porn actor Jamie Gillis. She was also close friends with Craig Claiborne and, though their relationship did not involve sex with each other, it involved lots of shared sexual humor. Unsurprisingly, Greene's reviews in *New York* magazine were frankly sensual. She also wrote erotic books including the non-fiction *Sex and the College Girl* (1964), a dirty novel, *Blue Skies, No Candy* (1976), and a "recipe book" for joyous erotic encounters, *Delicious Sex* (1985).[75]

In *Blue Skies, No Candy*, Greene captured the ethos of the straight, swinging foodie culture coming to prominence on both sides of the Atlantic in the mid-eighties. The novel is a wish-fulfillment fantasy about a forty-year-old brilliant, sexy female screenwriter with an insatiable sexual appetite who cheats on her doting husband and has mind-blowing sex with a series of partners, including a tall, domineering cowboy with a massive penis. The screenwriter and the cowboy first flirt over a meal together at Brasserie Lipp on the Left Bank in Paris, where he sweet-talks her by saying, "Everything turns you on. This brie. The wine. My fingers," and "Look how you touch yourself. How you eat. I'm watching your tongue on the edge of the glass."

Because it's a wish-fulfillment fantasy, her husband is also great in the sack and "a born cook" who makes her breakfast in bed. She watches him "studying Craig Claiborne's recipe for the week, contemplating a beef brisket, a carrot, some shallots and a bottle of wine." But, driven by her insatiable sexual needs, she sets off on a driving tour of France with the cowboy, during which they fuck endlessly and eat delicious food together at restaurants like Troisgros – a trip based on a *New York* magazine-funded driving tour of France that Mimi Sheraton took with one of her lovers, *Playboy* editor Murray Fisher. Sheraton thanks Fisher in the book's acknowledgments, and an excerpt was published in *Playboy*.[76] In her memoir, she boasted that they had sex before and after every great meal on the three-week trip.[77]

In *Delicious Sex*, Greene took her blending of food and sex one step further by suggesting various ways to incorporate food into sex play. In her chapter "How to Eat a Fig," Greene offered directions for arousing one's sensuality, beginning with a step-by-step tutorial on cutting, squeezing, admiring, smelling, and tasting that longstanding symbol for female genitalia. A list of "wonderful things to do with your mouth" included peeling a grape with your teeth, sucking on a passion fruit, and sucking on your lover's fingers. Her chapter on "Fork Play" expanded these instructions for incorporating food into sex play. She created seductive menus for different types of men, recommended edible panties as an aphrodisiac, and listed foods that people enjoyed incorporating into sex play, including whipped cream, honey, bananas, and popsicles. While declaring herself a food and sex purist who preferred keeping the two domains separated, Greene praised the recently released movie *9½ Weeks*, starring Mickey Rourke and Kim Basinger, for its kinky food and sex scene.[78]

Dude food

Sexualized foodie culture in the late twentieth century extended beyond cookbooks, professional kitchens, and food writing to aspects of popular culture like films, television, and merchandise. Early films had humorously mixed food and sex. A very early French pornographic film, *Mousquetaire au Restaurant* (*c*.1908), interspersed clips of a lusty musketeer having sex with two enthusiastic barmaids at a tavern, with title screens bearing food-related sexual puns like "dans la pot de moutarde" (in the mustard pot), "la moule ouverte," (the open mussel), and finally "sirop cordom" (man's body syrup).[79] The meeting of Lady and the Tramp's muzzles over a shared bowl of spaghetti is the 1955 Disney classic's most iconic image.[80] The 1963 film adaptation of the classic novel *Tom Jones* is famous for its scene in which the youthful Jones, played by Albert Finney, is seduced over a tavern meal by the mature Mrs. Waters, played by Joyce Redman.[81] In the 1980s, food and sex appeared together with growing frequency in films both comedic and overtly erotic.

The comedic tradition continued in *Neighbors*, a 1981 comedy starring John Belushi and Dan Aykroyd, which includes a scene in which the actress playing Belushi's punk daughter shows off her edible panties to Aykroyd and tells him that all the girls at high school are wearing them. Aykroyd delightedly reads the list of flavors off the packaging – banana, peach, mint, and of course, cherry – adding an extra leer to the final flavor. Belushi punches him in the face.[82] Another unforgettable comic treatment of food and sex comes from the 1982 film *Fast Times at Ridgemont High*, when the character played by Phoebe Cates uses a carrot to demonstrate how to give a blow job for her friend played by Jennifer Jason Leigh.[83]

The themes of food and sex also received more serious treatment in several erotic movies from the decade.[84] Although Adrian Lyne's *9½ Weeks* was completed in 1984, concerns about its explicitness delayed the film's release for two years. The scenes in which the Wall Street arbitrageur played by Rourke introduces food into his sexual encounters with the art gallerist played by Basinger begin humorously, but turn disturbing when Rourke feeds Basinger hot peppers, making her cry. To cool her mouth, she pours milk down her throat until she gags.[85] Another 1980s film with a dark take on food and sex is Peter Greenaway's *The Cook, the Thief, His Wife and Her Lover* (1989), the initial cut of which could only be released with an X rating or as unrated. The movie's plot revolves around a sadistic gangster, played by Michael Gambon, whose wife, played by Helen Mirren, conducts an affair at a restaurant he owns. Discovering the betrayal, Gambon murders Mirren's lover by force-feeding him pages from a book, after which Mirren asks the restaurant's chef to cook the body and then forces Gambon to eat it before she shoots him.[86] Both films depict the dark side of foodie masculinity, as Gambon's and Rourke's characters use food in their sexualized domination of their female partners.[87]

While Lyne and Greenaway offered disturbing critiques of heterosexual foodie culture, enthusiastic celebrations of these consumerist erotics were far more common. During the 1970s and 1980s, a wave of new products mixing food and sex hit the shelves. The edible panties that appeared in *Neighbors* were invented in 1972 by a Chicago chemist named John Anderson. When the underwear made of food starch, glycerin, inverted sugar, artificial coloring, and artificial flavoring became available for sale in 1976, they quickly emerged as a cultural phenomenon. College newspapers reported on the underwear as a new trend hitting campuses.[88] Don DeLillo included them in one of his novels of the times.[89] An erotic spa advertised that "our girls now wear edible panties. Three delicious flavors. Wild cherry. Passion fruit. BANana."[90] Sex stores stocked the undies for customers. At the Pleasure Chest in Los Angeles, they could be found with the lingerie, chastity belts, and massage oils.[91] At Come Again in midtown Manhattan, Helen Wolff sold them alongside raspberry "flavo-cept contraceptive cream."[92]

Fruit-flavored creams and lotions proved bestsellers in the 1980s at sex-paraphernalia parties that women hosted in their homes, updating the Mary Kay and Tupperware parties of earlier decades.[93] The most popular food-themed sex product was probably flavored condoms, first developed in the 1970s. A 1974 sex guide for adolescents explained that "with increasing public acceptance of oral–genital stimulation," there was a range of new products including "flavored douches, male genital deodorants, [and] even flavored condoms."[94] While flavored condoms emerged out of the same entrepreneurial drive to make money off marketing food and sex to straight people as edible panties had, the arrival of the AIDS epidemic soon made flavored condoms a favorite among safe-sex advocates in the queer community.[95] Like edible panties, flavored condoms became a cultural phenomenon, appearing frequently in novels and sex guides. Safe-sex advocates also handed out flavored dental dams, but the product didn't capture the imagination the same way.[96] The creativity of capitalism did not end at flavored contraceptives. Other products that found willing buyers included sex rocks, basically pop rocks to place in the mouth immediately before performing fellatio, flavored massage oils to lick off a partner, and flavored body creams for the same purpose.[97]

Even at the height of their popularity, fruit-flavored sex products were often treated as a punchline. In a *Playboy* comic strip from 1980, Holistic Harry seduces a woman with talk of herbs, vibes, and biorhythms, before recoiling in the final panel when he goes down on her and detects "artificial strawberry flavoring."[98] A *Hustler* humor piece joked that "the money-making possibilities for marketing erotic food" went way beyond "strawberry-flavored douches." What America needed was a "fast fucking food chain!" An accompanying illustration showed a man biting into a burger, with women's breasts pasted in the place of buns.[99]

The *Hustler* article may have been intended as a joke, but a number of entrepreneurs shared its vision. In 1983, the first Hooters restaurant opened in Clearwater, Florida, offering garden-variety bar food, like

A June 1980 comic strip from *Playboy* magazine captures the transition from the hippie counter-culture of the 1970s, with its focus on organic food and natural living, to the consumerist 1980s, with its processed consumerist products including strawberry-flavored douches and contraceptive creams.

wings, burgers, and shrimp, served by chesty waitresses wearing uniforms of cropped tank tops, orange booty shorts, flesh-colored tights, and white crew socks. The waitresses were encouraged to flirt with the male clientele. The restaurant was an immediate success and soon grew into a chain, with associated merchandise like pin-up calendars. The featured model in the first Hooters calendar, Lynne Austin, appeared as a *Playboy* centerfold in 1986.[100] (Playboy Enterprises had operated its own clubs since 1960, which included dining rooms, although the clubs were more focused on drinking and shows than on food.[101])

Hooters eventually expanded to over 450 restaurants. Later, more chains joined the "breastaurant" market sector, including the Tilted Kilt, founded in 2003, and Twin Peaks, founded in 2005. Many breastaurants sold branded merchandise, including tee-shirts, baseball caps, and hot sauces.[102] Hooters eventually launched an airline, with two Hooter Girls aboard every flight. While breastaurants hardly seem exemplary of foodie good taste, they represent an ongoing strategy to heterosexualize food culture for corporate profits. The food studies scholar Emily Contois has described this as the "dude food" marketing strategy, which endeavors "to distinguish straight male interest in food and cooking from perceptions of femininity or gayness" by using masculine and sexualized imagery.[103] Common themes in dude food advertising include appetites, pleasure, and the seduction of women. As distant as dude food might seem from gastronomy, the two shared many of the same preoccupations.

The foodie revolution also prompted the influx of machismo into celebrity chef culture. The gay gourmets who had dominated Anglo-American food media from Marcel Boulestin to Craig Claiborne were supplanted by a new wave of male cooks who were known in the industry as "chunks," a portmanteau of *chefs* plus *hunks*. The sexy suave restaurateur or chef became a celebrity icon in the 1980s and then exploded in popular culture with the rise of the Food Network in the 1990s.

The opportunity to launch a channel came first, the subject matter came second. Two executives working for a cable TV provider were looking to start a channel that focused on a profitable but underserved industry, and they settled on food as their subject matter. One of the Network's first hires was Emeril Legasse, who had won the Best Chef in the Southeast award from the James Beard Foundation in 1991, and more importantly – in the words of a female Network executive – was "a hunk," with his thick dark hair, trim waist, and sweet, growly, working-class accent. The executives cast the Network's early shows with their male talents' sex appeal foremost in mind, reasoning that women would be the primary audience and that "females will tune in to watch hunks." An early episode of chef David Rosengarten's show, where he discussed the aphrodisiacal properties of oysters, pushed the formula a little too far. Bobby Flay, who joined the network in 1994, personified the approachable sex appeal the Network aimed for, a persona carried through in the punning title of his long-running show and cookbook series, "Boy Meets Grill." According to Heidi Diamond, senior vice-president of marketing, viewers peppered the network with "indecent proposals" addressed to Flay, not just requests for recipes.[104]

The marketing of female food celebrities in the early 2000s exaggerated their heterosexual appeal even more explicitly than the marketing of male food celebrities.[105] Television show hosts like Giada De Laurentiis, Padma Lakshmi, and Nigella Lawson appeared in magazine pictorials licking their fingers, or their bodies dripping in syrups, echoing the semen-over-skin shots popularized in pornography.[106] The image of Lawson placing a piece of food in her mouth on the cover of her cookbook *Nigella Bites* (2002) has been described as an act of symbolic fellatio: "Her penchant for solitary consumption of the food she has prepared accompanied by orgasmic noises and visual references to fellatio ensure that the carni-valesque associations between food, sex and the body's orifices are more than suggested."[107] So-called food-porn imagery of De Laurentiis and Lakshmi similarly goes beyond suggestiveness.

Lakshmi, a former model, has been pictured licking burger juice from her hand in a Carl's Junior commercial; eating pizza naked in a bathtub to promote Top Chef, one pepperoni slice positioned just so over a breast; and eating ribs in bed dressed in a negligee and staring lustily at the camera for *GQ* magazine. The final image, which appeared in a spread headlined "Cook for Us, Padma," captures how the imagery of food and sex has been corralled for the production of a consumer-driven heterosexuality since the 1970s.[108] Lakshmi's indulgence of her alimentary appetite in the image is used not to signal her own hedonic orientation to embodied pleasures, but rather her ripeness to feed the alimentary-sexual appetites of the male readers of *GQ*. The pictorial appears as part of a feature section, "GQ Eats," that includes articles on "A Man's Guide to Mastering His Kitchen," "The Coolest Restaurant Neighborhood in America," and "The Hottest Dish on TV" (Lakshmi). Echoing Frank Lalli's *Forbes* article from thirty years before, the "GQ Eats" feature promises readers that they can be masters in the kitchen and connoisseurs of restaurants without undermining their heterosexuality.

The sexualized marketing of Lakshmi, De Laurentiis, Lawson and other women celebrity cooks reveals the gendered limits on the liberatory potential of foodie culture. The valuing of women foodies as consumable subjects according to heterosexual norms set limits on the women's expression of their own appetites.[109] To maintain the figures that male admirers desired – specifically, small waists and large breasts – often required the denial of their own alimentary appetites through restrictive dieting.

The female foodie ideal called on women to express pleasure in food while also denying themselves that same pleasure. The thousands of articles tracking Nigella Lawson's fluctuating weight over the decades of her celebrity testify to the challenge of meeting both incompatible demands. Although Lawson has valiantly pushed back, defending the right of women to have bellies, she's also given countless interviews about her diet tips.[110] The old gourmand motto, *bien vivre et mourir gras* – live well and die fat – which Marcel Boulestin had sighted on the sign of an Alpine inn in the early 1900s, remains out of reach for women a century later.[111]

Epilogue: Good Sex, Bad Food

In 2011, a self-published e-book, which originated as *Twilight* fan fiction, skyrocketed to the top of the bestseller lists. The wild success of E. L. James's *Fifty Shades of Grey*, about an innocent college girl and a bondage-loving billionaire, received breathless coverage in the press, which was seemingly astounded by the discovery of a popular taste for kink among ordinary Americans. The book's commercial success inspired countless imitations: endless romance novels about dominating billionaires; a pornographic film, creatively titled *Fifty Shades of Grey: A XXX Adaptation*; a musical, creatively titled *50 Shades! The Musical*.

The sexcapades of Christian Grey and Anastasia Steele also inspired more than thirty-five cookbooks, most of them self-published. Many had punning titles that signaled their design as gag gifts. Four different books appeared with the title *Fifty Shades of Gravy*. Three additional books shared the similar titles *50 Shades of Coq*; *Fifty Ways to Eat Cock*; and *Fifty Shades of Chicken*. The first of these books used a quote from Julia Child's character in the movie *Julie & Julia* as a blurb: "these damn things are as hot as a stiff cock." The last of the three was written by *New York Times* food editor Amanda Hesser, under the pen name F. L. Fowler, and had a front cover illustrated with a trussed-up bird on a platter, as well as excellent recipes. Several adaptations had earnest titles that promised readers real erotic rewards, like *50 Shades of Herbs: The Best Natural Remedies for Better Sex, Better Sleep, and More Energy* and *50 Shades of Dessert: The 50 Greatest Recipes for Steamy, Passion-Filled Nights*. There were also titles that used the "fifty shades" formula to introduce ingredients with hedonic associations, including three different books titled *50 Shades of Bacon*. The front cover of Jack River's *50 Shades of Bacon* featured the titular ingredient being dipped in chocolate, another hedonic food to get the "fifty shades" treatment from several authors. Chocolate's appearance in the "fifty shades" cookbook genre is unsurprising, considering that chocolate's aphrodisiac reputation can be traced back to pre-Columbian origins and has persisted since its earliest introduction into the European larder. The *50 Shades of Chocolate* cookbook, driven by a logic connecting alimentary and erotic pleasure, is only the latest expression of an alimentary-sexual regime that stretches back centuries.[1]

The fifty shades formula, however, also appeared in book titles that broke from this long tradition. Several cookbooks used the phrase "fifty shades" to introduce foods that had no hedonic associations at all, or even had anti-hedonic associations with self-denial and diet culture, like *50 Shades of Hummus, 50 Shades of Quinoa*, and *Fifty Shades of Kale*.[2] These last three titles hint at the emergence of a new alimentary-sexual regime in the twenty-first century, what might be called a shift away from "Good Food, Bad Sex" ("bad" as in wicked) to "Good Sex, Bad Food." The belief driving these texts is not that sensually indulgent foods will amplify the sexual appetites, but that nutritionally minded diets will make sexier bodies for better erotic encounters. At a simplified level, this new regime functions on the logic that good sex, redefined as pleasurable rather than moral sex, depends on bad food, or in other words, the renunciation of pleasure at the table.

The components of the old "good food, bad sex regime" began to crumble in the late twentieth century. The definition of bad sex shifted. No longer did it refer to sexual acts that occurred outside the moral norms, however shifting. During the sexual revolution, "bad sex" began to appear in popular writing as a shorthand for unsatisfactory sexual encounters. Bad sex was non-orgasmic sex, abbreviated sex, unimaginative sex.[3] A 1972 article in Britain's *She* magazine warned readers against the "downward plunge of bad-sex, unhappy life, worse sex, misery."[4] If the old definitions of bad sex created moral anxieties about how to discipline desires that strayed beyond appropriate boundaries, the new definition of bad sex ratcheted up anxieties about how to discipline the body into a desirable subject. In *Sex and the Single Girl*, a bible of the early sexual revolution, the notoriously skinny Helen Gurley Brown explained to readers that "the foods that make you sexy, exuberant, full of the *joie de vivre* are also the ones that keep you slender."[5] If women aspired to follow her example of enjoying orgasmic sex with multiple partners, they should also follow her calorie restrictive diet, which she laid out in the *Single Girl's Cookbook*, including a recipe for her daily breakfast shake made with powdered liver, orange juice, and salad oil.[6]

Overeating shifted from being seen as a sign of a proclivity to illicit sex toward being seen as a sign of unfitness for good sex, understood as pleasure-oriented sex.

The old indulgent alimentary-sexual regime hardly vanished. The twinned pleasures of good food and good sex remained a popular cultural theme. The rise of the foodie archetype sparked new erotic fantasies. Linda Jaivin's 1995 novel *Eat Me* described the erotic exploits of four female friends in Sydney, Australia, with each chapter named for a different indulgent food: veal, roast lamb, Peking duck. In the first chapter, Philippa visits a local supermarket and begins penetrating herself with fruits and vegetables in the produce aisle. The store security guard comes along and soon she is penetrating him with a cucumber as well. Later, over a meal, the four friends agree that "to revel in food and enjoy eating" is to enjoy life itself.[7] Nora Ephron, a famous foodie whose 1983 novel *Heartburn* helped invent the "novel with recipes" genre, and whose screenplay for the 1989 film *When Harry Met Sally* called for Meg Ryan to fake an orgasm over a deli sandwich, hit box office gold in the twenty-first century with her film *Julie & Julia*, which alternated scenes of a young Brooklyn hipster's attempts to cook all of the recipes in *Mastering the Art of French Cooking* with scenes from Julia and Paul Child's marriage, including Julia's sexual awakening over shared gourmet meals.[8]

Julie & Julia proved popular with audiences, but its drooling depictions of rich butter- and cream-based French cuisine also inspired disparaging attacks that the film was "food porn."[9] This expression, which had first emerged in twentieth-century attacks on women food writers like M. F. K. Fisher and Julia Child, increasingly came to be applied against depictions of high-calorie foods in the twenty-first century. The weight of the moral stigma shifted from the sexual to the alimentary side of the phrase. The website ReelGood used a still shot from *Julie & Julia* of Amy Adams mixing a chocolate cake to top its list, "Food Porn: 7 Films to Avoid when Dieting." Other entries included Jon Favreau's 2014 film *Chef*, whose "orgasmic" food truck cuisine "will make you want to stop aspiring for a bikini body" and lather your body with butter instead, and the 1996 *Big Night*, whose spaghetti and meatballs will make you think "screw being skinny for summer or shredded for film festivals."[10] While firmly tongue-in-cheek, ReelGood's listicle illustrates the shift from the regime of good food/bad sex to good sex/bad food. In the new logic, to achieve the bikini body or shredded physique requisite for good sex, a person had to give up good food.

A new genre of erotic cookbooks emerged in the 2000s, which promoted "clean" eating as the secret to a good sex life. Juan-Carlos Cruz, a pastry chef who became famous after his appearance on a Discovery Channel weight-loss show, joined forces with Amy Reiley, author of several aphrodisiac cookbooks, to co-author *The Love Diet* (2010). The book's bright red endsheet featured a woman's hand holding an apple, with the slogan "eat it up, take it off, get it on" printed over and over again. In Cruz's introduction he explained how his weight loss gave him an "unexpected gift," in short, "the more fit I am the better the quality of erection." A section of the book titled "Cook Me Sexy" focused on "lower calories foods," with the promise that eating from those recipes would give the reader the sort of body that would make them feel comfortable to cook with a lover while wearing nothing more than an apron. Another section titled "Romantic Weekend" included recipes that were "indulgent (but within reason)" and attached the stern warning to eat them only rarely if one wanted to sport a sexy body.[11] The ethos of *The Love Diet* marked a striking departure from twentieth-century erotic cookbooks like Mimi Sheraton's *The Seducer's Cookbook*, with its recipes for lobsters, herb butter, and baguettes.

Cruz and Reiley's recipe for good sex through calorie restriction was echoed in other titles from the early 2000s. Crystal Guthrie's *Paleo Sex Recipes and Positions Guide: Eat and F**k like a Caveman* (2015) promised readers that a paleo diet would help them regain their manhood and improve their performance in the bedroom. On its front cover, a smorgasbord of raw lean meats and vegetables previewed recipes free from fattening ingredients like butter or cream.[12] Lisa Davis's *Clean Eating, Dirty Sex* (2019) flipped the traditional moral stigma against kink and upended the historic association between sensual foods and sexual appetites. Having great sex, according to Davis, depended on eating a limited diet that excluded carbohydrates, sugars, animal products, and most fats. In the book's foreword, Australian juice-fast promoter Joe Cross described his own transformational journey in which he "juiced just plants for sixty days, then I ate just plants for another three months," which restored his sex drive and the vitality of his erections. Using the acronym SAD, Lisa Davis explained that the Standard American Diet, heavy on carbohydrates, meat, and sugar, "kills your libido which results in a SAD sex life," not just for men but for women too, who lost their sex drives as a direct consequence of bingeing on potato chips, ice cream, burgers, and French fries. Equally deleterious to one's sex life, the standard American diet caused "weight gain. Not sexy." Sexy sex required skinny bodies which required restrictive eating.[13]

The fantasy of good sex runs throughout contemporary discourse on "clean food." This twenty-first-century nutritional discourse preaches "freedom from" diets that avoid supposed toxic foods including, typically, gluten, sugar, "bad" fats, and processed foods.[14] Canadian wellness advocate Tosca Reno's *The Eat-Clean Diet* (2006), one of the first cookbooks to promote clean eating, opened with the inspiring story of how the right diet led Reno's "interest in life, love, even sex" to be suddenly reawakened. The right diet, as the book revealed, consisted of small meals of 300–400 calories, heavy on protein and complex carbohydrates and light on sugar or fat. After following this plan, "Was it possible that I was a little bit sexy again?" Reno asked, a question that pointed to the double erotic promise of eating clean: it would increase the sex drive while shaping a more sexually attractive body. Reno also added a third logic connecting clean food and good sex, "the release of male and female sex hormones causes an increase in metabolic rate." Having sex could raise one's basal metabolic rate – or the energy burn rate of the resting body – by "as much as 15 percent." Reno didn't supply a citation for this figure.[15]

Reno is one among many lifestyle influencers who hold out the promise that a moral diet will lead to erotic bliss. James Duigan, a celebrity trainer and another early promoter of clean food, promised readers of his 2010 *The Clean & Lean Diet* that following his advice would not only deliver a healthier, leaner, body, but "your concentration will improve, along with your sex drive and your mood."[16] On her website Peace Love & Kale, Carly Shankman, a "holistic health coach" with over one hundred thousand followers on Instagram, gives a long list of reasons that "clean, real food" will improve your sex life. At the top of the list: healthy foods, like dark, leafy greens, will make you "feel more comfortable in your body" and lead to "increased sexy time." Translation: if you lose weight, you will be sexier. Shankman's list also incorporates moral arguments that both echo and flip traditional arguments. Eating clean food, she promises, will make you into the type of person capable of good sex: "as you detox the negative emotions and toxic build up in your body with a clean diet, life becomes brighter, easier, happier, more fun, precious and expressive," allowing for better sexual connections with your partners.[17]

On the other hand, as the cultural critic Flavia Dzodan has pointed out, older moral logics remain deeply embedded in clean food discourse. For the women who are its primary targets, the linkage made in clean-eating discourse between the consumption of pleasurable foods like sugar and female dirtiness has a familiar ring.[18] The clean food movement also replicates race and class hierarchies deeply familiar to the older alimentary-sexual regime. Foods promoted as "clean" are those most associated with white women of means, such as quinoa. Clean food grammars reinscribe white, heteronormative middle- and upper-class privilege, finds a 2020 study of digital food influencers in the United Kingdom. The digital food influencers most associated with the clean food movement are themselves almost entirely white, slim, and privileged. Visit their websites and one will find photographs of large, bright, fashionable kitchens.[19] The photographs illustrating articles, blogposts, and books about clean food typically feature slim white women alongside raw vegetables.

Looking at the histories of food and sex in conjunction brings a new perspective to the seeming shift away from restrictions on the bodily appetites during the past half-century. While the relaxation of censorship laws, the spread of the sexual revolution, and the achievements of the gay rights movement have greatly widened the discussion and acceptance of a wide range of sexual behaviors including pre-marital sex, same-sex sex, non-monogamous sex, and kinky sex, norms around eating for pleasure appear to be tightening once more, after a period of post-Victorian relaxation. New counter-discourses have emerged to challenge normative frameworks. Queer body positivity influencers have pushed back against the equation of good sex with skinny calorie-deprived bodies, but they are minority voices struggling to be heard above the din of a widespread and growing consensus that alimentary indulgence makes unfit sexual subjects.

"In eating, pleasure offers itself to be problematised," Elspeth Probyn astutely points out.[20] During the nineteenth and twentieth centuries, the moral concern with pleasurable eating focalized around its proclivity for stimulating illicit sexual appetites. In the twenty-first century, the moral concern with pleasurable eating has shifted to its potential desexualizing effects. If the good life has come to be redefined as one that centers pleasurable sex, indulgence in the alimentary appetites now carries the stigma of threatening that ideal. Food and sex remain coupled in the Anglo-American imagination as problems for the construction of the moral subject. The consequences of this imaginative coupling can be severe. An obsession for clean eating can shade into orthorexia, or a harmful fixation on eating according to strict rules. At a systemic level, the new regime updates old hierarchies and provides new logics for gender, racial, and class orders. For too many of us, pleasure inflicts distress where it could produce joy.

The connection between food and sex has been a universal theme across continents and centuries. Often problematized, following as many divergent logics as human cultures can conceive, the potential pleasure of mixing the alimentary and erotic appetites remains an embodied truth that cannot be erased. Raspberries floating in a cold glass of plum wine shared with a lover in a hot bath. Rich dark chocolate snacked on with a lover on a couch in a hotel room between bouts of passion. Each reader has their memories and future interludes to enjoy. *Bon appétit.*

Notes

Introduction: Good Food, Wicked Sex

1 John Milton, *Paradise Lost: A Poem in Twelve Books* (London: Miles Flesher, 1688), 250–1.

2 *Women in Love*, dir. Ken Russell (United Kingdom: United Artists, 1969). The dialogue comes from "Figs," D. H. Lawrence, *Birds, Beasts and Flowers: Poems* (London: Martin Secker, 1923), 18–21.

3 *Call Me by Your Name*, dir. Luca Guadagnino (Sony Pictures Classics, 2017).

4 Paul R. Goldin, *The Culture of Sex in Ancient China* (Honolulu: University of Hawai'i Press, 2002), 8.

5 Judith Farquhar, *Appetites: Food and Sex in Post-Socialist China* (Durham, NC: Duke University Press, 2002), 1, 28. William Reddy argues that medieval Bengali and Japanese cultures did not have equivalent notions connecting the appetite and sexuality; William M. Reddy, *The Making of Romantic Love: Longing and Sexuality in Europe, South Asia, and Japan, 900–1200 CE* (Chicago: University of Chicago Press, 2012).

6 James N. Davidson, *Courtesans and Fishcakes: The Consuming Passions of Classical Athens* (New York: St. Martin's Press, 1997), 8, 17, 310.

7 Veronika Grimm, "The Good Things that Lay at Hand: Tastes of Ancient Greece and Rome," in Paul Freedman (ed.), *Food: The History of Taste* (Berkeley, CA: University of California Press, 2007), 71, 83.

8 The editor of food studies journal *Gastronomica* recently acknowledged that "sex rarely pops up explicitly" in its pages; James Farrer, "Editor's Letter, Spring 2023," *Gastronomica: The Journal of Food and Culture* 23(1) (March 6, 2023). A few important exceptions of scholars whose work combines these lines of inquiry include Philippa Pullar, *Consuming Passions: Being an Historic Inquiry into Certain English Appetites* (Boston: Little, Brown, 1970); Stephen Vider, "'Oh Hell, May, Why Don't You People Have a Cookbook?': Camp Humor and Gay Domesticity," *American Quarterly* 65(4) (December, 2013); Lola Gonzalez-Quijano, "'La chère et la chair': gastronomie et prostitution dans les grands restaurants des boulevards au xix siècle," *Genre, sexualité & société* 10 (Autumn, 2013); Katharina Vester, *A Taste of Power: Food and American Identities*, ed. Darra Goldstein. California Studies in Food and Culture (Berkeley, CA: University of California Press, 2015). See also John Birdsall, "America, Your Food Is So Gay: The Story of How Three Gay Men – James Beard, Richard Olney, and Craig Claiborne – Became Architects of America's Modern Food Culture," *Lucky Peach* 8 (September 27, 2013); John Birdsall, *The Man who Ate Too Much: The Life of James Beard* (New York: W. W. Norton, 2020).

9 "Three's Company," *ABC Wiki*. https://abc.fandom.com/wiki/Three%27s_Company/

10 This book brings together a diverse range of sexual expressions that are often treated separately by historians, who frame histories of sexuality from the viewpoint of present categories of sexual identity. Critics have argued that these categories are anachronistic, and that even the idea of "sexuality" as a principle of personal individuation is a modern

invention. David Halperin, "Is there a History of Sexuality?," *History and Theory* 28(3) (October 1989): 271; Jeffrey Weeks, "Sexuality and History Revisited," in Kim Phillips and Barry Reay (eds.), *Sexualities in History* (New York: Routledge, 2002); Kim M. Phillips and Barry Reay, *Sex before Sexuality: A Premodern History* (Cambridge: Polity, 2011). Using food as a lens opens the possibility for a historicist approach to embodied appetites that is structured by past frameworks rather than present categories.

11 Dana E. Amiraian and Jeffery Sobal, "Dating and Eating: Beliefs about Dating Foods among University Students," *Appetite* 53 (2009): 226–32.

12 Elspeth Probyn credits the term "alimentary-sexual regime," which refers to specific historical belief systems linking food and sex, to Gilles Deleuze and Félix Guattari's work *A Thousand Plateaus* (1987), in Elspeth Probyn, "Beyond Food/Sex: Eating and an Ethics of Existence," *Theory, Culture & Society* 16(2) (1999): 224. This book answers Probyn's call to scholars to "follow the line of sex as it intersects with that of food," which she argues can expose "the limits of sex as the sole optic through which to elaborate an ethics of existence." See also Elspeth Probyn, *Carnal Appetites: FoodSexIdentities* (London: Routledge, 2000).

13 Teresa M. Shaw, *The Burden of the Flesh: Fasting and Sexuality in Early Christianity* (Minneapolis: Fortress Press, 1998).

14 William Ian Miller, "Gluttony," *Representations* 60 (Autumn, 1997); Shaw, *The Burden*, 130.

15 Francine Prose, *Gluttony: The Seven Deadly Sins* (New York: Oxford University Press, 2003), 19.

16 Rachel Laudan, *Cuisine and Empire: Cooking in World History* (Berkeley, CA: University of California Press, 2013), 207–47.

17 Sabrina Strings, *Fearing the Black Body: The Racial Origins of Fat Phobia* (New York: New York University Press, 2019), 122–46. Also Doris Witt, *Black Hunger: Food and the Politics of US Identity* (New York: Oxford University Press, 1999), 183–210; Kyla Wazana Tompkins, "'Everything 'cept Eat Us': The Antebellum Black Body Portrayed as Edible Body," *Callaloo* 30(1) (2007): 202; Kyla Wazana Tompkins, *Racial Indigestion: Eating Bodies in the 19th Century* (New York: New York University Press, 2012).

18 Stephen Mennell, "On the Civilizing of Appetite," *Theory, Culture & Society* 4 (1987).

19 Laura Gowing, *Domestic Dangers: Women, Words, and Sex in Early Modern London* (New York: Oxford University Press, 1998), 91.

20 *The Arraignment, Conviction, and Imprisoning, of Christmas: on St. Thomas Day Last.* (London: Simon Minc'd Pye, for Cissely Plum-Porridge, 1646).

21 Quotes in Pullar, *Consuming Passions*, 126.

22 Samuel Danforth, *The Cry of Sodom Enquired Into; upon Occasion of the Arraignment and Condemnation of Benjamin Goad, for his Prodigious Villany* (Cambridge, MA: Marmaduke Johnson, 1674).

23 Douglas L. Winiarski, *Darkness Falls on the Land of Light: Experiencing Religious Awakenings in Eighteenth-Century New England* (Published for the Omohundro Institute of Early American History and Culture by the University of North Carolina Press, Chapel Hill Williamsburg, VA, 2017), 464.

24 Elaine G. Breslaw, *Lotions, Potions, Pills, and Magic: Health Care in Early America* (New York: New York University Press, 2012), 69; David Judson, *Timely Warning, against Surfeiting and Drunkenness* (New York: Henry De Foreest, 1752).

25 Louis Golding and André L. Simon (eds.), *We Shall Eat and Drink Again: A Wine & Food Anthology* (London: Hutchinson, 1944), 134–5. Also David Strauss, *Setting the Table for Julia Child: Gourmet Dining in America, 1934–1961* (Baltimore, MD: Johns Hopkins University Press, 2011).

26 Pullar, *Consuming Passions*, 118–30; David Hackett Fisher, *Albion's Seed: Four British Folkways in America* (New York: Oxford University Press, 1989), 135; Jean-Pierre Poulain, "French Gastronomy, French Gastronomies," in D. Goldstein and K. Merkele (eds.), *Culinary Cultures of Europe: Identity, Diversity and Dialogue* (Strasbourg, France: Council of Europe Publishing, 2005).

27 Richard Godbeer, *Sexual Revolution in Early America* (Baltimore, MD: Johns Hopkins University Press, 2002); Keith Stavely and Kathleen Fitzgerald, "Plainness and Virtue in New England Cooking," in Susan R. Friedland (ed.), *Food and Morality: Proceedings of the Oxford Symposium on Food and Cookery 2007* (Blackawton, UK: Prospect Books, 2008).

28 Jeremy Taylor, *The Golden Grove, or, a Manuall of Daily Prayers and Letanies, Fitted to the Dayes of the Week Containing a Short Summary of What Is to Be Believed, Practised, Desired* (London: Printed by R. Norton for Richard Royston, 1655).

29 Thomas Wright, *The Passions of the Mind* (London: Valentine Simmes, 1601), 128.

30 Swapan Chakravorty, *Society and Politics in the Plays of Thomas Middleton* (Oxford: Clarendon Press, 1996), 185.

31 Jean-Robert Pitte, *French Gastronomy: The History and Geography of a Passion*, trans. Jody Gladding (New York: Columbia University Press, 2002).

32 Stephen Mennell, *All Manners of Food: Eating and Taste in England and France from the Middle Ages to the Present* (Champaign, IL: University of Illinois Press, 1985), 106. Astrid Franke similarly argues against "Puritanism" as the explanation for American anti-alcohol sentiment; Astrid Franke, "Drinking and Democracy in the Early Republic," in Christa Buschendorf and Astrid Franke (eds.), *Civilizing and Decivilizing Processes: Figurational Approaches to American Culture* (Newcastle-upon-Tyne: Cambridge Scholars Publishing, 2011), 63.

33 Eliza Leslie, *Miss Leslie's Behavior Book: A Guide and Manual for Ladies* (Philadelphia: T. B. Peterson and Brothers, 1859), 120–32.

34 Byron's objections were commented upon by contemporaries, like John Sanderson, "The French and English Kitchen," *Godey's Magazine and Lady's Book*, 1844: 18–21.

35 John Murray (ed.), *Lord Byron's Correspondence, Chiefly with Lady Melbourne, Mr. Hobhouse, the Hon. Douglas Kinnaird, and P. B. Shelley*, 2 vols., vol. 1 (London: John Murray, 1922), 84.

Chapter 1 The Pleasures of the Table

1 Elizabeth David, *An Omelette and a Glass of Wine*, ed. Jill Norman (Guilford, CT: The Lyons Press, 1987), 19–22.

2 John Wesley, *Primitive Physick: Or an Easy and Natural Method of Curing Most Diseases* (London: W. Strahan, 1761), xvii, xix.

3 Vicesimus Knox, *The Works of Vicesimus Knox, D. D.*, 7 vols., vol. 6 (London: J. Mawman, 1824), 278–91.

4 Gilbert Chinard, *Benjamin Franklin on the Art of Eating: Together with the Rules of Health and Long Life and the Rules to Find Out a Fit Measure of Meat and Drink, with Several Recipes* (Philadelphia: American Philosophical Society, 1958).

5 Eric T. Carlson, "Benjamin Rush and Mental Health," *Annals of the New York Academy of Sciences* 291(1) (April 1977).

6 Benjamin Rush, *Sixteen Introductory Lectures to Courses of Lectures upon the Institutes and Practices of Medicine* (Philadelphia: Bradford & Inskeep, 1811), 400, 55; Benjamin Rush, *Medical Inquiries and Observations* (1818), 139–40; Benjamin Rush, *Sermons to Gentlemen upon Temperance and Exercise* (Philadelphia: John Dunlap, 1777), 8–16.

7 Kathleen Brown, *Foul Bodies: Cleanliness in Early America* (New Haven, CT: Yale University Press, 2009), 188.

8 Quoted in Katharina Vester, *A Taste of Power: Food and American Identities*, ed. Darra Goldstein. California Studies in Food and Culture (Berkeley, CA: University of California Press, 2015), 28.

9 Mark McWilliams, *Food and the Novel in Nineteenth-Century Literature* (New York: Rowman & Littlefield, 2012), 8–46.

10 Linda Colley, *Britons: Forging the Nation, 1707–1837* (New Haven, CT: Yale University Press, 1992).

11 Eliza Smith, *The Compleat Housewife* (London: J. and J. Pemberton, 1739), n.p.

12 Andrew F. Smith (ed.), *The Oxford Companion to American Food and Drink* (New York: Oxford University Press, 2007), 237–9.

13 "Of Taste, Modern Table-Talk, and Luxury in Eating," *New-York Weekly Journal*, February 16, 1740.

14 Gilly Lehmann, *The British Housewife: Cookery Books, Cooking and Society in Eighteenth-Century Britain* (Totnes, UK: Prospect Books, 2003), 283.

15 John Adams to Abigail Adams, February 21, 1779; Adams Papers Digital Edition. Massachusetts Historical Society. See also Smith, *The Oxford Companion to American Food and Drink*, 237–9.

16 Rachel Hope Cleves, *The Reign of Terror in America: Visions of Violence from Anti-Jacobinism to Antislavery* (New York City: Cambridge University Press, 2009).

17 Jean-Robert Pitte, *French Gastronomy: The History and Geography of a Passion*, trans. Jody Gladding (New York: Columbia University Press, 2002), 123.

18 Pitte, *French Gastronomy*, 115–16; Rebecca L. Spang, *The Invention of the Restaurant: Paris and Modern Gastronomic Culture* (Cambridge, MA: Harvard University Press, 2000), 2.

19 Teresa M. Shaw, *The Burden of the Flesh: Fasting and Sexuality in Early Christianity* (Minneapolis: Fortress Press, 1998), 53–78.

20 Katie Rawson and Elliott Shore, *Dining Out: A Global History of Restaurants* (London: Reaktion Books, 2019), 30.

21 Spang, *The Invention of the Restaurant*, 80.

22 Rawson and Shore, *Dining Out*, 29.

23 Gonzalez-Quijano, "'La chère et la chair.'"

24 Priscilla Parkhurst Ferguson, *Accounting for Taste: The Triumph of French Cuisine* (Chicago: University of Chicago Press, 2004), 10, 85–91; Philippe Meyzie (ed.), *La Gourmandise entre péché et plaisir*, special issue of Lumières 11(1) (2008), 10.

25 E. C. Spary, *Eating the Enlightenment: Food and the Sciences in Paris, 1670–1760* (Chicago: University of Chicago Press, 2012).

26 Joseph de Berchoux, *La Gastronomie, ou, L'Homme des Champs à Table* (Paris: L'Imprimerie de Giguet, 1801).

27 Joseph de Berchoux, *Gastronomy, or The Bon-Vivant's Guide: A Poem, in Four Cantos* (London: J. Booth, 1810).

28 Quotation from an early English translation; Berchoux, *Gastronomy*, 1–2, 11.

29 Jean Anthelme Brillat-Savarin, *Physiologie du Gout, or Méditations de Gastronomie Transcendante* (Paris, 1826).

30 Francisque Michel and Édouard Fournier, *Histoire des Hôteliers, Cabarets, Hôtels Garnis, Restaurants et Cafés* (Paris, 1851), 305. All translations from French are my own.

31 Alfred Delvau, *Histoire anecdotiques des cafés et cabarets de Paris* (Paris: E. Dentu, 1862), 158; Albert de La Fizelière, *Vins à la mode et cabarets au XVIIe siècle* (Paris: Chez René Pincebourde, 1866), 57–8.

32 Spang, *The Invention of the Restaurant*, 208.

33 Georges Touchard-Lafosse, *Le Lutin Couleur de Feu, ou Mes Tablettes d'une Année* (Paris: Chez Mongie Jeune, 1821), 96.

34 Pierre Larousse, *Grand Dictionnaire Universel du XIX Siècle*, 15 vols., vol. 3 (Paris: Édouard Blot, 1867), 16.

35 M. Xavier and M. Duvert, *Les Cabinets Particuliers: Folie-Vaudeville en un Acte* (Paris: Barba, 1832), 5, 9.

36 Touchard-Lafosse, *Le Lutin Couleur de Feu, ou Mes Tablettes d'une Année*, 99–101.

37 Alfred Boyer, *Mémoires d'un Cabinet Particulier* (Paris: Librairie Cournol, 1863), 22.

38 Gustave Flaubert, *Sentimental Education*, trans. Robert Baldick (New York: Penguin, 1964), 326; Joseph J. B. Rienti, "Reading the Restaurant: Social Class, Identity, and the Culture of Consumption in the Nineteenth Century French Novel" (PhD, City University of New York, 2014), 121.

39 Larousse, *Grand Dictionnaire Universel du XIX Siècle*, 3, 16.

40 Gabrielle Houbre (ed.), *Le Livre des Courtisanes: Archives secrètes de la police des moeurs (1861–1876)* (Paris: Tallander, 2006), 28.

41 Andrew Israel Ross, *Public City/Public Sex: Homosexuality, Prostitution, and Urban Culture in Nineteenth-Century Paris* (Philadelphia, PA: Temple University Press, 2019), 184–9.

42 Gustave Macé, *La Police Parisienne: Gibier de Saint-Lazare*, La Police Parisienne (Paris: G. Charpentier, 1888), 100–2.

43 Taxile Delord, Arnould Frémy, and Edmond Auguste Texier, *Les petits-Paris. Paris-restaurants / par les auteurs des "Mémoires de Bilboquet"* (Paris: A. Taride, 1854), 73–6.

44 "Decline of French Cooking," *Times-Picayune*, July 6, 1885, p. 8.

45 Émile Goudeau, *Paris qui consomme* (Paris: Henri Beraldi, 1893), 228.

46 Larousse, *Grand Dictionnaire Universel du XIX Siècle*, 3, 16.

47 William Melmoth, *The Letters of Pliny the Consul: With Occasional Remarks*, vol. I (London: J. Dodsley, 1786), 36–8. This letter is discussed in Philippa Pullar, *Consuming Passions: Being an Historic Inquiry into Certain English Appetites* (Boston, MA: Little, Brown, 1970), 241.

48 Chiara Sulprizio, *Gender and Sexuality in Juvenal's Rome: Satire 2 and Satire 6* (Norman, OK: University of Oklahoma Press, 2020).

49 Kate Lister, *A Curious History of Sex* (London: Unbound, 2020), 157.

50 Giacomo Casanova, *History of My Life*, trans. Willard R. Trask, vols. 11 and 12 (New York: Harcourt Brace Jovanovich, 1971), 65.

51 Alfred Delvau, *Dictionnaire érotique moderne* (Bale: Karl Schmidt, 1891), 222.

52 Eugène Briffault, *Paris à Table*, 2018 edn, ed. J. Weintraub (New York: Oxford University Press, 1846), 137–50.

53 John F. Donahue, *Food and Drink in Antiquity: A Sourcebook* (London: Bloomsbury Publishing, 2014), 201.

54 Root and Courtine are both quoted in Glen Pitre, *The Crawfish Book: The Story of Man and Mudbugs Starting in 25,000 BC and Ending with the Batch Just Put On to Boil* (Jackson, MS: University of Mississippi Press, 1993), 106.

55 Jacques Normand, *Les Écrivisses: Fantasie en Vers dite par M. C. Coquelin, de la Comédie-Française, Dessins de S. Arcos* (Tresse: Paris, 1879).

56 Rachel Hope Cleves, "*Vocabula Amatoria*: A Glossary of French Culinary Sex Terms," *American Historical Review* 125(4) (October, 2020): 1332.

57 Norman Douglas, *Paneros: Some Words on Aphrodisiacs and the Like* (London: Chatto & Windus, 1931), 22.

58 Marika Galli, "Conceptions diététiques anciennes et appétits charnels: effets de la nourriture sur la sphère sexuelle," *Persée* 7 (2011).

59 Sarah Gordon, "Sausages, Nuts, and Eggs: Food Imagery, the Body, and Sexuality in the Old French Fabliaux," in Albrecht Classen (ed.), *Sexuality in the Middle Ages and Early Modern Times: New Approaches to a Fundamental Cultural-Historical and Literary-Anthropological Theme* (Berlin: Walter de Gruyter, 2008), 513.

60 From M. F. K. Fisher's translation of Jean Anthelme Brillat-Savarin, *The Physiology of Taste: Or Meditations on Transcendental Gastronomy*, trans. M. F. K. Fisher (New York: Vintage, 2011), 159. The Fisher translation of Brillat-Savarin is the subject of withering criticism by Justin Spring, but I like it. Justin Spring, *The Gourmands' Way: Six Americans in Paris and the Birth of a New Gastronomy* (New York: Farrar, Straus and Giroux, 2017), 76–8. For the original, see Jean Anthelme Brillat-Savarin, *Physiologie du Gout, ou Méditations de Gastronomie transcendante* (Paris: Charpentier, 1840), 154.

61 Jean Anthelme Brillat-Savarin, *The Physiology of Taste; or, Transcendental Gastronomy*, trans. Fayette Robinson (Philadelphia: Lindsay & Blakiston, 1854), 103–6.

62 Brillat-Savarin, *The Physiology of Taste*, 127.

63 Paul Mahalin, *Le Bougeoir, lanternes des dames* (Paris, 1868), 26–7. Cited in Gonzalez-Quijano, "'La chère et la chair,'" 27.

64 Macé, *La Police Parisienne*, 103.

65 Boyer, *Mémoires d'un Cabinet Particulier*, 11.

66 Jules Boyer, *Nocturnal Paris or Paris after Dark: Containing a Description of the Fast Women, Their Haunts, Habits, etc. to which is Added a Faithful Description of the Night Amusements and Other Resorts Also All Particulars Relative to the Working of the Social Evil in the French Metropolis* (Boulogne (Seine), 1877), 56–8.

67 Albert Barrère, *Argot and Slang: A New French and English Dictionary of the Cant Words, Quaint Expressions, Slang Terms and Flash Phrases Used in the High and Low Life of Old and New Paris* (London: Whittaker & Co., 1889), 433. See also Barrère's extensive list of synonyms for "prostitute" on p. 170.

68 A. Coffignon, *Paris Vivant: La Corruption à Paris: Le Demi-Monde, Les Souteneurs, La Police des Moeurs, Brasseries de Femmes, Filles Galantes, Saint-Lazare, Le Chantage etc. etc.* (Paris: Jules Tallandrier, 1888), 125–39. For a definition of *ogresse*, see Jill Harsin, *Policing Prostitution in Nineteenth-Century Paris* (Princeton, NJ: Princeton University Press, 1985), 289.

69 Nérée Desarbres, *Deux Siècles à L'Opéra* (Paris: E. Dentu, 1868), 251–2.

70 Harsin, *Policing Prostitution*, 291.

71 Coffignon, *Paris Vivant*, 125–39.

72 Gonzalez-Quijano, "'La chère et la chair.'"

73 John Stephen Farmer, *Vocabula Amatoria: A French–English Glossary of Words, Phrases, and Allusions occuring in the works of Rabelais, Volatire, Molière, Rousseau, Béranger, Zola and Others* (London: privately printed for subscribers only, 1896), 246. For more, see Cleves, "*Vocabula Amatoria.*"

74 Macé, *La Police Parisienne*, 102–6.

75 Charles Virmaitre, *Supplément au Dictionnaire d'Argot fin-de-siècle* (Paris: A. Charles, 1894), 106.

76 Eugene Furpille, *Paris à Vol de Canard* (Paris, 1857), 143.

77 Alphonse Esquiros, *Les Vierges Folles* (Paris: P. Delavigne, 1842), 46–8; Alphonse Esquiros, *Les Vierges Folles* (Paris: E. Dentu, 1873), 128–33. There are significant differences between the discussion of prostitutes' appetites in these two editions. The first edition offers more details about phrenology, and also describes the organ of amativity (love) as having a role in the prostitute's makeup. The later edition focuses entirely on the appetite for food and offers an expanded list of physical characteristics of the prostitute. Esquiros's theories are discussed in Virginia Rounding, *Grandes Horizontales: The Lives and Legends of Four Nineteenth-Century Courtesans* (London: Bloomsbury, 2003), 27. See also Jann Matlock, *Scenes of Seduction: Prostitution, Hysteria, and Reading Difference in Nineteenth-Century France* (New York: Columbia University Press, 1994), 123–4.

78 Rounding, *Grandes Horizontales*.

79 Auguste Escoffier, *Memories of My Life*, trans. Laurence Escoffier (New York: Van Nostrand Reinhold, 1997), 13–14.

80 Rounding, *Grandes Horizontales*, 236–7.

81 Pitte, *French Gastronomy*, 123.

82 Zed (Charles-Albert comte de Maugny), *Le Demi-Monde sous le Second Empire: Souvenirs d'un Sybarite* (Paris: Ernest Kolb, 1892), 43–8. See also "'La chère et la chair,'" 18, 9.

83 *Les Joyeuses Dames de Paris* (Paris, 1867), 164.

84 Philibert Audebrand, *Les Gasconnades de L'Amour* (Paris: E. Dentu, 1881), 327–8.

85 Alfred Delvau, *Les Plaisirs de Paris: Guide Pratique des Étrangers* (Paris: Achille Faure, 1867), 122–3.

86 Quoted in Ross, *Public City/Public Sex*, 184.

87 *Paris at Night: Sketches and Mysteries of Paris High Life and Demi-Monde. Nocturnal Amusements: How to Know Them! How to Enjoy Them!! How to Appreciate Them!!!* (Boston: Boston and Paris Publishing Company, 1875), 32.

88 Edmond de Goncourt, Jules de Goncourt, *Journal des Goncourt: Mémoires de la Vie Littéraire*, vol. 6 (Paris; E. Flammarion, 1956): 147; Joanna Richardson, *The Courtesans: The Demi-monde in Nineteenth-Century France* (London: Weidenfeld & Nicolson, 1966), 30.

89 Julian Field Osgood, *Things I Shouldn't Tell* (Philadelphia, PA: L. B. Lippincott, 1925), 200.

90 "Marquise de Fontenoy," *Chicago Daily Tribune*, February 5, 1909; "Marquise de Fontenoy," *Chicago Daily Tribune*, April 20, 1913.

91 Rienti, "Reading the Restaurant," 3.

92 Alexandre Dumas, *Grand Dictionnaire de Cuisine* (Paris: Éditions Pierre Grobel, 1873).

93 Albert Dresden Vandam, *An Englishman in Paris* (New York: D. Appleton & Company, 1899), 44.

94 Dorsey, "The Gourmet's Paradise," *The Argonaut* (San Francisco), November 20, 1895, p. 5.

95 William, "Lolo," *La Vie Parisienne* (October 8, 1864), 576–7.

96 Henri Meilhac and Ludovic Halévy, *La Vie Parisienne: Pièce en Cinq Actes* (Paris: Michel Lévy, 1867), 110.

97 Martin Priestman, *Detective Fiction and Literature: The Figure on the Carpet* (New York: Palgrave Macmillan, 1991), 56–73; Guillaume Foussard, "The Emergence of French Crime Fiction during the Nineteenth Century," *Journal of Publishing Culture* 4 (2015).

98 Adolphe Belot, *Le Drame de la Rue de la Paix* (Paris: Michel Lévy Frères, 1872), 166. For more about Belot, see Gretchen Schultz, *Sapphic Fathers: Discourses of Same-Sex Desire from Nineteenth-Century France* (Toronto: University of Toronto Press, 2014), 65–104.

99 Pierre Alexis Ponson du Terrail, *Les Voleurs du Grande Monde: Le Seigneur de la Montagne* (Paris: E. Dentu, 1870), 161–2.

100 Charles Mérouvel, *Les Secrets de Paris: Angèle Méraud* (Paris: E. Dentu, 1883), 162.

101 Fortuné du Boisgobey, *La Bande Rouge: Adventures d'une Jeune Fille pendant le Siège* (Paris: E. Dentu, 1886), 66.

102 Honoré de Balzac, *Le Père Goriot* (Paris: Michel Lévy, 1875), 229; Flaubert, *Sentimental Education*, 209–15; Émile Zola, *Nana* (Paris: G. Charpentier, 1880), 231, 234; Émile Zola, *La Curée* (Paris: A. Lacroix, 1871), 163–71; Alphonse Daudet, *Les Rois en Exil: Roman Parisien* (Paris: E. Dentu, 1879), 150. See also the mention of the Café Anglais in the Guy de Maupassant short story "Bijoux," first published in *Gil Blas* in 1883, and in Marcel Proust's volume 2 of *Remembrance of Things Past* (1919).

103 Ernest A. Vizetelley, *Émile Zola: Novelist and Reformer* (London: John Lane, 1894), 144–6.

104 "Frogs and Snails," *Once a Week* 63 (March 13, 1869), 184–5.

105 Mary Elizabeth Braddon, *Ishmael: A Novel* (London: J. and R. Maxwell), 270.

106 X. L. "A Kiss of Judas," *Pall Mall Magazine*, vol. 1 (1893): 345; X. L. "A Waltz of Chopin," in *Aut Diabolus Aut Nihil and Other Tales* (London: Methuen & Co., 1895), 64; Osgood, *Things I Shouldn't Tell*, 183.

107 Francis Bourne-Newton, *Gastronomic Guide to Paris* (New York: The Caterer Publishing, 1903); Nathaniel Newnham-Davis, *The Gourmet's Guide to Europe*, 2nd edn (New York: Brentano's, 1908), 5–7.

108 Barbara Cartland, *The Golden Illusion* (New York: Bantam Books, 1976), 81; Frank Wilkinson, *Bygones* (New York: Zebra Books, 1981), 217.

109 Ferguson, *Accounting for Taste*, 84.

Chapter 2 Innocents Abroad

1 Francis William Blagdon, *Paris as It Was and as It Is; or A Sketch of the French Capital*, vol. 1 (London: C. and R. Baldwin, 1803), 437–60.

2 Benjamin Colbert, "Bibliography of British Travel Writing, 1780–1840: The European Tour, 1814–1818," *Romantic Textualities: Literature and Print Culture, 1780–1840* 13 (2013).

3 Harvey Levenstein, *Seductive Journey: American Tourists in France from Jefferson to the Jazz Age* (Chicago: University of Chicago Press, 1998), 22.

4 John Scott, *A Visit to Paris in 1814: Being a Review of the Moral, Political, Intellectual, and Social Condition of the French Capital* (London: Longman, Hurst, Rees, Orme, and Brown, 1815), 51.

5 Henry Matthews, *Diary of an Invalid: Being the Journal of a Tour in Pursuit of Health in Portugal, Italy, Switzerland, and France in the Years 1817, 1818 and 1819* (Paris: A. and W. Galignani, 1825), 394.

6 Edward Planta, *A New Picture of Paris; Or, The Stranger's Guide to the French Metropolis* (London: Samuel Leigh, 1816), 54–5.

7 Ian Littlewood, *Sultry Climates: Travel & Sex* (Cambridge, MA: Da Capo Press, 2001).

8 Blagdon, *Paris as It Was*, 1, 442.

9 *Oeuvres Complètes de Diderot*, vol. 19 (Paris: Garnier Frères, 1876), 235.

10 *The Pictorial French Dictionary* (London: Charles Tilt, 1839), 306.

11 Grimod de La Reynière, "Almanach des Gourmands ou Calendrier Nutritif," *Chez Maradan*, 1803.

12 Grimod de La Reynière, *Almanach des Gourmands: Sixième Année* (Paris: Chez Maradan, 1808), 261.

13 César Gardeton, *Nouveau guide des dîneurs ou Répertoire des restaurants à la carte et à prix fixe*, quoted in Laurent Baridon, "*La Carte vivante du Restaurateur de Grandville*: les appétits d'une période de crise," in Bertrand Marquer and Éléonore Reverzy (eds.), *La Cuisine de l'Oeuvre au XIXe Siècle: Regards d'Artistes et d'Écrivains* (Strasbourg: Presses universitaires de Strasbourg, 2013), 16. Also Rebecca L. Spang, *The Invention of the Restaurant: Paris and Modern Gastronomic Culture* (Cambridge, MA: Harvard University Press, 2000), 199.

14 Scott, *A Visit to Paris in 1814*, 52, 93, 128, 32.

15 Stephen Weston, *A Slight Sketch of Paris; Or, Some Account of the French Capital in Its Improved State, since 1802* (London: Robert Baldwin, 1814), 32–3.

16 Thomas Rowlandson, *La Belle Liminaudiere au Caffe de Mille Collone. Palais Royal Paris* (1814). National Gallery of Art. Rosenwald Collection, 1945.5.1254.b.

17 *La Belle limonadière ou le Trône des milles Colonnes* (1816), Bibliothèque Nationale de France, département Arsenal, EST-204 (93). See also the portrait by Parfait Augrand, *La belle Limonadière* (1819).

18 Alfred Delvau, *Dictionnaire érotique moderne* (Bale: Karl Schmidt, 1891), 77.

19 An 1817 erotic print titled *Lady Cauchemar au Café des Mille Colonnes* by Georges-Jacques Gatine seems to depict a successor to Romain. In the picture, the woman is seated behind a mirrored counter which reflects the legs of the men standing around it, giving the appearance that she is naked from the waist down. Bibliothèque nationale de France, département Arsenal, EST-204 (94).

20 Nathaniel H. Carter, *Letters from Europe, Comprising the Journal of a Tour through Ireland, England, Scotland, France, Italy, and Switzerland, in the Years 1825, '26, and '27* (New York: G. & C. Carvill, 1827), 421.

21 Blagdon, *Paris as It Was*, 1, 119–20.

22 Thomas Rowlandson, *Madame Very Restauranteur, Palais Royal Paris, and La Belle Liminaudiere au Caffee de Mille Collone, Palais Royale Paris* (1814). The Elisha Whittelsey Collection, 1959, Metropolitan Museum of Art.

23 Louis Marie Yves Queverdo, *Milord Bouffi payant sa Carte à Madame Veri*, c. 1815. The British Museum. 1979, U.559. Queverdo also sketched *La Belle Limonadière*. See Louis Marie Yves Queverdo, "Portraits fidèles des maisons à la mode No 4/La Belle Limonadière ou le café des milles colonnes" (1817). Musée Carnavalet, Histoire de Paris. G10953.

24 Aaron Martinet, *Le goût du jour, No. 25, le gastronôme après diner*, 1814. The British Museum 1861. 1012.379.

25 Baridon, "*La Carte vivante du Restaurateur de Grandville*: les appétits d'une période de crise," 18.

26 John Sanderson, *Sketches of Paris: In Familiar Letters to His Friends* (Philadelphia: E. L. Carey and A. Hart, 1838), 57.

27 F. Lloyd, *The Paris Estafette; or, Pilferings from the Paris and Dover Post-Bag* (London: G. Biggs, 1842), 184. See also N. Parker Willis, *Pencillings by the Way: Written during Some Years of Residence and Travel in Europe* (New York: Charles Scribner & Sons, 1856), 112.

28 Susan Hale (ed.), *Life and Letters of Thomas Gold Appleton* (New York: D. Appleton & Company, 1885), 130.

29 J. G. Millingen, *Recollections of Republican France, from 1790 to 1801* (London: Henry Colburn, 1848), 239.

30 Stanley T. Williams, "Washington Irving's First Stay in Paris," *American Literature* 2(1) (March, 1930).

31 "Le facheux contretems ou l'anglais surpris par sa femme," 1818, published by Gault de Saint-Germain. British Museum. 2009, 7032.3.

32 Rachel Hope Cleves, "*Vocabula Amatoria*: A Glossary of French Culinary Sex Terms," *American Historical Review* 125(4) (October, 2020): 1330.

33 Hezekiah Hartley Wright, *Desultory Reminiscences of a Tour through Germany, Switzerland, and France* (Boston: William D. Ticknor, 1838), 13, 236, 92, 322.

34 David McCullough, *The Greater Journey: Americans in Paris* (New York: Simon & Schuster, 2011), 132.

35 L. J. Frazee, *The Medical Student in Europe* (Maysville, KY: R. H. Collins, 1849), 40, 69.

36 McCullough, *The Greater Journey*, 122–3.

37 See chapter 6.

38 Mark Twain, *The Innocents Abroad, or, The New Pilgrims' Progress* (San Francisco: H. H. Bancroft and Company, 1869), 150–1.

39 "A 'Good American,'" *The Critic* 70 (May 2, 1885): 206.

40 Julia Ward Howe, *Reminiscences, 1819–1899* (Boston: Houghton, Mifflin, 1899), 432.

41 "A 'Good American,'" 206; Howe, *Reminiscences, 1819–1899*, 434.

42 Hale, *Life and Letters of Thomas Gold Appleton*, 301, 37.

43 Jane Moore, "Thomas Moore, Anacreon and the Romantic Tradition," *Romantic Textualities* 21 (Winter 2013).

44 John Russell (ed.), *Memoirs, Journal, and Correspondence of Thomas Moore*, vol. 1 (New York: Appleton & Company, 1857), 317–429, esp. 323, 350.

45 Russell, *Memoirs, Journal, and Correspondence of Thomas Moore*, 317.

46 Brian Cowan, *The Social Life of Coffee: The Emergence of the British Coffeehouse* (New Haven, CT: Yale University Press, 2005), 246–54.

47 Planta, *A New Picture of Paris*, 40, 140.

48 William Shepherd, *Paris, in Eighteen Hundred and Two, and Eighteen Hundred and Fourteen* (London: Longman, Hurst, Rees, Orme, and Brown, 1814), 175. See also Richard Boyle Bernard, *A Tour through Some Parts of France, Switzerland, Savoy, Germany and Belgium, during the Summer and Autumn of 1814* (London: Longman, Hurst, Rees, Orme, and Brown, 1815), 59.

49 Scott, *A Visit to Paris in 1814*, 129.

50 W. Stewart, *Diary of an Excursion to France in the Months of August and September 1814* (Edinburgh: Manners and Miller, 1814), 38, 120, 24.

51 John Sanderson, "The French and English Kitchen," *Godey's Magazine and Lady's Book*, 1844: 18–21.

52 Frazee, *The Medical Student in Europe*, 40, 116–17.

53 A. Coffignon, *Paris Vivant: La Corruption à Paris: Le Demi-Monde, Les Souteneurs, La Police des Moeurs, Brasseries de Femmes, Filles Galantes, Saint-Lazare, Le Chantage etc. etc.* (Paris: Jules Tallandrier, 1888), 133.

54 Emma Willard, *Journal and Letters: From France and Great-Britain* (Troy, NY: N. Tuttle, 1833), 82.

55 Caroline Kirkland, *Holidays Abroad, or Europe from the West*, 3 vols., vol. 1 (New York: Charles Scribner, 1854), 133–4.

56 Caroline W. Cushing, *Letters, Descriptive of Public Monuments, Scenery, and Manners in France and Spain* (Newburyport, MA: E. W. Allen & Co., 1832), 8–10.

57 Jane Bigelow Diary, November 1858–December 1858, p. 27. Bigelow Family Papers, New York Public Library.

58 Laure Katsaros, "Greenhorns and She-Devils: George Foster on Prostitution in Mid-Nineteenth-Century New York," *Médias* 19 (2018): 16. Marguerittes performed under the stage name Madame Bozzi.

59 Julie de Marguerittes, *The Ins and Outs of Paris: Or, Paris by Day and Night* (Philadelphia: Wm. White Smith, 1855), 64, 118–27, 255.

60 Eric G. E. Zuelow, *A History of Modern Tourism* (London: Palgrave Macmillan, 2016), 76–90.

61 J. Steward, *The Stranger's Guide to Paris* (Paris: Baudry's European Library, 1837), 30.

62 Wideawake, *Paris and Brussels after Dark: The Cocottes, or, Gay Women of Paris and Brussels* (Paris, 1865), 20–2. Café le Brebant remains in operation, and travelers' reviews on websites like Google and TripAdvisor still warn potential diners not to get scammed by the high prices.

63 Alfred Delvau, *Les Plaisirs de Paris: Guide Pratique des Étrangers* (Paris: Achille Faure, 1867), 109.

64 Peeping Tom, *Paris by Gaslight: Being a Complete Description of the Amusements, &c., Illustrative of Life in the French Metropolis* (Thomas & Co., 1867), 40–52. The book cites M. Reboux's *Ces Dames du Casino* as the original source of information about the sob trick, which is also included in Wideawake, *Paris and Brussels*, 27–8.

65 Jules Boyer, *Nocturnal Paris or Paris after Dark: Containing a Description of the Fast Women, Their Haunts, Habits, etc. to which is Added a Faithful Description of the Night Amusements and Other Resorts Also All Particulars Relative to the Working of the Social Evil in the French Metropolis* (Boulogne [Seine], 1877), 20–2, 46.

66 Captain Wray Sylvester, *The Nocturnal Pleasures of Paris: A Guide to the Gay City.* (Paris: The Byron Library, 1889), 91–111.

Chapter 3 Perverted Appetites

1 "For the Norwich Courier," *Norwich Courier*, September 24, 1828. The word "gastronomy" first appeared in American newspapers in 1817; "Second Course of French Readings & Recitations," *The Repertory*, Boston, MA, August 5, 1817, 4.

2 Joan Jacobs Brumberg, "The Appetite as Voice," in Carole Counihan and Penny Van Esterik (eds.), *Food and Culture: A Reader* (New York: Routledge, 1997), 166.

3 For the Norwich Courier," *Norwich Courier*, September 24, 1828.

4 Isaac Appleton Jewett, *Passages in Foreign Travel*, 2 vols., vol. 2 (Boston: Charles C. Little and James Brown, 1838), 31.

5 Frances Milton Trollope, *Domestic Manners of the Americans*, 2 vols., vol. 1 (London: Whittaker, Treacher, & Co., 1832), 67.

6 E. Mannering, *Christian Consistency; or, The Connexion between Experimental and Practical Religion* (Philadelphia: Presbyterian Board of Publication of Tracts and Sabbath School Books, 1839), 118.

7 Sylvester Graham, "A Lecture on Epidemic Diseases Generally, and Particularly the Spasmodic Cholera; Delivered in the City of New York, March, 1832, and repeated, June, 1832, and in Albany July, 1832, and in New York, June, 1833" (Boston: David Campbell, 1838), 49. For more on Graham, see Stephen Nissenbaum, *Sex, Diet, and Debility in Jacksonian America: Sylvester Graham and Health Reform*, Contributions in Medical History (Westport, CT: Greenwood Press, 1980); Adam D. Shprintzen, *The Vegetarian Crusade: The Rise of an American Reform Movement, 1817–1921* (Chapel Hill, NC: University of North Carolina Press, 2013), 21–2.

8 Sylvester Graham, *A Treatise on Bread, and Bread-Making* (Boston: Light & Stearns, 1837), v, 61, 25, 105, 36.

9 Stephen Mennell, *All Manners of Food: Eating and Taste in England and France from the Middle Ages to the Present* (Champaign, IL: University of Illinois Press, 1985), 214.

10 Lydia Maria Child, *The Frugal Housewife* (Boston: Marsh & Capen, 1829), 8, 45.

11 Yvonne Elizabeth Pelletier, "Strawberries and Salt: Culinary Hazards and Moral Education in *Little Women*," in Monika Elbert and Marie Drews (eds.), *Culinary Aesthetics and Practices in Nineteenth-Century American Literature* (New York: Palgrave Macmillan, 2009), 189–204.

12 Carolyn Daniel, *Voracious Children: Who Eats Whom in Children's Literature* (New York: Routledge, 2006), 42.

13 William Andrus Alcott, *The Young House-Keeper, or, Thoughts on Food and Cookery* (Boston: George W. Light, 1839), 18, 43, 37, 88, 160, 90.

14 Michel Foucault, *The History of Sexuality: An Introduction*, trans. Robert Hurley, 3 vols., vol. 1 (New York: Vintage Press, 1990), 12.

15 Dio Lewis, *Chastity; or, Our Secret Sins* (Philadelphia: George Maclean & Co., 1874), 20.

16 Dio Lewis, "Notes and Maxims about Health," *Scientific American* 23(22) (November 26, 1870): 337.

17 Lewis, *Chastity*, 30, 34, 265–73.

18 Lewis, *Chastity*, 23.

19 White and her husband knew Dio Lewis, and visited him at his home in Boston; Ellen G. White, *Manuscript Releases*, vol. 5 [Nos. 260–346] (Ellen G. White Estate, 2017), 308.

20 Terrie Dopp Aamodt, Gary Land, and Ronald L. Numbers (eds.), *Ellen Harmon White: American Prophet* (New York: Oxford University Press, 2014), 198–200.

21 Ellen Gould Harmon White, "Chapter 39: Health," in *Spiritual Gifts* (Battle Creek, MI: Seventh-day Adventist Publishing Association, 1864).

22 E. G. W., "Moral and Physical Law," *Good Health* 7(10) (October, 1872): 26–7; Ellen White, "Temperance in the Family," *The Signs of the Times*, September 22, 1881; Ellen White, "Controlling the Appetites and Passions," in *The Sanctified Life* (Battle Creek, MI: Review and Herald Publishing Association, 1937).

23 See, for example, William A. Alcott, *Letters to a Sister; or Woman's Mission* (Buffalo, NY: G. H. Derby, 1850), 295; William A. Alcott, *Gift Book for Young Ladies; Or, Familiar Letters on Their Acquaintants, Male and Female, Employments, Friendships, &c.* (Buffalo, NY: G. H. Derby and Co., 1852), 295; William A. Alcott, *The Young Woman's Book of Health* (Auburn, NY: Miller, Orton, & Mulligan), 184.

24 "I Can't and I Won't," *Graham Journal of Health* 1(14) (July 4, 1837): 1; "Reflections," *Graham Journal of Health* 2(5) (March 3, 1838), 15; "Physical Suffering the Consequence of Violated Physical Law," *Graham Journal of Health* 2(17) (August 18, 1838): 8; William Metcalfe, "Diet," *American Vegetarian and Health Journal* 1(5) (May, 1851): 85; Daniel Lott, "Who is Right?," *American Vegetarian and Health Journal* 1(9) (September, 1851): 155.

25 Committee, "Vegetarian Progress," *American Vegetarian and Health Journal* 1(5) (May, 1851): 92.

26 Lewis, *Chastity*, 269.

27 Aamodt, Land, and Numbers (eds.), *Ellen Harmon White: American Prophet*, 199–201. White also decried "fleshy lusts," a term she took from the New Testament and defined as "wrong habits of eating and drinking."

28 Brian C. Wilson, *Dr. John Harvey Kellogg and the Religion of Biologic Living* (Bloomington, IN: Indiana University Press, 2014).

29 Wilson, *Dr. John Harvey Kellogg*, 50.

30 Wilson, *Dr. John Harvey Kellogg*, 30–61.

31 A few examples from the journal's first year: E. G. W., "Parents Their Own Physicians," *Good Health* 1(3) (October, 1866): 3–5; Miss Dr. Lamson, "Happiness a Natural Condition," *Good Health* 1(10) (May, 1867): 9–10; J. H. Waggoner, "White and Brown Bread," *Good Health* 1(11–12) (June, 1867): 4–5; D. M. Canright, "Nothing Fit to Eat," *Good Health* 1(11–12) (June, 1867): 12.

32 D. T. Bourdeau, "Health. No. 6: Eating and Drinking," *Good Health* 1(8) (March, 1867): 1–4.

33 J. F. Meigs and William Pepper, "Treatment of Chronic Diarrhea in Children," *The Monthly Abstract of Medical Science* 55 (July, 1872): 272; Jerome Walker, "Do Children Over-Eat?" *The Home-Maker* 1(3) (December, 1888): 75–8; "Helpful Suggestions for Mothers," *Everyday Housekeeping* 19(6) (September, 1903): 87.

34 Simplicitas, "Cookery: A Word against Pickles," *The Woman Worker* 4(13) (September, 29, 1909): 14.

35 "Self," *All the World; A Monthly Record of the Work of the Salvation Army in All Lands* 6(10) (October 1, 1890): 2.

36 "A Fad No Longer," *Sunderland Daily Echo and Shipping Gazette*, December 22, 1892.

37 J. F. Clymer, *Food and Morals: A Sermon Preached by Rev. J. F. Clymer in the First Methodist Episcopal Church at Auburn, New York* (New York: Fowler & Wells, 1888).

38 Quoted in Rachel Rich, *Bourgeois Consumption: Food, Space and Identity in London and Paris, 1850–1914* (Manchester: Manchester University Press, 2011), 27.

39 Archibald Alison, *Travels in France during the Years 1814–1815*, vol. 2 (Edinburgh: Macredie, Skelly, and Muckersy, 1816), 282–3.

40 Bigelow Diary Transcripts, 1843–1860. Bigelow Family Papers, Box 102, New York Public Library.

41 January 10, 1860 entry; Transcript of Jane Bigelow Diary, July 1859–January 1860. For a description of her as "cheerfully unconventional," see 1895 clipping from the *Chicago Tribune* included in a volume from the "Assorted ledgers and diaries assoc'd with Jane Poultney Bigelow." Bigelow Family Papers, Box 34, New York Public Library.

42 November 28, 1858, entry in Jane Bigelow Diary, November 1858–December 1858; June 13, 1865, entry in Jane Bigelow Diary. Bigelow Family Papers. New York Public Library.

43 Hugh R. Haweis, *Travel and Talk 1885–93–95: My Hundred Thousand Miles of Travel through America, Canada, Australia, New Zealand, Tasmania, Ceylon, and the Paradises of the Pacific*, vol. 1. (New York: Dodd, Mead, & Company, 1897), 97–102.

44 July 12, 1867, entry in Jane Bigelow Diary. April 1867–August 1869. Bigelow Family Papers. New York Public Library.

45 November 4, 1838, entry in Sylvia Drake Diary. Charity Bryant–Sylvia Drake Papers, Henry Sheldon Museum.

46 Rachel Hope Cleves, *Charity and Sylvia: A Same-Sex Marriage in Early America* (New York: Oxford University Press, 2014).

47 Frances Shimer to Caroline Nash, May 17, 1853. Frances W. Shimer College Collection, Box 3, Folder 5, Regional History Center, Northern Illinois University.

48 Rachel Hope Cleves, "Six Ways of Looking at a Trans Man?: The Life of Frank Shimer (1826–1901)," *Journal of the History of Sexuality* 27(1) (January, 2018).

49 Harriet Sanderson Stewart Diary, "Western Wanderings," 1906–1907, vol. 2, 364–5. Sallie Bingham Center for Women's History & Culture.

50 Carolyn A. Day, *Consumptive Chic: A History of Beauty, Fashion, and Disease* (London: Bloomsbury Academic, 2017).

51 Helena Michie, *The Flesh Made Word: Female Figures and Women's Bodies* (New York: Oxford University Press, 1987), 15; Abigail Dennis, "'A Study in Starvation': The New Girl and the Gendered Socialisation of Appetite in Sarah Grand's *The Beth Book*," *Australasian Journal of Victorian Studies* 12(1) (2007).

52 Abba Goold Woolson, *Woman in American Society* (Boston: Roberts Brothers, 1873), 136.

53 Ada Clare, *Only a Woman's Heart* (New York: M. Doolady, 1866), 14–15, 106, 286.

54 Edith Wharton, *False Dawn (The 'Forties)* (New York: D. Appleton and Company, 1924), 22–3.

55 Lauren Christie Navarro, "Feast, Famine, and 'Such Queer Things to Eat': The Decline of Lily Bart," *Edith Wharton Review* 33(1) (2017): 1–29.

Chapter 4 Private Rooms and Rooms Private

1 Isaac Appleton Jewett, *Passages in Foreign Travel*, 2 vols., vol. 1 (Boston: Charles C. Little and James Brown, 1838), 227, 309.

2 David S. Shields, *The Culinarians: Lives and Careers from the First Age of American Fine Dining* (Chicago: University of Chicago Press, 2017), 25–9.

3 Andrew F. Smith, *Eating History: 30 Turning Points in the Making of American Cuisine* (New York: Columbia University Press, 2009), 16–26; Paul Freedman, *Ten Restaurants*

that Changed America (New York: Liveright Publishing, 2016), 3–48; Shields, *The Culinarians*, 107–9.

4 "New-York Daguerreotyped," *Putnam's Monthly Magazine of American Literature, Science, and Art* (April, 1853): 135. The presence of prostitutes at Delmonico's is also alluded to in N. Parker Willis, *The Rag-Bag: A Collection of Ephemera* (New York: C. Scribner, 1855), 132.

5 Frederick A. Pottle (ed.), *Boswell's London Journal 1762–1763*, 1991 edn (New York: McGraw-Hill Book Company, 1950), 240, 68; Brenda Assael, *The London Restaurant, 1840–1914* (New York: Oxford University Press, 2018).

6 Charles Dickens, *Dickens's Dictionary of London: An Unconventional Handbook* (London: Macmillan & Co.), 224.

7 Gregory Houston Bowden, *British Gastronomy: The Rise of Great Restaurants* (London: Chatto & Windus, 1975).

8 John DeFerrari, *Historic Restaurants of Washington, DC: Capital Eats* (Charleston, SC: History Press, 2013).

9 "American and French Restaurants," *National Intelligencer*, January 1, 1838.

10 Padraig Riley, "The Lonely Congressmen: Gender and Politics in Early Washington, DC," *Journal of the Early Republic* 34(2) (Summer, 2014): 264.

11 Cindy R. Lobell, "'Out to Eat': The Emergence and Evolution of the Restaurant in Nineteenth-Century New York City," *Winterthur Portfolio* 44(2/3) (2010).

12 Members of the New York Press, *The Night Side of New York: A Picture of the Great Metropolis after Nightfall* (New York: J. C. Haney & Co., 1866), 77–9.

13 "A Most Capital Place," *The Pick* (New York), February 2, 1852: 3.

14 "Dinners and Diners," *New York Clipper*, May 5, 1866.

15 George Ellington, *The Women of New York; Or, the Under-World of the Great City* (New York: New York Book Co., 1869), 272–7.

16 New York Press, *The Night Side of New York*, 79.

17 "Mssrs. Shelley & Dupignac," *National Police Gazette*, May 11, 1850: 3.

18 William M. Bobo, *Glimpses of New York City by a South Carolinian (who Had Nothing Else to Do)* (Charleston: J. J. McCarter, 1852), 54.

19 Katie M. Hemphill, *Bawdy City: Commercial Sex and Regulation in Baltimore, 1790–1915* (New York: Cambridge University Press, 2020), 74, 92–3. Welsh also rented out rooms to prostitutes.

20 "Parisian Restaurant," *Daily Inter Ocean*, December 21, 1890.

21 "Where to Dine," *Portland Oregonian*, August 7, 1892; August 14, 1892; August 24, 1892.

22 "Maison Dorée," *Harvard Lampoon* 6(1), October 4, 1878.

23 "Notice to the Public," *Vicksburg Herald*, July 22, 1864. For Vicksburg, see Christopher Morris, *Becoming Southern: The Evolution of a Way of Life, Warren County and Vicksburg, Mississippi, 1770–1860* (New York: Oxford University Press, 1995), 121.

24 "Hotel du Globe. Restaurant Francais!!" *Polynesian*, April 17, 1852.

25 Shields, *The Culinarians*, 415. Shields notes many nineteenth-century restaurants with private rooms, and doesn't distinguish which were devoted to the sex trade.

26 "Restaurant du Commerce," *Sacramento Bee*, November 30, 1869.

27 Angela C. Fitzpatrick, "Women of Ill Fame: Discourses of Prostitution and the American Dream in California, 1850–1890." PhD, Graduate College of Bowling Green State University: 2013.

28 The unpublished memoir of Ben-Ezra Stiles Ely comments on the frequency with which men conducted business in brothels during San Francisco's early days, because they were some of the only well-furnished houses in the city; "Memoir of Ben Ezra Stiles Ely," Curtis Dahl Papers, Marion B. Gebbie Class of 1901 Archives. Wheaton College, Norton, Massachusetts.

29 Erica J. Peters, *San Francisco: A Food Biography* (Lanham, MD: Rowman & Littlefield, 2013), 114.

30 Clarence E. Edwords, *Bohemian San Francisco, Its Restaurants and Their Most Famous Recipes: The Elegant Art of Dining* (San Francisco: Paul Elder and Company Publishers, 1914), 16–17.

31 *Out in Frisco*, 1900–.

32 Old Poodle Dog Restaurant Ephemera, approximately 1906–1922, Box 2, Bancroft Library, University of California, Berkeley.

33 Sally Stanford, *The Lady of the House: The Autobiography of Sally Stanford* (New York: G. P. Putnam's Sons, 1966), 67.

34 Stanford, *The Lady of the House*, 67.

35 Robert Clark, *James Beard: A Biography* (New York: HarperCollins, 1993), 42.

36 "The Williams' Fete," *The Whip*, December 10, 1842; "Next Week," *The Whip*, December 10, 1842; "Queen Sweets Assembly," *The Whip*, December 31, 1842; "The Belvidere," *The Whip*, December 31, 1842. Thanks to Robert Davis for pointing me toward these sources. See also a description of a "cocotte" ball in New York City in 1870; "New York Is Getting 'High' Indeed," *Wilmington Post*, NC, February 27, 1870, p. 2.

37 https://www.theamericanmenu.com/2013/01/dining-at-love-hotel-in-gilded-age.html/

38 Pamela D. Arsenaux, *Guidebooks to Sin: The Blue Books of Storyville, New Orleans* (New Orleans: The Historic New Orleans Collection, 2017), 28.

39 Alecia P. Long, *The Great Southern Babylon: Sex, Race, and Respectability in New Orleans, 1865–1920* (Baton Rouge, LA: Louisiana State University Press, 2004); Emily Epstein Landau, *Spectacular Wickedness: Sex, Race, and Memory in Storyville, New Orleans* (Baton Rouge, LA: Louisiana State University Press, 2013).

40 "Pino's Oyster Saloon and Restaurant," *Daily Picayune*, December 29, 1864, p. 3; "French Restaurant, 72 Charles Street," *Daily Picayune*, December 9, 1866, p. 10; "Forget's Restaurant," *Daily Picayune*, November 17, 1867, p. 10; "Reopened! Leon's Restaurant," *Daily Picayune*, October 9, 1886, p. 4.

41 "Charles Boster's Casino Beer Saloon and Restaurant," *Daily Picayune*, December 7, 1860, p. 2.

42 "Denechaud's Restaurant," *Daily Picayune*, October 19, 1877, p. 5.

43 "Personal and General Notes," *Daily Picayune*, November 5, 1884, p. 2. The Denechauds were a prominent restaurant family, who likely had connections to the previously mentioned Denechaud's in Vicksburg.

44 "The Maison Doree," *Daily Picayune*, November 21, 1866, p. 4.

45 "A Suit for Libel," *Daily Picayune*, November 4, 1882, p. 2.

46 Poppy Tooker, *Tujague's Cookbook: Creole Recipes and Lore in the New Orleans Grand Tradition* (Gretna, LA: Pelican Publishing Company, 2015), 52–3.

47 J. S. W. Harmanson, *Mme. Begué's Recipes of Old New Orleans Creole Cookery* (New Orleans: Harmanson, 1937), 7.

48 Rachel Hope Cleves, "The Erotic Poetry of Begué's Breakfast Register," *Victorian Review* 45(2) (2019).

49 Elizabeth Kettenring Begué and H. M. Mayo, *Mme. Begué and Her Recipes: Old Creole Cookery* (San Francisco, CA: Southern Pacific Co., 1900).

50 Eugenié Lavedan Maylié, *Maylié's Table D'Hote Recipes* (*c.*1940), 2.

51 Menu for "The Gem. Old Number. 17 Royal," Tulane Digital Library Menus Collection; Leonard V. Huber, *Mardi Gras: A Pictorial History of Carnival in New Orleans* (Gretna, LA: Pelican Publishing, 2003), 9.

52 "The New Era Restaurant," *Piqua Daily Call*, August 14, 1891, p. 7; "D. Rennick Thayer," *The Republican* (Oakland, MD) 39(18) (July 2, 1914): 5.

53 T. Max Kniesche, "Schroeder's Cafe and the German Restaurant Tradition in San Francisco. 1907–1976," interview by Ruth Teiser, *Regional Oral History Office*, 1976, 73.

54 John Drury, *Chicago in 7 Days* (New York: Robert M. McBride & Company, 1928), 121.

55 Edward Hungerford, *The Story of the Waldorf-Astoria* (New York: G. P. Putnam's Sons, 1925), 139.

56 "Diary of a Congressman," *Biloxi Daily Herald*, April 20, 1900, p. 2.

57 "On the Wing," *Philadelphia Inquirer*, April 20, 1896, p. 11.

58 "Little Egypt's Hot Dance," *St. Louis Post-Dispatch*, December 27, 1896, p. 1; Lucius Beebe, *The Big Spenders* (Garden City, NY: Doubleday & Company, 1966), 110–15.

59 M. H. Dunlop, *Gilded City: Scandal and Sensation in Turn-of-the-Century New York* (New York: W. Morrow, 2000), 169–71.

60 Rohan McWilliam, *London's West End: Creating the Pleasure District, 1800–1914* (New York: Oxford University Press, 2020), 256.

61 Peter Cunningham, *Handbook for London: Past and Present*, 2 vols. (London: John Murray, 1849), xxiii.

62 Tabitha Tickletooth (Charles Selby), *The Dinner Question: Or, How to Dine Well and Economically* (London: Routledge, Warne, & Routledge, 1860).

63 "Housekeeping, English and American," *Appleton's Journal* 5 (July–December 1878): 335.

64 Charles Eyre Pascoe, *London of To-day: An Illustrated Handbook for the Season* (Boston: Roberts Brothers, 1885), 45.

65 Pascoe, *London of To-day*, 49–51.

66 Robin Maugham, *Escape from the Shadows* (London: Hodder & Stoughton, 1972), 27.

67 Nathaniel Newnham-Davis, *Dinners & Diners* (London: Grant Richards, 1899), 291–6. Also, Francis Charles Philips, *As in a Looking Glass* (Leipzig: Berhard Tauchnitz, 1886), 90.

68 Bowden, *British Gastronomy*, 22.

69 Newnham-Davis, *Dinners & Diners*, 295.

70 McWilliam, *London's West End*, 256.

71 Assael, *The London Restaurant*, 194.

72 Auguste Escoffier, *Memories of My Life*, trans. Laurence Escoffier (New York: Van Nostrand Reinhold, 1997), 91.

73 Rachel Rich, *Bourgeois Consumption: Food, Space and Identity in London and Paris, 1850–1914* (Manchester: Manchester University Press, 2011), 137, 158.

74 Assael, *The London Restaurant*, 194.

75 Pascoe, *London of To-day*, 45.

76 Dorothy L. Sayers, *Murder Must Advertise* (London: Hodder & Stoughton, 2016), 64.

77 Nathaniel Newnham-Davis, *The Gourmet's Guide to London* (New York: Brentano's, 1914), 10.

78 Assael, *The London Restaurant*, 46.

79 Alice L. McLean, *Aesthetic Pleasure in Twentieth-Century Women's Food Writing: The Innovative Appetites of M. F. K. Fisher, Alice B. Toklas, and Elizabeth David* (New York: Routledge, 2012), 43.

80 George G. Foster, *New York in Slices: By an Experienced Carver* (New York: William H. Graham, 1849), 72.

81 "New-York Daguerreotyped."

82 Bobo, *Glimpses of New York City*, 159.

83 "A Scene at Taylor's Restaurant," *New York Pick*, April 29, 1854, p. 2.

84 "The Cream-Vender's Crime," *New York Clipper*, July 3, 1875.

85 Tortoni's was attracting sex workers at least by the 1860s, according to Alfred Delvau, *Les Plaisirs de Paris: Guide Pratique des Étrangers* (Paris: Achille Faure, 1867), 115. See also *Paris at Night: Sketches and Mysteries of Paris High Life and Demi-Monde. Nocturnal Amusements: How to Know Them! How to Enjoy Them!! How to Appreciate Them!!!* (Boston: Boston and Paris Publishing Company, 1875), 11.

86 "Baltimore Correspondent of the Whip," *Whip and Satirist of New-York and Brooklyn*, June 11, 1842, p. 1.

87 "Alice Hoag Again," *National Police Gazette*, July 20, 1861, p. 3.

88 "Philadelphia," *Whip, and Satirist of New-York and Brooklyn*, December 3, 1842, p. 1.

89 "A Novelty Indeed: Women Eating Their Lunch Sitting on Hard Stools," *True Republican* (Sycamore, Illinois), February 18, 1891, p. 3.

90 Francis McKee, "Ice Cream and Immorality," in Harlan Walker (ed.), *Oxford Symposium on Food and Cookery 1991: Public Eating* (London: Prospect Books, 1991).

91 "The Sorosis Society: Discussion of the 'Social Evil' at Delmonico's – the Male Monsters Served Up after Lunch," *New York Times*, May 19, 1869.

92 "Sorosis: Annual Meeting of the Ladies' Lunch Party," *New York Times*, March 22, 1870.

93 J. C. Croly, *Jennie June's American Cookery Book* (New York: Excelsior, 1878), 306, 334–43.

94 Newnham-Davis, *The Gourmet's Guide to Europe*, 132.

95 Em'ly (Annie S. Wolf), *Pictures and Portraits of Foreign Travel* (Philadelphia: E. Claxton & Company, 1880), 195–8.

96 Henry Haynie, "Paris Pencilings," *Daily Picayune*, November 2, 1890. A 1900 guidebook published by the Northern Trust Company Bank of Chicago warned American tourists to "in no case take a private room" at a restaurant. Not only were the prices twice those in the main salons, the *cabinets* were "distinctly not respectable"; Barrett Eastman and Frédéric Mayer, *The American Guide to the City and Exposition* (Northern Trust Company Bank: Chicago, 1900), 119.

97 F. Berkeley Smith, *The Real Latin Quarter* (New York: Funk & Wagnalls, 1901), 168–71.

98 Elizabeth Dryden, *Paris in Herrick Days* (Paris: Dorbon-Aîné, 1915), 11.

99 Valerie Mars, "Experiencing French Cookery in Nineteenth-Century London," in Debra Kelly and Martyn Cornick (eds.), *A History of the French in London: Liberty, Equality, Opportunity* (London: Institute of Historical Research, 2013).

100 Violet Hunt, *Affairs of the Heart* (London: S. T. Freemantle, 1900), 45–71.

101 H. G. Wells, *Ann Veronica* (London: Virago Press, 1980), 161–72. Also Assael, *The London Restaurant*, 195–6.

102 "Wells Portrays the New Woman," *New York Times*, October 22, 1909.

Chapter 5 Pretty Waiter Girls

1 Peter Bailey, "Parasexuality and Glamour: The Victorian Barmaid as Cultural Prototype," *Gender & History* 2(2) (Summer, 1990): 148; Brenda Assael, *The London Restaurant, 1840–1914* (New York: Oxford University Press, 2018), 117.

2 Frank Soulé, John H. Gihon, and James Nisbet, *The Annals of San Francisco: Containing a Summary of the First Discovery, Settlement, Progress, and Present Condition of California and a Complete History of All the Important Events Connected with Its Great City* (New York: D. Appleton & Company, 1855), 641–2.

3 Marion S. Goldman, *Gold Diggers and Silver Miners: Prostitution and Social Life on the Comstock Lode* (Ann Arbor, MI: University of Michigan Press, 1981), 90.

4 For an overview, see Brooks McNamara, *The New York Concert Saloon: The Devil's Own Nights* (New York: Cambridge University Press, 2002). Also Chloë R. Edmonson, "Under the Influence: Drinking and Immersion in New York City Theatre and Popular Entertainment, 1850 to Present" (PhD, City University of New York, 2018), 25–52.

5 Junius Henri Browne, *The Great Metropolis; A Mirror of New York* (Hartford: American Publishing Company, 1869), 326.

6 Robert Clyde Allen, *Horrible Prettiness: Burlesque and American Culture* (Chapel Hill, NC: University of North Carolina Press, 1991), 73–4.

7 Gustav Lening, *The Dark Side of New York Life and Its Criminal Classes from Fifth Avenue Down to the Five Points* (New York: Fred'k Gerhard, 1873), 372.

8 "City Summary," *New York Clipper*, December 28, 1861.

9 Browne, *The Great Metropolis*, 326.

10 "Gaieties Concert Room," *New York Daily Herald*, January 25, 1860, p. 7; "Great National Concert Saloon," *New York Daily Herald*, April 17, 1860.

11 "Gaieties Concert Room," *New York Daily Herald*, January 5, 1861, p. 14.

12 "Gaieties Concert Room," *New York Daily Herald*, January 15, 1861, p. 7.

13 "Gaieties Concert Room," *New York Daily Herald*, March 10, 1861, p. 7.

14 "Official Advertisement of the Concert Saloons," *New York Times*, January 5, 1861, p. 4.

15 "Amusements," *Baltimore Sun*, November 1, 1861, p. 2.

16 "Miscellaneous," *New York Times*, May 23, 1962, p. 11.

17 "Prostitution in the American Metropolis," *New York Clipper*, February 8, 1868, p. 848.

18 Lening, *Dark Side of New York*, 378.

19 Goldman, *Gold Diggers and Silver Miners*, 58.

20 Edward Winslow Martin (James D. McCabe), *The Secrets of the Great City: A Work Descriptive of the Virtues and the Vices, the Mysteries, Miseries and Crimes of New York City* (Philadelphia: Jones, Brothers & Co., 1868), 312.

21 Mark Mills Pomeroy, *Brick-Dust: A Remedy for the Blues, and a Something for People to Talk About* (New York: G. W. Carleton & Co., 1871), 213.

22 George Ellington, *The Women of New York; Or, the Under-World of the Great City* (New York: The New York Book Co., 1869), 469; William F. Howe and Abraham H. Hummel, *Danger! A True History of a Great City's Wiles and Temptations* (Buffalo, NY: Courier Company, 1886).

23 Martin (James D. McCabe), *The Secrets of the Great City*, 208.

24 Ellington, *The Women of New York*, 461–4.

25 Pomeroy, *Brick-Dust*, 224.

26 Lening, *Dark Side of New York*, 374; Howe and Hummel, *Danger! A True History.*

27 Pomeroy, *Brick-Dust*, 217.

28 McNamara, *The New York Concert Saloon*, 89.

29 "Saturday Night in the Bowery," *New York Clipper*, May 25, 1861. P45.

30 "Illustration 34: Interior of a Concert Saloon," in Ellington, *The Women of New York*.; The Miriam and Ira D. Wallach Division of Art, Prints and Photographs: Picture Collection, The New York Public Library. "The sights and sensations of New York," New York Public Library Digital Collections. https://digitalcollections.nypl.org/items /510d47e1-2cbd-a3d9-e040-e00a18064a99/

31 Lening, *Dark Side of New York*, 374.

32 Browne, *The Great Metropolis*, 326.

33 Pomeroy, *Brick-Dust*, 217.

34 Ellington, *The Women of New York*, 464.

35 Lening, *Dark Side of New York*, 378.

36 Pomeroy, *Brick-Dust*, 219.

37 Quoted in Herbert Asbury, *The Gangs of New York: An Informal History of the Underworld* (New York: Blue Ribbon Books, 1939), 188.

38 "Tragedy at One of the Broadway Concert Saloons," *National Police Gazette*, April 12, 1862, p. 1.

39 *Susie Knight, or, the True History of the Pretty Waiter Girl: A Fancy Poem in Three Cantos* (New York: C. Mackey & Co., 1863). For publishing, see Marcus A. McCorison, "Risqué Literature Published in America before 1877," *Bibliographical Society of America*, 19.

40 Martin (James D. McCabe), *The Secrets of the Great City*, 310; Pomeroy, *Brick-Dust*, 219.

41 "The Fashionable Concert Saloon," *Nashville Union and American*, January 2, 1866, p. 4.

42 Bailey, "Parasexuality and Glamour," 165.

43 "Pretty Waiter Girls," *Delaware State Journal*, May 10, 1861, p. 3.

44 "Waiting Girls Going to Albany," *Janesville Daily Gazette*, February 1, 1862, p. 2.

45 "The Concert Saloons: A 'Pretty Waiter Girl' in Trouble," *New York Times*, April 26, 1862, p. 3.

46 "The Result of the 'Pretty Waiter-Girls' Case in the Supreme Court," *New York Times*, May 20, 1862, p. 2.

47 McNamara, *The New York Concert Saloon*, 17–19.

48 "Academy of Music," *Evening Star*, January 10, 1862, p. 3; "The Broadway Varieties," *New York Clipper*, March 3, 1866, p. 375; "Pretty Waiter Girls," *Daily Missouri Republican*, September 9, 1866, p. 2; "The Olympic Music Hall," *New York Clipper*, December 29, 1866; "Fighting for a Feminine," *New York Clipper*, May 9, 1868; "Effects of Jealousy," *New York Clipper*, July 2, 1870, p. 100; "Local Miscellany," *Chicago Tribune*, June 11, 1874, p. 5;

49 Hannah Rosen, *Terror in the Heart of Freedom: Citizenship, Sexual Violence, and the Meaning of Race in the Postemancipation South* (Chapel Hill, NC: University of North Carolina Press, 2009), 41.

50 "Kansas Items," *Weekly Herald and Tribune*, April 3, 1862, p. 4; "'Pretty Waiter Girls' to Be Abolished," *Columbia Democrat and Bloomsbury General Advertiser*, January 30, 1864, p. 2; "Exit Waiter Girls," *Baltimore Sun*, May 4, 1864.

51 "Vermont," *Burlington Free Press*, September 13, 1865, p. 2; "A Plucky and Pretty Waiter Girl," *New York Dispatch*, February 4, 1866, p. 1; "A Waiter-Girl Romance," *Memphis Daily Appeal*, June 11, 1873, p. 2.

52 "The Pretty Waiter Girls of the White Mountains," *Rutland Weekly Herald and Globe*, August 24, 1860, p. 4.

53 "Annual Dinner of the St. Nicholas Society," *Brooklyn Daily Eagle*, December 16, 1863, p. 2; "Unitarian Festival and Fair," *Burlington Daily Times*, July 1, 1864, p. 3; "A New England Dinner at Alden," *Buffalo Courier*, March 3, 1864, p. 3.

54 "A Gay Deceiver," *New York Clipper*, April 15, 1865, p. 3. The news went national. See "A Dashing Young Canadian," *Richmond Whig*, April 20, 1865, p. 8; "Metamorphosis in a Saloon," *Contra Costa Gazette*, May 20, 1865, p. 1.

55 "A Man in Cleveland Personating a Woman for Fourteen Years," *New York Times*, July 2, 1865, p. 6. Addie's story became international news; "A Curious Case," *Chicago Tribune*, June 29, 1865, p. 3. "A Man Personating a Female," *Preston Chronicle and Lancashire Advertiser*, August 19, 1965, p. 2.

56 Lois M. Foster, *Annals of the San Francisco Stage, 1850–1880*, vol. 1, (San Francisco: Federal Theatre Projects, 1936) 300; Carolyn Grattan Eichin, *From San Francisco Eastward: Victorian Theater in the American West* (Reno, NV: University of Nevada Press, 2020); Jonathan Verbeten, "'Trashy Music' in the Halls: A Cultural–Geographical History of Music Making in San Francisco during the Gold Rush Years (1849–1869)" (PhD, Texas Tech University, 2020), 168.

57 February 19, 1868 entry in Book No. 36 of *The Journals of Alfred Doten, 1849–1903*, vol. 2, ed. Walter Van Tilburg Clark (Reno, NV: University of Nevada Press, 1973), 979.

58 "Coney Island: The Big Elephant," *New York Times*, July 12, 1885, p. 11.

59 Jan MacKell, *Red Light Women of the Rocky Mountains* (Albuquerque, NM: University of New Mexico Press, 2009), 106.

60 "Dramatic," *New York Clipper*, July 9, 1864, p. 102.

61 "Miss Jennie Lamont," *San Francisco Chronicle*, July 14, 1866, p. 3.

62 "California Comicques," *Chicago Tribune*, November 8, 1866, p. 4.

63 "Shelby's Comicque," *Buffalo Sunday Morning News*, September 27, 1874, p. 1; "Madame Rentz's Minstrels," *Fort Scott Daily Monitor*, January 12, 1876, p. 4.

64 Allen, *Horrible Prettiness: Burlesque and American Culture*.

65 "Our Dramatic Portrait Gallery: Francis Leon," *New York Clipper*, March 2, 1867, p. 370.

66 "Negro Minstrelsy," *New York Clipper*, October 19, 1867, p. 223; "Negro Minstrelsy," *New York Clipper*, August 8, 1868, p. 142.

67 "Negro Minstrelsy," *New York Clipper*, September 9, 1865, p. 175; "Negro Minstrelsy," *New York Clipper*, December 8, 1866, p. 279; "Negro Minstrelsy," *New York Clipper*, July 3, 1869, p. 103.

68 Katherine Mullin, *Working Girls: Fiction, Sexuality, and Modernity* (New York: Oxford University Press, 2016), 176.

69 Laurence Senelick, "Boys and Girls Together: Subcultural Origins of Glamour Drag and Male Impersonation on the Nineteenth-Century Stage" in Lesley Ferris (ed.),

Crossing the Stage: Controversies on Cross-Dressing (London: Routledge, 1993), 83. These "male barmaid" acts may have also played off the notoriety of an infamous 1860s English transmasculine cross-dresser, Tommy Walker, known popularly as the "female barman."

70 Havelock Ellis, *Studies in the Psychology of Sex* (Philadelphia: F. A. Davis Company, 1908), 174.

71 Hugh Ryan, *When Brooklyn Was Queer* (New York: St. Martin's, 2019), 92–104.

72 "Broadway below the Sidewalk: Pretty Waiter Girls and Underground Concert Halls. No. 12. The Reveille," *New York Clipper*, April 9, 1864, p. 412. In December 1864, either the Reveille reopened in a new location, or a new establishment, also called the Reveille, opened at 627 Broadway, staffed apparently with women. See "Complaint against a Broadway Saloon," *New York Times*, November 28, 1865, p. 2.

73 Clare Sears, *Arresting Dress: Cross-Dressing, Law, and Fascination in Nineteenth-Century San Francisco* (Durham, NC: Duke University Press, 2015), 1–2.

74 Edward Van Every, *Sins of New York: As "Exposed" by the Police Gazette* (New York: F. A. Stokes Co., 1930), 215. McGlory's Armory Hall has been a source of fascination for chroniclers of New York history ever since the 1870s. See, for example, Asbury, *Gangs of New York*, 188; Lloyd Morris, *Incredible New York: High Life and Low Life from 1850 to 1950* (Syracuse, NY: Syracuse University Press, 1951), 51.

75 "Billy M'Glory's Mardi-Gras: A Night of Rude and Rapid Fun in Armory Hall," *Cincinnati Enquirer*, December 31, 1882, p. 16; "Revelry Wild and Shameless," *Alexandria Gazette*, March 19, 1883, p.1; "A Disgusting Performance," *Daily Register*, February 13, 1884, p. 2.

76 There is extensive information on Paresis Hall in George Chauncey, *Gay New York: Gender, Urban Culture, and the Making of the Gay Male World, 1890–1940* (New York City: Basic Books, 1995). See also McNamara, *The New York Concert Saloon*, 79.

77 R. A. Witthaus and Tracy C. Becker, *Medical Jurisprudence, Forensic Medicine and Toxicology*, vol. 2 (New York: William Wood & Company, 1894), 311–12.

78 Ellis, *Studies in the Psychology of Sex*, 174. This passage is also cited in Aaron S. Lecklider, *Love's Next Meeting: The Forgotten History of Homosexuality and the Left in American Culture* (Berkeley, CA: University of California Press, 2021), 116.

79 Coffignon, *Paris Vivant*, 91–108; Jill Harsin, *Policing Prostitution in Nineteenth-Century Paris* (Princeton, NJ: Princeton University Press, 1985), 317.

80 Andrew Israel Ross, "Serving Sex: Playing with Prostitution in the *Brasseries à femmes* of Late Nineteenth-Century Paris," *Journal of the History of Sexuality* 24(2) (May, 2015).

81 Captain Wray Sylvester, *The Nocturnal Pleasures of Paris: A Guide to the Gay City*. (Paris: The Byron Library, 1889), 73.

82 Ross, "Serving Sex"; A. Coffignon, *Paris Vivant: La Corruption à Paris: Le Demi-Monde, Les Souteneurs, La Police des Moeurs, Brasseries de Femmes, Filles Galantes, Saint-Lazare, Le Chantage etc. etc.* (Paris: Jules Tallandrier, 1888), 96.

83 *Pleasure Guide to Paris for Bachelors: Paris by Day, Paris by Night, How to Enjoy One's-Self, Where to Enjoy One's-Self, What to See, What to Do*, trans. George Day (London: Nilsson, 1903), 118–19.

84 Coffignon, *Paris Vivant*, 312.

85 Sommerville Story, *Dining in Paris: A Guide to Paris à la Carte and Table d'Hôte* (New York: Robert M. McBride & Company, 1925), 95.

86 "New Year in Paris," *Owosso Times*, January 1, 1897.

87 "A Waitress at Duval's Restaurant," *c*.1875. The Metropolitan Museum of Art, Gallery 824. https://images.metmuseum.org/CRDImages/ep/original/DT1488.jpg

88 Thomas de Quincey, *Selections Grave and Gay from Writings Published and Unpublished: Autobiographic Sketches* (Edinburgh: James Hogg, 1854), 188. In fact, the term "waitress" had appeared in English as early as the sixteenth century to describe servant girls; "Waitress" entry in the *Oxford English Dictionary* online.

89 Quoted in Mullin, *Working Girls*, 167.

90 "The Maid of the Inn," in R. E. Egerton-Warburton, *Poems, Epigrams and Sonnets* (London: Basil Montagu Pickering, 1877), 106–7; "Pretty Waitress," *The Insurance Journal: A Monthly Review of Fire and Life Insurance* 14 (Hartford, CT: H. R. Hayden, 1886), 343; Eli Perkins, "A Very Bright Girl," in Melville D. Landen (ed.), *Wit and Humor of the Age* (Chicago: Star Publishing Company, 1890), 665.

91 Quoted in Assael, *The London Restaurant*, 117.

92 C. H. M. Wharton and Alfred Taylor, *The Bachelors: An Original Modern Comic Opera* (Manchester, UK: T. Sowler & Co., 1880), 7.

93 Assael, *The London Restaurant*, 114.

94 Sterling Heilig, "Waiter Girls," *St. Louis Globe-Democrat*, August 24, 1894, p. 13.

95 Mary Lee Spence, "They Also Serve who Wait," *Western Historical Quarterly* 14(1) (1983): 9, 23.

96 Frances Donovan, *The Woman who Waits* (Boston, MA: Richard G. Badger, 1920), 211–12.

97 Donovan, *The Woman who Waits*, 169.

98 Donovan, *The Woman who Waits*, 219–20.

99 Donovan, *The Woman who Waits*, 27.

100 Dorothy Sue Cobble, *Dishing It Out: Waitresses and Their Unions in the Twentieth Century* (Urbana, IL: University of Illinois Press, 1991), 24–7.

101 See, for example, Richard von Krafft-Ebing, *Psychopathia Sexualis: With Especial References to the Antipathic Sexual Instinct*, trans. Franklin Klaf (Philadelphia: F. J. Rebman, 1894), 298, 340, 416, 18; Lewis M. Terman and Catharine Cox Miles, *Sex and Personality: Studies in Masculinity and Femininity* (New York: McGraw-Hill, 1936), 286, 95, 99, 311, 12, 13.

102 Chauncey, *Gay New York*, 165; Matt Houlbrook, *Queer London: Perils and Pleasures in the Sexual Metropolis, 1918–1957* (Chicago: University of Chicago Press, 2005), 85. More discussion of gay waiters in the twentieth century follows in chapter 9.

103 Alison Owings, "Hey, Waitress!," *Gastronomica* 3(1) (Winter, 2003).

Chapter 6 Dinners in Bohemia

1 "The Late Charles Astor Bristed," *New York Times*, January 16, 1874, p. 4.

2 Carl Benson (Charles Astor Bristed), "Table Aesthetics," *Knickerbocker; or, New-York Monthly Magazine of Literature, Art, Politics & Society* (April 1, 1848): 292. Despite Bristed's reputation for indifference to public opinion, he published this essay and other works under a pen name, Carl Benson, perhaps out of respect for his more respectable Astor relations. His identity was not a secret, however, and he also signed pieces with both names.

3 "Art. II – Five Years in an English University," *North American Review* 75 (July, 1852).

4 Charles Astor Bristed, "A New Theory of Bohemians," *The Knickerbocker*, 1861.

5 Robert Darnton, "Finding a Lost Prince of Bohemia," *New York Review of Books* (April 3, 2008).

6 James Gatheral, *The Bohemian Republic: Transnational Literary Networks in the Nineteenth Century* (New York: Routledge, 2021), 24.

7 Henri Murger, *The Latin Quarter ("Scènes de la Vie de Bohème")*, trans. Ellen Marriage and John Selwyn (London: Grant Richards, 1901), 21, 295. The scenes were first printed as a serial in 1845, then adapted as a musical in 1849, and ultimately collected in a single volume in 1851.

8 The first installment is Carl Benson (Charles Astor Bristed), "The Gypsies of Art: Translated for the Knickerbocker from Henry Murger's 'Scenes de la Boheme,'" *The Knickerbocker* 411 (January 1853): 12–23.

9 Charles Astor Bristed, "The Gypsies of Art," *The Knickerbocker: Or, New-York Monthly Magazine*, 1854.

10 "Literary Notices: The Physiology of Taste," *The Knickerbocker: Or, New-York Monthly Magazine* 43 (1854): 68–71.

11 Charles Astor Bristed, "A New Theory of Bohemians," in César Graña and Marigay Graña (eds.), *On Bohemia: the Code of the Self-Exiled* (New York: Routledge, 2017), 78–85.

12 It's unclear how much Bristed inherited from his grandfather. In his first book, about attending Cambridge, he claimed not to have the resources to support his studies as he would have liked. In reference to this fact, his obituarist noted Bristed's "absolute independence of character," "The Late Charles Astor Bristed," *New York Times*, January 16, 1874, p. 4.

13 Carl Benson (Charles Astor Bristed), "Casual Cogitations: Will the Coming Americans Eat and Drink?," *The Galaxy* (September 1, 1873).

14 Junius Henri Browne, *The Great Metropolis: A Mirror of New York* (Hartford, CT: American Publishing Company, 1869).

15 Eve Kosofsky Sedgwick, *Epistemology of the Closet*, 2008 edn (Berkeley, CA: University of California Press, 1990), 193.

16 Antonia Harland-Lang, "Thackeray and Bohemia" (PhD, University of Cambridge, 2010).

17 William Makepeace Thackeray, *The History of Pendennis* (London: Bradbury & Evans 1850), 405. See also Andrew Dowling, *Manliness and the Male Novelist in Victorian Literature* (London: Routledge, 2001), 62–81.

18 Harland-Lang, "Thackeray and Bohemia," 64.

19 Gatheral, *Bohemian Republic*, 154.

20 William Winter, *Old Friends: Being Literary Recollections of Other Days* (New York: Moffat, Yard and Company, 1909), 309.

21 N. Parker Willis, *Pencillings by the Way: Written during Some Years of Residence and Travel in Europe* (New York: Charles Scribner & Sons, 1856).

22 Mark A. Lause, *The Antebellum Crisis and America's First Bohemians* (Kent, OH: Kent State University Press, 2009), 19.

23 Lause, *The Antebellum Crisis*, 49–57.

24 Walt Whitman, *New York Notebook*. Thomas Biggs Harned Collection, Library of Congress, 1861.

25 See, for example, "A Hasty-Pudding Supper," March 26, 1859, p. 1; "Tea in Russia," May 7, 1859, p. 1. The first article was a reprint from a British magazine, *Chambers's Journal of Popular Literature* (13 November, 1858): 305–30.

26 "On the Death of the Temperance Movement," *New York Saturday Press*, December 11, 1858, p. 2.

27 "Harmony in the Kitchen," *New York Saturday Press*, December 11, 1858, pp. 2–3.

28 "A Souvenir of a Dinner," *New York Saturday Press*, January 8, 1859, p. 4.

29 "Pfaff's, New York City, 1866," theamericanmenu.com, September 23, 2017.

30 Albert Parry, *Garrets and Pretenders: A History of Bohemianism in America* (New York City: Covici Friede Publishers, 1933), 22–3.

31 Parry, *Garrets and Pretenders*, 21.

32 S. Frederick Starr, *Louis Moreau Gottschalk* (Springfield, IL: University of Illinois Press, 2000), 244–56. There is some uncertainty about when Clare gave birth to her son, Aubrey. She gave different dates. Gottschalk's biographer argues that the birth most likely took place in Paris (and the illegitimate pregnancy explains her decision to leave the United States).

33 "A Letter from Ada Clare – No. 6," *New York Musical World* 18(346) (November 14, 1857): 711.

34 Getty Gay, "The Royal Bohemian Supper," *New York Saturday Press*, December 31, 1859, p. 2.

35 Diary of Thomas Butler Gunn, vol. 14, September 23, 1860–December 31, 1860, p. 13. Missouri History Museum. This quotation and the subsequent quotations from Gunn's diaries are referenced in "Gay, Getty (1840?–1860)," *The Vault at Pfaff's*. https://pfaffs.web.lehigh.edu/node/54147

36 Diary of Thomas Butler Gunn, vol. 11, June 1, 1859–December 31, 1859, p. 152. Missouri History Museum.

37 Diary of Thomas Butler Gunn, vol. 14, September 23, 1860–December 31, 1860, p. 13. Missouri History Museum. Gay's extreme youth led one chronicler of bohemianism to call her a "rare-ripe," A. L. Rawson, "Bygone Bohemia," *Frank Leslie's Popular Monthly*, January–June 1896: 102.

38 Justin Martin, *Rebel Souls: Walt Whitman and America's First Bohemians* (New York: Da Capo Press, 2014), 249.

39 Franklin Ottarson, "Drama: Bohemianism," *The Round Table* 1(8) (February 6, 1864).

40 Frank Bellew, "Bohemians as they are – described by one of their own number" and "As they were said to be by a knight of the Round Table," *Demorest's New York Illustrated News*, February 6, 1864.

41 Most historians of same-sex sexuality follow the lead of George Chauncey and date the appearance of a queer subculture in New York City to the late nineteenth century, but Jonathan Ned Katz and others have highlighted attacks on "sodomites" in the city's flash newspapers in the 1840s; George Chauncey, *Gay New York: Gender, Urban Culture, and the Making of the Gay Male World, 1890–1940* (New York City: Basic Books, 1995); Jonathan Ned Katz, *Love Stories: Sex between Men before Homosexuality* (Chicago: University of Chicago Press, 2003); Marc Stein, "Introduction: Sodomites and Gender Transgressors in 1840s New York," *Queer Pasts* (2022).

42 Some scholars have definitively treated this group as queer; Ed Folsom and Kenneth M. Price, *Re-Scripting Walt Whitman: An Introduction to His Life and Work* (Malden,

MA: Blackwell Publishing, 2005), 62. Stephanie M. Blalock's scholarship on Gray has been more circumspect about the circle's sexuality; Stephanie M. Blalock, "'My Dear Comrade Fredrickus': Walt Whitman and Fred Gray," *Walt Whitman Quarterly Review* 27(1) (2009); Stephanie M. Blalock, "'Tell What I Meant by *Calamus*': Walt Whitman's Vision of Comradeship from Fred Vaughan to the Fred Gray Association," in Joanna Levin and Edward Whitley (eds.), *Whitman among the Bohemians* (Iowa City: University of Iowa Press, 2014). For more on Whitman's relationship to the Fred Gray Association, see Christine Stansell, "Whitman at Pfaff's: Commercial Culture, Literary Life and New York Bohemia at Mid-Century," *Walt Whitman Quarterly Review* 10(3) (Winter, 1993). The literary critic Allan Bloom argued that the repression of sexual alterity in the nineteenth century had served a positive good by forcing bohemia "to justify its unorthodox practices by its intellectual and artistic achievement." Repression gave rise to creative genius. Bloom disdained scholarship that focused on "so insignificant a fact" as a writer's sexual attachments. But Bloom's former student Eve Kosofsky Sedgwick pushed back against her mentor's defense of the closet to argue in favor of "the naming as what it is" of the homoerotic male canon. Sedgwick made the closet itself a subject of analysis, exploring how the structured opposition of bohemianism versus respectability stood in for another binary opposition, homosexuality versus heterosexuality; Sedgwick, *Epistemology of the Closet*, 53–6, 184.

43 "Walt Whitman to Hugo Fritsch, before 7 August 1863," in Matt Cohen, Ed Folsom, and Kenneth M. Price (eds.), *The Walt Whitman Archive*. http://www.whitmanarchive.org/ See also Whitman's 1863 letter to Nathaniel Bloom about longing for "those hot spiced rums & suppers" they used to share as a group, "Walt Whitman to Nathaniel Bloom, 5 September 1863."

44 Horace Traubel, *Walt Whitman in Camden* (New York: Mitchell Kennerley, 1914), vol. 3, 388.

45 Willis, *Pencillings by the Way*, 112–17.

46 Cindy R. Lobell, "'Out to Eat': The Emergence and Evolution of the Restaurant in Nineteenth-Century New York City," *Winterthur Portfolio* 44(2/3) (2010): 216. See also Maura D'Amore, "Suburban Men at the Table: Culinary Aesthetics in the Mid-Century Country Book," in Monika Elbert and Marie Drews (eds.), *Culinary Aesthetics and Practices in Nineteenth-Century American Literature* (New York: Palgrave Macmillan, 2009), 21–33.

47 "Minute Philosophies," *American Monthly Magazine* 1(8) (November, 1829): 520.

48 Law Reporter of the New York Herald, *The Forrest Divorce Case: Being a Verbatim Report of the Testimony Taken in the Action for Divorce by Catharine N. Forrest vs. Edwin Forrest* (New York: Dewitt and Davenport, 1851), 24.

49 Thomas N. Baker, *Sentiment and Celebrity: Nathaniel Parker Willis and the Trials of Literary Fame* (New York: Oxford University Press, 1999), 48–9, 131. *The Century Dictionary and Cyclopedia*, vol. 5 (New York: The Century Co.), 3798.

50 Dominic James, "A Queer Taste for Macaroni," *The Public Domain Review* (2017). https://publicdomainreview.org/essay/a-queer-taste-for-macaroni/

51 N. Parker Willis, *The Rag-Bag: A Collection of Ephemera* (New York: C. Scribner, 1855), 28–31.

52 Thomas Butler Gunn Diaries, vol. 12, January 1–May 31, 1860, pp. 126, 131. Missouri History Museum.

53 Edward Whitley, "The Southern Origins of Bohemian New York: Edward Howland, Ada Clare, and Edgar Allan Poe," *Poe Studies* 49 (2016).

54 Arthur Bartlett Maurice, *Fifth Avenue* (New York: Frank Dodd, 1918), 183–98.

55 Thomas Butler Gunn Diaries, vol. 9, 53, 56. Missouri History Museum, 1857. https:// pfaffs.web.lehigh.edu/

56 "The Bohemians of Paris," *The Golden Era* 8(2) (December 18, 1859): 5. The article is a reprint from the *Boston Gazette*.

57 Harland-Lang, "Thackeray and Bohemia," 78.

58 Joanna Levin, *Bohemia in America, 1858–1920* (Stanford, CA: Stanford University Press, 2009), 121.

59 Bret Harte, "Bohemian Days in San Francisco," in *The Writings of Bret Harte* (Boston and New York: Houghton Mifflin Company, 1902), 144.

60 Marcus Clarke, "Lower Bohemia in Melbourne [by the Peripatetic Philosopher]," *Wallaroo Times*, August 14, 1869, p. 2.

61 Clarence E. Edwords, *Bohemian San Francisco, Its Restaurants and Their Most Famous Recipes: The Elegant Art of Dining* (San Francisco: Paul Elder and Company Publishers, 1914), ix.

62 Edwords, *Bohemian San Francisco*, 6.

63 Edwords, *Bohemian San Francisco*, 12.

64 Joanna Levin, "The Double Dealers in Bohemian New Orleans," in Shawn Chandler Bingham and Lindsey A. Freean (eds.), *Bohemian South: Creating Countercultures, from Poe to Punk* (Chapel Hill, NC: University of North Carolina Press, 2017).

65 Elizabeth Stevenson, *The Grass Lark: A Study of Lafcadio Hearn* (New York: Routledge, 1999), 81. Also, Elizabeth Bisland, *Life and Letters of Lafcadio Hearn*, 2 vols., vol. 1 (Boston: Houghton Mifflin, 1906), 176.

66 Bisland, *Life and Letters of Lafcadio Hearn*, 1, 199.

67 Stevenson, *The Grass Lark: A Study of Lafcadio Hearn*, 86–7.

68 Quoted in Valérie Loichot, "Cooking Creoleness: Lafcadio Hearn in New Orleans and Martinique," *Journal of French and Francophone Philosophy – Revue de la philosophie française et de langue française* 20(1) (2012): 8.

69 Lafcadio Hearn, *La Cuisine Creole: A Collection of Culinary Recipes from Leading Chefs and Noted Creole Housewive, who Have Made New Orleans Famous for Its Cuisine* (New Orleans: F. F. Hansell & Bro., 1885). Many of Hearn's recipes were stolen from other cookbooks, according to Paul Freedman; Paul Freedman, *American Cuisine: And How It Got This Way* (New York: Liveright, 2019). Two years later, he traveled to the French West Indies, settling in Martinique. He wrote about that island's cuisine in his *Two Years in the French West Indies*, and sent letters to friends rhapsodizing over the beauty of its mixed-race population, male and female, whose skin tones he likened to mangoes, bananas, lemons, and other fruits. Loichot, "Cooking Creoleness," 8–10. Loichot notes in footnote 50 that no one has yet made a study of Hearn's homoerotic descriptions, which is a missed opportunity.

70 Kevin Fox Gotham, *Authentic New Orleans: Tourism, Culture, and Race in the Big Easy* (New York: New York University Press, 2007), 59.

71 Parry, *Garrets and Pretenders*, 168: 56–7.

72 John Drury, *Chicago in 7 Days* (New York: Robert McBride & Company, 1928), 124–6; John Drury, *Dining in Chicago* (New York: John Day Company, 1931), 26–30. Women

NOTES TO PP. 122–129

were seated in an upstairs room with a cracked ceiling, peeling wallpaper, and only an old coal stove for heating.

73 Parry, *Garrets and Pretenders*, 196.

74 Chad Heap, *Slumming: Sexual and Racial Encounters in American Nightlife, 1885–1940* (Chicago: University of Chicago Press, 2009), 248.

75 Maurice, *Fifth Avenue*, 185–6.

76 George du Maurier, *Trilby: A Novel* (London: George Bell & Sons, 1896), 32, 111–12, 54.

77 Sedgwick, *Epistemology of the Closet*, 192. This panic followed the emergence of the modern sexual identity category of the homosexual in the late nineteenth century.

78 In another homage to Thackeray, the Laird sings verses from Thackeray's 1849 poem "The Ballad of the Bouillabaisse," a paean to a Paris restaurant that Thackeray visited in his youth; William Makepeace Thackeray, *Ballads and Verses and Miscellaneous Contributions to "Punch"* (London: Macmillan, 1911), 47–8.

79 Du Maurier, *Trilby*, 142.

80 Denis Denisoff addresses the novel's homoerotic themes in Dennis Denisoff, *Aestheticism and Sexual Parody, 1840–1940* (New York: Cambridge University Press, 2001), 85–93.

81 L. Edward Purcell, "Trilby and Trilby-Mania: The Beginning of the Bestseller System," *Journal of Popular Culture* 11(1) (1977).

82 Maurice, *Fifth Avenue*, 184–5.

83 Begué's Breakfast Register, October 13, 1902. Begué's and Tujagues Restaurant Collection, Historic New Orleans Collection, MSS 778, Boxes 1–6.

84 Annette M. Magid, "A Taste of Wilde: Food Issues in the Life and Works of Oscar Wilde," *The Victorian Web: Literature, History, & Culture in the Age of Victoria*, 2009. http://www.victorianweb.org/authors/wilde/magid1.html

85 Oscar Wilde, "Dinners and Dishes," *Pall Mall Gazette* (London), March 7, 1885.

86 Steve Bradshaw, "London's Café Royal," in Graña and Graña, *On Bohemia: The Code of the Self-Exiled*, 477–85.

87 Frank Harris, *Oscar Wilde: His Life and Confessions*, 2 vols., vol. 1 (New York: Brentano's, 1916), 153, 88–9. Harris also used the private rooms of the Café Royal for sex with his many lovers, which he described in his notorious pornographic multivolume autobiography, Frank Harris, *My Life and Loves* (Paris: privately printed, 1922).

88 Katie Rawson and Elliott Shore, *Dining Out: A Global History of Restaurants* (London: Reaktion Books, 2019), 54.

89 John Paul Bocock, "Dinners in Bohemia and Elsewhere," *North American Review* 172(534) (May, 1901).

Chapter 7 Greedy Women

1 Mary MacLane, *The Story of Mary MacLane* (Chicago: Herbert S. Stone and Company, 1902), 60, 140.

2 The book was eventually published under MacLane's chosen title by the publisher Melville House in 2013.

3 MacLane, *The Story of Mary MacLane*, 80–6.

4 Cathryn Halverson, "Mary MacLane's Story," *Arizona Quarterly: A Journal of American Literature, Culture, and Theory* 50(4) (Winter, 1994).

5 Agnes Repplier, *In Our Convent Days* (Boston: Houghton, Mifflin and Company, 1905), 76, 79, 104, 88–9.

6 After many years of obscurity, Pennell has recently become a subject of renewed schol-arship. See Judith Schaffer, "The Importance of Being Greedy: Connoisseurship and Domesticity in the Writings of Elizabeth Robins Pennell," in Janet Floyd and Laurel Forster (eds.), *The Recipe Reader: Narrative Contexts Traditions* (Aldershot, UK: Ashgate, 2004); Alice L. McLean, *Aesthetic Pleasure in Twentieth-Century Women's Food Writing: The Innovative Appetites of M. F. K. Fisher, Alice B. Toklas, and Elizabeth David* (New York: Routledge, 2012); Kimberly Morse Jones, *Elizabeth Robins Pennell: Nineteenth-Century Pioneer of Modern Art Criticism* (New York: Routledge, 2015); Julieta Flores Jurado, "From 'The Diary of a Greedy Woman' to Food Porn: Appetite and Pleasure in the Discourse of Women Gastronomes," *Genesis* 16(1) (2017); J. Michelle Coghlan, "The Art of the Recipe: American Food Writing Avant la Lettre," in Gitanjali G. Shahani (ed.), *Food and Literature* (New York: Cambridge University Press, 2018).

7 Jones, *Elizabeth Robins Pennell*, 39–40.

8 Schaffer, "The Importance of Being Greedy," 108.

9 *The Yellow Book: An Illustrated Quarterly* 10 (July 1896).

10 Elizabeth Robins Pennell, *The Feasts of Autolycus: The Diary of a Greedy Woman* (London: John Lane, 1896), 9–16. See also Jurado, "From 'The Diary of a Greedy Woman' to Food Porn," 9.

11 Robert Clark, *James Beard: A Biography* (New York: HarperCollins, 1993), 22.

12 Jamie Horrocks, "Camping in the Kitchen: Locating Culinary Authority in Elizabeth Robins Pennell *Delights of Delicate Eating*," *Nineteenth-Century Gender Studies* 13(2) (Summer, 2007).

13 Pennell, *The Feasts of Autolycus*.

14 Isadora Duncan, *My Life by Isadora Duncan* (New York: Horace Liveright, 1927), 9, 31, 44.

15 Duncan, *My Life*, 74, 100–1.

16 Quoted in Lisa Cohen, *All We Know: Three Lives* (New York: Farrar, Strauss, Giroux, 2012), 179.

17 "Comment BiB [Georges Breitel] a vu Isadora Duncan au Trocadéro."

18 Duncan, *My Life*, 152, 327.

19 Katharina Vester, "'Somewhat Inclined to Embonpoint': Introducing Female Slenderness in Late 19th-Century Short Stories and Serial Novels" (March 1, 2020). https://foodfat-nessfitness.com/

20 William Banting, *Letter on Corpulence: Addressed to the Public* (San Francisco: A. Roman & Co., 1865). Banting's advice to wash down meals with great amounts of alcohol, including several glasses of claret at dinner and supper and for a nightcap, fits less well with modern dietary advice.

21 Harriet Beecher Stowe, *The Writings of Harriet Beecher Stowe: With Biographical Introductions, Portraits, and Other Illustrations*, 16 vols., vol. 8 (Cambridge, MA: Houghton Mifflin & Co., 1896), 322.

22 Susan Dunning Power, *The Ugly-Girl Papers; or, Hints for the Toilet* (New York: Harper & Brothers, 1874), 3, 14, 132.

23 Helen Zoe Veit, *Modern Food, Moral Food: Self-Control, Science, and the Rise of Modern American Eating in the Early Twentieth Century* (Chapel Hill, NC: University of North Carolina Press, 2013), 23.

24 Charlotte Biltekoff, *Eating Right in America: The Cultural Politics of Food and Health* (Durham, NC: Duke University Press, 2013), 20–3.

25 Biographical details about Barney are drawn from Suzanne Rodriguez, *Wild Heart: A Life: Natalie Clifford Barney and the Decadence of Literary Paris* (New York: HarperCollins, 2009).

26 Shari Benstock, *Women of the Left Bank: Paris, 1900–1940* (Austin, TX: University of Texas, 1986), 47–8.

27 Rodriguez, *Wild Heart*, 91–4, 112, 13, 248, 302–3.

28 Djuna Barnes, "Lament for the Left Bank," *PMLA* 130(1) (January, 2015): 114.

29 Rodriguez, *Wild Heart*, 198. When plovers' eggs became scarce later in the century, Barney did not give up the hunt for them. The writer Sybille Bedford mentioned in a 1953 letter to a friend that Barney had asked her to buy plovers' eggs on a visit to Holland, "the last place in Europe where you can get them." Sybille Bedford to Evelyn Gendel, April 5, 1953. Sybille Bedford Papers, 1911–2006, Box 19, Folder 1, Harry Ransom Center.

30 Cohen, *All We Know*, 55.

31 Rodriguez, *Wild Heart*, 302–3.

32 For overviews of the Lesbian Left Bank, see Benstock, *Women of the Left Bank*; Andrea Weiss, *Paris Was a Woman: Portraits from the Left Bank* (Berkeley: Counterpoint, 2013). Katharina Vester includes several Left Bank figures in Katharina Vester, *A Taste of Power: Food and American Identities*, ed. Darra Goldstein. California Studies in Food and Culture (Berkeley, CA: University of California Press, 2015), 137–95.

33 Hemingway recalled the "good things to eat" at Stein's salon in Ernest Hemingway, *A Moveable Feast* (London: Arrow Books, 2004), 8–9.

34 Gertrude Stein, *Paris France* (New York: W. W. Norton & Co, 1970), 1; Gertrude Stein, *The Autobiography of Alice B. Toklas* (New York: Vintage, 1933), 71.

35 Robert McAlmon and Kay Boyle, *Being Geniuses Together 1920–1930* (San Francisco: North Point Press, 1984), 295–6.

36 Weiss, *Paris Was a Woman*, 93.

37 Belinda Bruner, "A Recipe for Modernism and the Somatic Intellect in the *Alice B. Toklas Cook Book* and Gertrude Stein's *Tender Buttons*," *Papers on Language & Literature* 45(4) (Fall, 2009).

38 Gertrude Stein, *Lifting Belly*, ed. Rebecca Mark (Tallahassee: Naiad Press, 1995), 3. See also Katharina Vester's analysis of food discourse in Stein's *Tender Buttons* in Vester, *A Taste of Power*, 150–5.

39 Stein, *The Autobiography of Alice B. Toklas*, 7, 14, 41, 99, 104–5. Some scholars hypothesize that Toklas did, in fact, author the autobiography; see Bruner, "A Recipe."

40 Vester, *A Taste of Power*, 155.

41 "We eat. A Cookbook by Alice Toklas and Gertrude Stein," Series I. Writings of Gertrude Stein, Gertrude Stein and Alice B. Toklas Papers, Box 82, Folder 1494, American Literature Collection, Beinecke Rare Book and Manuscript Library. Interestingly, the manuscript also includes a memory belonging to French historian Bernard Faÿ, the Nazi collaborator who protected Stein and Toklas, two Jewish lesbians, from being murdered in the Holocaust.

42 Alice Toklas, *The Alice B. Toklas Cookbook*, 1984 edn (New York: Harper Perennial, 1954), 29.

43 Toklas, *The Alice B. Toklas Cookbook*, 23, 90, 97, 118, 19, 208.

44 McLean, *Aesthetic Pleasure*, 92–117; Elspeth Probyn, *Carnal Appetites: FoodSexIdentities* (London: Routledge, 2000); Justin Spring, *The Gourmands' Way: Six Americans in Paris*

and the Birth of a New Gastronomy (New York: Farrar, Straus and Giroux, 2017), 45–64, 170–98.

45 Elspeth Probyn, "An Ethos with a Bite: Queer Appetites from Sex to Food," *Sexualities* 2(4) (1999). See also Probyn's description of Toklas as one of her "favourite mistresses of the 'alimentary-sexual' as guide for life." Probyn, "Beyond Food/Sex," 224.

46 Sylvia Beach, *Shakespeare & Company* (Lincoln: Bison Books, 1991), 112–15.

47 Brigitte Mahuzier, "Colette's 'Écriture gourmande,'" in Lawrence R. Schehr and Allen S. Weiss (eds.), *French Food on the Table, on the Page, and in French Culture* (New York: Routledge, 2011), 104–5.

48 GLOBAL French-English Dictionary. https://dictionary.cambridge.org/dictionary/french-english/gourmandise; Collins Beginner's French–English Dictionary https://www.collinsdictionary.com/dictionary/french-english/gourmandise/ See also Ferguson's definition of *gourmandise* as the excessive love of good food; Priscilla Parkhurst Ferguson, "A Cultural Field in the Making: Gastronomy in Nineteenth-Century France," in Lawrence R. Schehr and Allen S. Weiss (eds.), *French Food on the Table, on the Page, and in French Culture*, ed. (New York: Routledge, 2001), 14.

49 Janet Flanner, *Paris Was Yesterday (1925–1939)*, ed. Irving Drutman (New York: Popular Library, 1972), journalism, ix.

50 Adrienne Monnier, *The Very Rich Hours of Adrienne Monnier*, trans. Richard McDougall (New York: Charles Scribner's Sons, 1976), 196, 403.

51 Beach, *Shakespeare & Company*, 116.

52 Monnier, *The Very Rich Hours*, 196, 201.

53 https://www.themorgan.org/exhibitions/online/ulysses/adrienne-monniers-d%C3%A9jeuner-ulysse

54 Sylvia Beach to Adrienne Monnier, September 27, 1942; Beach to Monnier, October 15, 1942; Beach to Monnier, October 20, 1942; Beach to Monnier, November 11, 1942; Beach to Monnier, December 30, 1942; Maurice Saillet Collection of Sylvia Beach and Shakespeare and Company, 1917–1976, Series II, Box 264, Folder 3, Harry Ransom Library. Adrienne Monnier's occupation journal shows a similar sustained attention to what she was eating; Monnier, *The Very Rich Hours*, 391–403. Stein commented acerbically in her war book *Paris, France* about a French neighbor in Bilignin who, like Monnier, never lost sight of the importance of good food: "it was French of her with a son at the front to be worried about her quenelles"; Stein, *Paris France*, 37.

55 Adrienne Monnier to Tudor Wilkinson, January 20, 1943; Maurice Saillet Collection of Sylvia Beach and Shakespeare and Company, 1917–1976, Series II, Box 264, Folder 3, Harry Ransom Library.

56 Sylvia Beach, "Inturned"; Maurice Saillet Collection of Sylvia Beach and Shakespeare and Company, 1917–1976, Series II, Box 264, Folder 3, Harry Ransom Library.

57 Flanner, *Paris Was Yesterday*, viii, xii.

58 Weiss, *Paris Was a Woman*, 81–6.

59 Violet Trefusis, *Don't Look Round* (London: Hutchinson, 1952), 89.

60 There is a lengthy description of the Marquise and her relationship with Colette in X. Marcel Boulestin, *Myself, My Two Countries . . .* (London: Cassell and Company, 1936), 85–6.

61 Weiss, *Paris Was a Woman*, 81–6.

62 Mahuzier, "Colette's 'Écriture gourmande,'" 99.

63 "Lunch with Colette," in Monnier, *The Very Rich Hours*, 196–200. Colette's health is described in Judith Thurman, "Introduction," Colette, *The Pure and the Impure*, trans. Henri Briffault, ed. Judith Thurman (New York: New York Review of Books, 2000), xiii.

64 Spring, *The Gourmands' Way*, 278.

65 Alice B. Toklas, *Aromas and Flavors of the Past and Present: A Book of Exquisite Cooking* (New York: Harper & Brothers, 1958).

66 Janet Flanner, "Recipes of Alice B. Toklas," *The New Republic* (December 15, 1957): 20.

67 Alice B. Toklas to Poppy Cannon, October 13, 1954. Walter Francis White and Poppy Cannon White Papers, Series I, Box 11, Folder 98, Beinecke Library.

68 Cannon's conformity was more a matter of appearance than fact. For example, her *Bride's Cookbook* included love poems that the married Cannon had written for her married lover, Walter White, a Black activist and leader of the NAACP; Spring, *The Gourmands' Way*, 222.

69 Flanner, *Paris Was Yesterday*, xvii.

70 Djuna Barnes, *Nightwood* (London: Faber and Faber, 1936), novel, 31, 34.

71 Barnes, "Lament for the Left Bank," 112.

72 Phillip Herring, "Djuna Barnes and Thelma Wood: The Vengeance of 'Nightwood,'" *Journal of Modern Literature* 18(1) (Winter, 1992).

73 Thanks to Wood's great-nephew, Matthew Marchesani, who sent me scans of Wood's copy of Samuel Chamberlain's book *Bouquet de France*. Private correspondence, Matthew Marchesani to Rachel Hope Cleves, August 31, 2015.

74 Barnes, *Nightwood*, 24.

75 Katie Rawson and Elliott Shore, *Dining Out: A Global History of Restaurants* (London: Reaktion Books, 2019), 50. Newburg is sometimes spelled -erg and sometimes spelled -urg. There are apocryphal stories about the name's origins (supposedly, it was named for a ship captain named Wenburg who later angered Ranhofer, causing him to rename the dish Newburg). Samuel Chamberlain may have switched out the lobster for langoustine to make it seem even more French.

76 Lobster Newburg was the sort of French dish that *Playboy* food editor Thomas Mario would later recommend bachelors cook to seduce young women; "Food by Thomas Mario," *Playboy* 13(2) (February, 1966): 105. For more on Thomas Mario, see chapter 10.

77 Leila Rupp, *Sapphistries: A Global History of Love between Women* (New York: New York University Press, 2009), 179.

78 Michel Foucault, *The History of Sexuality: An Introduction*, trans. Robert Hurley, 3 vols., vol. 1 (New York: Vintage Press, 1990), 1.

79 Djuna Barnes, *Ladies Almanack Showing Their Signs and Their Tides; Their Moons and Their Changes; the Seasons as It Is with Them; Their Eclipses and Equinoxes; as well as a Full Record of Diurnal and Nocturnal Distempers. Written & Illustrated by a Lady of Fashion.* (New York: Harper & Row, 1972); Colette, *The Pure and the Impure*; Radclyffe Hall, *The Well of Loneliness* (Anchor Books, 1990, 1928).

80 Sylvia Beach wrote about meeting "the ladies with high collars and monocles" at Barney's salon; Beach, *Shakespeare & Company*, 112–15. There was even a lesbian bar in Paris in the thirties called Le Monocle; Rupp, *Sapphistries*, 179.

81 Gertrude Stein, *Fernhurst, Q.E.D., and Other Early Writings* (New York: Liveright, 1971), 55.

82 F. Scott Fitzgerald, *Tender Is the Night*, 1948 edn (New York: Charles Scribner's Sons, 1933). In point of fact, the Divers diverged radically from the Murphys, with Fitzgerald painting Nicole as a schizophrenic and Dick as an alcoholic, resembling Zelda and himself far more closely than Sara and Gerald. Hemingway wrote to Fitzgerald about *Tender Is the Night*, "I liked it and I didn't like it. It started off with that marvelous description of Sara and Gerald . . . then you started fooling with them, making them come from things they didn't come from, changing them into other people"; Ernest Hemingway to F. Scott Fitzgerald, May 28, 1934, copy enclosed within Sara & Gerald Murphy Papers, Box 4, Folders 68–9, Beinecke Library. And Sara said, "I reject categorically any resemblance to us or to anyone we knew"; Calvin Tomkins, "Living Well Is the Best Revenge: The Couple who Inspired F. Scott Fitzgerald's 'Tender Is the Night,'" *New Yorker*, July 20, 1962.

83 Amanda Vaill, *Everybody Was So Young: Gerald and Sara Murphy, A Lost Generation Love Story* (New York: Broadway Books, 1998), 113, 19.

84 Fitzgerald, *Tender Is the Night*, 72.

85 Tomkins, "Living Well Is the Best Revenge."

86 Kathryn Price, 'The "Juice of a Few Flowers': Gerald and Sara Murphy's Life of Beautiful Things," *Gastronomica* 7(2) (May 4, 2007).

87 Sara & Gerald Murphy Papers, Box 15, Folders 211–26, Beinecke Library.

88 As it happens, both Gerald's sister Esther Murphy and Sara's sister Hoytie Wiborg were lesbians who mixed in Parisian artistic circles. Esther Murphy, referenced above, was part of Natalie Barney's larger circle and is caricatured in Djuna Barnes's *Ladies Almanac*. The Murphys had somewhat tenuous relationships with both sisters, unrelated to their sexualities.

89 Vaill, *Everybody Was So Young*, 101, 26, 54.

90 Vaill, *Everybody Was So Young*, 272–4.

91 Morley Callaghan provides a firsthand account of the complex relationship between Hemingway and Fitzgerald in his memoir; Morley Callaghan, *That Summer in Paris*, 2006 edn (Toronto: Exile Editions, 1963). See also Cody Delistraty, "Distinctly Emasculated: Hemingway, Fitzgerald, and Sexual Anxiety," *Paris Review*, April 24, 2015.

92 Flanner, *Paris Was Yesterday*, xix.

93 McAlmon and Boyle, *Being Geniuses Together*, 15, 66, 125, 40, 216.

94 For a great capsule account of Boyle's biography, see Sandra Spanier, "Kay Boyle Knew Everyone and Saw It All," *Humanities* 39(2) (2018). https://www.neh.gov/humanities/2018/spring/feature/kay-boyle-knew-everyone-and-saw-it-all

95 Linda Hamalian, "Kay Boyle and Caresse Crosby: Devoted Friendship," *e-Rea: Revue électronique d'études sur le monde anglophone* 10(2) (2013).

96 Geoffrey Wolff, *Black Sun: The Brief Transit and Violent Eclipse of Harry Crosby* (New York: New York Review of Books, 2003), 81, 147, 69–70, 83–4. Attitudes toward the Crosbys varied enormously. Sylvia Beach called them "among the most charming people I ever knew," but other people thought them insufferable frauds. Harry Crosby ultimately killed himself and his girlfriend, Josephine Rotch Bigelow, in New York in 1929.

97 John Glassco, *Memoirs of Montparnasse* (New York: New York Review of Books, 2007), 32–3. According to Glassco, he slept with Wood and was seduced by Boyle.

98 Glassco, *Memoirs of Montparnasse*, 123.

Chapter 8 Mistresses of Gastropornography

1 Details of David's life come from her authorized biography Artemis Cooper, *Writing at the Kitchen Table: The Authorized Biography of Elizabeth David* (London: Faber and Faber, 2011). See also the more gossipy unauthorized biography, Lisa Chaney, *Elizabeth David: A Biography* (London: Macmillan, 1998). David obscured many things about her life, making an accurate biography challenging. Even her autobiographical notes in her archived papers are inaccurate; "Biographical notes, resumes, etc. 1945–1990." Elizabeth David Papers, Box 2, Folder 7, Schlesinger Library.

2 "Profile: Elizabeth David," *New Statesman*, August 9, 1968. Elizabeth David Papers, Box 2, Folder 12, Schlesinger Library.

3 A. A. Gill, "Elizabeth David," in *Table Talk: Sweet and Sour, Salt and Bitter* (London: Weidenfeld & Nicolson, 2007), 152–8.

4 Stephen Mennell, *All Manners of Food: Eating and Taste in England and France from the Middle Ages to the Present* (Champaign, IL: University of Illinois Press, 1985); Gilly Lehmann, *The British Housewife: Cookery Books, Cooking and Society in Eighteenth-Century Britain* (Totnes, UK: Prospect Books, 2003); Alice L. McLean, *Aesthetic Pleasure in Twentieth-Century Women's Food Writing: The Innovative Appetites of M. F. K. Fisher, Alice B. Toklas, and Elizabeth David* (New York: Routledge, 2012; Samantha Presnal, "Art to Table: The Power of Aesthetics in Women's Cookbooks of the Belle Époque," *Historical Reflections/Réflexions Historiques* 43(3) (2017).

5 M. F. K. Fisher, *The Art of Eating: M. F. K. Fisher's Five Most Famous Books in One Volume* (New York: Vintage Books, 1976), 320.

6 McLean, *Aesthetic Pleasure*, 73–5.

7 Elizabeth David, *Is There a Nutmeg in the House?*, ed. Jill Norman (New York: Penguin, 2001), 1–7; Chaney, *Elizabeth David*, 21.

8 Judith Jones, *The Tenth Muse: My Life in Food* (New York: Anchor Books, 2007), 5.

9 Betty Fussell, *My Kitchen Wars* (New York: North Point Press, 1999), 31.

10 Betty Fussell, *Masters of American Cookery: M. F. K. Fisher, James Andrews Beard, Craig Claiborne, Julia McWilliams Child* (New York: Times Books, 1983), 15.

11 M. F. K. Fisher to family, September 25, 1929. M. F. K. Fisher Papers, Box 1, Folder 8, Schlesinger Library.

12 M. F. K. Fisher to family, October 4, 1929. M. F. K. Fisher Papers, Box 1, Folder 8, Schlesinger Library.

13 M. F. K. Fisher to family, October 5, 1929. M. F. K. Fisher Papers, Box 1, Folder 8, Schlesinger Library.

14 Elizabeth David, *French Provincial Cooking* (New York: Penguin Books, 1970), 22–5. The family were actually named Barette; Cooper, *Writing at the Kitchen Table*, 29. David used the word "greedy" to describe the Barettes in a two-page handwritten account of her life included in her personal papers; "Biographical notes, resumes, etc. 1945–1990." Elizabeth David Papers, Box 2, Folder 7, Schlesinger Library.

15 Chaney, *Elizabeth David*, 119–20.

16 Cooper, *Writing at the Kitchen Table*, 60–3.

17 Rachel Hope Cleves, *Unspeakable: A Life beyond Sexual Morality* (Chicago: University of Chicago Press, 2020).

18 Elizabeth David, *An Omelette and a Glass of Wine*, ed. Jill Norman (Guilford, CT: Lyons Press, 1987), 120–33. See also David's assertion of Douglas's influence on her cooking in

"Profile: Elizabeth David," *New Statesman*, August 9, 1968. Elizabeth David Papers, Box 2, Folder 12, Schlesinger Library.

19 Theodora FitzGibbon, *A Taste of Love: The Autobiographies* (Gill & Macmillan, 2015), 165–9, 242–56, 351.

20 Julia Child and Alex Prud'homme, *My Life in France* (New York: Anchor Books, 2006), 15–29.

21 Jones, *The Tenth Muse*, 17–33.

22 Fussell, *Masters of American Cookery*, 15–17.

23 Hibben's food writing is the subject of a recent dissertation; Meaghan Elliott Dittrich, "Toward a Feminist Rhetorical Strategy of Sass: Sheila Hibben as America's Early 20th Century Culinary Influencer" (PhD, University of New Hampshire, 2021).

24 Some sources give Hibben's birth year as 1888, but others list 1884 and, considering that she made the fourth grade honor roll in 1894, the latter date seems more likely; "Four Grade – Minnie Taylor, Teacher," *Montgomery Advertiser*, June 1, 1894, p. 7. Also, contrary to what some online biographies assert, she was not raised in Italy and France, but in Montgomery, Alabama.

25 Keri Walsh (ed.), *The Letters of Sylvia Beach* (New York: Columbia University Press, 2012), 8.

26 "French Cross Given Alabama Woman Worker," *Evening Independent*, June 10, 1919.

27 Her first article "Miss Cecile Craik Writes of 'To Have and to Hold,'" appeared in *The Montgomery Advertiser*, March 25, 1900, p. 12. During World War I, she contributed articles to the *New York Sun* that were published without her byline. Dittrich, "Toward a Feminist Rhetorical Strategy," 8.

28 Sheila Hibben, "Food Is to Eat," *Outlook and Independent*, March 20, 1929. She also briefly served as the associate editor of a progressive magazine, "Women Head New Magazine," *Cumberland Evening Times*, MD, February 11, 1930, p. 6.

29 Sheila Hibben, *The National Cookbook: A Kitchen Americana* (New York: Harper & Brothers, 1932).

30 "Sheila Hibben, 76, a Food Authority," *New York Times*, February 21, 1964; Jon Michaud, "Sheila Hibben," *New Yorker*, November 16, 2010. There are errors in the *Times* obituary about her publishing history. At her death, Hibben lived at 171 West 12th Street, the same building where James Beard lived.

31 Hibben, "Food Is to Eat," 477.

32 Sheila Hibben, "Foreign Cheese and What Ails Them," *New Yorker*, June 2, 1934, pp. 75–7; Sheila Hibben, "Eating American," *New Republic*, April 6, 1932.

33 Sheila Hibben, "Picnic Lunches for Assorted Tastes," *New Yorker*, July 13, 1934.

34 Sheila Hibben, "The Infant Gourmet," *Vogue Magazine*, July 15, 1942, pp. 53, 78.

35 Dittrich, "Toward a Feminist Rhetorical Strategy," 3.

36 Sylvia Lovegren, *Fashionable Food: Seven Decades of Food Fads* (Chicago: University of Chicago Press, 2005), 150.

37 Edward Bunyard and Lorna Bunyard, *The Epicure's Companion* (London: J. M. Dent, 1937), 15. The fact that his book was co-authored with his sister Lorna Bunyard, and illustrated by their other sister Frances Bunyard, did not take away from this stated conclusion about the "average" English woman.

38 Fisher, *The Art of Eating*, 119.

39 Joan Reardon, *Poet of the Appetites: The Lives and Loves of M. F. K. Fisher* (New York: North Point Press, 2004).

40 Fisher, *The Art of Eating*, 5, 7.

41 Fisher, *The Art of Eating*, 8, 17, 22, 25, 26, 27, 67. This list does not exhaust the sexual material included in *Serve It Forth*. See also Fisher's references to pederasty (33), to eating food being like sexual play (42), to virgins as the best truffle hunters (48), to the cooks of famous courtesans (76), etc.

42 K. W., "About the Various Pleasures of Eating," *New York Times*, June 20, 1937.

43 Edward Larocque Tinker, "The Great Pleasures Inherent in Oysters," *New York Times*, November 9, 1941, p. 38. The epicurean writer Lucius Beebe also mistook M. F. K. Fisher for a man when *Serve It Forth* was published; McLean, *Aesthetic Pleasure*, 67.

44 Fisher, *The Art of Eating*, 128, 46, 75.

45 Fisher, *The Art of Eating*, 369.

46 Fisher, *The Art of Eating*, 369; Krafft-Ebing, *Psychopathia Sexualis*.

47 The scholarship on this culture is extensive. See, for example, Martha Vicinus, "Distance and Desire: English Boarding-School Friendships," in Estelle B. Freedman et al. (eds.), *The Lesbian Issue: Essays from SIGNS* (Chicago: University of Chicago Press, 1985); Sherrie A. Inness, "Mashes, Smashes, Crushes, and Raves: Woman-to-Woman Relationships in Popular Women's College Fiction, 1895–1915," *NWSA Journal* 6(1) (Spring, 1994); Lillian Faderman, *Surpassing the Love of Men: Romantic Friendship and Love between Women from the Renaissance to the Present* (New York: Quill, 1998).

48 Fisher, *The Art of Eating*, 368–77.

49 Reardon, *Poet of the Appetites*, 30.

50 Fisher's grand-nephew, the author Luke Barr, believes that Fisher and Lord did not consummate their relationship; Luke Barr, *Provence, 1970: M. F. K. Fisher, Julia Child, James Beard and the Reinvention of American Taste* (New York City: Random House, 2014), 107. Having no evidentiary basis on which to judge, my own interpretive bias is to assume that mutually attracted adolescents probably did act on their desires. I don't think male writers necessarily have the best insight into what the internal dynamics of adolescent female erotic relationships might be like.

51 Reardon, *Poet of the Appetites*, 262–3; Spring, *The Gourmands' Way*, 71. For a queer reading of Fisher's oeuvre, see Elspeth Probyn, "Eating Athwart and Queering Food Writing," in Gitanjali G. Shahani (ed.), *Food and Literature* (New York: Cambridge University Press, 2018), 186–200.

52 Reardon, *Poet of the Appetites*, 334.

53 Selina Hastings, *Sybille Bedford: A Life* (New York: Alfred A. Knopf, 2021), 51.

54 Sybille Bedford to Sheila Hodges, 1952. Sybille Bedford Papers, Box 23, Folder 8, Harry Ransom Library.

55 Sybille Bedford, *Jigsaw: An Unsentimental Education* (London: Hamish Hamilton, 1989), 138.

56 Sybille Bedford to Allanah Harper, November 13, 1946; Bedford to Harper, June 10, 1949. Sybille Bedford Papers, Box 23, Folder 8, Harry Ransom Library.

57 Sybille Bedford to Allanah Harper, November 13, 1946; Sybille Bedford to Allanah Harper, August 9, 1942. Sybille Bedford Papers, Box 23, Folder 8, Harry Ransom Library.

58 Esther Murphy to Sybille Bedford, October 3, 1949. Sybille Bedford Papers, Box 25, Folder 6, Harry Ransom Center.

59 Bedford describes learning to cook Italian and Provençal food in Bedford, *Jigsaw*, 63, 91.

60 I've discussed the long and complicated history of this cookbook in Rachel Hope Cleves, "Philotes in the Kitchen: Norman Douglas' Friendships with Faith Compton Mackenzie, Elizabeth David, Sybille Bedford and Theodora FitzGibbon," in Wilhelm Meusburger (ed.), *Norman Douglas: 9. Symposium, Bregenz und Thuringen, Vlbg., 7./8.10.2016* (Bregenz: Norman Douglas Forschungsstelle, Vorarlberger Landesbibliothek, 2017).

61 Sybille Bedford, *The Sudden View: A Mexican Journey* (London: Victor Gollancz, 1953). For her regret, see Sybille Bedford to Allanah Harper, December 4, 1952; Sybille Bedford to Evelyn Gendel, March 28, 1953. Sybille Bedford Papers, Box 19, Folder 1; Box 25, Folder 6, Harry Ransom Center.

62 For example, Sybille Bedford, *A Legacy*, 2015 edn (New York: New York Review of Books, 1956), 109–13; Sybille Bedford, *A Compass Error* (London: Collins, 1968), 40–1; Bedford, *Jigsaw*, 18, 63.

63 Andrew Barrow, "Sybille Bedford: Secret History," *Independent* (UK), May 22, 2004.

64 Hastings, *Sybille Bedford: A Life*. Elsewhere she blamed "hedonism and sloth for her not producing more books over a 50-year career," Eleanor Wachtel, "Being Sybille," *Globe and Mail*, December 24, 2005.

65 Sybille Bedford, *Quicksands: A Memoir* (New York: Counterpoint, 2005), 142.

66 "Evelyn Gendel, 61, Senior Editor with Bobbs-Merrill since 1952," *New York Times*, December 20, 1977; Evelyn Gendel, *Pasta! Spaghetti, Macaroni, Ravioli. Cannelloni, Linguini, Lasagne, and All Kinds of Noodles: How to Buy, Cook and Serve Them – with 50 Recipes for Sauces, Baked Dishes and Other Good Things* (New York: Simon & Schuster, 1966); *Vintage Soup!* (New York: Simon & Schuster, 1967).

67 Sybille Bedford Papers, Box 24, Folders 3–4, Harry Ransom Library.

68 Bedford, *Quicksands*, 273–4.

69 Sybille Bedford to Elizabeth David, September 15, 1964. Sybille Bedford Papers, Box 15, Folder 30, Harry Ransom Center.

70 Sybille Bedford to Elizabeth David, July 9, 1963. Elizabeth David Papers, Box 15, Folder 30, Schlesinger Library.

71 Elizabeth David to Sybille Bedford, September 3, 1963. Sybille Bedford Papers, Box 26, Folder 6, Harry Ransom Center.

72 Sybille Bedford, "Elizabeth David Profile for the *Sunday Times*." Sybille Bedford Papers, Box 10, Folder 5, Harry Ransom Center.

73 Julia Child to James Beard, February 21, 1967. Julia Child Papers, Box 10, Folder 128, Folder 129, Schlesinger Library.

74 Julia Child to James Beard, November 19, 1961. Julia Child Papers, Box 10, Folder 128, Folder 129, Schlesinger Library.

75 Reardon, *Poet of the Appetites*, 338.

76 Reardon, *Poet of the Appetites*, 379; Cooper, *Writing at the Kitchen Table*, 301, 19.

77 Christopher Driver, "The Writers Are Off," *Spectator*, November 10, 1990. Elizabeth David Papers, Box 2, Folder 15, Schlesinger Library.

78 James Beard, "Beard on Food," January 2, 1972. Elizabeth David Papers, Box 15, Folder 29, Schlesinger Library.

79 Jane Howard, "Cookery Crusader," *Quest* 81: 38–41. Elizabeth David Papers, Box 2, Folder 14, Schlesinger Library.

80 Sybille Bedford to Elizabeth David, May 11, 1967. Elizabeth David Papers, Box 15, Folder 30, Schlesinger Library. Funnily enough, in her final years Bedford herself preferred a diet of processed foods: powdered mash potatoes, Bovril, and tin corned beef; Hastings, *Sybille Bedford: A Life*, ch. 13.

81 M. F. K. Fisher's nephew Luke Barr argues that 1970 was the critical year in this network, but that's only true from Fisher's point of view; Barr, *Provence, 1970*. See also David Kamp, *The United States of Arugula: The Sun-Dried, Cold-Pressed, Dark-Roasted, Extra Virgin Story of the American Food Revolution* (Broadway Books, 2006).

82 Helen Evans Brown to James Beard, June 6, 1958. James Beard Papers, Box 11, Folder 6, Fales Library, New York University.

83 "Myself with Others: Claudia Roden," *London Review of Books Podcast*, January 18, 2018.

84 Fussell, *My Kitchen Wars*, 126–7, 54–5, 216.

85 Fussell, *Masters of American Cookery*. According to Fussell's website, she is now, at age ninety-six, working on a second memoir, titled *How to Cook a Coyote*, after M. F. K. Fisher's World War II cookbook *How to Cook a Wolf*. https://www.bettyfussell.com/

86 André Simon Memorial Fund press release, March 15, 1973. Elizabeth David Papers, Box 2, Folder 1, Schlesinger Library.

87 McLean, *Aesthetic Pleasure*, 128.

88 David Lazar (ed.), *Conversations with M. F. K. Fisher* (Jackson, MS: University of Mississippi Press, 1992), 12.

89 Quoted in Barr, *Provence, 1970*, 142–3.

90 Fussell, *Masters of American Cookery*, 25. See also Fussell's description of a Fisher passage about eating snails as "erotic," 27.

91 Anthony Bourdain, "Foreword," in Marilyn Hegarty, *Grand Forks: A History of American Dining in 128 Reviews* (New York: Ecco/Anthony Bourdain Books, 2013).

92 Rosalind Coward, "Naughty but Nice: Food Pornography," in *Female Desires: How They Are Sought, Bought and Packaged* (New York: Grove Weidenfeld, 1985), 99–106.

93 "Elizabeth David Talks to the Editor," *Wine & Food* (September, 1968).

94 Julian Barnes, "The Land without Brussels Sprouts," in *Something to Declare: Essays on France and French Culture* (New York: Random House, 2002), 46–55; "Diana Simmonds Samples Some Food Porn," *Weekend Australian*.

95 Kyla Wazana, "She Brought Food Porn to the People," *Globe and Mail*, October 18, 1997, D14.

96 Lisa Rosman, "Julia Child: Recipe for Culinary Revolution," *Signature: Making Well-Read Sense of the World*, August 11, 2014.

97 Mark Kurlansky, *Choice Cuts* (New York: Ballantine Books, 2002), 35; Spring, *The Gourmands' Way*.

98 James McWilliams, "Sex and a Cheese Sandwich: The Once and Future Brilliance of Food Writing," *The Awl* (January 24, 2018).

Chapter 9 Gay Gourmets

1 X. Marcel Boulestin, *Myself, My Two Countries* . . . (London: Cassell and Company, 1936), 25.

2 Boulestin, *Myself*, 93.

3 Quoted in Maria Bustillos, "The Chef for Every Age," *Eater* (July 6, 2016). https://www.eater.com/2016/7/6/12095640/marcel-boulestin-chef-cookbook-history/ The French

term *pédéraste* was commonly used for men who had sex with men at the turn of the century, and did not mean the equivalent of today's term "pedophile," used for adults who desire sex with children. That said, the eroticization of male youths was central to male same-sex erotics at that time. See William A. Peniston, *Pederasts and Others: Urban Culture and Sexual Identity in Nineteenth-Century Paris* (New York: Harrington Park Press, 2004); Andrew Israel Ross, *Public City/Public Sex: Homosexuality, Prostitution, and Urban Culture in Nineteenth-Century Paris* (Philadelphia, PA: Temple University Press, 2019); Rachel Hope Cleves, *Unspeakable: A Life beyond Sexual Morality* (Chicago: University of Chicago Press, 2020).

4 Reggie Turner to Max Beerbohm, March, 1904. bMS Eng 1220 (1–104), Houghton Library; Boulestin, *Myself*, 77.

5 Boulestin, *Myself*, 151.

6 *Elysium Books*, shortlist #10, https://www.elysiumpress.com/

7 X. Marcel Boulestin, "Londres Satirisé," *Cambridge Magazine*, February 22, 1913. 359.

8 Boulestin, *Myself*, 287.

9 X. Marcel Boulestin, *Simple French Cooking for English Homes* (London: William Heinemann, 1924); X. Marcel Boulestin, *A Second Helping, or More Dishes for English Homes* (London: William Heinemann, 1925).

10 Boulestin, *A Second Helping*, 11–13.

11 X. M. Boulestin, "The Way of All Flesh, Fish and Fowl," *Daily Telegraph* (London), March 15, 1929, p. 9.

12 Joan Russell Noble (ed.), *Recollections of Virginia Woolf by Her Contemporaries* (New York: William Morrow & Company, 1972), 173–4.

13 X. Marcel Boulestin, *Ease and Endurance*, trans. Robin Adair (London: Van Thal, 1948).

14 Noble, *Recollections of Virginia Woolf*, 38.

15 Virginia Woolf, "Old Bloomsbury" (1922), quoted in Jans Ondaatje Rolls, *The Bloomsbury Cookbook: Recipes for Life, Love, and Art* (London: Thames & Hudson, 2014), 43.

16 E. M. Forster, "Porridge or Prunes, Sir?," in André L. Simon and Louis Golding (eds.), *We Shall Eat and Drink Again: A Wine & Food Anthology* (London: Hutchinson, 1944).

17 Rolls, *The Bloomsbury Cookbook*, 18, 231; Philippa Pullar, *Consuming Passions: Being an Historic Inquiry into Certain English Appetites* (Boston: Little, Brown, 1970), 215.

18 Boulestin, *Ease and Endurance*, 81.

19 Phil Lyon, "Good Food and Hard Times: Ambrose Heath's Contribution to British Food Culture of the 1930s and the War Years," *Food & History* 12(2) (2014).

20 Elizabeth David, "Having Crossed the Channel: The Work of X. Marcel Boulestin," in Elizabeth David, *An Omelette and a Glass of Wine*, ed. Jill Norman (Guilford, CT: Lyons Press, 1987), 162–74. See also Elizabeth David 1977 notebook, Elizabeth David Papers, Box 8, Folder 8, Schlesinger Library.

21 Martin Gayford, "A Whiff of Wine and Garlic," *Spectator*, April 28, 2018.

22 D. D. Cottington-Taylor, *Subtle Seasoning: A Little Book of Recipes* (Worcester: Lea & Perrins, 1926); "Boulestin Broadcast," *Evening Standard*, November 28, 1938, p. 16.

23 Jane Stern and Michael Stern, *American Gourmet: Classic Recipes, Deluxe Delights, Flamboyant Favorites and Swank "Company" Food from the '50s and '60s* (New York: HarperCollins, 1991), 5, 61, 189.

24 Lewis M. Terman and Catharine Cox Miles, *Sex and Personality: Studies in Masculinity and Femininity* (New York: McGraw-Hill, 1936), 269, 278, and 281; Jennifer Terry, *An American Obsession: Science, Medicine, and Homosexuality in Modern Society* (Chicago: University of Chicago Press, 1999), 168–75.

25 Byron MacFadyen, "Give a Man Man's Food," *Good Housekeeping* 112(3) (March, 1941): 106–8.

26 Jean Freeman, "A Good Egg," *House & Garden* 85 (March, 1944): 59.

27 Mark McWilliams, *Food and the Novel in Nineteenth-Century Literature* (New York: Rowman & Littlefield, 2012), xiv.

28 David Strauss, *Setting the Table for Julia Child: Gourmet Dining in America, 1934–1961* (Baltimore, MD: Johns Hopkins University Press, 2011), 25; Katharine Parkin, *Food Is Love: Food Advertising and Gender Roles in Modern America* (Philadelphia, PA: University of Pennsylvania Press, 2011), 144, 99. "Sissy" is a complex term. Used to denote cowardly femininity, it could be applied to girls as well as boys, but the term always carried a derogatory imputation of homosexuality when used for boys; https://greensdictofslang.com/entry/4cmq4ma

29 For the creativity explanation, see Daniel Isengart, "The Joy of Gay Cooking," *Slate*, July 13, 2015. John Birdsall makes a much more compelling cultural argument in John Birdsall, "America, Your Food Is So Gay: The Story of How Three Gay Men – James Beard, Richard Olney, and Craig Claiborne – Became Architects of America's Modern Food Culture," *Lucky Peach* 8 (September 27, 2013).

30 John Birdsall, *The Man who Ate Too Much: The Life of James Beard* (New York: W. W. Norton, 2020), 245.

31 Robert Clark, *James Beard: A Biography* (New York: HarperCollins, 1993), 22.

32 Barbara Kafka, *The James Beard Celebration Cookbook: Memories and Recipes from His Friends* (New York: William Morrow & Company, 1990), 16–35.

33 Clark, *James Beard*, 41.

34 James Beard, *Delights and Prejudices* (New York: Manufacturers Hanover Trust Company, 1964; repr. 1990), 3–56, 174–5; Evan Jones, *Epicurean Delight: The Life and Times of James Beard* (New York: Simon & Schuster, 1990), 40, 43–4; Clark, *James Beard*, 42; Birdsall, *The Man who Ate Too Much*, 72–3.

35 Clark, *James Beard*, 64–6.

36 Jones, *Epicurean Delight: The Life and Times of James Beard*, 15.

37 Jones, *Epicurean Delight: The Life and Times of James Beard*, 86. Ruth Norman co-authored a cookbook with another gay male friend, George Bradshaw and Ruth Norman, *Cook until Done: A Collection of Unexpected Recipes* (New York: M. Barrows & Co., 1962).

38 William Rhode, *Of Cabbages and Kings* (New York City: Stackpole Sons, 1938).

39 Lucius Beebe, "This New York," *Oakland Tribune*, May 7, 1939, p. 24; Birdsall, *The Man who Ate Too Much*, 105–11.

40 Sheila Hibben, "Markets and Menus," *New Yorker*, June 24, 1939, p. 61.

41 Kafka, *James Beard Celebration Cookbook*, 57.

42 "William Rhode; Expert on Food Preparation Had Been Magazine Writer," *New York Times*, November 28, 1946, p. 27.

43 James Beard, *Hors d'Oeuvre and Canapés* (Philadelphia: Running Press, 1999), xiii.

44 Kafka, *James Beard Celebration Cookbook*, n.p.

45 Jeanne Owen, *A Wine Lover's Cook Book* (New York: M. Barrows and Company, 1940), 132. Evan Jones's biography of Beard suggests that the "Bachelor Brotherhood of Cooks" was the name of an actual organization; Jones, *Epicurean Delight: The Life and Times of James Beard*, 94. If so, I can't find any information about them.

46 Ann Barr and Paul Levy, *The Official Foodie Handbook* (London: Ebury Press, 1984), 119.

47 Birdsall, *The Man who Ate Too Much*, 284.

48 James Villas, *Between Bites: Memoirs of a Hungry Hedonist* (New York: John Wiley & Sons, 2002), 177. Tales of Beard's gluttony are abundant. See for example the recollections of many of his food industry friends in Kafka, *James Beard Celebration Cookbook*.

49 Betty Fussell, *Masters of American Cookery: M. F. K. Fisher, James Andrews Beard, Craig Claiborne, Julia McWilliams Child* (New York: Times Books, 1983), 31.

50 Birdsall, *The Man who Ate Too Much*, 125, 59.

51 Mimi Sheraton Falcone, "Oral History Interview," interview by Sarah Dziedzic, *West Village Oral History Project* (2019), p. 7. Sheraton mentions how her mother was upset that she moved to the Village in 1945 because it was filled with "fairies" (and communists and mixed-race couples).

52 Kafka, *James Beard Celebration Cookbook*, 254.

53 Kafka, *James Beard Celebration Cookbook*, 110.

54 "Lucky Pierre," *Green's Dictionary of Slang* https://greensdictofslang.com/search/basic ?q=lucky+pierre/ The term could also be used for the middle person in a threesome involving two women and a man, but this was less common.

55 Clark, *James Beard*, 4.

56 Birdsall, *The Man who Ate Too Much*, 319, 25.

57 Villas, *Between Bites*, 136.

58 David Kamp, *The United States of Arugula: The Sun-Dried, Cold-Pressed, Dark-Roasted, Extra Virgin Story of the American Food Revolution* (Broadway Books, 2006), 73.

59 Villas, *Between Bites*, 138.

60 Gael Greene, *Insatiable: Tales from a Life of Delicious Excess* (New York: Warner Books, 2006), 149.

61 Cathy Crimmins, *How the Homosexuals Saved Civilization: The True and Heroic Story of How Gay Men Shaped the Modern World* (New York: Penguin, 2004).

62 "Times Has Man Food Editor? So Have We. For Many Years," *Commercial Appeal* (Memphis), October 20, 1957, p. 89; "Craig Claiborne Food Editor of New York Times," *Enterprise-Tocsin*, October 31, 1957, p. 1; "New York Times Food Editor's Authority Remains Unchallenged," *Greenwood Commonwealth* (MS), April 16, 1954, p. 7.

63 "Revolutionary News," *Fort Payne Journal*, November 26, 1957, p. 6. See also "Times Has Man Food Editor? So Have We. For Many Years," *Commercial Appeal* (Memphis), October 20, 1957, p. 89; "Craig Claiborne Food Editor of *New York Times*," *Enterprise-Tocsin*, October 31, 1957, p. 1; "Trend of the Times?" *Miami Herald*, November 8, 1957, p. 73.

64 Kimberly Wilmot Voss, *The Food Section: Newspaper Women and the Culinary Community* (London: Rowman & Littlefield, 2014), 23, 123.

65 Helen Evans Brown to James Beard, August 7, 1957. James Beard Papers, Box 11, Folder 5, Fales Library, New York University.

66 Helen Evans Brown to James Beard, September 12, 1957. James Beard Papers, Box 11, Folder 5, Fales Library, New York University.

67 Helen Evans Brown to James Beard, July 20, 1957. James Beard Papers, Box 11, Folder 5, Fales Library, New York University. Claiborne later became friends with Brown and Beard. See James Beard to Helen Evans Brown, January 24, 1959; July 7, 1959. Helen Evans Brown to James Beard, March 13, 1960; May 22, 1963. James Beard Papers, Box 11, Folders 7, 8, 11, Fales Library, New York University.

68 Craig Claiborne, *Craig Claiborne's a Feast Made for Laughter* (New York: Doubleday & Company, Inc., 1982), 37.

69 Craig Claiborne (ed.), *A Cookbook for Booksellers* (New York: New York Times Company, 1965). For Strutwell, see Juliet Shields, "Smollett's Scots and Sodomites: British Masculinity in 'Roderick Random'," *The Eighteenth Century* 46(2) (2005). For Thackeray, see Joseph Litvak, *Strange Gourmets: Sophistication, Theory, and the Novel* (Durham, NC: Duke University Press, 1997), 6, 16

70 Litvak, *Strange Gourmets: Sophistication, Theory, and the Novel*, 6, 56.

71 José, August 19, 1975 note. James Beard Collection, Box 1, Folder 14, Fales Library, New York University. For the hustler bar, see Villas, *Between Bites*, 183.

72 Beard, *Delights and Prejudices*, 173; Kafka, *James Beard Celebration Cookbook*, 24.

73 Claiborne, *A Feast Made for Laughter*, 20. For the memoir's shocking impact, see Liz Smith, "Gourmet Day! Claiborne to Tell All in Bio," *Daily News*, April 5, 1982, p. 8; Barbara Hodge Hall, "'Feast' of a Memoir," *Anniston Star*, August 22, 1982, p. 53.

74 Oddly, one reviewer thought that Claiborne hadn't outed himself enough; Harvey Steiman, "Schizophrenic Memoirs," *San Francisco Examiner*, October 3, 1982, p. 107.

75 Noel Riley Fitch, *Appetite for Life: The Biography of Julia Child* (New York: Anchor, 1997), 225–6.

76 Judith Jones, *The Tenth Muse: My Life in Food* (New York: Anchor Books, 2007), 50–61; David K. Johnson, *The Lavender Scare: The Cold War Persecution of Gays and Lesbians in the Federal Government* (Chicago: University of Chicago Press, 2004).

77 Laura Shapiro, *Julia Child: A Life* (New York: Penguin, 1997), 135–41.

78 Fitch, *Appetite for Life*.

79 Robert Carrier, *Great Dishes of the World* (New York: Random House, 1964); Robert Carrier, *The Connoisseur's Cookbook* (New York: Random House, 1967). For biographical information about Carrier, see Jay Rayner, "Cook Dinner with Robert Carrier," *Guardian*, April 4, 2021; Ann Barr and Paul Levy, *The Official Foodie Handbook* (London: Ebury Press, 1984), 123. Rayner describes Carrier's Wikipedia entry as notoriously inaccurate.

80 Jane Grigson, *Fish Cookery*, 1984 edn (New York: Pengun Books, 1973), 37.

81 *Bon Viveur's London and the British Isles* (London: Andrew Dakers, 1955), 61.

82 See also a wonderful story by the record producer Simon Napier-Bell about the time he got a would-be thug a job at Le Matelot. https://www.huffingtonpost.co.uk/simon-napierbell/one-of-lifes-little-succe_b_1070847.html

83 Matt Houlbrook, *Queer London: Perils and Pleasures in the Sexual Metropolis, 1918–1957* (Chicago: University of Chicago Press, 2005), 68–92.

84 George Chauncey, *Gay New York: Gender, Urban Culture, and the Making of the Gay Male World, 1890–1940* (New York City: Basic Books, 1995, 164–6.

85 Sara B. Franklin (ed.), *Edna Lewis: At the Table with an American Original* (Chapel Hill, NC: University of North Carolina Press, 2018), 49–54, 70–3. For the bronze, see Marian Burros, "An Innovator in Café Décor and Food," *New York Times*, March 10, 1982, p. C3. Also Paul Freedman, *American Cuisine: And How It Got This Way* (New York: Liveright, 2019), 304.

86 Craig Claiborne, "Restaurant on Review," *New York Times*, July 29, 1963; "Cafe Nicholson: Food Is Almost Afterthought," *New York Times*, August 22, 1967.

87 Christopher Blake, *52 Recipes: No Week's Complete without a New Orleans Seafood Recipe*, vol. 1 (New Orleans: Blake, 1975).

88 Craig Claiborne, "Writer Achieves Success as a Cook," *New York Times*, April 6, 1965, p. 35. For more information about Blake, see https://sofab.fandom.com/wiki/Christopher_Blake and http://www.tankdestroyer.net/honorees/b/496-blake-christopher-s-706th6th-grp

89 Kenny Lopez, "The Secrets of CellarDoor: From Brothel to Bar," *WGNO*, July 14, 2015.

90 Richard H. Collin, *The New Orleans Underground Gourmet* (New York: Simon & Schuster, 1970), 92–4.

91 This list is extracted from the wonderful digital humanities project https://www.mappingthegayguides.org/ For more about gay guidebooks see David K. Johnson, *Buying Gay: How Physique Entrepreneurs Sparked a Movement* (New York: Columbia University Press, 2019), 196–8.

92 Menu for Flamingo's Café & Bar, Tulane Digital Library Menus Collection; Poppy Tooker, interview by Rien Fertel, *Women Cookbook Writers*, March 29, 2018, 19–21.

93 Michael Lynch, "By-Products of Liberation: Gay Eateries," *Body Politic* 59 (December 1979/January 1980): 26.

94 Mike Hippler, "Working, Dining, and Funning in a Gay Beanery," *Bay Area Reporter* 12(31) (August 5, 1982): 13.

95 John Birdsall, "The Forgotten Queer Legacy of Billy West and Zuni Café," *New York Times*, May 28, 2021.

96 "The Finding Aid of the Robert Lawrence Balzer Papers," California State Polytechnic University, Pomona, Special Collections and Archives.

97 Birdsall, *The Man who Ate Too Much*.

98 Robert D. McFadden, "Chuck Williams, Founder of Williams-Sonoma, Dies at 100," *New York Times*, December 5, 2015.

99 James Beard to Elizabeth David, June 10, 1974. James Beard Collection, Box 11, Folder 24, Fales Library.

100 Richard Olney to Eda Lord, October 14, 1976. Sybille Bedford Papers, Box 36, Folder 1, Harry Ransom Library. Also Charles E. Williams, "Williams-Sonoma Cookware and the American Kitchen: The Merchandising Vision of Chuck Williams, 1956–1994," interview by Lisa Jacobson and Ruth Teiser, *Regional Oral History Office, The Bancroft Library*, 1995, 135.

101 Artemis Cooper, *Writing at the Kitchen Table: The Authorized Biography of Elizabeth David* (London: Faber and Faber, 2011).

102 Bert Greene and Denis Vaughan, *The Store Cookbook: Recipes and Recollections from "The Store in Amagansett"* (Chicago: Henry Regnery Company, 1974), 4, 15.

NOTES TO PP. 184–188

103 Kamp, *The United States of Arugula*, 202.

104 "Gino P. Cofacci, Chef, 75," *New York Times*, March 11, 1989, p. 33.

105 Richard Olney, *The French Menu Cookbook* (New York: Simon & Schuster, 1970); Richard Olney, *Reflexions* (New York: Brick Tower Press, 1999). Sybille Bedford described Olney as a key figure in the food "establishment" by 1970; Sybille Bedford to Elizabeth David, December 23, 1970. Elizabeth David Papers, Box 15, Folder 30, Schlesinger Library.

106 Kafka, *James Beard Celebration Cookbook*, 383.

107 Kafka, *James Beard Celebration Cookbook*, 52, 140, 68, 212, 389.

108 James Beard to Julia Child, December 20, 1966. Julia Child Papers, Box 10, Folder 129, Schlesinger Library.

109 Richard Olney to James Beard, October 1, 1970. James Beard Papers, Box 11, Folder 18, Fales Library.

110 Olney, *Reflexions*, 127. On the topic of Olney's memoir, I can't leave out the story of when Olney met English poet W. H. Auden in the 1950s. Auden showed him the jars of honey and jam he always carried in his pocket and said that given the opportunity he "liked to smear the stuff on boys' cocks and lick it off."

111 M. F. K. Fisher to James Beard, February 2, 1978. M. F. K. Fisher Papers, Box 2, Folder 13, Schlesinger Library.

112 Olney, *Reflexions*, 196.

113 Julia Child to James Beard, December 12, 1962; James Beard to Julia Child, December 4, 1966; Julia Child to James Beard, November 18, 1966; Julia Child to James Beard March 29, 1967; Julia Child to James Beard, June 16, 1967; Julia Child to James Beard, August 1, 1967. Julia Child Papers, Box 10, Folders 128–9, Schlesinger Library.

114 Ryan Linkhof, "'These Young Men who Come Down from Oxford and Write Gossip': Society Gossip, Homosexuality and the Logic of Revelation in the Interwar Popular Press," in Brian Lewis (ed.), *British Queer History* (Manchester: Manchester University Press, 2017), 111.

115 Gavin Duff, *Between You and Me: Queer Disclosures in the New York Art World, 1948–1963* (Durham, NC: Duke University Press, 2005), 12.

116 Robert C. Doty, "Growth of Overt Homosexuality in City Provokes Wide Concern," *New York Times*, December 17, 1963.

117 "The Homosexual in America," *Time*, January 21, 1966.

118 Lou Rand Hogan, *The Gay Cookbook* (Los Angeles: Sherbourne Press, 1965), vi–vii; Vider, "'Oh Hell, May.'"

119 Howard Austen and Beverly Pepper, *The Myra Breckinridge Cookbook* (Boston: Little, Brown and Company, 1970), 111, 17, 22, 207.

120 The Bloodroot Collective et al., *The Political Palate: A Feminist Vegetarian Cookbook* (Bridgeport, CT: Sanguinaria Publishing, 1980); Rick Leed, *Dinner for Two: A Gay Sunshine Cookbook* (San Francisco: Gay Sunshine, 1981); Rick Karlin, *The Gay Gourmet Cookbook* (Chicago: Richard E. Karlin, 1980); Bob Drake and Carol Carlson, *Sweet Music: A Collection of Delectable Desserts from the Windy City Gay Chorus* (Chicago: Windy City Gay Chorus, 1981); Maya Contenta and Victoria Ramstetter, *The Whoever Said Dykes Can't Cook Cookbook* (Cincinnati: Dinah, 1983); Bode Noonan, *Red Beans & Rice: Recipes for Lesbian Health and Wisdom* (Trumansburg, NY: Crossing Press, 1986); Billi Gordon, *You've Had Worse Things in Your Mouth Cookbook* (Los Angeles: West

Graphics, 1985), 13. Thanks to Alex Ketchum for sharing her scans of the Bloodroot Collective cookbook with me. See also Alex D. Ketchum, *Ingredients for Revolution: A History of American Feminist Restaurants, Cafes, and Coffeehouses* (Montreal: Concordia University Press, 2022); Maria McGrath, "Living Feminist: The Liberation and Limits of Countercultural Business and Radical Lesbian Ethics at *Bloodroot Restaurant*," *The Sixties: A Journal of History, Politics and Culture* 9(2) (2016).

121 Gail Sausser, *Lesbian Etiquette: Humorous Essays*, The Crossing Press Feminist Series, (Trumansburg, NY: Crossing Press, 1986), 33–6.

122 See, for three geographically disparate examples, Lesbian Group, Chicago Women's Liberation Union, June 20–9, 1975. MS ORGFIL0904, Organization Files from the Lesbian Herstory Archives; North Carolina, General. 1976–March, 1997. MS GEOUSA0033, Geographic Files from the Lesbian Herstory Archives; "Calendar." *Pandora* (1974): 14. *Archives of Sexuality and Gender.*

123 Food, August 17, 1995–October, 1997 and undated. August 17, 1995–October, 1997; n.d. TS Lesbian Herstory Archives: Subject Files: Part 3: Feminism-International Lesbian Movement Folder No.: 05270. Lesbian Herstory Archives. *Archives of Sexuality and Gender.* See also Reina Gattuso, "How Lesbian Potlucks Nourish the LGBTQ Movement," *Gastro Obscura*, May 2, 2019.

124 "Epicures Unlimited, 1987–1989," N. A. Diaman Papers. GLBT Historical Society. See for example 17(36), September 3, 1987.

125 "Gay Gourmet Group," *Bay Area Reporter* 17(36) (September 3, 1987).

126 "The Gay Gourmet," *The Body Politic* 77 (October, 1981): 41.

127 "Voice Bulletin Board," *The Village Voice* (June 5, 1978), p. 2.

128 Birdsall, "The Forgotten Queer Legacy of Billy West and Zuni Café."

129 Zuni Cafe hosted its first political fundraiser by June 1979; "Gay Vote News from the Harvey Milk Gay Democratic Club June 1979." *Gay Vote*, June 1979, p. 3. By the mid-1980s, it was participating in AIDS fundraising; "Gay Vote News from the Harvey Milk Lesbian & Gay Democratic Club January 1986." *Gay Vote*, January 1986, p 5; "Bay Area Chefs 'Aid & Comfort.'" *Mom Guess What*, June 1987, p. 12; "Restaurant Benefit for AIDS." *Mom Guess What*, July 1987, p. 3. *Archives of Sexuality and Gender.*

130 "Open Forum," *Bay Area Reporter* XI(10) (May 7, 1981), 6.

131 "Writer Mike Hippler, 1951–1991," 21(15) (April 11, 1991), 11.

132 Judith Michaelson, "Television: Finally, the Band Will Play," *Los Angeles Times*, March 21, 1993.

133 Danny Meyer, *Setting the Table: The Transforming Power of Hospitality in Business* (New York: HarperCollins, 2006), 33.

134 "Stephen Spector, 49, Dead; Art Consultant and Collector," *New York Times*, August 7, 1985; Clark, *James Beard*, 297.

135 Molly O'Neill, "Felipe Rojas-Lombardi, 46, Dies; Chef Known for Spanish Cuisine," *New York Times*, September 11, 1991. Section B, p. 12; Mayukh Sen, "The Gay Man who Brought Tapas to America," *Taste* (October 18, 2018).

136 Kirk Johnson, "Richard Sax, 46, Chef and Prolific Cooking Writer," *New York Times*, September 3, 1995, p. 36; John Birdsall, "Richard Sax and the Silence of AIDS," *John Birdsall*, 2020. https://www.john-birdsall.com/stories/richard-sax-aids-queer-food-history/.

137 "Bill Neal," *Associated Press*, October 24, 1991; Brett Anderson, "Crook's Corner, a Landmark North Carolina Restaurant, Has Closed," *New York Times*, June 9, 2021.

138 Michael Adno, "The Short & Brilliant Life of Ernest Matthew Mickler," *The Bitter Southerner*. https://bittersoutherner.com/the-short-and-brilliant-life-of-ernest-matthew -mickler

139 Dirk Fullmer, "Obituary." *Mom Guess What* (February, 1987), 2.

140 "Special Report: One Year in the Epidemic," *Newsweek*, July 1987, p. 37.

141 "Obituaries," *Outlines: The Voice of the Gay and Lesbian Community* 6(9): 39. For other examples of obituaries of chef that cite AIDS as the cause of death, see "Obituary," *Gay and Lesbian Times*, March 25, 1999, 21; "Obituary." *Gay and Lesbian Times*, December 23, 1999, 22.

142 See, for example, "AIDS Rumor Hurts Restaurant & Employee." *The Front Page* 9(18), (October 18–31, 1988): 19. The article mentions several cases, in Kentucky, Florida, and Virginia. Also, "Woman Sues Restaurant over AIDS Rumor." *Update*, February 19, 1997: A-3.

143 Dirk Fullmer, "Obituary." *Mom Guess What* (February, 1987), 2.

144 "Bounty Offered on Gay Waiters," *Bay Area Reporter* 18(26) (June 30, 1988): 13.

145 "Organization to Fight against Gay Rights Bill." *International Gay Association Bulletin* 2 (1985): 15.

146 "Ok GOP Says 'No.'" *Update*, May 6, 1987, A-3.

147 Jeremiah Tower, *California Dish: What I Saw (and Cooked) at the American Culinary Revolution* (New York: Free Press, 2003), 177, 211.

148 "Ruth Brinker, 89; Gave AIDS Patients Meals," *New York Times*, August 21, 2011, p. 18.

149 *Out of Our Kitchen Closets: San Francisco Gay Jewish Cooking* (San Francisco: Congregation Sha'ar Zahav, 1987), 151.

150 *Twenty-Five Years and Still Cookin' at Metropolitan Community Church of San Francisco* (Kearney, NE: Morris Press, 1995).

151 Robert H. Lehmann, *Cooking for Life: A Guide to Nutrition and Food Safety for the HIV-Positive Community* (New York: Random House, 1996); Mubarak S. Dahir, "The Gay '90s," *Update*, April 2, 1997, p. 14; Burkhard Bilger, "Nature's Spoils: The Underground Food Movement Ferments Revolution," *New Yorker*, November 22, 2010.

152 Daniel Isengart, "The Joy of Gay Cooking: The Gay Party's Over," *Slate.com*, July 13, 2015.

153 Jonathan Kauffman, "Get Fat, Don't Die," *Hazlitt* (April 28, 2020).

Chapter 10 Foodies

1 Frank Lalli, "'The Kitchen: America's Playroom,'" *Forbes*, March 15, 1976.

2 "Display Ad 62," *New York Times*, March 24, 1976, p. 40.

3 Leslie Brenner, *American Appetite: The Coming of Age of a Cuisine* (New York: Avon Books, 1999), 299–300.

4 Paul Levy, "What Is a Foodie?," *Guardian*, June 14, 2007.

5 Neil Hogg to Elizabeth David, August 22, 1985. Box 20, Folder 5, Schlesinger Library. See also Helen Gougeon, "Grande Dame of Britain's Kitchen Culture," *Globe and Mail*, February 26, 1986.

6 Laura Davenport, *The Bride's Cook Book: A Superior Collection of Thoroughly Tested Practical Recipes Specially Adapted to the Needs of the Young Housekeeper* (Chicago: Reilly & Britton Co., 1908).

7 John Douglass Louderback, *The Bride's Cook Book* (San Francisco: Douglass Publishing Co., 1909), 17.

8 Louise Bennett Weaver and Helen Cowles LeCron, *A Thousand Ways to Please a Husband: With Bettina's Best Recipes* (New York: A. L. Burt Company, 1917).

9 *The Bride's Cook Book* (San Francisco: The Original Bride's Cook Book Publishing Co., 1912).

10 *For the Bride* (Memphis: American Advertising Association, n.d.).

11 *The Bride's Cook Book: A Gift from the Merchant* (Los Angeles: Chase-Phillips Company, 1918); *The Bride's Cook Book: A Gift from the Merchants of San Francisco* (San Francisco: Pacific Coast Publishing, 1918); *The Bride's Cook Book: A Gift from The Merchants of Seattle* (San Francisco: Pacific Coast Publishing, 1918); *The Bride's Cook Book: A Gift from The Merchants of Portland* (San Francisco: Pacific Coast Publishing, 1918).

12 https://digitalcollections.lib.washington.edu/digital/collection/imlsmohai/id/8223

13 *Cupid's Book* (Oakland, CA: Kiessling, 1929).

14 Poppy Cannon, *The Bride's Cookbook* (New York: Holt, 1954); Myra Waldo, *1001 Ways to Please a Husband* (Princeton, NJ: D. Van Nostrand Company, 1958).

15 Robert H. Loeb, Jr., *Wolf in Chef's Clothing: The Picture Cook and Drink Book for Men* (Chicago: Wilcox & Follett Company, 1950), 8, 35. See also Elizabeth Fazakis, "Esquire Mans the Kitchenette," *Gastronomica* 11(3) (2011).

16 Robert H. Loeb, Jr., *She Cooks to Conquer* (New York: Wilfred Funk, 1952), 9, 31, 45, 59.

17 Robert H. Loeb, Jr., *Date Bait: The Younger Set's Picture Cookbook* (Chicago: Wilcox and Follett Company, 1952).

18 Joanne Hollows, "The Bachelor Dinner: Masculinity, Class and Cooking in *Playboy*, 1953–1961," *Continuum: Journal of Media & Cultural Studies* 16(2) (2002).

19 Aptekar took his pen name from Thomas Mann's short story "Mario the Magician"; Jane Aptekar, *Evolution of a Nonagenarian Culinarian: Life Stories of Thomas Mario* (Rhinebeck, NY: Epigraph Books, 2010), 62.

20 Thomas Mario, *The Face in the Aspic: Tales of Club Life among the Overfed* (New York: Simon & Schuster, 1944), 55–67.

21 The first issue of *Playboy* included a food and drink article by a different author; Bob Roderick, "Matanzas Love Affair," *Playboy* 1(1) (1953): 33.

22 Aptekar, *Evolution of a Nonagenarian Culinarian*, 108, 29–30.

23 Aptekar, *Evolution of a Nonagenarian Culinarian*, 112–13.

24 Ian Fleming, *Casino Royale* (New York: Penguin, 2006), 64.

25 Quoted in Carrie Pitzulo, *Bachelors and Bunnies: The Sexual Politics of Playboy* (Chicago: University of Chicago Press, 2011), 72.

26 Thomas Mario, "Playboy at the Chafing Dish," *Playboy* 1(10) (September 1954): 29, 36.

27 Thomas Mario, "Santa Claus in a Bottle," *Playboy* 2(1) (December 1954) 37, 46. See also a column by another *Playboy* columnist; Ken W. Purdy, "Liqueurs," *Playboy* 10(10) (October 1963): 101, 174–5.

28 Thomas Mario, "The Sophisticated Cheese," *Playboy* 2(5) (May 1955): 17–18, 40, 52. See also Thomas Mario, "The Cocktail Hour," *Playboy* 2(10) (October 1955): 22–4, 58.

29 Thomas Mario, "The Elegant Omelet," *Playboy* 5(2) (February 1958): 32–4, 70.

30 Thomas Mario, *The Playboy Gourmet: A Food and Drink Handbook for the Host at Home* (New York: Crown Publishers, 1961), 5.

31 Aptekar was married to his wife Rose, the love of his life, for sixty-nine years; Aptekar, *Evolution of a Nonagenarian Culinarian*.

32 Helen Gurley Brown, *Sex and the Single Girl* (New York: Pocket Books, 1962), 8, 124, 29.

33 Paula D. Hunt, "Editing Desire, Working Girl Wisdom, and Cupcakeable Goodness: Helen Gurley Brown and the Triumph of *Cosmopolitan*," *Journalism History* 38(3) (2012).

34 Helen Gurley Brown, *Single Girl's Cookbook* (Greenwich, CT: Fawcett Crest, 1969), 90.

35 Jinx Kragen and Judy Perry, *Saucepans and the Single Girl: The Cookbook with All the Ingredients for that Light-Hearted Leap from Filing Cabinet to Flambé* (Garden City, NY: Doubleday, 1965).

36 Jinx Kragen and Judy Perry, *The How to Keep Him (After You've Caught Him) Cookbook* (New York: Doubleday & Company, 1968).

37 For example, Mimi Sheraton, "Seductive Cookery: Part II," *Cosmopolitan* 160(1) (January 1966): 36; Mimi Sheraton, "Seductive Cookery: Part VIII," *Cosmopolitan* 161(1) (July 1966): 28; Mimi Sheraton, "Seductive Cookery: Part XII," *Cosmopolitan* 161(5) (November 1966): 32.

38 Mimi Sheraton, *The Seducer's Cookbook: Helpful and Hilarious Hints into which Men May Lure Women and Vice Versa – including Décor, Dress, Dialogue, Drink and Delicious Recipes* (New York: Random House, 1963), 3, 8, 11, 13, 99.

39 Pierre Le Poste and David Thorpe, *Rude Food* (New York: Ballantine Books, 1978). Actually, *Playboy* misprinted the first sentence of Aptekar's first essay to read "You can talk about oysters and leave out sex," which he later complained about and corrected in the *Playboy Gourmet* (1961).

40 Pierre Le Poste and David Thorpe, *Vin Rude: An Alcoholic Alphabet* (London: Macmillan, 1980); Pierre Le Poste and David Thorpe, *Rude Cocktails* (London: Macmillan, 1983); Pierre Le Poste and David Thorpe, *More Rude Food* (London: Macmillan, 1984).

41 Ron Stieglitz and Sandy Lesberg, *Saucy Ladies* (New York: Peebles Press, 1977).

42 Sandy Lesberg, *The Cookbook for Swinging Singles or How to Make It in the Kitchen* (Newport Beach, CA: Quail Street Publishing, 1976). Lesberg also authored many non-sex-related cookbooks and established several food-related organizations and events including the Master Chefs Institute and the International Chocolate Festival. https://blogs.timesofisrael.com/author/sandy-lesberg/

43 Jon Paul Frascone and Mark Allen David, *Aphrodisiac Meals to Pep Up Your Love Life* (Dallas: Candle Productions, 1975). The book's original artwork is credited to Robert Houle; it's unclear if this is the same as the Sandy Bay First Nation artist by this name; https://www.aci-iac.ca/art-books/robert-houle/biography/ The copyright for the cookbook is recorded as John Robert Frascone, rather than Jon Paul Frascone.

44 Billie Young, *The Naked Chef: An Aphrodisiac Cookbook* (Port Washington, NY: Ashley Books, 1971). For the hoax, see Margalit Fox, "Mike McGrady, Known for a Literary Hoax, Dies at 78," *New York Times*, May 14, 2012. Young also wrote other pornographic texts under the pen name Penelope Ashe, including *Viva La Difference: An Erotic Romp*

through the Wonderful World of Ultra Sex (New York: Ballantine Books/Penthouse International, 1976).

45 Louise Woolf and Susan Sky, *The X-Rated Cookbook* (New York: R. H. Brown & Co, 1977).

46 https://www.abebooks.it/prima-edizione-autografata/X-Rated-Cookbook-Susan-Sky -Louise-Woolf/31359827887/bd/ A listing for the shop can be found in Pemela Williams, *The Women's Traveller* (Damron, 1991).

47 Bridget, Martin Riskin, and Martin Cornel, *Bridget's Diet Cookbook* (Waltham, MA: American Publishing, 1972). The cookbook also includes funny sketches of Bridget.

48 Bridget, Martin Riskin, Martin Cornel, *Bridget's Organic Cookbook* (Waltham: American Publishing Corporation, 1973); Bridget, Martin Cornel, Martin Riskin, *Bridget's Basic Sex* (Waltham: American Publishing Corporation, 1973).

49 Greg Frazier and Beverly Frazier, *Aphrodisiac Cookery, Ancient and Modern* (San Francisco: Troubador Press, 1970); Adam Gottlieb, *Sex Drugs and Aphrodisiacs: Where to Obtain Them, How to Use Them, and Their Effects* (New York: High Times/Level Press, 1974); Robert Hendrickson, *Lewd Food: The Complete Guide to Aphrodisiac Edibles: How to Sate All the Hungers of the Bawdy* (Radnor, PA: Chilton Book Company, 1974); Gary Selden, *Aphrodisia: A Guide to Sexual Food, Herbs, and Drugs* (New York: Plume, 1979).

50 Munroe Howard, *Sex Pots and Pans: The Single Girl's Guide to Hooking Her Man – through Cooking* (New York: Paperback Library, 1970); Cory Kilvert, *The Male Chauvinist's Cookbook* (New York: Winchester Press, 1974); Marilyn Hase and Al Lerman, *The Happy Cooker* (London: Heinrich Hanau, 1977).

51 Abragail and Valaria, *How to Become a Sensuous Witch* (New York: Paperback Library, 1971); Jack S. Margolis and Daud Alani, *Cooking for Orgies and Other Large Parties* (Los Angeles: Cliff House Books, 1972); Peggy Holt, *The Lovers' Astrology Cookbook* (Los Angeles: Price/Stern/Sloan, 1974); Jane George, *How to Have an Affair: A Mischievous Cookbook* (Burbank, 1978).

52 Irene Ashley, *The Newd Cook Book: Sketched, Compiled, and Published by These Artists* of Torana Art League Santa Ana, California* (Santa Ana, CA: Torana House, 1971); Yvonne Young Tarr, *Love Portions: A Cookbook for Lovers* (Seacaucus, NJ: Citadel Press, 1972). Some art cookbooks weren't *about* sex but contained significant sexual imagery; Dana Crumb and Shery Cohen, *Eat It* (San Francisco: Bellerophon Books, 1972); Salvador Dali, *Les Dîners de Gala*, trans. Captain J. Peter Moore (New York: Felicie, 1973).

53 Sophia Loren, *In the Kitchen with Love* (New York: Doubleday & Company, 1972).

54 Peter Worthington and Ben Wicks, *The Naked Gourmet* (New York: Simon & Schuster, 1970), cook book.

55 Kilvert, *The Male Chauvinist's Cookbook*, ix.

56 Lionel H. Braun and William Adams, *Fanny Hill's Cook Book* (New York: Taplinger Publishing, 1971), 3, 15, 36. See also the recipe for Asso Buco, p. 58.

57 Bruce Feirstein, "Real Men Don't Eat Quiche (and Other Guidelines for the Modern Male," *Playboy* (May, 1982): 138–40, 184–8.

58 Jane Stern and Michael Stern, *American Gourmet: Classic Recipes, Deluxe Delights, Flamboyant Favorites and Swank "Company" Food from the '50s and '60s* (New York: HarperCollins, 1991), 230; James Beard, *Hors d'Oeuvre and Canapés* (Philadelphia: Running Press, 1999), 14, 135, 425.

59 For a handful of examples, see Craig Claiborne, "Lorraine Is a Palatable Entrée," *New York Times*, September 11, 1958, p. 41; Craig Claiborne, "Custard Is for Eating," *New York Times*, February 19, 1961, p. 152; Craig Claiborne and Pierre Franey, "And Then There's Quiche Alsace," *New York Times*, December 8, 1974, p. 398. Claiborne also included recipes for quiche in multiple editions of his cookbooks; Craig Claiborne, *New York Times Cook Book* (New York: Harper, 1961), 27–8; Craig Claiborne (ed.), *New York Times Menu Cook Book* (New York: Harper & Row, 1966), 17, 47, 91; Craig Claiborne, *New York Times International Cook Book* (New York: Harper & Row, 1971), 141. Sidney Aptekar also published quiche recipes in *Playboy*, describing it as excellent bachelor cooking; Thomas Mario, "Eggspo '68," *Playboy* 15(10) (October, 1968): 100–2, 108.

60 Robert Patrick, "Primal Scream: Elegant New York? No, Thank You," *Philadelphia Gay News*, October 2–5, 1981, p. 8.

61 See also the queer radical student group founded at Wesleyan College in 1991 which used the acronym QUICHE, for "Queers United in Crushing Homophobia Everywhere."

62 Bruce Feirstein, *Real Men Don't Eat Quiche: A Guidebook to All that Is Truly Masculine*, special forthright True Brit edn (London: New English Library, 1982); Scott Redman and Bruce Feirstein, *Real Men Don't Cook Quiche: The Real Man's Cookbook* (New York: Pocket Books, 1982); Scott Redman and Bruce Feirstein, *Real Men Don't Cook Quiche* (London: New English Library, 1983). For more on this complicated text, see Rachel Hope Cleves, "*Real Men Don't Eat Quiche*: Queer Food and Gendered Nationalism in the Late Twentieth-Century USA," *Gender & History* 34(3) (2022); Emily J. H. Contois, "Real Men Don't Eat Quiche, Do They? Food, Fitness, and Masculinity Crisis in 1980s America," *European Journal of American Culture* 40(3) (September, 2021).

63 Ann Barr and Paul Levy, *The Official Foodie Handbook* (London: Ebury Press, 1984), 123. 7, 10–11, 20, 27.

64 Stern and Stern, *American Gourmet*, x; Brenner, *American Appetite*, 4; David Kamp, *The United States of Arugula: The Sun-Dried, Cold-Pressed, Dark-Roasted, Extra Virgin Story of the American Food Revolution* (Broadway Books, 2006), 144; Thomas McNamee, *Alice Waters & Chez Panisse: The Romantic, Impractical, Often Eccentric, Ultimately Brilliant Making of a Food Revolution* (New York: Penguin, 2007); David Strauss, *Setting the Table for Julia Child: Gourmet Dining in America, 1934–1961* (Baltimore, MD: Johns Hopkins University Press, 2011), 249.

65 Paul Freedman, *American Cuisine: And How It Got This Way* (New York: Liveright, 2019), 292–9. Waters has had her detractors as well, including James Villas, who disliked her food and called her "fatuous," and Karen Hess, who called her "so stupid"; James Villas, *Between Bites: Memoirs of a Hungry Hedonist* (New York: John Wiley & Sons, 2002), 219, 78; Kamp, *The United States of Arugula*, 280.

66 McNamee, *Alice Waters & Chez Panisse*, 251.

67 Jim Beard, "Back to the Old Grind," *San Francisco Examiner*, December 11, 1974, p. 31. See also Jim Beard, "Tastes Recollected," *San Francisco Examiner*, December 30, 1974, p. 24.

68 Elizabeth David to Alice Waters, November 23, 1976, Box 1, Folder 6, Bancroft Library; Richard Olney, *Reflexions* (New York: Brick Tower Press, 1999), 226.

69 Elizabeth David to Alice Waters, December 15, 1978; Elizabeth David to Alice Waters, April 6, 1981. Chez Panisse Records, Box 1, Folder 6, Bancroft Library.

70 M. F. K. Fisher to Alice Waters, March 17, 1978. Chez Panisse Records, Box 1, Folder 8, Bancroft Library.

71 M. F. K. Fisher to Alice Waters, July 27, 1978; M. F. K. Fisher to Alice Waters, January 14, 1979; M. F. K. Fisher to Alice Waters, November 30, 1981. Chez Panisse Records, Box 1, Folders 8, 9, 10, Bancroft Library.

72 Kamp, *The United States of Arugula*, 144–56.

73 David Lance Goines, "(#65) Garlic," (June 27, 1977). For his description of the poster, see https://www.goines.net/Poster_art3/poster_65.html

74 Ruth Reichl, *Comfort Me with Apples: More Adventures at the Table* (New York: Random House, 2001), 14, 42, 157.

75 Gael Greene, *Insatiable: Tales from a Life of Delicious Excess* (New York: Warner Books, 2006), 21.

76 Gael Greene, *Blue Skies, No Candy* (New York: William Morrow, 1976), 12, 39, 124.

77 Greene, *Insatiable: Tales from a Life of Delicious Excess*, 99. See, for an example of Greene's reportage from this trip, Gael Greene, "The Insatiable Critic: Losing My Head at Marie-Antoinette's," *New York* 7(24) (June 17, 1974): 90–3.

78 Gael Greene, *Delicious Sex: A Book for Women . . . and the Men who Want to Love Them Better* (New York: Prentice Hall Press, 1986), 23–5, 55–67.

79 *Mousquetaire au Restaurant.* https://en.wikipedia.org/wiki/File:Mousquetaire_au_restaurant_part_1.ogvhttps://commons.wikimedia.org/wiki/File:Mousquetaire_au_restaurant_part_2.ogv

80 *Lady and the Tramp*, dir. Clyde Geronomi, Wilfred Jackson, and Hamilton Luske (Walt Disney Animation Studios, 1955).

81 *Tom Jones*, dir. Tony Richardson (Woodfall Film Productions, 1963).

82 *Neighbors*, dir. John G. Avildsen (Columbia Pictures, 1981).

83 *Fast Times at Ridgemont High*, dir. Amy Heckerling (Universal Pictures, 1982).

84 Barry Forshaw, *Sex and Film: The Erotic in British, American and World Cinema* (London: Palgrave Macmillan, 2015), 168–74; Laura Lindenfeld and Fabio Parasecoli, *Feasting Our Eyes: Food Films and Cultural Identity in the United States* (New York: Columbia University Press, 2017), 93–118.

85 *9½ Weeks*, dir. Adrian Lyne (Producers Sales Organization, 1986).

86 *The Cook, the Thief, His Wife, and Her Lover*, dir. Peter Greenaway (Allarts, 1989).

87 Maria Angel and Zoë Sofia, "Cooking Up: Intestinal Economies and the Aesthetics of Specular Orality," *Cultural Studies* 10(3) (1996).

88 "Itsy-Bitsy Bite Size Bikini," *The Harvest* (McGill) 48(4) (December 14, 1976): 5. See also the edible panties joke in "Hays to Nation," *National Lampoon*, August 1976. They made news in gay newspapers as well, which emphasized that they could be worn by men or women; "Rare, medium, or well done?" *Philadelphia Gay News*, March 6, 1976, pp. B4, B6; Joe Venuti, "For Sure!" *Philadelphia Gay News*, April 1, 1976, p. A19.

89 Don DeLillo, *Amazons: An Intimate Memoir by the First Woman Ever to Play in the National Hockey League* (New York: Holt, Rinehart and Winston, 1980), 359.

90 Classified for Golden Touch. *Berkeley Barb*, November 19–25, 1976, p. A8.

91 Christian Millau, *The Best of Los Angeles* (New York: Crown Publishers, 1984), 419.

92 Hillary Ray, "Ask for Raspberry," *Columbia Daily Spectator*, December 7, 1981.

93 Barbara Ehrenreich, Elizabeth Hess, and Gloria Jacobs, "Women and Erotica," *New Woman* 16(9) (September 1986), 120.

94 Elaine Catherine Pierson and William V. D'Antonio, *Female and Male: Dimensions of Human Sexuality* (Philadelphia: Lippincott, 1974), 84.

95 For flavored condoms as consumerist excess, see C. E. Crimmins, *Entrechic: The Mega-Guide to Entrepreneurial Excellence* (New York: American Management Association, 1985), 6; Howard Lewis Russell, *Rush to Nowhere* (New York: D. I. Fine, 1988), 239. For an example of flavored condoms and safe sex, see E. G. Martin, "Hot & Healthy: A Second Coming Out," *Gay Community News* 14(22) (December 14–20, 1986), 7.

96 Ted McIlvenna, *The Complete Guide to Safe Sex* (PreVenT Group: 1987), 162; "How to Use a Dental Dam for Safer Oral Sex," in *The HIV Pyramid* (Washington, DC: Department of Veterans Affairs, 1989) n.p.

97 Nannette LaRee Hernandez, *Creative Screwing: A Woman's Guide to Becoming an Erotic Enchantress of Superlustful Sex* (Richardson, TX: Brilliant Creations Publishing, 1993), 97–9.

98 "Holistic Harry," *Playboy* 27(6) (June, 1980): 200.

99 "Titburger," *Hustler* (February, 1976), 16.

100 Dean Boyer, "Hooters of America, Inc." in *The International Directory of Company Histories* 69 (Gale Thomson, 2005): 211–14; "Lights, Camera, Austin!" *Playboy* 33(7) (July, 1986): 88–101, 148.

101 Pitzulo, *Bachelors and Bunnies: The Sexual Politics of Playboy*, 61–4.

102 Jason Daley, "Billion-Dollar Boys' Club," *Entrepreneur* (June, 2011): 101–5; Tim Walker, "Wings over America," *Independent*, December 13, 2014, pp. 133–7; Dianne Avery, "The Female Breast as Brand: The Aesthetic Labor of Breastaurant Servers," in Marion G. Crain, Winifred R. Poster, and Miriam A. Cherry (eds.), *Invisible Labor: Hidden Work in the Contemporary World* (Berkeley, CA: University of California Press, 2019).

103 Emily J. H. Contois, *Diners, Dudes, & Diets: How Gender and Power Collide in Food Media and Culture* (Chapel Hill, NC: University of North Carolina Press, 2020), 23.

104 Allen Salkin, *From Scratch: Inside the Food Network* (New York: G. P. Putnam's Sons, 2013), 55, 73, 217.

105 Josée Johnston, Alexandra Rodney, and Phillipa Chong, "Making Change in the Kitchen? A Study of Celebrity Cookbooks, Culinary Personas, and Inequality," *Poetics* 47 (2014): 12.

106 Forshaw, *Sex and Film: The Erotic in British, American and World Cinema*, 154.

107 Maggie Andrews, "Calendar Ladies: Popular Culture, Sexuality and the Middle-Class, Middle-Aged Domestic Woman," *Sexualities* 6(3–4) (November, 2003): 400.

108 Adam Rapoport, "Cook for Us, Padma," *GQ Magazine* (August, 2007), pp. 122–3.

109 As sociologist Antje Lindenmeyer has argued, "women themselves are what is eaten – they are metaphorically represented as food." Antje Lindenmeyer, "'Lesbian Appetites': Food, Sexuality and Community in Feminist Autobiography," *Sexualities* 9(4) (2006): 470.

110 Examples of both sides of the coin: https://twitter.com/Nigella_Lawson/status/10740 0892835316121; https://www.express.co.uk/life-style/diets/1576637/nigella-lawson-weight-loss-two-stone-transformation-how-to-lose-weight-easy-changes

111 X. M. Boulestin, *Having Crossed the Channel . . .* (London: William Heinemann, 1934), 48.

Epilogue: Good Sex, Bad Food

1 Daniel Grubb and Gabi Grubb, *Fifty Shades of Gravy: You've Witnessed the Crazy, Now Whip Up the Gravy, 50 Saucy Recipes for the Sexiest of Socialites* (East Yorkshire, UK: Fantastic Books Publishing, 2012); Jenny Ric, *Fifty Shades of Gravy* (Kindle Edition, 2012); I. M. Pliant, *Fifty Shades of Gravy: The Cookbook: Rude Recipes for Dirty Dinner Parties* (CreateSpace Independent Publishing Platform, 2012); Halle Bridgeman, *Fifty Shades of Gravy: A Christian Gets Saucy!* (House of Bread Books, 2013); A. F. Owlpun and E. L. Poppycock, *50 Shades of Coq: A Parody Cookbook for Lovers of White Coq, Dark Coq, and All Shades Between* (CreateSpace Independent Publishing Platform, 2015); Adrienne N. Hew, *50 Ways to Eat Cock: Healthy Chicken Recipes with Balls!* (CreateSpace Independent Publishing Platform, 2013); F. L. Fowler, *Fifty Shades of Chicken: A Parody in a Cookbook* (New York: Clarkson Potter, 2012); Michelle O'Shaughnessy, *50 Shades of Herbs: The Best Natural Remedies for Better Sex, Better Sleep, and More Energy* (Granger, IN: TCK Publishing, 2013); E. J. Grayle, *50 Shades of Dessert: The 50 Greatest Recipes for Steamy, Passion-Filled Nights* (Kindle, 2014); Benjamin Myhre, *Fifty Shades of Bacon* (CreateSpace Independent Publishing Platform, 2012); Jack Rivers, *50 Shades of Bacon: The Ultimate Cookbook for Bacon Lovers* (Kindle, 2015); I. M. Bacon, *Fifty Shades of Bacon* (CreateSpace Independent Publishing Platform, 2015); Claire Preen, *50 Shades of Chocolate: A Sexylicious Book of Delicious Chocolate Recipes with Handy Hints on How to Enjoy Them in the Bedroom* (CreateSpace Independent Publishing Platform, 2014). For chocolate's aphrodisiac reputation, see Martha Few, "Chocolate, Sex, and Disorderly Women in Late-Seventeenth- and Early-Eighteenth-Century Guatemala," *Ethnohistory* 52(4) (Fall, 2005); Ken Albala, "The Use and Abuse of Chocolate in 17th Century Medical Theory," *Food and Foodways* 15(1–2) (2007); Marcy Norton, *Sacred Gifts, Profane Pleasures: A History of Tobacco and Chocolate in the Atlantic World* (Ithaca, NY: Cornell University Press, 2008); Kate Loveman, "The Introduction of Chocolate into England: Retailers, Researchers, and Consumers, 1640–1730," *Journal of Social History* 47(1) (Fall 2013).

2 Drew Ramsey and Jennifer Iserloh, *Fifty Shades of Kale: 50 Fresh and Satisfying Recipes that Are Bound to Please* (New York: Harper Wave, 2013); Jonathan Doue, *50 Shades of Quinoa* (CreateSpace Independent Publishing Platform, 2014); Lallah Rowe, *Fifty Shades of Hummus: A Cookbook* (Rose Ink Publishers, 2013).

3 Nona Willis Aronowitz, *Bad Sex: Truth, Pleasure, and an Unfinished Revolution* (New York: Random House, 2022).

4 Quoted in Ian Robinson, *The Survival of English: Essays in Criticism of Language* (New York: Cambridge University Press, 1973), 179.

5 Helen Gurley Brown, *Sex and the Single Girl* (New York: Pocket Books, 1962), 62.

6 Helen Gurley Brown, *Single Girl's Cookbook* (Greenwich, CT: Fawcett Crest, 1969)

7 Linda Jaivin, *Eat Me* (New York: Bantam Books, 1995), 159.

8 *Julie & Julia*, dir. Nora Ephron (Columbia Pictures, 2009); Julia Moskin, "Nora Ephron Never Forgot the Food," *New York Times*, June 27, 2012.

9 See, for example, Toby Young "Julie & Julia," *Times*, September 11, 2009.

10 https://reelgood.com.au/articles/food-porn-films-avoid-dieting/

11 Juan-Carlos Cruz and Amy Reiley, *The Love Diet: With Simple Recipes (Cocktails, Too) for a Healthy, Happy, Sexy You* (Life of Reiley, 2010), 11, 16, 19. Juan-Carlos Cruz was arrested shortly before the publication of the book for soliciting homeless people to murder his wife, and sentenced to nine years in prison; Michael Martinez, "Former Food Network

Chef Sentenced in Murder Plot," December 13, 2010. CNN.com. https://www.cnn.com/2010/CRIME/12/13/california.tv.chef.case/index.html

12 Crystal Guthrie, *Paleo Sex Recipes and Positions Guide: Eat and F**k like a Caveman* (CreateSpace Independent Publishing Platform, 2015).

13 Lisa Davis, *Clean Eating, Dirty Sex: Sensual Superfood Recipes and Aphrodisiac Practices for Ultimate Sexual Health* (New York: Skyhorse Publishing, 2019), n.p.

14 Bee Wilson, "Why We Fell for Clean Eating," *Guardian* (August 11, 2017).

15 Tosca Reno, *The Eat-Clean Diet* (Mississauga, ON: Robert Kennedy Publishing, 2006), 7, 25.

16 James Duigan, *The Clean & Lean Diet: 14 Days to Your Best-Ever Body* (London: Kyle Cathie, 2010), 8.

17 https://carlyshankman.com/6-reasons-real-food-improves-increases-your-sex-life/

18 https://medium.com/this-political-woman/clean-eating-and-dirty-women-9ac223278abd/

19 Michael K. Goodman and Sylvia Jaworska, "Mapping Digital Foodscapes: Digital Food Influencers and the Grammars of Good Food," *Geoforum* 117 (2020).

20 Elspeth Probyn, "An Ethos with a Bite: Queer Appetites from Sex to Food," *Sexualities* 2(4) (1999): 426.

Index